QUEEN MARGARET
UNIVERSITY COLLEGE

100 172 689

RMPSM06

D1420996

Withdrawn from
Queen Margaret University Library

QUEEN MARGARET UNIVERSITY LIBRARY

BUSINESS AND PUBLIC MANAGEMENT IN THE UK 1900-2003

Business and Public Management in the UK 1900-2003

DUNCAN McTAVISH
Glasgow Caledonian University, UK

ASHGATE

QUEEN MARGARET UNIVERSITY LIBRARY

© Duncan McTavish 2005

All rights reserved. No part of this publication may be reproduced, stored in a retrieval system, or transmitted in any form or by any means, electronic, mechanical, photocopying, recording or otherwise without the prior permission of the publisher.

Duncan McTavish has asserted his right under the Copyright, Designs and Patents Act, 1988, to be identified as the author of this work.

Published by
Ashgate Publishing Limited
Gower House
Croft Road
Aldershot
Hampshire GU11 3HR
England

Ashgate Publishing Company
Suite 420
101 Cherry Street
Burlington, VT 05401-4405
USA

Ashgate website: http://www.ashgate.com

British Library Cataloguing in Publication Data
McTavish, Duncan
Business and public management in the UK, 1990-2003
1.Public utilities - Great Britain - Management - History -
20th century 2.Industrial management - Great Britain -
History - 20th century 3.Public utilities - Scotland -
Management - Case studies 4.Industrial management -
Scotland - Case studies
I.Title
658'.00941'0904

Library of Congress Cataloging-in-Publication Data
McTavish, Duncan.
Business and public management in the UK 1900-2003 / by Duncan McTavish.
    p. cm.
Includes bibliographical references and index.
ISBN 0-7546-4335-2
  1. Industrial management--Great Britain--History--20th century. 2. Industrial management--Great Britain--Case studies. 3. Government ownership--Great Britain--History--20th century. 4. Government ownership--Great Britain--History--Case studies.
I. Title.

  HD70.G7M38 2005
  658'.00941'0904--dc22

2005009772

ISBN-10: 0 7546 4335 2

Printed and bound in Great Britain by Athenaeum Press, Ltd.,
Gateshead, Tyne & Wear.

Contents

List of Figures

List of Tables

Acknowledgements

This book started life as a PhD thesis at the University of Glasgow. The support given there through the supervision process and in particular advice given by Dr Duncan Ross in the Department of Economic and Social History was much valued. Much of the research is based on archive material, some of which falls within the 30 year public disclosure protocol. Special permission was given to examine Strathclyde Regional Council departmental and directorate records and papers. Dr Irene O'Brien, archivist with Glasgow City Archives, was particularly helpful in helping me gain access to this material. Similar permission was also granted for a range of Greater Glasgow Health Board documentation. Other primary documentation was used and the support of staff in the Scottish Business History Centre staff in making this material available is recognised.

The support of Linda and Iain was immense in many ways, not least of which is an understanding of the concentration and focus, indeed mild obsession, required for work of this nature.

Introduction

This book is framed by two important areas of study critical for an understanding of twentieth century British management. First, management and broader structural issues surrounding British business and economic history from 1900, and second, the management of the public sector in the growth years from 1945 and the dynamic created here between traditional internal and more generic 'imported' management practices.

Business management has been a topic of active research by business and economic historians. Considerable research and literature has appeared on internal and external management structures and arrangements, management control and the relationship between the economic-business environment and company management. Study and research of management in the public sector (at least prior to the late 1970s) has been relatively limited, though various government led investigations like the Fulton Commission on the civil service, the Wheatley and Maud Commissions on local government and various Royal Commissions and other reports on the NHS, have contributed important source material.

The book contributes towards the research base and debates in business and public sector management through an examination of the literature and original case study research. This is achieved by:

- researching management practices in British business within the context of the British economic and competitive environment. The nature and extent of internal management structures, the significance, scope and scale of external management including the management of business and societal relationships is a primary focus of the study.

In the public sector, this contribution will be achieved by:

- identifying the internal contextual environments in various parts of the public sector (local government, civil service and the National Health Service) and researching specific internal management practices in each of these areas. The import and use of external management, especially in the post 1970s public policy environment is an important dimension of the study.

The range of case studies is justified below. Both chronological and thematic approaches were adopted.

Chronology

The book concentrates on business management from 1900 and public sector management from 1945. When exploring public sector management, a broad chronological and thematic approach was used. Although there are themes, trends and practices which cross chronological boundaries, there is nonetheless a powerful consensus view that dates are important: 1945 to the 1970s were the years of the post war settlement which saw broad political consensus and growth in the public sector (Kavanagh 1987; Marquand 1988; Marwick 1990); the years after the mid-1970s saw the breakdown of this settlement and deliberate attempts by governments to introduce managerialism (often influenced by 'new right' thinking) into public sector service provision.

The work was based on business management from around 1900. Significant pre-1900 developments in management have been well documented, yet the turn of the century was nonetheless important: from then the size of business unit required increased management resource to manage throughput. Chronologically-evolutionary based approaches to management in the twentieth century have tended to look at the development of scale and 'big business'; the organisational form, structure and practices required to manage this; the evolution of multinational companies (Chandler 1962, 1977, 1990; Wren 1994). These approaches focus on the development, after the first decades of the twentieth century, of 'soft' management practices like human relations and 'human factors', almost as a reaction or an emollient to the hard edge of big business efficiency driven capitalism (Pollard 1974; Wren 1994). Chronologies too explain much of the post-1970 years in terms of the evolution of globalisation, the integration of product and capital markets across geographical boundaries increasingly eased by information and communication technologies, the collapse of early-mid twentieth century multidivisional structures and the development of structures and human resource management strategies to manage such businesses (Bartlett and Ghoshal 1989; Stalk, Evans and Schulman 1992; Yip 1995; Micklethwaite and Wooldridge 1996; Clarke and Clegg 1998).

There are attractions (with considerable supporting evidence) of narrative chronologies and evolutionary explanations of business management. But such an approach presents problems. Unlike the public sector, there is less agreement on the 'key dates'. For example, the variety of 'non modern' (but clearly appropriate) institutional forms found in British companies until well into the twentieth century indicated that at key points the chronological – evolutionary paradigm was at best qualified (Schmitz 1993; Jones 1994; Wilson 1995). Of course, businesses failing to develop the recognised hierarchical structures and organisational form may be seen as chronological aberrations or 'backward'. Certainly many British businesses did not develop internal hierarchies and M form structures as the world's leading companies did in the first half of the twentieth century, and may indeed have been backward; it may simply be that the labour-technological environment or factor endowments in Britain were different and more suited to market and external co-ordination of business activity.

Thematic Approaches

The key themes are internal and external management. When analysing internal management in the business sector, market-environmental influences are important: since business is driven by the need to perform in the market (whether optimally or not is another matter) its internal management is arranged towards this end. Since Chandler's work, debate has addressed the role played by managerial hierarchies and structures, which are in effect mechanisms to co-ordinate and control managerial and other resources in the organisation. This consequently leads to a focus on the management of human resources, an emphasis particularly apt in Britain where traditionally the labour technology mix was dominated by the craft system, even more so in the shipbuilding case given the industry's domination by the craft system; the focus is equally justified in analysing contemporary business and management practice, acknowledging the importance of value added by the human resource.

The study of internal management in the public sector is also important. In contrast with the business sector, growth in the public sector was not by market environmental determination, but by government initiated public policy. Analysis of internal management is vital since governments chose to increase resources and grow the public sector through the existing internal administrative, professional and managerial arrangements in the relevant sectors. Addressing human resource issues is important given the labour intensity of the public sector. Despite the contextual differences, internal management is conceptually relatively straightforward in both business and public sectors: it is the management practiced within the internal boundaries of the organisation.

External management has greater subtleties and complexities. In business it refers to management co-ordination through external relationships and is often defined as market co-ordination distinct from internal bureaucratic methods (e.g. through the 'visible hand'). In the public sector, externalisation has a nuanced meaning: like in business, it can refer to management co-ordination through external (sometimes marketised) relationships; it can also refer to management practices externally imposed or imported, thereby superimposing or even replacing traditional administrative and professional internal arrangements.

Within these broad definitions, there are a series of questions which the book addresses. In the business sector:

- How was business managed in the changing growth oriented market environment of the early twentieth century? Was there a change from external market co-ordination practice to the strengthening of internal structures and practices?
- Was there a shift from internal management control with the externalisation of much business activity from the 1970s?
- Was the wider societal dimension of business aimed mainly at business related concerns?

- Did business management's societal engagement in corporate-state machinery affect management practices at company level?

In the public sector:

- How did the professional-administrative structures in the three main parts of the public sector (civil service, local government, NHS) manage the politically inspired resource growth in the post war years to the 1970s?
- Was there an attempt by government in these years to introduce alternative management practices and structures?
- Were there any discernible and substantial differences between Scotland and England?
- How successful was the new managerialism as an externally generated instrument in radically altering existing management practices?
- How substantially is public sector management now framed by externalisation – the management of external relationships?

A related issue, specifically focused on Y College case study:

- Has the new managerial agenda led to the fracturing of public policy and the management of service provision?

Selected Case Studies

Primary research was carried out through a series of case studies. Public sector and business cases were chosen. The nationalised industries were excluded. Since these were an important part of the post 1945 public sector, it is important to justify exclusion. The state run sector comprised in the main some basic infrastructural industries and utilities, and were distinguished from the major public sector services by the fact of their market operations. Like other parts of the public sector, they were subject to government policy goals - not always successfully implemented: for example nationalised industries were used as an instrument to curb inflation in the 1970-74 years; to protect employment from 1974-76; to stimulate economic growth 1964-1970 (Robson 1977). Yet for all this, the Morrisonian inspired governance structures of the public corporation board made it very difficult for governments to exert control, as illustrated graphically by the leading Conservative Cabinet Minister Geoffrey Howe in 1981:

> The Morrisonian constitution grants our nationalised corporations a degree of autonomy, which is probably unique in the Western World. In the strict sense of the word they are constitutionally 'irresponsible'...the Government's only real weapon is the threat to reduce or cut off external funds. This is far too drastic to be effective. It is like equipping traffic wardens with anti tank guns but depriving them of the right to leave parking tickets. (1)

So even though state owned businesses could be used as instruments of public policy, they were different from other parts of the public sector with greater levels of operational independence. They were different too from private business, the purpose of which was to survive and perform in the competitive marketplace. Public sector owned industries were charged to 'engage' rather than 'perform' in the market for a variety of reasons and in a variety of ways. Government initiatives for example were used in municipal enterprises often to guarantee health and safety (Milward 1989). Government action could be motivated by the difficulties of regulating natural monopolies other than by nationalisation (Chick 1994). State action was also used (through the nationalised Central Electricity Board and the Grid) to break local monopolies (Chick 1994). Political frustration and inability of private sector firms in key industries (e.g. coal and iron and steel) to restructure and consolidate to achieve proper economies of scale also led to state ownership (Burn 1961; Supple 1987; Tolliday 1987; Chick 1995) – based of course on a belief in the desirability and achievability of this (Greasley 1995). Nationalised industries and related initiatives therefore had a much broader scope than private business.

Once established, practice and experience in nationalised industries was also diverse. Some had strong management structures at the centre (e.g., the electricity industry); some had relatively weak centres (e.g. gas); others, like rail, had over complex and over bureaucratised structures, which appeared to impede clear decision making (Chester 1975; Gourvish 1991; Tolliday 1991). Various measures of managerial performance gave a heterogeneous picture: 1948-1978, coal and steel had poor growth and productivity records, but electricity, gas and airlines did well (Ashworth 1991); profitability tended to be poorer than in the private sector (Gourvish 1991) but much of this may be attributed to the basis of calculation (Jeremy 1998); coal, gas and electricity did very well in terms of research and development by international comparison but the railways did not. Indeed there is a strong justification for a collective case study approach to management in the nationalised industries per se to consolidate and develop the work already in place.

Case 1: Clydeside Shipbuilding was an important industry for Scotland, especially west Scotland, and Britain. Although the industry only employed a small proportion of Glasgow's industrial workforce even at its peak in 1913, the figure reached almost 25% when allied engineering and metal working were included (Rodger 1996); the industry's linkages with other sectors and its difficulties in the inter war years came to symbolise the problems of the Scottish economy; it persisted into the increasingly competitive post second world war decades and in these years was considered to be over traditional in its structure and management as well as highly visible from the 1960s in attempts to rationalise, modernise and restructure (Geddes 1966). The case researches the organisation of markets, production and human resources and highlights the extent to which management practice was in keeping with the rest of British business or rather particular to shipbuilding.

The main sources used were the archives of Fairfield Shipbuilders and John Brown Shipbuilders. Both company archives were used in complementary fashion, both strong on the activities of the Board of Directors, the latter stronger on aspects of human resource management. Some records of the Shipbuilding Employers Federation and the Clyde Shipbuilders Association were also used.

Case 2: X plc is a company operating in the films sector, producing packaging and other cellulose based products. The company's profile provides justification for selection: it is based in the UK in the north west of England and is part of a Belgian owned multinational group which is included in Europe's top 250 companies by turnover; the three main activities of the group are pharmaceuticals, chemicals (both of which are headquartered in Belgium) and films, which is headquartered in north-west England. The scope and nature of the company's activities will be analysed to assess the extent to which management arrangements display practices in line with current frameworks as generally outlined in research and literature.

Meetings and interviews with all levels of management in the firm were arranged and carried out over a three month period. The top three levels of management in the company completed a detailed questionnaire. This research instrument provided the basis for the discussions with managers. Restricted access was also given to some confidential company documentation.

Case 3: National Health Service Management: the hospital service in greater Glasgow 1947-1987 focuses on the management of the hospital service at local level. This is particularly apt since the legislation establishing the health service gave executive authority for hospital service management to area hospital boards. The value of research based on one such board is evident. The degree to which this case highlights themes particular to Glasgow or Scotland as a whole, or contributes more generally to the extant literature largely English based, is assessed.

Sources used were based in the Greater Glasgow Health Board archive, and included the minutes and working papers of the Western Regional Hospital Board from 1947 to 1987, the constituent hospital management boards and specialist sub committees. Papers of the successor body, the Greater Glasgow Health Board, and in particular the Strategy and Policy Committee of that board and its associated material are also used. Special permission was given (with some conditions) to view and use material post 1970.

Case 4: Management of Education in Glasgow and Strathclyde 1955-1992, explores the management of education in Glasgow, run by Glasgow Corporation until the reform of local government in 1974, and from then by Strathclyde Regional Council. This latter body, with a remit beyond Glasgow, contained about half of Scotland's population within its boundaries and was one of Europe's largest education authorities. The scale clearly makes this a significant case. The study informs and highlights practice in local authority management in the context of the current literature and research; it also addresses issues of Scottish exceptionalism.

Sources used were Glasgow Corporation Education Department papers mainly those relating to the work of the Directorate. Strathclyde Education Department papers, especially the Directorate's have been used extensively; material relating to education from the Chief Executive's Department has also been consulted. Special permission was required to view much of the archive, which to my knowledge has not previously been used for academic research. Personal interviews were also held with Strathclyde's second and last Director of Education, and with the Personal Assistant to the Chief Executive of Strathclyde 1988-92; some of these interviews were held on a confidential basis.

Case 5: Y College is a further education college, which like all further education colleges was transferred from mainstream public sector (controlled and managed by local authorities) through legislation in 1992 and 1993, into a corporate body with a locally selected Board of Management. Colleges are in effect Local Public Spending Bodies (LPSBs) created as such by central governments' thrust of new managerialism in the 1980s and 1990s. The college studied is Scotland's median college in terms of size and turnover. The case relates to the existing and growing literature on LPSBs and non governmental agencies. Research was based on an interview programme with college managers and Board of Management members. Some access was granted to Board of Management and sub committee papers and proceedings.

Case studies 1, 3 and 4 made extensive use of archive material. Some primary archive material is also used in other chapters: chapters 2 and 3 draw on material from the private papers of Viscount Weir, chapter 6 - various Glasgow Corporation Departmental papers, and chapter 7 - Strathclyde Region Chief Executive's Departmental minutes and papers.

Note

1. Howe, G. (1981), *Privatisation: The Way Ahead*: Conservative Political Centre, p. 3. Geoffrey Howe was Chancellor and Foreign Secretary in Thatcher led governments and for a period was her Deputy Prime Minister. Howe's devastating speech in the House of Commons in November 1990 played a significant role in Thatcher's downfall.

Part A
Management of Business in Britain 1900-2003

Overview

The growth and increased size of business unit from around the turn of the century, with the subsequent challenge to manage increased throughput, led to a search for managerial and business efficiency. The link between market growth, increased size of business unit, structural integration of value and supply chains and the development of supportive management practices was evident in Britain, yet different environmental factors meant that in large sections of British business, the quest for efficiency was less apparent than elsewhere. Chapter 1 gives an overview of the business competitive environment in Britain from 1900. The internal management of business in Britain is the focus of chapter 2. The issues researched are the growth of management structures; an analysis of the way in which the human resource was managed including examination of the craft system and management training; identification of the various stages and approaches of internal management control including personnel and welfarist frameworks, human relations, control in regulated and deregulated (often 'human resource management'- HRM-influenced) workplace environments. In the pre 1970s years supply factors and wider environmental determinants provide an explanatory context for the British experience: factors ranging from managerial failure, restrictive practices, persistence of the craft based production system as well as institutional factors have all been offered on the supply side; the business environment from the 1930s through the post war decades in effect insulated management practice from the need to change. Aspects of the shipbuilding case illustrate this.

Chapter 3, addressing the external aspects of management poses the question: the externalisation of British business management? External management includes an examination of the wider societal engagement of business from 1900. The nature of this engagement, which differed over time, is explored. The other aspect of external management is the business dimension. Here a paradigm shift occurred after the 1970s. Changes in transaction costs and the pattern of multinational activity led to the fall from grace of the internally integrated organisational form. Though there is debate about the extent of the break with the past, externalisation strategies like lean production and just in time have had impact on the organisation of business activity, less concerned with asset specific growth strategies. There is no real sense in which the quest for efficiency in this 'externalisation era' saw

British business isolated from the competitive environment as powerful engines of change, as was arguably the case pre 1970s. The contemporary case exemplifies this.

Within these broad categorisations (the internalisation years pre 1970s and externalisation thereafter, though in many respects the British experience qualifies this generalisation), Part A researches external and internal management of British business. Research of the former: examines the 'Chandlerian paradigm' in the British context; analyses the conceptual background to externalisation; outlines the way in which the 'post M form' as an externally focused organisation integrates management activities; identifies the development of societal engagement of business management, an engagement which spread over the entire period from 1900 to present. Research of internal management looks primarily at: management and organisational control and focuses on the management of the human resource, justified by current debate and research of the traditional British business environment, much of which was labour intensive and craft dominated; the contemporary centrality of aspects of human resource management to internal management.

Case studies 1 and 2 are researched within these parameters. The shipbuilding case covers the period 1900-1965. This was an industry, which in Britain largely failed to develop the optimal use of integrated value and supply chains, and invested relatively little in its internal management. The case shows how the companies operated through externalisation strategies and made minimal investment in strengthening internal management. However the case also shows it is far too simplistic to define these practices as 'backward': at times many practices, internal and external were appropriate to the business-economic environment, at other times perhaps not.

The contemporary case (X Films plc) researched a range of internal and external practices within the firm itself, X's relationship with other companies in the value chain, wider societal relationships and the nature of connection with multi national group headquarters. The research indicated strong internal management though arguably under developed managerial capability in HRM terms; extensive externalisation of a range of value chain activities; a relationship with group headquarters not entirely explained by Bartlett and Ghoshal's 'post M' model; societal engagement consistent with the concept of stakeholder company - though much of this explained by the nation state governmental environment.

Chapter 1

Introduction and Context: Overview of the Business-Competitive Environment from 1900

- The quest for business efficiency and concern for throughput management.

'In the Wealth of Nations, Adam Smith advocated a system of production based on employee specialisation and economies of scale...industrialists such as Henry Ford and Alfred Sloan perfected the system building the assembly line. But Sloan wished to invent a company that could run itself. He thus invented the modern multidivisional firm in which businesses are divided into a set of semi autonomous operating units. Although the Sloanist firm was decentralised there was a rigid and internally integrated command and control system and a professional class to do this' (Micklethwaite and Wooldridge (1996). (1)

'...to generalise it [a universally valid business model] to other societies smacks of an ethnocentricity that neglects a host of vital national specific determinants of productivity and competitive success. Differences in corporate structures and managerial hierarchies are undoubtedly relevant to the discussion of national economic performance. But so are resource and factor endowment....indeed in the last resort, big business is at least as much a product as a cause of economic and social activity' (Supple 1992). (2)

'....our integrated structures worked very well for us. But it is an idea whose time has past' (Bob Allen, ATT's Chief Executive Officer, 1995). (3)

'...the Sloanist model has disintegrated – or more accurately an extreme version of one of Sloan's beliefs, decentralisation, has triumphed over two of his other tenets, the emphasis on formal controls and self sufficiency' (Micklethwaite and Wooldridge p 106). (4)

Background

By the end of the nineteenth century, two dimensions of economic and business development provided the backdrop for management practice. The first was the growing importance of the USA. The United States' average annual growth rate (at 4.1%) 1860-1913 was double Britain's (Pollard 1989) and by 1900 America was the world's leading industrial nation with national income from industry now exceeding agriculture (Cameron 1997). There was also an impetus towards the increased scale of business unit: transportation and communications improvements enabled volume production for the supply of large geographically dispersed markets; in the capital goods industries in particular, the logic of scale economies to produce at the lowest unit cost was attractive (Chandler 1962,1977,1990). The Sherman Anti Trust Act of 1890 also played a critical role in encouraging large scale corporate structures (Chandler 1976). It is not surprising that America led the way in the systematic development of 'modern' management practice, though the antecedents of many of these practices originated elsewhere (Wren 1994).

Second, was Britain's relationship to this. While the impediments to scale and 'modernisation' of business structure have been well aired ranging from market characteristics (e.g., Payne 1988; Kirby 1994) to familial ownership (e.g. Chandler 1976, though over-simplification and indeed a range of counter evidence has considerably modified the traditionally negative airing given to 'personal capitalism' – see e.g., Fitzgerald 2000, Mackie 2001) and socio cultural factors (e.g., Coleman 1973; Sanderson 1972; Locke 1993) of great significance was the international scope of much British business activity, thereby providing over time exposure to an increasingly competitive environment and the consequent need for a strategic response. Of all the large nations at this time, Britain was most dependent on imports and exports. From the last decades of the nineteenth century the emergence of extensive foreign competition was a major feature of the international trading environment, an increase in the scale of enterprise being a key feature of this with much of the pace being forced by the USA. This environment provided the context of the quest for business efficiency, revealing American and British parallels and contrasts.

The Quest for Business Efficiency

At its fundamental level, the increasing size of business unit from the end of the nineteenth century meant that efficient throughput management was imperative. Increase in scale, though occurring differently country to country brought a complexity qualitatively distinct from management practices in smaller (often proprietor run) companies prior to this time. (5) Payne (1967) described an appreciable increase in business size in Britain, though far outdone by the United States where by 1900 there were 1500 companies with more than 500 employees, one third of these employing over 1000. The concomitant increase in market spread both in volume and geographically has provided much of the theoretical explanation for the motivation towards internalisation of management and the supercession of market functions by hierarchical co-ordination: the emergence of internal hierarchies facilitated higher volumes and frequencies of transaction leading to further growth (Williamson 1981).

Growth via horizontal growth and vertical integration were both significant features of the three decades from 1890. In the USA, Chandler traced the 15 year period after 1880 as significant in terms of horizontal growth in business with an accelerated period of vertical growth from 1898-1914 (Chandler 1962; 1977;

1990). He argued strongly that the key to organisational success lay not so much in capacity (the potential to produce and sell) but in how well throughput was managed. Others have argued that managed control of the labour process went hand in hand with this (e.g., Braverman 1974). It is highly significant that companies in sectors which experienced growth (and in Chandlerian terms throughput management needs) 'prematurely' (i.e. before the last quarter of the nineteenth century) were indeed pioneers of modern management techniques. The railroads were early practitioners of management practices later to be written as 'principles' in early management thought: Andrew Carnegie's early experience on the Pennsylvania Railroad led to organisational arrangements for delegating authority as early as the mid nineteenth century; (6) in Britain the railways with their extensive route networks, passengers and goods carrying business required complex systems for rate fixing, freight, passenger and rolling stock handling, accentuated when the amalgamation movement gathered momentum after the mid 1840s (Dyos and Aldcroft 1974). Gourvish's study of the London and North Eastern Railway which indicated a strong centrally imposed management capability aimed at controlling a geographically divided structure also showed that the early trunk line railway companies 'made the first concerted attempt to solve the overriding problems of large scale businesses and developed important and possibly novel forms of business management' (Gourvish 1972).

The British and American merger movements ran in parallel (Wilson 1995), though the difference in degree was striking. 150 firms valued at £42 million were involved in the British merger mania peak of 1898-1900, while 979 American firms with a value of over £400 million merged in one year alone, 1898 (Hannah 1983). Most importantly, in the USA vertical integration and diversification were common, 98% of all mergers in Britain were horizontal combinations (Hannah 1974). Consequently, the 'need' for Tayloristic and scientific management approaches to job control, measurement and precision was less in the Britain than in America. The case of steel highlighted this most vividly.

Prior to the introduction of the Bessemer process, the iron and steel industry was particularly fragmented: some firms owned the furnaces that smelted the ore into pig iron; others had the rolling mills and forges that converted the pig iron into bars or slabs; still others took the bars or slabs and rolled them into rails, sheets, nails and wire. Between each of these independent operations, an intermediary took the output of one and sold it on to the next producer. From 1872, using the Bessemer process, Carnegie decided to concentrate on steel production. Using Bessemer converters he integrated operations, integrating vertically too into coal and iron mines. Until 1908 and the perfection of the open hearth process, the Bessemer process was the basis of the world's steel industry. When Carnegie started producing, iron rails cost $100 per ton, by 1900 $12. Steel production in the USA in 1868 was 8500 tons (Britain 110000); in 1902 it was 9,000,000 (Britain 1,800,000) (Wren 1994). The steel industry in Britain, and especially in Scotland, exhibited little integration even during the inter war years except in the sense of iron masters intensifying their existing activities in coal mining (Payne 1992). Regional amalgamations and integration devised by US consultants failed when heavy steel-makers perhaps inevitably adopted a defensive stance behind a tariff wall in 1932 (Tolliday 1984; Kirby 1994).

US-UK differences have been well documented. Both supply and demand factors were important. Private companies with limited liability provided the legal-institutional framework, which enabled family firms and partnerships to sustain themselves by controlling share capital. While there was the emergence of mass markets in Britain towards the end of the nineteenth century, this has to be placed in context compared with the USA, concisely expressed by some historians:

> Although the later nineteenth century witnessed the emergence of embryonic mass markets for small scale items of common consumption, these were far from ubiquitous. They were also far narrower in extent than their counterparts in the United States. Moreover, the generality of markets for British firms, both at home and abroad, remained sufficiently fragmented to preclude access to dynamic economies of scale. (7)

Unsurprisingly then, full vertical integration of value chain activities in many sectors of the economy failed to occur despite ownership conglomeration and amalgamation until well into the second half of the twentieth century (Channon 1973). But although throughput management needs were therefore less than in leading US companies-illustrated dramatically with steel-it would be quite wrong to suggest throughput efficiency practices were insignificant. Even in the steel sector, very modern and up to date practices took place. Bolckow Vaughan and Company of Middlesbrough, John Brown and Company of Sheffield had acquired ore and coal mines as an essential complement to their own activities (Wilson 1995); the formation in 1902 of Guest Keen and Nettlefolds and Company saw the integration of the collieries, Spanish ore mines and blast furnaces of Guest Keen and Company with the steel and components business of Nettlefolds, creating a firm with a nominal capital of £4 million (Jones 1978). Also, in terms of managerial practices, some steel firms developed cost accounting techniques comparable to those employed in many US corporations (Boyce 1992). By 1920, J and P Coats the largest manufacturing enterprise was valued at £45 million; just over a decade later, 5 firms exceeded this (Unilever, Imperial Tobacco, ICI, Courtaulds and Distillers) by which time at least 10 British firms employed in excess of 30000, and ICI and Unilever had workforces of around 50000 (Kirby 1994). There was also evidence of managerial innovation with the use of functional management specialists, especially accountants (Hannah 1974). More recent research indicated that efficiency and scientific management practices (if not strictly Taylorism) did have an impact on British industry to an extent not recognised previously (e.g., Littler 1985;Whitson 1996); analysis of the engineering press in Britain showed that such views were well covered - with the assumption that subscribers were aware of the new methods (Boticelli 1997). A recent study of the Leeds clothing industry has shown the success of applying mass production and scientific management principles to a non uniform product, the made to measure suit, from the 1920s. Customers were measured in manufacturer owned retail shops and their orders were transmitted to large well equipped factories in which work was organised along Fordist lines. At its peak, Burton's Hudson Road factory in Leeds employed over 10000 turning out 50000 suits per week (Honeyman 2000). Some business sectors though showed much scepticism (Zeitlin 1983; Gospel 1992; Tailby 2000).

Similar trends were evident in the service sector. Some mass retailers adopted strategies of backward vertical integration. Firms like Lipton's, the Cooperative Wholesale Society and Home and Colonial Stores acquired manufacturing operations and integrated production and distribution on a scale much more ambitious than even the USA, though their managerial hierarchies were less developed than in American firms (Chandler 1990; Wilson 1995). Similar integration of production and distribution strategies were also evident in the branded and packaged goods sector in leading companies like Rowntree and Cadbury, Huntley and Palmer, Peak Freens, WD & HO Wills, Guinness and Watneys, Lever Bros, J J Coleman, Crosse and Blackwell (Wilson 1954; 1965; 1995a). In banking too, Britain did not lag in the development of modern forms of organisation and management. By the eve of World War 1, banking was dominated by a small number of large banking companies with head offices and nationwide branch networks. As one writer has put it the form of ownership that most closely encapsulates Chandler's concept of personal capitalism was largely displaced in the retail banking sector and the corporate form of ownership came to dominate at what was for Britain an early date. (8) This had come about according to the same writer because of the economies of scale, the operation of intermediary and remittance services which drove expansion by way of mergers and the build up of extensive branch networks (Collins 1995).

The efficient management of throughput continued as a major theme in management and business practice throughout the twentieth century, associated with integration of operational activities, rational and scientific approaches to business management, well exemplified in the view of the World Economic Conference of 1927. Its industry sub committee held the following view:

> Rationalisation by which we understand the methods of technique and of organisation designed to secure the minimum waste of effort and material. They include the scientific organisation of labour, standardisation of both materials and products, simplification of process and improvements in the system of transport and marketing. (9)

The post second war Anglo-American Council on Productivity which organised visits to the United States by leading British businessmen and trade unionists often issued reports expressing the view that British workers worked as hard as their American counterparts but that poor production flow bad plant layout and inefficient management practices were responsible for relatively low UK productivity (Tomlinson 1991). Although the methodology adopted by the Council was such that we should be circumspect about the findings (e.g., visits were often to best practice rather than 'average' American firms), there was nonetheless a strong concern that efficiency practices should be propagated in Britain. After 1949 the TUC took steps to encourage the spread of scientific management in Britain. In the following decades, government led initiatives in various sectors (e.g., cars, shipbuilding, aerospace, engineering) attempted to encourage integration, rationalisation and support more efficient and effective throughput management. In some instances, nationalisation was the chosen policy instrument to achieve these ends. The Ministry of Technology supervised the Shipbuilding Industry Act of 1967, which created Upper Clyde Shipbuilders merging four existing shipyards; this and the later nationalisation of the shipbuilding industry used the strong argument of efficient integration of constituent shipyards and research facilities (though this failed) as a spur to efficiency and competitiveness (Sawyer 1991; 1992).

To summarise and contextualise British practice in the post war period to the 1970s, the historiography now indicates the linkages between throughput management practices and the competitive environment. Compromises between management and labour helped reinforce restrictive practices (Barnett 1986; Bean and Crafts 1996). There was an inability of British employers in many sectors to control the labour process, often linked to the persistence of a craft system which frustrated technological innovation and automation (Lewchuk 1987). All of this was underpinned by managerial failure (e.g., markedly in the car industry – Church 1994; Foreman-Peck, Bowden and McKinlay 1995). More recent work on the car industry, some of which is transferable to other sectors (Bowden, Foreman-Peck and Richardson 2001), has placed the failure to develop efficient throughput management in the context of longer run trends in the international competitive environment: world economic collapse in 1931 led to a long period of insulation from foreign competition but allied to this was the fact that many sectors were too small to create adequate domestic competition; the competitive environment therefore was not an engine for change and modernisation (see also Foreman-Peck and Hannah 1999). In the immediate post war years, the economy's need to export (to compensate for decline in net foreign assets) led to manufacturing expanding to the largest ever share of GDP; until the revival of effective foreign competition, management practice was insulated from the need to change, though work by Broadberry and Crafts examining a range of British industrial ventures in the 1950s and 1960s did not find that competitive markets were good for innovation per se (Broadberry and Crafts 2001). This is a reminder that managerial, institutional, governance and labour practices were not in themselves important in explaining failure to manage throughput efficiently, and suggests that performance be viewed in the context of a multi-layered economic-competitive environment.

Although the writing and research on post 1980 business is less comprehensive than the earlier period, contextual underpinnings can still be recognised with observed linkages between management of throughput, Britain's wider economic-competitive environment and managerial practice; this is expanded and detailed in chapter 3. From the mid 1970s, two significant factors in the business-economic environment had an impact on business management: movement in transaction costs and changes in the international competitive environment.

As detailed in chapter 3, the balance of internal and external transaction costs shifted towards the latter. In consequence, not only was more of the supply and value chain managed externally, but there were ramifications for internal management of businesses: decreasing numbers meant less justification for the strong hierarchical structures associated with the internally integrated firm. In many sectors of manufacturing, the focus of throughput management shifted significantly from integration to concerns about managing suppliers, information technology, and within the factory, team based production. The market-environmental context of this is outlined below. Lean production techniques (spectacularly successful in sustaining many Japanese companies' ability to penetrate western markets especially in motor cars and electronic goods), with the emphasis on just in time, demand pull production and supplier relationships had by the 1980s replaced internal integration of supply and value chain activities as the leading practices (Womack, Jones and Roos 1990). In the USA, most automobile factories adopted at least some aspects of lean production, with 25% attempting to adopt the entire system (Milkman 1997). This should be tempered by a recent study of changing practices in a diesel plant during the 1990s which showed that while just in time was the imagery, random and uncoordinated changes were the reality (Malloch 1997). There is though no consensus on the extent to which lean production was a break with the past tradition of throughput management control: some work indicated a 'progressive' and different proto-democratic and participative view of organisation was predicated on such practices (Adler 1993); in other instances it was labelled a new form of Taylorism, or criticised thus, 'in the eyes of the workers, when the production system is lean, many see it as mean'. (10)

There was still considerable unidirectionality of control, very familiar to scientific management and Taylorism (Jackson and Carter 1998). Foucaultian accounts of factory control systems in the 1980s and 1990s indicated that often 'objectives echo classical Taylorism' (11) even though implementation was rather different, based on large elements of self discipline and control, rather than Taylorist managerial control (Poster 1990). But some research in the US auto sector indicated that practice was not uniform, with wide variations in the degree of supervision of the production process within the plant (Shaiken, Lopez and Mankita 1997). Research in other sectors showed that contemporary throughput management was less concerned by internal management control but very much defined by the management of linkages and relationships. In clothing manufacture and retailing, company studies indicated that value adding activities occurred in the management of design, manufacture and the operational aspects of retailing, each function often undertaken by separate companies. In food retailing, research on the main supermarket chains in Britain illustrated the main market developments from the 1970s were the link between asset specific investment (like the building of new stores) and relational contracts with independent companies to supply own branded goods. (12) Studies of the British general insurance sector showed that pre existing capabilities could not manage growth and competition necessitated by the expansion of computerisation and electronic data bases from the 1980s with the required levels of efficiency: throughput management here meant a break with existing managerial processes and operations and led to the creation of new and separate organisations to capture and manage computer and electronically generated business (Westall 1997).

A key development in the international competitive environment was the globalisation of key areas of activity. Jones (1996) outlined the significant movement in multinational company activity from strategies of regional integration to globalisation and a rapid growth in intra-firm trade. Allied to this was a substantial increase in foreign direct investment by multinationals. Britain was a major recipient of direct investment by foreign owned companies. The post war decades were previously shown to be years when the international competitive environment initially enabled large sections of British industry to perform well enough with little need for radical change. The international competitive environment and effective competition were not engines for change for much of the 1945-1970s period. However, in the subsequent years, the picture is rather different. Research indicates high levels of inward investment in UK manufacturing 1972-1995 have helped encourage transfer of innovative production and the convergence of 'best practice' techniques to the UK economy and also to UK owned companies due to 'transmission effects' (Barrell and Pain 1997; DTI 1998; Hubert and Pain 2001).

Summary, Conclusion and Preview of Chapters 2-5

The increased size of business unit and the growth in both horizontal and vertical integration presented scale economies of a quite unprecedented nature. However, the full realisation of these economies necessitated the development of efficient practices to manage the increased throughput. These trends, developments and practices occurred in the USA and in Britain, to a greater extent in the former. Although there were many examples of significant modernising practices in British companies, there were nonetheless strong environmental factors which provided a background, against which management practice in the generality (specifically in manufacturing) was rarely designed to achieve the most efficient and optimal outcomes in the pre 1970s era of the internally integrated hierarchically organised business. The competitive environment changed from the 1970s with shifts in transaction costs and geographical patterns of production and trading within multinational companies. Consequently, less reliance was placed on the management of internal integrated processes and more on external management: that is management of extended value and supply chains often external to the company.

In the following chapters, the two themes of internalisation and externalisation of management are developed in detail. Although the economic-business environment has been presented as a broad historical sweep (pre 1970s and post 1970s), the approach adopted and themes explored reflect a complexity of internal and external management which cannot be captured solely by chronological analysis. Aspects of external management, for instance the societal dimension, were highly important aspects of managerial and business practice throughout. Chapter 3 and case studies 1 and 2 (chapters 4 and 5) highlight this. Chapter 3 critically analyses the integration/external co-ordination dichotomy in the British context in some detail; and assesses the form and scope of externalisation of business management to the present, particularly whether externalisation and the management of the external dimension of business is significant enough to justify the term 'externalisation of management'.

Similarly the complexity of internal management is addressed. The strengthening of internal management has been associated with the development of hierarchies required by the large scale growth and integration depicted as typical of the 70 or so years from the turn of the twentieth century. Chapter 2's analysis of internal management and the case studies in chapters 4 and 5 go beyond this. In so doing the research and analysis is focused largely on management/organisational control structures and various aspects of the management of human resource. There are compelling reasons for analysing internal management in this way. First, much of the debate in the business history and management research and literature has been framed by Chandler's and others' work on the importance of investment in hierarchies and strategic control structures. Second, management of the human resource was highly significant in Britain given the high labour input in the labour technology mix, with high levels of labour intensity. This was especially important in the context of a highly craft oriented production system reflected in the choice of case. Third, the management of the human resource has important explanatory significance in debates surrounding issues of restrictive practices, management control, inadequate management and the economic-competitive environment. Fourth, although the craft system and high levels of labour intensity have much reduced in significance, management of the human resource is still vitally important given the apparently radical change to management approaches based on autonomous teams, delegated decision making, 'empowerment'.

Notes

1. Micklethwaite, J. and Wooldridge, A. (1996), *The Witch Doctors. Making Sense of the Management Gurus*, London: Heinemann, p. 105.
2. Supple, B. (1992), 'Introduction' in B.E. Supple (ed), *The Rise of Big Business*, Aldershot: Elgar, p. xxxv.
3. Bob Allen, AT&T's Chief Executive Officer, *Business Week* 23 April 1995, p. 92.
4. Micklethwaite, J. and Wooldridge, A. (1996), *The Witch Doctors. Making Sense of the Management Gurus*, London: Heinemann, p. 106.
5. There were of course significant strides towards what we would call modern managerial practices prior to this. For example during the industrial revolution as outlined in Pollard's classic study. But even here, '—there were few isolated examples of conscious thought on management and the attempt to systematise it' (Pollard, S 1965, *The Genesis of Modern Management*, Harmondsworth: Pelican p. 292) and '---as far as we know the management pioneers were isolated and their ideas without great influence' (Ibid p. 295).
6. Andrew Carnegie learned the trade of a telegrapher with the western division of the Pennsylvania Railroad. On one occasion when Thomas A Scott the superintendent of that division was absent, Carnegie untangled a traffic tie up after a derailment by

sending out orders using Scott's initials-unauthorised. This initiative led to a major change in the organisation by providing for the delegation of dispatching authority. Formerly, only the superintendent had the authority (cited in Wren 1994, *The Evolution of Management Thought,* New York and London: Wiley).

7. Kirby, M.W. and Rose, M.B. (1994), 'Introduction' in M.W. Kirby and M.B. Rose (eds) *Business Enterprise in Modern Britain From the Eighteenth to the Twentieth Century* London: Routledge, p. 10.

8. Collins, M. (1994) 'The growth of the firm in the domestic banking sector' in M.W. Kirby and M.B Rose (eds) *Business Enterprise in Modern Britain From the Eighteenth to the Twentieth Century* p. 276, London: Routledge.

9. World Economic Conference 1927 Industry Sub Committee, cited in Wilson, J.F (1995), *British Business History 1720-1994*, Manchester: Manchester University Press p. 142.

10. Babson, S. (1993) 'Lean or   mean: the MIT model and lean production' *Labour Studies Journal*, 18 (Summer) p. 3.

11. McKinlay, A. and Taylor, P. (1998) 'Through the looking glass: Foucault and politics of production', in A. McKinlay and K. Starkey (eds), *Foucault, Management and Organisation Theory*, London: Sage p. 179.

12. Carlo Morelli, Managing the Value Chain in Supermarket Retailing, Seminar paper delivered at University of Glasgow 11 December 1997.

Chapter 2

Internal Management of Business in Britain

Synopsis

The central debate on the role played by internal management-the debate surrounding the visible hand of managerial capitalism – in developing Chandlerian styled strength in managerial form and structure is addressed. This explanatory model had important qualifications in Britain. The internal management of post-M form structures is also analysed, indicating managerial integration if not internalisation practices. Various aspects of human resource management, particularly important features of the British business management context, are analysed. Included in this is an examination of the craft system and the extent to which management was bounded by this system; the key role given to the foreman indicated a rational management strategy, though this was less successful in the later decades of the twentieth century. The position of management training and development in the strengthening of management is assessed, though local company material suggested that generally accepted failings in this area did not apply in all cases. While considerable increases in the volume of training had increased since the 1980s, corporate management training was still underdeveloped in Britain. Finally, some other human resource management practices are analysed, particularly in the context of managerial control: personnel and welfarist approaches often associated with managerial responses to heightened trade union activity and to concerns for production; 'human relations', focused largely on managerial control and relatively ineffectual in relation to management practice in Britain (though more important in the USA); regulation and deregulation of the workforce; Human Resource Management (HRM) with its strong emphasis on managerial initiative though not without aspects of democratisation.

- Internal Management: structures and control.
- Internal Management: managing human resource- the craft/technical system; management training.
- Internal Management: management control-personnel and welfare; human relations; workplace regulation; deregulation and HRM.

Introduction

Organisation and management structure was a major instrument used to strengthen and control firms in an era of growth. Hierarchies were used to address the support required for the internally integrated companies, which developed in the various phases of horizontal and vertical integration. The term used-'visible hand'-was apt, for this represented a deliberate attempt to control business and its markets by managerial action rather than working with the 'invisible hand' of market co-ordination. But there were other dimensions of internal management, which illustrated the means by which managers attempted to control and strengthen their position within firms. As argued above, management of the human resource is of greatest significance for the purposes of this research, and this chapter will assess practices to strengthen management and also analyse issues of management control, by examining: management of the craft/technical resource; training and development of managers; the significance of a range of human resource and personnel management practices in the context of management control.

Structures and Control

The Chandlerian paradigm fully articulated in 1977, further developed in 1990, linked the growth of big business, increasing efficiency of national economies and the replacement of family owned enterprise with corporate structures administered by salaried managers. This has largely focused the debate on the role of management and organisation structures in the running of business. Significantly, Chandler's book published in 1977 was entitled 'The Visible Hand'. Company staffed professional hierarchies of salaried managers were superimposed on the market as an instrument for co-ordinating business activity. Leading business practice in the competitive environment was represented as evolving from external market co-ordination practices to the internalisation of key managerial functions. Internalisation was prioritised in business development terms over externalisation. The apotheosis of this was the multidivisional (M) form of company, a structure with a strategic centre and a series of operating divisions (including international divisions) each with a managerial hierarchy supported and controlled by managerial levels intervening between the centre and operations. The value of this internalisation/professional manager model in providing a comprehensive explanation of British practice is addressed later, but there are major qualifications to the model: serious doubt has been expressed about the supposedly damaging effects of family owned and run businesses since there was no obvious and direct correlation between the decline of this organisational form and business and economic growth and efficiency (Church 1993; Jones and Rose 1993). The accentuation of the M form by Chandler and other writers (e.g., Williamson 1975) also represented a rather ethnocentric view: if this structure/model was fundamental to business development it did not address aspects of corporate success elsewhere (in Germany and Japan for example) where different managerial and structural forms were adopted (Dyos and Thanhauser 1976; Hannah 1976; Suzuki 1991; Yui 1998). Indeed it was claimed that British business achieved much before 1920 without US management models and arguably less thereafter with (Jones 1997). Nevertheless, Chandler's work has clearly shown that the M form arose because the rudimentary hierarchies suited to growth up to c1914 could not efficiently and effectively sustains growth and expansion. According to Chandler, 'managerial hierarchies that had been created to co-ordinate, monitor and allocate resources for one line of products had great difficulty in administering the processing of several sets of products for new and different markets.' (1) The M form saw the creation of relatively autonomous operating divisions each having their own levels of management, with a general office acting as the focal point for corporate strategy, supervision and reporting. The 'typical' M form is illustrated:

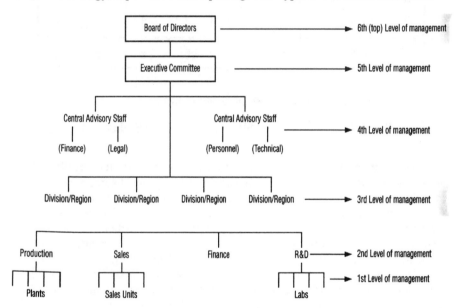

**Figure 2.1 The Multidivisional Form of Organisation
(adapted from Schmitz 1993)**

The speed and extent to which these managerial and organisation structures were adopted in Britain has been charted in Table 2.1.

Table 2.1 Diversification and Multidivisional Structures in the Largest 100 Firms 1950-1970

Product Type	1950		1960		1970	
	A	B	A	B	A	B
Single	31	2	18	1	6	1
Dominant	38	4	35	8	34	24
Related	21	6	39	19	54	43
Unrelated	2	0	4	1	6	4
Total	92	12	96	29	100	72

Source : Channon (1973)

A = Number of firms in the product range

B = Number of firms with the M form structures

The spread of the M form has been outlined in other work too: by the 1970s according to Gospel (1992), 75% of British firms had adopted some variant of the multidivisional form. However, the picture was rather more complex than the figures suggest. In reality, in Britain these large scale corporations tended to evolve from holding (H) companies-a form which proliferated in Britain in the inter war years (Gourvish, 1987)-making structures weaker than in US counterparts, with smaller managerial hierarchies and weaker central planning organisations. Studies of internal management practices also revealed less than optimal practices. There were deficiencies in effective accounting procedures both within and between divisions, weaknesses in marketing and technical innovation and in the case of holding companies transforming to the M form, a tendency to insert a 'cosmetic' layer of management falling far short of the fundamental internalisation of managerial structures and practices (Pagnamenta and Overy 1984; Clark and Tann 1986; Alford 1988; Payne 1990). The apparent conversion to the M form by 1970 was partly explained by the increasing number of American multinational subsidiaries implanted in the UK (Bostock and Jones 1994) and by the activities of American management consultants. Moreover, there was considerable evidence that such structural forms did not always ground themselves in British company life. Channon (1973) showed that the relationship between the central office or board and the divisions was not that of the headquarters-decentralised business unit, and the failure to develop a core of strategic staff specialists at the centre was considered a major shortcoming compared to the classic M form. In addition, concentration of ownership which did occur in Britain was not always accompanied by concentration of plants especially in engineering, electrical goods, chemicals and metal manufacture. So rather than strengthening internal management, this led to a fragmentation and a loss of some scale economies (Hughes 1976; Prais 1976).

Contemporary 'modern' structures differ markedly from the M form. After the 1970s most multinational companies abandoned corporate wide international divisions and globalised. In the most advanced cases this meant a deepening of regional integration of production systems to global integration (Jones 1994) and the subcontracting of production in many cases (Casson 1995). The sharing of risk, research and development costs, and accessing new technologies led to a substantial growth in strategic alliances (Morris and Hergert 1987; Lorange and Roos 1992).

Table 2.2 Growth in International Strategic Alliance Formation in Manufacturing 1980-1989

Industry	No. of Alliances	
	1980-84	1985-89
Automobile		
US - Europe	26	79
US - Japan	10	24
Europe - Japan	10	39
Total	**6**	**16**
Biotechnology		
US - Europe	108	148
US - Japan	58	124
Europe - Japan	45	54
Total	**5**	**20**
Information Technology		
US - Europe	348	445
US - Japan	158	256
Europe - Japan	133	132
Total	**57**	**57**
Chemicals		
US - Europe	103	80
US - Japan	54	31
Europe - Japan	28	35
Total	**21**	**14**

Source : United Nations 1994 (cited in Jones 1996 p 144)

The internal management structures and controls required in these environments differed from those developed in the multidivisional form and in some respects (in some cases) reflected the externalisation of management (Miles, Snow and Coleman 1992), addressed in chapter 3. The key to internal management control was the integration of diverse and disparate activity, often occurring relatively far down the organisation at first and second levels of management, calling looser, more federal, and in some cases much more decentralised structural forms, than the typical multidivisional (Bartlett and Ghoshal 1998). The contrast with the M form is illustrated in Figure 2. Not only had the post M company reduced levels of management, but it also devolved functions and business activities to lower levels in the organisation. This had implications for managerial roles within the company structure, analysed in chapter 3 and in the case study in chapter 5.

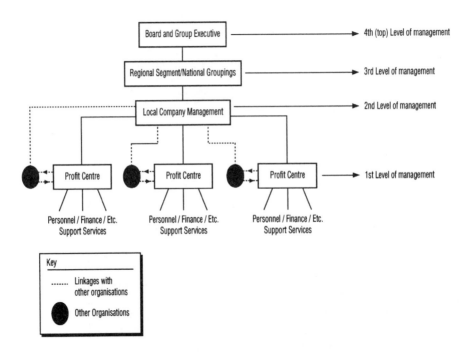

Figure 2.2 The Post M Form Structure
(adapted from Bartlett and Ghoshal 1998)

Managing Human Resource and Management Control

As a means of strengthening internal management, the methods and strategies employed to manage human resource were vital. Three aspects of this will be examined: the extent to which management was strengthened or bounded by the craft, technical resource; the extent and nature of managerial training and development; the importance and significance of management control in personnel and human resource management practices.

Management Bounded by the Craft/Technical Resource?

The technical-productive resources of the firm in Britain were organised, in substantial measure, through the craft system. Management of this craft-technical human resource, and the extent to which this constrained management, is key to an understanding of internal management. Management was influenced by factor endowment. Labour intensive practices were used in many manufacturing sectors precisely because the labour-technology environment made this an appropriate and rational basis for managerial action. In contrast to the USA where high investment in new technologies was linked to scarcity of skilled labour and tight managerial control over the machine process (Braverman 1974), Britain often adopted greater labour intensity with profits maintained at acceptable levels in a relatively low productivity environment only by pressurising wages (Kirby 1994) and in some cases (e.g., in coal mining) through the intensification of labour sub contracting, (Melling, 1996a). Consequently, labour organisations were able to control the pace of work in many industrial sectors (Lewchuck 1987), mirrored in the various industrial disputes over the issue of managerial control (McKinlay and Zeitlin 1989). Disputes over control of fundamental work practices and processes surfaced with some intensity, especially when capital investment was proposed, thereby challenging the traditional craft labour-technology mix. The Weir Company's new foundry investment in the west of Scotland after World War 1 illustrated this. The investment was presented in the following terms:

> [We] propose to initiate a system by which the individual moulder or group of moulders can increase earnings according to results--is it right that the complicated frame of a sewing machine is moulded by unskilled labour at Kilbowie while a plain blind flange has to be moulded at Cathcart by a man who has served 7 years apprenticeship? (2)

In this initiative, Weir made his thinking and plans very clear to the Minister of Labour:

> I regard wage rate payable to the unskilled man as of small importance-- because of my belief in payment by results, there is no reason why unskilled men at coremaking or on moulding machines should not earn 50% over the skilled man's earnings--[there was] failure of attempts to obtain co-operation through the Moulders union. After this failure, we applied ourselves to the problem from the technical standpoint. We have now designed and have 85% completed an entirely new foundry wherein the work will be carried out under entirely new processes and methods--. The necessity for skilled men has been eliminated. We will lay down the conditions for employment in this foundry. (3)

The Weir Group historian suggested that the experience with the ironmoulders stimulated Weir's attempts to break down traditional building industry craft practices in the company's housing project (Reader 1971).

The position of craft unions up to and including the 1930s vis a vis managerial prerogative indicated not so much an all powerful craft trade union constituency, or a sustained managerial assault on unions but an employee group whose power fluctuated from time to time: for example the major dispute in 1897 between the ASE and the engineering employers led to the acceptance of managerial prerogative (Zeitlin 1983); ten years later traditional craft practices had been reasserted; Lewchuk (1987) outlined trade union control over work practices in the motor vehicle industry in the 1930s. (4) On the other hand, craft unions apparently accepted 'scientific management' in Weir's engineering works by 1915 after some hostility (McLean 1983). The same company's house building venture, aimed as an attack on traditional building craft unionism was in the long run unsuccessful in these terms since building trade union conditions were maintained. And although Weir's attempt to depart from traditional craft practices in his foundry operations was clear and sustained, (5) his foundries remained unionised under craft conditions.

There was however evidence of an appreciation amongst opinion formers of a particularistic British labour-technology mix. It was significant that some of the leading management thinkers and practitioners went some way towards recognising the difficulties which craft based trade unions had with raw scientific management. Urwick for example noted:

> The objectives raised by trades unions to many forms of scientific management are often set down hastily to mere ignorance and perversity. But if we take account of the fact that the very existence of the craft unions is threatened by the erasure of the craft distinctions; and that the skilled workers thus risk losing the outlet for the creative impulse, the dignity of skilled work, we cannot help seeing, unless wilfully blind, that the workers are contending for a type of civilisation higher than that which it is intended to force upon them. (6)

The National Institute of Industrial Psychology chose its name very carefully, in conjunction with trade union leaders, to avoid any association with 'human efficiency' or 'scientific management' (Welch and Myers 1932). Oliver Sheldon, company secretary of Rowntree and ' first to lay claim to developing an explicit philosophy of management' (7) was anxious that trade unions should become partners with management and enlisted into corporate life instead of apart from it (Sheldon 1930). All this ran counter to Child's view 'that by the mid 1920s, management thinkers ignored the role of the unions'. (8)

The prevailing labour-technology mix in Britain did display a dynamic and strength for management of human resource in two key areas. First, close attention must be paid to the role played by internal labour markets in management of the craft technical resource. Recent work has shown the development of internal labour markets in the railway and other sectors of the British economy from the last quarter of the nineteenth century into the first two decades of the twentieth.

Sectors, which evolved internal labour markets, were mainly those with large stable markets relatively unaffected by the vicissitudes of the business cycle and who could therefore build up large permanent workforces and invest in training knowing the investment would pay off (Drummond 1995; Howlett 2000). Other research also showed that some firms in sectors affected by fluctuations in the business cycle did at least internalise much training. This was the case with the Mather and Platt textile machinery makers (Fitzgerald 1988) and in companies in the cotton and steel sectors (Moore 1996). The growth in internalisation of work processes which (like negotiation with the workforce) had previously been undertaken externally helped explain the fierce struggle at times for control of the workplace (Turner 1985). It should also be noted that the persistence of an externally modulated system-the craft system-may in part be explained by the distinct advantages to business owners of organising the human resource in this way: a plentiful supply of cheap labour trained within the craft obviated the need for large fixed capital investment, especially attractive in the cyclical and uncertain environment of shipbuilding (McKinlay 1989; Lorenz 1991). Some writers have gone further and linked management strategies of internal control (or their absence) to product-market mix in a rather deterministic way. For example, stable markets with relatively homogeneous products permitted the establishment of internal control systems: the absence of these conditions (in e.g. shipbuilding) led to employers externalising this function to employers' organisations (Gospel 1992). This is explored in some detail in chapter 4 case study 1.

Second, management of the key craft/technical resource-the craft worker-was vitally important. The role of the foreman was critical. Not seen simply as a co-ordinator of craft activity, a craft worker who had progressed through the craft system, key managerial practices were developed to ensure this post was identified as 'managerial' rather than 'craft worker employee'. This surely qualified as an investment in internal control systems. Archive material shows that William Weir's company had a clear view about the role played by foremen in the co-ordination of production and other functions in the engineering works. The role was more than just organising craft activities. In a paper delivered to the International Engineering Congress in Glasgow in 1901, Weir referred to the establishment in his engineering works of 'friction clubs' composed of foremen, administrative heads of department, drawing office staff, costing department personnel led by foremen,

> on the principle that its mission was to eliminate friction. Its business was to discuss shop problems and decide on solutions, to institute improvements and provide the means of carrying them out. Meetings are held once a month and minutes recorded. (9)

At the outset of the First World War, the shortage of skilled men led to Weir adopting a range of strategies including recruitment in the US, and although Weir would

> pay at no more than the local rate, there was to be a bonus system and,
> if we find good workers it is in the foreman's discretion to pay them more. (10)

The discretionary powers of the foremen were significant.

As case 1 indicates, in shipbuilding in the first half of the twentieth century, there was evidence that the strategy of foreman managerial identification was largely successful but less so after the 1950s. Interesting research is now appearing on the role of the career in gaining loyalty and hence easing managerial control (Savage 1998). There is some evidence of this process occurring in shipbuilding, though the limitations of job advancement and restricted hierarchies in this industry made the process rather different and indeed minimalist compared to other sectors (see case study 1).

However a human resource training system based on craft technical training faced much criticism by the 1960s; so too did the education system's approach to technical education (Baxter and McCormick 1984). Attempts were made to improve company technical training generally with the creation of Industrial Training Boards after the passage of the Industrial Training Act in 1964. Although enjoying only mixed success (Fitzgerald 1993) attempts were made to systematise and formalise technical and craft training: the key Clydeside shipyards for example all established craft technical training centres and liaised closely with the formal and rapidly growing further education sector. Later studies, though, indicated shortcomings in the training of craft and technical resource. Matched studies of firms in the German and British machine tool industry in the 1980s showed technical competence levels of skilled workers lacking in Britain compared to German counterparts (Daly et al 1985); other studies indicated serious skills and technology training gaps at various levels in business from workforce to management (Porter 1990; Mason et al 1992). In 1999 a survey by the Confederation of British Industry found severe skills shortages in construction, engineering, information technology; although this had much to do with buoyant economic growth (though not in some parts of the Britain, for example locations in Scotland and the north east of England), a significant part of the problem was the difficulty in re-skilling the existing workforce (CBI 1999).

Strengthening the Managerial Resource: Training and Development of Managers

The senior managers of larger businesses were from 1880 often   professionally trained as accountants. This profession played a very important part in the running of large companies, due to the absence of any other sources of managerial professionalism (Matthews, Anderson and Edwards 1997). In the USA the first business school dedicated to the training and education of professional managers, Wharton, was set up at the University of Pennsylvania in 1881. The Universities of Chicago and California both established undergraduate schools of commerce in 1889. New York University's Stern School of Business Administration, Dartmouth's Amos Tuck School of Administration and Harvard's Graduate School of Business Administration followed in the next decade. This contrasted sharply with Britain where very low priority was given to management training (an exception being the railways with the formation of the Railways Department at the London School of Economics in 1904).

In technical and scientific education and training, although the strong and symbiotic relationship between the civic universities and technical-scientific needs of business should not be ignored (Sanderson 1988), it has been shown that these universities responded largely to local rather than national needs (Rose 1994). However, the national (indeed international in many cases) scope of many 'local' businesses qualifies this local/national dichotomy. The Weir Company firmly rooted on Clydeside was very much a national firm being the main supplier of pumping equipment to the British merchant and naval fleets. Weir's works manager in 1887, CR Lang graduated from Glasgow University (Reader 1971). This started a trend of graduate recruitment of managers by the company. Nonetheless, the inappropriateness of the British approach to further and higher education, particularly the cultural/institutional barriers to the managerial, business, scientific and technical sophistication required for the early twentieth century, has been well documented (Locke 1993). In the few institutions, which ran business related degree courses, establishment was not an easy process (Keeble 1992). The financial struggle to establish the Manchester Business School in 1965 has been outlined by Wilson (1992), yet this was after generations of similar business school provision in America.

The conventionally accepted view was that management training was largely informal or non existent until well into the last three decades of the twentieth century. It was experience based and often disdainful of formal qualifications of any sort (Keeble 1992). It did not attract priority as a call on business resource:

> In the context of increasingly difficult trading conditions-- management training is likely to come very low in the determination of priorities at a time of greater competition for very scarce resources. (11)

Again, though, the experience of the Weir Group did not sit easily with this picture. The Weir Bulletin in 1953 indicated a number of middle and senior managers were university educated: at that date the apprentice training officer held a BSc; the works manager was educated at Glasgow's Royal College and Cambridge University, holding an MSc from the latter; senior engineering management staff were also graduates; indeed a strong core of university educated engineers in the Anglo Iranian Oil Company were 'ex Weir men'. (12)

Yet despite the experience of some individual businesses and their managers, it cannot be denied that even by the late 1980s British managers were ill qualified. At that time, only 24% of senior British managers were graduates (of any discipline) compared with 85% in the USA and Japan (Ackrill 1988). There has been significant change in the last decade. The provision of business and management education at university level (both under and postgraduate) is well established and can no longer be said to lag. A British university business school (Open University Business School) claimed in the late 1990s to be the biggest in Europe, educating many of its students/managers in Britain. However, it has been argued that the efficacy of business school led management training and development should be questioned: it is recognised that Germany and Japan did not initially adopt (and still do not in large numbers) the US style business school to train and develop managers, with few apparent ill effects on managerial strength or performance; Handy (1988) argued that by eventually going down the business school and academic route, Britain failed to reinforce attempts by firms to develop highly advanced corporate training regimes so successful in Germany and Japan. Nevertheless, published research indicated by the late 1990s significant improvements in management development at company level since the Constable McCormick Report in 1987 (Constable and McCormick 1987; Thomson 2001).

Management Control

Management Control and Personnel

In the development of internal management, personnel management and human relations strategies illustrated twin themes of personal/business development and management control. There is an interesting literature on the proliferation of development of personnel, welfare and human relations practices indicating that many such approaches were motivated by a management control agenda. The expansion of such schemes into the early twentieth century has been well documented (Fitzgerald 1988). It also appeared that the impetus for the introduction of welfare schemes could be antagonism to the growth of trade unions. The Great Eastern Railway's pension scheme was motivated in this way (Howlett 2000). Such schemes were often more than peripheral or fringe to the total remuneration package (Melling 1983). Welfarist approaches were also linked to the control of production and productivity concerns (human factors concerns) especially in a wartime environment. The Industrial Fatigue Board and the Health of Munitions Workers Committee saw a link between, on the one hand, the individual's physical health, mental development, his/her relationship to other employees in the group and, on the other, management's ability to control productivity (Thomas 1978); similar concerns were expressed in the Chief Factory Inspector's Reports in the 1940s (cited in Child 1969); the Tizard Committee set up in 1946 was interested in the 'human factors' aspects of production and efficiency and influenced the Chancellor of the Exchequer Sir Stafford Cripps (Tomlinson 1996). The Committee on Industrial Productivity established in 1948 had a Human Factors Panel containing 9 members, 3 government representatives, delegates from the British Employers Federation, delegates from the Trades Union Congress, an independent member and 3 representatives from independent social science research institutions.

Management Control and Personnel: Human Relations

Funding and research into human relations practices had an early agenda of workforce-management consultation. The Glacier Metal research project, highly significant in the development and application of human relations approaches in the workplace, was approved and supervised by the Human Factors Panel. However, although various employee representation mechanisms were set up as part of the project, these were quickly subsumed within the systems approach of the research: the organisation was viewed as an interacting system, with elaborate procedures developed to initiate a 'felt fair' pay system and to break with past practices. The researchers believed that once the group (employees) had gained experience and familiarisation they would in the early stages:

> develop insight and skill in recognising forces related to status, prestige, security, authority, suspicion, hostility and memories of past events these forces no longer colour subsequent discussions nor impede progress to the same extent as before. (13)

The focus of the research thereafter was mainly based on the legitimation of management action. By 1951,

> this consultative structure is now clearly distinguished from the executive structure. The General Manager's monthly report assumes considerable importance as providing the main link between the factory executive and consultative systems. The management brings a regular report on its work and in this way the management receives constantly renewed sanction for its work from all sections. (14)

In effect, like the earlier welfarist approaches activity was largely influenced by a managerial control agenda. In this case the context was the development of Jacques own evolving system of 'felt fair' pay and time span analysis, which was an approach based on developmental psychology with the matching-and importantly, the development- of individuals' capabilities to the time span of specific jobs and roles in the organisation. (15) Jacques' approach achieved a degree of uptake and support internationally but very little in Britain. His methodology was used by pre privatised British Gas and ICI and he was retained as a consultant by the Department of Health through the 1970s reforms of the NHS (Webster 1996). His work though was used more extensively elsewhere: by the US military, Whirlpool, a major American white goods manufacturer, the Toronto Police Force and C.R.A. an Australian mining company owned by Rio Tinto.

The broader human relations movement in Britain was synonymous with Eliot Jacques and the Tavistock Institute-a very significant factor in explaining the restricted impact of human relations thinking in Britain. (16) Jacques' work at the Tavistock sought to use research and consultancy in work settings to enable management to understand, tackle, and thereby control effectively a range of people related issues and problems. Research was disseminated through the journal *Human Relations*. The editorial policy outlined in the first issue in 1947 was

> the practical application of social science in response to community needs – the recent war gave urgency and opportunity for work on large scale problems and gave experience in handling interpersonal and inter group tensions.

The approach to be adopted was to be of practical use,

> to draw people from different academic disciplines in an effort to collaborate with those responsible for problems. (17)

In the United States, Human Relations was much more explicitly (indeed ideologically) influenced by a management control agenda. In a wide ranging article, O'Connor (1999) has illustrated a key driving force in the development of Human Relations (and its acceptance by Harvard Business School supported by a business elite) was its position as an alternative to both labour movement unrest and the anti business ideologies on offer:

> The case of the Harvard Business School and Human Relations shows a number of agendas at the institutional level, at the corporate industry levels and at the political level the support for the reinforcement of managerial over worker authority – it also reveals a case in which leaders in academe, industry, research and government sought solutions to management-labour conflicts that would not jeopardise managerial control. (18)

Conceptually similar arguments have been presented with regard to the Jacques Glacier project in Britain. This initiative was identified as 'managerial manipulation', at the expense of the employees' chosen representatives with a degree of hostility to trade unionism and organised labour (Child 1969). Human Relations was less influential in managerial practice in Britain than America. In the latter, considerable research was undertaken: the much cited Hawthorne enquiries kindled further research and study into human relations because these studies were marshalled into a coherent form, most notably by Roethslisberger and Dickson (1939), followed by more research from the Harvard Graduate School of Business Administration. In Britain, the anti pluralistic underpinnings failed to gain support of key professionals in management. An important Institute of Personnel Management study group

> deplored the managerial social mission and the attempt to absorb the whole man into hours of work. (19)

This was a criticism aimed at the Glacier work. In addition, the human relations movement in Britain was dealt a severe blow with the disintegration of much of the Tavistock Institute's work after Jacques departure. It was hardly surprising therefore that the key piece of Human Relations work in Britain, socio-technical systems, had little impact and failed to develop. The Human Relations journal in 1965 stated:

> in systems theory we have the growth of an interdisciplinary concept, but so far application has been abstract and tentative. (20)

Management Control and Personnel: Workplace Regulation

By far the most significant post 1945 development, almost diametrically opposed to the unidirectionality of human relations, was the development of a regulated workplace environment with increasing degrees of negotiation and authority taking place at factory level. Managers could find it difficult to exercise control and take hard decisions to overhaul production processes (Clutterbuck and Crainer 1988); there was a failure of management to introduce the most recent innovations in labour and production control (Hawkins 1976). This was exacerbated by labour market conditions and the development of industrial relations practices in post war decades. The Donovan Commission on Industrial Relations painted a picture of workplace bargaining, which gave local union officials, especially shop stewards, considerable power at workplace level. Some company studies have indicated the lack of control exercised by managers: British Leyland (perhaps the most extreme case) had 900 separate bargaining units covering 17000 employees and worked with a payment system which had been in existence since before the war. This limited severely the ability of management to introduce new ideas (Lewchuk 1987). But even in less extreme instances, managerial control was qualified. Recent studies of shop floor politics of productivity in engineering in the decades after 1950 revealed a continuous struggle over the effort bargain with outcomes that failed to maximise productivity (McKinlay and Melling 2000).

Management Control and Personnel: Management Control and the Rise of Human Resource Management; Deregulation of the Workforce

From the late 1970s there was a significant shift in the managerial-business environment in favour of managerial control. Industrial relations legislation in 1980, 1982 and 1984 reduced trade union influence and power; added to this was the uncertainty created within the workforce by the sharp rise in unemployment to 3 million by 1983 (Roberts 1989). This enabled managers in many firms to undertake job redesign, scrap 'custom and practice', negotiate and / or impose new staffing levels, increase flexibility and reduce demarcation (Richardson 1992). There was the decline since the late 1970s of employee relations practices based on negotiation and accommodation of the Donovan era (Scott 1994). Some have argued that many of these measures would have been unacceptable without the reduction in trade union power (Littler and Salaman 1984), others that the changing focus and nature of the trade union constituency enabled the appearance of management led initiatives like total quality management (TQM) and quality circles (Beaumont 1985). Managing the human resource in large sections of British business in fact changed substantially from a regulated, often collectivised, approach to a more individualised human resource management (HRM) approach which identified human resource practices much more closely with business, organisational and managerial goals (Storey 1989). Many HRM practices though have been given a 'Jekyll and Hyde' label (Sison 1994), with 'hard' and 'soft' versions. (21) The hard was typified by managerial action with a very clear view that HRM is business centred, rational, calculative and rooted in managerial concerns for efficiency and economy. Softer views emphasised the importance of concepts like devolution and responsibility for decision making (self development and empowerment), self managing or autonomous teams. These stressed the value of a committed and adaptable though integrated labour force rather than one, which was 'controlled' (Terry1986; MacInnes1987). There were clearly elements of democratisation as well as normative integration in much of this. Yet large-scale national surveys carried out 1992-1997 have indicated weak levels of employee commitment to their firms 'due to the notable decline in the discretion that employees were allowed to exercise over their work' (Gaillie and Felstead 2001, p. 1953). The evidence surrounding the actual practice of teamwork is mixed. The objectives are clear enough:

> Team-work must rest on changes in the normative (e.g. socialisation of team members) and governance dimensions (e.g., increased responsibilities and decision making. (22)

Some evidence on team-work suggests instances where normative integration has occurred (e.g., Barker 1993); other studies show managerial intentions failing through employee suspicion and abuse (perceived or otherwise) of team-working arrangements (McKinlay and Taylor 1996; Findlay, Hine, McKinlay, Marks and Thompson 2000); recent research in the Scottish spirits industry has shown that even where there was a link between normative integration and team autonomy, this was very significantly contextualised by factors such as the boundaries of acceptable normative intervention being set by team members (Findlay, McKinlay, Marks and Thompson 2000). There are also studies showing systems including autonomous teams and TQM were often aimed directly at compliance rather than commitment (Edwards and Whitson 1989; Knights and Morgan 1990; Jones 1992; Edwards et al 1998).

Summary and Conclusion

The strengthening of internal management occurred through the development of management/organisational structures, and strategies to manage and control the human resource. In the former, multi-divisional structures, though evident in Britain, were not as comprehensively or systematically applied as elsewhere. Since the 1970s, such internally integrated forms and structures have become less common with internal structures and controls more decentralised and dispersed.

Strategies to manage and control human resource showed in Britain the importance of the craft method of production. This led to practices, which could make the exertion of strong managerial control difficult, though the advantages of craft production to business were important. More recent shortcomings of craft training were indicated. The role of management training and education in facilitating managerial capability, traditionally viewed critically in terms of the volume (minimal) and lack of formality, was not entirely borne out by experience of at least one major business in the west of Scotland. In any case, most recent work indicates substantial increases in both quantity and quality of management development and training.

The importance of human resource management to the strengthening of internal management was seen through the contribution made by personnel practices to management control. Early developments in personnel and welfare practices were closely linked to attempts at improving or strengthening control. So too with the development of Human Relations, though this failed to have any significant impact in Britain; its unidimensionality and non pluralistic perspective ran counter to the regulated workplace environment of the 1950s to 1970s. These decades saw workplace practices, which often gave power to organised labour at a local level, thereby defining managerial control within negotiated parameters. Deregulation of large sections of the workforce and the growth of HRM from the late 1970s enabled an assertion of control, though there are elements in HRM of workforce responsibility and control alongside that of company managers.

The themes outlined in this chapter will be used to research the internal management of the cases, Clydeside Shipbuilding and X Films plc. In the former, considerable attention is paid to the management of the craft production system and the role played by managerial hierarchies, and support structures and managerial training. In the latter, the extent of internal integration of throughput management is analysed, as well as the management of the craft/technical resource, managerial training and development and the use of Human Resource Management practices.

Notes

1. Chandler, A.D. (1980), 'The United States: seedbed of managerial capitalism' in A.D. Chandler and H. Daems (eds) *Managerial Hierarchies: Comparative Perspectives on the Rise of the Modern Industrial Enterprise,* Cambridge MA. p. 32.
2. DC 96 2/20 Speech by W Weir to the institute of Mechanical Engineers 3 April 1919.
3. DC 96 1/251 File 1V Letter from W Weir to JJ MacNamara Minister of Labour 13 November 1920.
4. There is interesting comparative work. The powerful craft union tradition with its impact on industrial relations and managerial environment in Britain was not the case internationally. In New South Wales, the introduction of scientific management in the Railway and Transportation Department precipitated a general strike in 1917 leading to changes affecting the traditional solidaristic craft culture (Taska 1997). Significantly, it was often the case that the Bedaux system (a variant of scientific management) was not applied in craft union environments in Britain, but mainly in processes employing unskilled labour (Littler 1982; Wilson 1996).
5. Material in the Weir archive make it clear that Weir's attempts to alter union practices in one of his foundries (see 5 above) was intensified-with the possibility of a non union operation seriously considered in 1932: DC 96 1/251 File V Letter from JRR to William Weir in Ottawa.
6. Urwick, L. (1922), 'Experimental psychology and the creative impulse' *Psyche,* Vol 111, No. 1 p. 32-33.
7. Wren, D.A. (1994), *The Evolution of Management Thought, fourth edition,* London and New York: Wiley p. 215.

8.   Child, J (1969), *British Management Thought: A Critical Analysis*, London: George Allen and Unwin, p. 24.

9.   DC 96 2/4 Some Efficiency Factors in an Engineering Business. Paper delivered by W Weir and J Richmond, International Engineering Congress Glasgow 1901.

10.   Reader, W.J (1971), *The Weir Group*, London: Weidenfield and Nicholson, p. 72.

11.   National Economic Development Council (1972), *Education for Management. A Study of resources*, London: HMSO p. 36.

12.   DC 96 28/12. The Weir Bulletin No. 77 April 1953.

13.   Jacques, E (1951), *The Changing Culture of a Factory*, London: Tavistock p. 307.

14.   Ibid p. 319.

15.   See *International Encyclopaedia of Business and Management* 1998.

16.   Jacques had a particularly influential role in the Tavistock's work in industry and the development of socio-technical systems theory. He led most of the Institute's consultancy work, which was the main source of the Tavistock's income. When he left the Tavistock, mid way through the Glacier study in the 1950s, he took about 50% of the consultancy staff with him and over 60% of income. I am grateful to Dr. Martyn Dyer-Smith of the University of Northumbria (ex Tavistock Institute and author of a forthcoming biography of Jacques) and Professor Gillian Stamp of the Brunel Institute of Organisation and Social Studies, Brunel University for this information.

17.   *Human Relations* 1947-1948, Vol 1, Editorial Statement pp. 1-11.

18.   O'Connor, E.S. (1999), 'The politics of management thought', *Academy of Management review*, Vol 24 No. 1 p. 129.

19.   Hunter, G (1957), The Role of the Personnel Officer: A Group Review, *IPM Occasional Paper*, London, p. 6.

20.   *Human Relations* 1965, Vol. 18, Restatement of Editorial Policy p. 1.

21.   Although the majority of researchers examine hard and soft approaches (Legge 1995), there is a discussion of different models of HRM (Poole 1990; Brewster 1995; Legge 1995; Budhwar 2000a). What is increasingly being called strategic HRM has two key features which can be viewed as bringing together some aspects of the hard and soft: the integration of HRM practices at the most senior and strategic levels of the organisation and the devolution of managing human resource to line managers (Schuler 1992; Budhwar 2000b).

22.   Findlay, P. McKinlay, A., Marks, A. and Thompson, P. (2000), 'In search of perfect people: teamwork and team players in the Scottish spirits industry', Human *Relations*, Vol. 53, No. 12 p. 1550.

Chapter 3

The Externalisation of British Business Management?

Synopsis

The externalisation of management is considered in two ways. First the business dimension, which analysed practices and methods used by business in the organisation of commercial activities. Second the engagement which business management had with wider society outwith the boundaries of the firm- the societal dimension. This chapter shows that the Chandlerian association of managerial form and structure and efficient business operation was not always apparent in Britain; alternative, externally co-ordinated arrangements were experienced. It is also argued that post-M form structures developing from the 1970s had relied on a series of external relationships ranging from strategic alliances to sub contractual relationships and global integration rather than the archtypal M form headquarters/ strategic business unit model. Nevertheless, post-M form structures while being very different from the internally integrated model were not typified by the comprehensive externalisation of business activities. Internal integration was still important, with many modern structures federal in nature and looser in the way they integrated a series of dispersed activities; this is shown to have significant impact on managerial roles in post-M form companies.
Early twentieth century business-societal relationships are identified, illustrating a range of motivations from self-interest to civic responsibility to the gestation of informal corporatist style networking at the highest levels of government. The extent to which government action regulated business organisation practice in the 40 years after 1920 is assessed, and found to be minimal. It is shown that post 1945 corporatist approaches to business policy had limited impact at individual company management level. Finally, the chapter outlines some elements of the post corporatist era including the legitimation of business managerial engagement in a broad range of public policy initiatives since the 1980s.

- The Business Dimension – The Externalisation of Value Chain Management?
- The Societal Dimension.

Introduction

Externalisation is conceptualised as a counterpoint to management activities the scope of which are internal to the firm. Internal management was framed by growth in vertical integration and the expansion of value chain activities within the firm; the development of managerial structures and hierarchies; other internal activities associated with internal labour markets or the organisation of production. This was outlined in chapters 1 and 2. This chapter analyses management outwith the firm, ranging from value chain relationships with other companies (the business dimension) to the activities of business managers with wider society at political, business and public policy levels (the societal dimension).

The Business Dimension

Externalisation of value chain management: the Chandlerian paradigm revisited

The Chandlerian paradigm accentuated the association of business growth and investment in managerial hierarchies and structures, resulting specifically in the multidivisional structure. In this context, the experience of management structures in British companies overseas was diverse. There were M form structures in British overseas business activity, the success of which can hardly be doubted: by the last decades of the twentieth century almost 50% of the earnings of the British corporate sector came from abroad (Jones 1994); since the early 1960s, when US firms were considerably more profitable in their foreign operations than British firms, the profitability of British firms abroad had risen sharply relative to those of other nations (Dunning 1970; 1986). But it was very evident that many such successes came without the M form structure as an accompaniment. The existence of a range of (non M form) structures pre and post 1945 may according to Jones (1994) have been just as effective as US style structures; research on BAT's activities in China in the first 40 years of the twentieth century indicated that distribution networks and later the creation of parallel distribution mechanisms through joint ventures with Chinese partners were the most appropriate and highly effective ways to structure business and management operations (Cox 1997).

This is not to say that the Chandlerian case was without foundation. There was considerable evidence of the continuation of underdeveloped management in British international business practice. There were examples of British free standing companies in the US proving unsuccessful before being transformed into successful American enterprises by 'removing British corporate structures' (Wilkins 1989); there were companies like Dunlop and Vickers which had haphazard management structures and inappropriate strategies (Jones 1986). Yet there were many instances where 'ragged managerial edges' (and family ownership and management) were not impediments to success. Studies showed that there was no link between personal capitalism and failure to introduce modern budgetary control in the inter war period: relatively sophisticated budgetary control was developed at Austin and Lever Bros, but absent at London, Midland and Scottish (LMS) and Imperial Chemical Industries (ICI) (Quail 1997). There has been a steady flow of studies (e.g., Mackie 2001) leading a prominent economic and business historian to urge British historians to 'stop beating the dead horse of Chandlerianism---British historians have amply shown the flaws of Chandler's model when extended to Britain' (Blackford 2003). Studies in some US business sectors also show the difficulty of establishing a universally applied link between family control and managerial weakness (e.g., Fitzgerald 2000). It is also worth noting there is diverse evidence on the generally accepted benign and modernising view of direct bank-company links in relation to British experience. The persistence of proprietary control and other structural features of British industry kept banks at arms length, exerting little influence over corporate affairs until well after 1945 (Lazonick and O'Sullivan 1997), though instances are cited of long term associations between British banks and companies which involved elements of organisational control not unlike the German experience in the inter war period (Sjogren 1997). These successful ragged edged and family owned companies fall short of the Chandlerian benchmark. Added to this, it has also been shown that from the nineteenth century to the present, joint ventures and loose managerial arrangements with other firms (often in clusters) were as important as strong internal managerial hierarchies when crossing borders (Wilkins 1986). Jones (1996) indicated that the interesting parallels with complex cross border relationships from the 1890s and from the1990s might suggest that in periods of fast and deep globalisation, flexible networks have advantages over firms with clearly defined boundaries. And of course it is difficult to classify British international business management practice, often eschewing strong internally integrated structures for looser more externalised relationships as a 'quirk' and exceptional to the Chandlerian paradigm, given the role and importance of multinational activity in the British economy: the contribution of foreign and domestic multinationals to Britain's gross national product, capital expenditure, employment, exports and profit has been far greater than in any other industrialised economy (Dunning 1985).

Externalisation strategies were not only significant in international business. Such strategies were indeed the preferred norm in large sections of British business life. Case study 1 indicates this in the shipbuilding industry. Elbaum and Lazonick (1986) have shown that the actual reality of corporate life was the family firm operating within a loose federation and strong trade association. Between 1914 and 1943 the number of trade associations rose from 500 to 2500 (Kirby 1994). Undoubtedly, there is evidence that the restrictive agreements of such bodies may have impeded the modernisation of substantial sections of manufacturing industry (Gribbin 1978). The encouragement of cartels and collusive agreements in the 1930s can be seen as a response to the complete failure of firms in the export sector to rationalise themselves in the 1920s. Although recent work has focused on the lack of potential to overcome constraints imposed by depressed markets rather than the failure or otherwise of rationalisation in the coal, steel, textiles and shipbuilding sectors (Garside and Greaves 1997), Lazonick (1991) argued that Britain's atomistic market and organisational inheritance formed a formidable institutional barrier to alternative more Chandlerian type approaches.

But the equation of management/organisation structure and performance in this way is problematic. The conduct of industry and its managers, rather than structures and strategies per se, was important in assessing performance (Broadberry and Crafts 1992). The Weir Group based on Clydeside with its national and international interests operated successfully using a relatively loose holding company (H) form and structure. Key acquisitions were made to achieve product synergy: for example, the purchase of Drysdale Pumps in 1919, then managed by the holding company added centrifugal pumps to Weir's existing turbine driven rotary machinery (Reader 1971); in later years the H format was used as a vehicle to lessen the company's dependence on shipbuilding (Reader 1971). Weir's chosen management and business format – an externalised H format – also showed a dynamic ability to strengthen managerial structures when necessary without following the multidivisional format. In 1940, the company created a 2 tier board with the 'upper' board advisory and strategic in nature, the other tier executive (Reader 1971). This was strengthened and consolidated by an infusion of professional managers in the early 1950s. By 1953 there was a strong line management arrangement in place, with machine shop superintendents, assistants and foremen. This was replicated in other production areas: there were 10 non production functions from inwards order department to inspection and costs departments each with supervisory and managerial line structures. (1) The board of the holding company was increased and by the mid 1950s was 8 strong (including 4 non executive directors from outwith Weirs, very senior business figures: Sir Charles Connel shipbuilder and shipowner; IM Stuart chairman of Hall Thermostats; JA Lumsden company lawyer; JH Lord, director of Dunlop Rubber Company). The group had 9 subsidiaries with group executive board members on the subsidiary boards. The current historical literature goes further in questioning the link between structure and performance: much of it focuses on the quality and cost of information flows and their impact on transaction costs (e.g., Boyce and Lepper 2002; Broadberry and Marrison 2002; Popp 2002).

The debate has shifted ground and can now be described as post Chandlerian. The 1970s were something of a watershed for Britain in this respect. Ironically as around 75% of the top 100 British companies adopted the M form (compared to only 10–15 in 1950, Channon 1973), the appropriateness and effectiveness of this form was becoming less obvious even in the US (Hannah 1980). Some sector studies in Britain have shown this. In the textile depression of the 1970s it was the medium size firms which performed best, while Courtaulds, the corporate giant with a relatively well developed multidivisional form and management hierarchy, suffered due to a market strategy which made it vulnerable to import penetration (Blackburn 1982; Toyne et al 1984). It should be noted, too, that in practice the management and structural form adopted in the United States' biggest companies could differ significantly from the Chandlerian-Sloanist model. During the 1960s, some leading American multinationals (e.g., IBM and Ford) were moving beyond the multidivisional form and integrating regional production activities. Ford of Europe in fact possessed considerable autonomy from its parent way beyond what the headquarters-strategic business unit model would suggest (Dassbach 1989; McKinlay and Starkey 1994). Many leading European multinationals had a much greater reliance on a decentralised parent-affiliate structure and informal personalised control; in contrast to the US model, personal relationships between the senior management of parent companies and managers of foreign ventures (with little standardisation in practice) were more common, with the higher proportion of home country expatriates as presidents of subsidiaries meaning written rules and instructions were used less, and there was a reliance on high levels of socialisation (Franko 1976; 1978; Egelhoff 1984). All this led an authoritative business historian to conclude in the early 1990s that the promulgation of a universally valid US model was misplaced, symptomatic of ethnocentricity (Supple 1992).

The case of British Leyland (BL) in the 1970s typified the watershed decade rather well. This firm was the outcome of a rather unsuccessful merger of the late 1960s, which failed to integrate activities and impose an effective divisional structure; it collapsed in 1975 and was passed to the government's agent for intervention, the National Enterprise Board. Sir Michael Edwards became chief executive, split the car division from trucks and buses, attempted to change the management culture from the Board (reduced from 16 to 6, all members selected after rigorous psychometric tests) down to the workforce. Much of his strategy was continued by his successor Graham Day. BL was later split up and sold off in parts, the car division (Rover) going to British Aerospace in 1988. But perhaps the most notable development of this era was the collaborative joint venture with an external producer, Honda the Japanese car giant. The hoped for technological and commercial success of Rover in the early to mid 1980s was very much predicated on that external relationship (Church 1994).

From Internal Integration to Externalisation

Since the 1970s there has been a change in leading practice in terms of the 'balance' struck between strong internal managerial hierarchies and structures on the one hand, and externalisation strategies on the other, in favour of the latter. There were various environmental forces behind this. There is broad agreement that transaction costs of internalisation increased relative to that of marketplace co-ordination. A slowdown in productivity growth, fierce international competition and upward pressure on wages squeezed profits (Clarke and Clegg 1998). In Britain, the institutional power of trades unions and the consequent inflexibility of labour were described as running counter to UK industries' quest for competitiveness, leading to outsourcing (Bassett 1986; Beatson 1995). This was also considered significant for firms in the USA, though to a lesser extent (Kochan, Katz and McKersie 1986). Certainly, companies, which had previously been strongholds of Fordism, outsourced and decentralised standardised production to new, dispersed localities (and later internationally) while keeping certain managerial and financial functions within existing areas and locations (Albertson 1988). The flexible firm model suggested that such outsourcing was strategic and heralded a significant trend towards flexible organisations (Atkinson 1984; Atkinson and Meager 1986; Ackroyd and Proctor 1998). This economic explanation however does not necessarily provide an explanatory framework for outsourcing decision making. It does not explain why activities as disparate as maintenance, information technology or catering were being selectively retained or outsourced (Pollert 1988; Cross 1990; 1995; Strauss 1992). In addition, the notion of asset specificity, key to understanding transaction cost theory (in that the assets specific to the firm or industry will remain internalised) can be problematic. Recent research in the oil refining sector, where outsourcing was significant, indicated no common agreement in the industry as to what was asset specific (Ritson 2000). There was, however, no doubt about the fact of externalisation.

Other pressures lay behind externalisation strategies and practices. The significant movement of multinational activity from regional integration to globalisation led to a rapid growth in intra firm trade. By the 1990s most US multinationals abandoned their corporate wide international divisions and globalised their product divisions (Jones 1996); many European multinationals moved from mother daughter structures towards global product divisions and generally there was a convergence of US, European and Japanese management and organisation structures, though considerable diversity still occurred (Humes 1993). Significantly, this integration led to the creation of networks between suppliers and producers and a considerable expansion in the number of strategic alliances and joint ventures and other external collaborative arrangements (see Table 3.1).

This enabled in particular the sharing of risk in research and development, facilitated access to new technologies (Morris and Hergert 1987; Lorange and Roos 1992), and represented a radical change in practice from the world's leading multinationals, which had previously sought to maintain sole control of their proprietary technology. Global integration provided a platform for strategic alliances to exploit research and development: exploitation of scale economies, filling of product line gaps and development of new geographical markets had been the motivation to use collaborative alliance type mechanisms and structures (Yoshino and Rangan 1995; Krubasik and Lautenschlager 1993). Research has shown that the collaborative approaches and arrangements required to exploit such opportunities are often related to the characteristics of business managers themselves (Buckley and Casson 1988) and in many cases models of business organisation based on tight financial control and ownership are replaced by partnerships based on complementary resources and skills and the development of business relationships (Lane and Beamish 1990; Glaister and Buckley 1997).

Table 3.1 Types of Global Alliance Option 1980-1991

	Acquisition	Merger	Core Business Joint Venture	Sales Joint Venture	Production Joint Venture	Development Joint Venture	Product Swap	Production License	Technological License	Development License
Penetrate New Geographical Market	●	●	●	●	●					
Fill Product Gap	●		●	●		●	●			
Economics of Scale	●	●	●		●		●	●		
Increase Capacity Utilisation	●	●	●	●	●	●		●		
Leap Frog Product Technology	●	●	●	●	●		●	●		
Share Development Costs		●	●			●	●	●		●
Share Upstream Risks		●							●	●
Develop Product Markets								●	●	●

Source : Krubasik & Lautenscholager, 'Forging Successful Strategic Alliances' (1993 p60)

There was wide recognition that the internally integrated M form was not appropriate to manage this external environment. Symbolically, by the 1990s at least two of the four innovators of the multidivisional form at the core of Chandler's work (General Motors and Sears) were problem cases (Bartlett and Ghoshal 1993). Chandler recognised that the 'corrupted multidivisional organisation' perhaps was not an exception but the state to which the dynamics of the form could lead (Chandler 1991). This was appreciated too in the management and managerial economics literature (e.g., Williamson 1975; Kanter 1983; Peters and Waterman 1982; Peters 1992a). The 'evolution to dysfunction' was seen in the significant post 1960s diversification and growth of conglomerates like ITT, Litton, Textron (Berg 1969) resulting in the development and diffusion of strategy and matrix structures caused by the difficulty of designating strategic business units as unambiguously discrete businesses, limiting them to the right number and dealing with the relatedness amongst them (Bettis and Hall 1983). Since the end of the 1970s levels of industry concentration and vertical integration, the ground base conditions for the multidivisional form have been falling. Over the 1954-1979 period, total employment in the Fortune 500 companies grew from 8 million to 16 million and their aggregate share of America's gross national product grew from 37% to 58%; by 1991 the figures had fallen to 12 million and 40% respectively (Peters 1992b). Britain's 50 largest employers in 1955 employed 3.9 million and in 1992, 2.8 million (Jeremy 1998). Concurrent with this was the emergence of various forms of inter organisational co-operation (Leavy 1999).

The Post-M form Company: Externalisation or Management of Dispersed Activities?

Just as studies of the largest companies of the first three decades of the twentieth century (General Motors, Du Pont, Sears and Jersey Oil) became a keynote for the development of the M form, experience of the business leaders in the late 1990s and early years of the twenty first century (General Electric (GE), Asea Boveri Brown (ABB); Minnesota Mining and Manufacturing (3M), Toyota and Cannon) gave some indication of dominant management structures and practices. Studies indicated that there was not necessarily a direct relationship between the relative decline of the vertically integrated multidivisional structure and pursuit of externalisation practices per se (Womack, Jones and Roos 1990; Bartlett and Ghoshal 1998; Williams, Haslam, Johal and Williams 1994; Oliver and Wilkinson 1988). And it is particularly significant that key agents did not see a direct relationship either. (2) Many managerial activities were still motivated by the attempt to integrate, if not internalise, dispersed managerial and business activities important for the firm's performance. Practice has nonetheless changed in leading companies. This has led to management of the constituent parts of the dispersed enterprise *as if* they were external enterprises (Bartlett and Ghoshal 1998). Federal structures have been created with the decentralisation of assets and resources. This has meant considerable responsibility being given to constituent parts of the 'federation'. In ABB, the Swedish owned multinational engineering group considered the epitome of the post-M form multinational (Bartlett and Ghoshal 1998; Micklethwaite and Wooldridge 1996; Financial Times 13 Aug. 1998) many operations were constituted in separate legal entities, each company responsible for its business plan, and enabled to retain one third of its profit for reinvestment in the company. In ABB, this came with considerable reduction of management levels and layers between operations level and corporate executive committee (Bartlett and Ghoshal 1998). The contrast with the classic M form and the post-M form is illustrated in figures 3.1 and 3.2.

Managerial Practices and Roles in Multi-divisional (M), Holding (H) and Post-Multi-divisional (post-M) Companies

Importantly the post-M form structure also differed from the holding company conglomerate structure (H form), where the holding company adopted a largely 'hands off' financial control role, leaving considerable areas of management externalised (Williamson 1975).

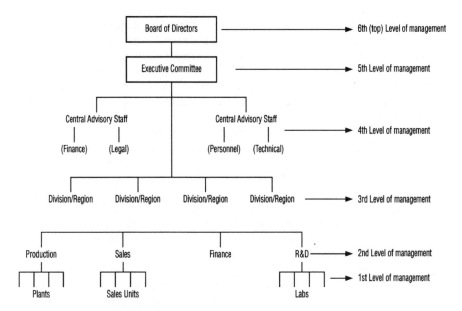

Figure 3.1 The Multidivisional Form of Organisation

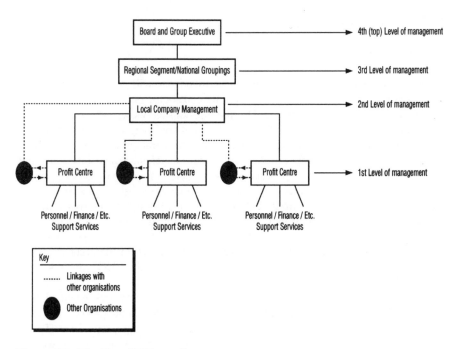

Figure 3.2 The Post-M Form Structure

In this sense, the H form was presented as a counter to the M form's erosion of front line entrepreneurialism and definition of front line managerial function in terms of implementation and planning, all directed and controlled by the internalisation of key strategic functions at central corporate level. Research suggests otherwise: federal style post-M form structures appear more complex, the relationship between the constituent businesses (treated in many respects as external dispersed businesses), and corporate executive level qualitatively different from either M or H formats. A key aspect of this was the redefinition of the intervening managerial role between front line and corporate executive, based partly on a belief, reflected in the literature, on the competitive advantages of devolved decision making and local capacity building (e.g., Birkinshaw, Hood and Johnson 1998;Martinez and Jarillo 1998; Birkinshaw and Hagstrom 2000; Birkinshaw 2000). This was in contrast to the long standing research which showed that the dominant role of middle managers in the multidivisional was internal budgeting, planning and controlling the decision process between front line strategic initiators and executive level strategic decision (Bower 1970). This managerial role has altered significantly (and the number of middle managers reduced), to being one of actively supporting, indeed advocating, front line managers' strategic and business development initiatives through resource winning and active support at corporate executive level (Ghoshal and Bartlett 1994). Case study 2 addresses this.

The Societal Dimension

Introduction and Context

In most businesses of whatever size, most managers will be preoccupied with managing the enterprise from a purely commercial focus, minimally engaged (if at all) with a wider societal dimension. Despite this, and the views expressed by some liberal political economists and others that managerial action should not have a social dimension at all, instead confining itself to commercial roles (Friedman 1962; Hayek 1979; Heilbroner 1972), the business-societal dimension is not one which can be ignored in an historical study of business and managerial practice. Increasing interest and research in the area of social action as a facet of business management is evident in Britain (Marinetto 1999), finding its way into the business policy arena largely (and ironically) through the enhanced societal role proposed for business during the liberal economic 'new right' agenda of the Thatcher years. A societal role is supported by an increasing literature on stake-holding (Wallman 1991; Allen 1992; Argenti 1997; Campbell 1997; Jacobs 1997; Freeman and Reed 1983; RSA 1995; Kay 1997).

Throughout the period under study, managers and/or owners engaged with wider society from philanthropic giving (e.g. Briggs 1959) to the promotion of self interest and involvement in the policy process (e.g., Middlemas 1979, 1983; Turner 1984; Abraham 1974). The business-management societal dimension will be analysed in terms of: early twentieth century business-societal relationships; the influence of government on business organisation, an important consideration from the 1920s to the 1960s; management practice in corporate and post-corporate environments, from the years immediately after World War Two to the present.

Early Twentieth Century Business-Societal Relationships from 1900-1930: Philanthropy, Self Interest and Neo-Corporatism

There were two dimensions to business-societal relationships in the first three decades of the twentieth century. First, there was a wide range of philanthropic giving with benefaction of schools, colleges, hospitals, churches and amenity areas in many cities and communities throughout Britain. This sometimes had a strong Christian motivation with the Christian Frontier Council established in 1932 forming strong Christian entrepreneurs' networks (Marinetto 1999). Local studies showed that such philanthropy might also have been driven by the desire for local visibility and paternalistic control of a deferential labour force (MacDonald 2000). In some instances of philanthropic giving it was difficult to distinguish philanthropy and self interest-as in the financial support by Fairfields Shipbuilding and Engineering Company to establish a chair in naval architecture at Glasgow University, thereby giving access to leading ideas and personalities in a discipline very important to the continuing success of the firm. In other areas, self interest appeared to play little role-for instance, Fairfields financial support to the Western Infirmary in Glasgow. While these initiatives do seem to have been taken by leading business people acting as individuals, such philanthropic and charitable giving often brought business figures together in association, thus reinforcing their position as part of a business elite (Johnston, R, 2000). Yet the view that such giving was an individually based initiative rather than a systematic business-management response to a local or nationally identified need was strongly supported by the evidence of decline in post war giving in Britain. This decline has been explained by the shift from family based to shareholder based firms thus making the financial autonomy to give more difficult; not that philanthropy was ruled out for lack of motivation or legitimacy in the eyes of the givers (Marinetto 1999).

Second, there was involvement in local socio-political governmental structures and institutions, increasingly at national political level too. Local studies of Birmingham (and Chamberlain's 'municipal socialism') and more recently Glasgow (Maver 2000), showed considerable civic engagement of business elites in municipal government. There was not much systematic or comprehensive evidence that this was motivated by narrow business self-interest, though such accusations were made-and substantiated-from time to time. Glasgow Corporation Transport was an exemplar of civic amenity efficiency. Far from being used for the self-interest of the councillors (in the early decades of the twentieth century predominantly business-men) the service was accused, at certain points in its development, of municipal empire building at the expense of private companies (Maver 2000). Self-interest was presumably not entirely absent: councillors as prominent business-men were aware that a cheap reliable public transport system was of immense benefit to business. And when Glasgow developed an underground system, its circular route was especially important for transporting men between home and shipyards in Govan and Partick. Although not municipally owned at the outset, the Corporation acquired the underground system in 1923.

Business involvement was extended to the national government arena in the decades after the first war. There was broad engagement of many leading business figures in aspects of the policy process extending in some cases from wartime experience. This has been seen as the genesis of neo-corporatism in Britain with

> a new form of political activity growing up [involving] governing institutions like the FBI, the NCEO and TUC working closely with government ministries. (3)

This view was challenged on the grounds that such institutions had not become

> governing institutions[because] industrial diplomacy aimed to achieve the very opposite, to attach the increasingly important trade and industry pressure groups to the existing parliamentary process'. (4)

There was, however, an informal grouping of prominent industrialists like Lord Weir, Sir Eric Geddes, Sir Charles Gardner, Sir Harry McGowan and Sir James Lithgow, who had influence on industrial and business policy. The pattern of influence and involvement though was not definitive in its purpose. Nor could it be accurately termed corporatist, since what occurred was a series of ad-hoc arrangements rather than a formal or semi formal state-business partnership or policy framework. However, this did seem to represent a step towards corporatist approaches, rather than purely sectionalist interests being followed by business or their representatives. Specific advice was offered by business leaders and accepted in some instances: the Central Electricity Board was established after the recommendation for a national distribution network (the National Grid) by the Committee led by Clydeside industrialist Lord Weir; the BBC was set up as a state monopoly after the recommendation of another industrialist, Lord Crawford. In other instances, leading business figures appeared to have an interest in exerting influence on leading political figures-in or out of office-on general politico economic issues. Lord Weir's advice to Churchill in a communication in 1928 was of such a nature, revealingly proto Keynesian in tone, though such views were not translated into policy:

> The government is not doing all that it might to protect industry-- what is to be done[is] use of £100 million of British credit to be directed along demonstrated lines in constructive enterprises (funded: £15 million National Insurance payment to mines conversion, capital value of this is £350 million credit). If a scheme for coal was agreed similar scheme for iron and steel and shipbuilding, accelerating 2 major Atlantic ships and new propelling machinery etc. (5)

Finally, out-with the peak policy level, business-men actively participated in government/administrative networks important in promoting the welfare of their businesses. The long line of Fairfields directors and chairmen who had spent time in the Admiralty was significant, reflecting the importance of Admiralty work to the company. The circumstances surrounding the Lithgow takeover of Fairfields in 1934 were intriguing given Lithgow's insider status within the machinery of government (see case study 1). The pursuit of specific business interests, however, was not always successful, as the experience of the Weir Company in house building indicates.

The Weir House Building Initiative

In the 1920s, Weir decided to diversify into house building, providing factory built houses using engineering labour at reduced rates, rather than building trade operatives. The intention was to use a mix of engineering craft and labourer rates as appropriate in the various phases of construction and assembly, realising that this was an attack on existing building trade craft practices (Reader 1971). Material in Weir's private papers also makes it clear that the skilled craft engineers were to be paid less than engineers elsewhere. (6) That Weir saw the scope of this initiative in much broader terms, as an attack on 'restrictive craft practices', is hinted in the company history (Reader 1971). Private correspondence showed his intention:

> Today we commence building 100 houses near Glasgow and the building trade say they are going on strike---but the thing I am trying to demonstrate is of far broader application than merely housing. As long as we have rigidity of practice in labour matters then we will never get out of our troubles in this country. (7)

Weir was willing to go to some length to impress his scheme on central government (against a lack of enthusiasm from local authorities) and to gain government subsidy to use unemployed labour. He organised a Prime Ministerial visit to Glasgow's slums in 1925, which was apparently successful. In a communication with Lord Stonehouse, Weir referred to

> ... the P.M's declaration that John Gilmour pay a premium of £40 per house on 4000 houses, 90% of labour to be unemployed, over the next 12 months. John Gilmour has fixed the 24 November as the date on which all local authorities must say how many they want. Behind this, I have another arrangement secretly which is to the effect that if the local authorities say they are too frightened, then the PM's scheme will be withdrawn and a dummy company formed by the government to order 1000 houses to be put down in Glasgow outside of the local authority altogether. (8)

He went even further. In another letter to Lord Stonehouse the following month:

> I thought there was a weakening on the whole question and accordingly I told the PM officially that unless they were prepared to see us through I would withdraw the whole scheme. This had an immediate effect and I have been given the necessary guarantee, which I cannot speak of at the moment. (9)

Guarantee or not, there were only 2900 homes built under this initiative, although Weir Homes continued to operate but under traditional building industry

QUEEN MARGARET UNIVERSITY LIBRARY

arrangements (Reader 1971). Weir's networking and operation at the highest level of government was not successful in this instance, as he himself wrote in 1928:

> There were 2900 Weir Houses erected in this country, but production has now ceased due to the opposition to the Weir scheme by the vested interests of the building trade and the trade unions. (10)

If philanthropy, pursuit of self-interest, nascent corporatism provide the conceptual frames for business's wider societal engagement, what of governments' attitude towards businesses as economic organisations having impact on economy and society as a whole?

Government Regulation of Business Organisation?

Governments in the 1920s sought to encourage mergers and rationalisations in key sectors like chemicals (in the1920s) and cotton, coal, iron and steel (in the1930s) (Hannah 1983). There was though in many businesses a strong preference for cartels rather than re-organisation and amalgamation (Mercer 1989; Johnman 1991). The distinction between policy intention and outcome has been explained by division among industrialists and the banks' failure to provide long term finance (Aldcroft 1986; Hall 1986; Tolliday 1986; Kirby 1987). Recent studies have focused on the difficulties of intervention and regulation through sheer industrial complexity, for example in the cotton industry (Greaves 2002). Elsewhere, industries' preferences were not always agreed. The compulsory cartelisation advocated by organisations representing large firms in 1934 and 1942 was vetoed by the governments of the day. Nevertheless, the cartelisation that was conducted (non compulsory and adherence to trade association rules unless a majority of firms in the industry wanted it) accorded with the view of the then peak representative association of business, the Federation of British Industry (FBI) (Mercer 1994).

After the second world war, there was a range of monopolies and restrictive practices legislation, which had an impact on business organisation. The first Monopolies and Restrictive Practices Commission 1949-1956 investigated restrictive practices and other single firm monopolies. Large firms were often shielded from enquiries with advice to ministers cautioning action against strategically important firms (Mercer 1991). This was underpinned by a referral procedure of the Board of Trade which gave considerable weight to countervailing business interests, giving some credence to a view that the system functioned as a 'businessman's court' (Mercer 1994). The 1956 Restrictive Trade Practices Act out-lawed a wide range of cartels and anti-competitive alliances but did not touch arrangements operated by single firm activity alone; mergers remained largely unregulated and evidence indicated that the Act contributed to the developing wave of mergers reaching its height in the 1960s. Industries with high levels of cartelisation before 1956 had a higher level of concentration afterwards (Aaronovitch and Sawyer 1975; Elliot and Gribbin 1977; Hannah 1983; Fairburn 1989).

In the realm of business organisation, it appeared that legislation reflected the grain of prevailing or developing practices - especially the trend towards scale in the 1960s - rather than causing serious disturbance or change in direction. In fact, the regulatory bias in favour of mergers against collusive activity remained largely intact through the 1980s and 1990s merger waves (Littlewood 1998; Toms and Wright 2002).

Management Practice in the Corporate and Post- Corporate Environments

The rise of corporatism   Post-1945   initiatives indicated willingness on the part of government to support a range of managerial practices in British industry. Building on war time experience, there was an attempt to introduce corporatist style tripartite employer, union, government consultation to address productivity. This led to the setting up of the Tizard Committee in 1946 (Tomlinson 1996). There is strong research suggesting employee representatives' enthusiasm for such initiatives at locality and firm levels (McKinlay 1996). Although such productivity and consultation initiatives were supported strongly at very senior levels in government (e.g., Sir Stafford Cripps saw consultation in industry as part of a modernisation agenda – Tomlinson 1996), no effective productivity coalition was built in British industry (Booth 1996). A key reason for this was that the main employers' organisation, FBI remained very firm on managerial prerogative and had a clear and regularly expressed view that production matters belonged to the domain of management (Melling 1996). It was not surprising that without legislative backing Joint Productivity Councils disappeared in the 1950s (Tomlinson 1996). There was a similar experience with the 1947 Industrial Organisation and Development Act. The Act allowed for voluntary tripartite development councils in specific industries to be set up to review questions of technical development and industrial structure, hoping to provide services 'essential to modern industrial development but which were sometimes available to large organisations but not to smaller organisations'. (11) The FBI opposed the measure and was particularly against bringing trade unions into managerial issues (Rogow and Shore 1955; Mercer 1991). However, the research concentration on employers' representative organisations perhaps underestimated the mood swing amongst key senior business figures, (well connected to government and policy machinery) in their attitudes to state-industry-employee relationships, often motivated by perceptions of enlightened self-interest. The personal views of some leading members of the British Employers Confederation and FBI (as distinct from the official views of these bodies) in the critical pre-1945 years were revealing. A memorandum written by Sir Ralph Wedgwood and Basil Sanderson to Sir Harry Brand (undated but likely to be 1942 or 1943) indicated an attitude to nationalisation motivated by self interest but not unequivocally oppositional:

> So much that is unreasonable and absurd has been said on the subject of 'exploitation' that there is a tendency to write off the whole question as a political slogan.

> In fact the exploitation completely colours the whole attitude of the workman to industry making him regard his employer as the representative of an opposing force. Such an attitude is bad for productivity and is generally quite unjustified, but it is there and in the professed view of labour the road to a remedy lies through nationalisation. We suggest there are certain steps which might be taken in this direction. Public Boards carrying on important utility services are an accepted feature of industry and have proved their efficiency; but they are subject to special dangers, political interference, internal dry rot and local ' interests'. If these can be eliminated there need be no danger in a gradual extension of public ownership. (12)

Attitudes to organised labour were often similarly motivated. A personal paper submitted by Basil Sanderson to the British Employers Confederation indicated that,

> another safeguard for the future and one we must do nothing to weaken is the influence of the enlightened trade union leader. We all know in the past there has been a strong-even bitter-antipathy in the Labour Movement between industrial and political sections. The one is realist, the other is not. The trade unions do not really want socialism. (13)

Another leading industrialist, Sir James Lithgow, also saw the value of bringing organised labour closer to the governmental process because he felt:

> unless we can get the TUC to co-ordinate its necessarily selfish point of view with the national interest or at least look at the two at one and the same time with employers and government, there is no likelihood of our being able to solve the various economic and employment problems which are bound to crop up. (14)

That this view was expressed by a leading Clydeside employer was highly significant, given that group's traditional antagonistic views to links between organised labour and state intervention (Melling 1989; Johnston, R 2000).

Consequently, by 1960, a leading employer organisation's policy 'conversion' on state-industry links favouring a partnership for long term planning and growth (Ingham 1984), should not have been entirely surprising. This view is consistent with some recent research on the FBI. (15) One outcome was the creation of the National Economic Development Council (NEDC). (16) That said though, there was little evidence that enthusiasm for a form of tripartism was reflected in consultative managerial practices at company level. Other key state-industry initiatives in the 1960s and 1970s 'corporatist' era appear to have had minimal impact on managerial practice at the company level. For example, studies of the Industrial Re-organisation Corporation (IRC) indicated that while that body was instrumental in funding and influencing important mergers, the most notable being GEC-AEI, it had much less impact on managerial practice within the rationalised companies after the resultant job losses (Young and Lowe 1974). The IRC was hardly in a position to be proactive in this regard: it had no more than 30 staff, of whom only 10 were executives. In fact it was suggested that the IRC achieved little else other than providing a forum for businessmen to discuss mergers 'without talking to government but knowing that public money would be forthcoming'. (17) Its role in promoting mergers should not be underestimated. Between 1966 and 1971 when it was wound up the IRC negotiated over 50 completed mergers involving more than 150 companies. This was less than 2% of the 3400 mergers 1967-1970 but many of the IRC inspired mergers were in key industries or sectors e.g., GEC, AEI and English Electric mergers 1967-68; British Motor Holdings and Leyland merger of 1968; rescue of Rolls Royce 1970 (Hague and Wilkinson 1983; Jeremy 1998). In the 1970s, in contrast to the pro-merger focus of the IRC, the National Enterprise Board (NEB) had the power to take holdings in private companies, rescue 'lame ducks' and promote planning agreements. Public ownership was also to be used to promote large-scale enterprise. The NEB was certainly proactive. It took over BL when it was nationalised in 1974 and drew up a modernisation plan implemented by Michael Edwards (also a NEB member). It also had a board which represented some of Britain's most senior business figures: the first chairman was Sir Donald Ryder former director of Reed International; Ryder's deputy Sir Leslie Murphy was a merchant banker (from Schroder Wagg). They were succeeded by Sir Arthur Knight, former chairman of Courtaulds and Council member of the Confederation of British Industry and Sir John (later Lord) King, head of Babcock International and later head of British Airways (Kramer 1988). But these initiatives had minimal impact at the level of company management: the nationalisation of shipbuilding with the formation of British Shipbuilders produced neither the integration of shipyards nor research facilities (Sawyer 1991; 1992). (18) National Enterprise Board planning agreements had virtually no impact at all (Wilks 1981). There is very strong evidence that while corporatist approaches accompanied by legislative enactment did have some impact on business development from merger to rationalisation, the impact on management practice was minimal.

The post-corporatist era: 'new right' state disengagement; business and management involvement in public policy From the end of the 1970s in Britain there was a marked change in governmental attitudes to corporatism as a platform for regulating government-business relationships. Corporatist frameworks and instruments of consultation and participation between union, employer organisation and government were dismantled. There was also the encouragement of a pro-market and pro-managerialist politico-economic agenda. This environment in Britain enabled the passage of industrial relations legislation, which reduced trade union power. Added to very high levels of unemployment (over 3 million by 1983) this led to significant changes in managerial practices. Not only could employers push through previously unacceptable measures (Littler and Salaman 1984) but also the changing nature and focus of the trade union constituency enabled the appearance of management led initiatives like Total Quality Management (TQM), Quality Circles and team working-initiatives (Beaumont 1985). The post 1970s decline of negotiation and accommodation-based industrial relations practices were replaced by overt and proactive managerialism (Scott 1994). According to some, existing employee rights, interests and established working practices had been re-articulated along managerial lines (Martinez and

Weston 1994). Specific research on working conditions in corporate cultures associated with quality initiatives has gone further and indicated that the dominance of managerial control has led to workloads which were high and stressful, with adverse consequences on employee health (Lewchuk and Robertson 1996). Many companies in the 1980s and 1990s saw employee commitment in this environment as a key to business success, but large scale national surveys carried out between 1992 and 1997 to assess whether worker commitment to their firms increased in the 1990s found that employees only had weak levels of commitment to their firms 'due to a notable decline in the discretion that employees were allowed to exercise over their work' (Gallie and Felstead 2001 p. 1053).

However, while this shift in the business-managerial environment was conceptually consistent and in the mind of some linked with a liberal economic de-statist philosophy, the post-corporatist era, despite the new right influence on governments after 1979, did not result in business-state disengagement, although liberal economic philosophy may have predicted so: the leading new right acolyte Milton Friedman believed that,

> if businessmen do have a social responsibility other than making maximum profit for their shareholders, how are they to know what it is? Can self selected private individuals decide what the social interest is? (19)

This thinking represented a narrow definition of what business's legitimate role was: certainly not defined in terms of social involvement or engagement. Practice was different. In 1981 Business in the Community, a private sector led initiative, was founded in Britain (along with Scottish Business in the Community) and it endorsed the US Business Roundtable, which had identified four business constituencies: customers; employers; communities and society at large, and shareholders. It was believed by Roundtable that business should play an active role not only in business and economic development but also in social rejuvenation and public life more generally (Cannon 1994). Some, like the Prime Minister, believed business should go further and take a lead role:

> The great news is that business is once again giving a lead, not only in your companies but also in the life of the community as a whole. (20)

This concept of business-societal linkages, and indeed an expanded role for business, rather than the Friedmanite approach had impact on practice. In Britain from the 1980s there was the deliberate attempt to apply a broad range of business and managerial practices as an instrument of public policy. In large measure, enthusiasm for the privatisation policy of the 1980s and 1990s was motivated by the desire to inject private sector practice into public sector bodies (Beesley and Littlechild 1986), though there was some doubt whether at key stages of the privatisation programme there was any rationale at all (Kay and Thompson 1986). But as chapter 8 shows, privatisation and marketisation of public sector services was driven largely by a desire for the transferability of leading (private sector) management practices into these services. Conversely areas of change in public policy likely to have a direct impact on management of business were usually subjected to active consultation with senior business managers: the level at which minimum pay levels were set in 1998; the percentage electoral support required from employees seeking trade union recognition; the 'New Deal' taskforce overseeing the training and job placement programme for key categories of unemployed labour comprised some of the Britain's leading business managers.

The last two decades witnessed the growth of business managers on the boards of the increasing number of non-governmental and non-departmental bodies from national economic development agencies, bodies in education and the arts, to local public spending bodies (LPSBs), some with sizeable public sector funded budgets. The number of business managers on the governing boards of these bodies in a non executive capacity went way beyond the level of the informal business networks in the years before 1945 or the more formal connections of the corporatist 1960s and 1970s (Flynn 1997). This suggested an embedding of managerial-social relationships, not restricted as in the past to economic and business development, and has altered the management of these organisations (as illustrated in case study 5). Some current research of LPSBs has revealed a 'new' public service ethos, encompassing practices which represent a synthesis of 'traditional' public sector approaches and private sector originated managerial practices (Brereton and Temple 1999); other research has shown a strong division between business-strategic management in LPSBs and policy matters, with a resulting evacuation of service management from public policy (Greer and Hoggett 1999) very much in keeping with Conservative Governments' objectives in the 1980s and 1990s (Clarke and Newman 1997; see also chapter 8).

Post-corporatism and the stake-holding company The migration of private managerial practices into the public sector and social sphere was in keeping with perspectives which gave the firm a domain of interest out-with the strictly commercial. This was legitimised by stake-holder theory. This is best described in contrast to the shareholder-agency model of the corporation which treats the company as a nexus of contracts through which various participants agree to transact with each other; assets of the company are the property of the shareholders; managers and directors were agents of the shareholders with the rights of creditors, employees and others limited to statutory contractual and common law rights (Friedman 1962). This view is still supported by those stating that shareholder return is overwhelmingly dominant in the corporate environment (Argenti 1997). Stake-holder theory was first used at the Stanford Research Institute in the USA, though Edith Penrose laid the intellectual foundations in her concept of the company as a bundle of human assets and relationships (Penrose 1959). Key academic underpinning was provided at a conference held on the subject in 1993 leading to a special edition of the Academy of Management Review in 1995, seminal in the development of stake-holding views of the firm:

> The firm is a system of stake-holders operating within the larger system of the host society that provides the necessary legal and market infrastructure for the

firm's activities. The purpose of the firm is to create wealth or value for its stake-holders by converting their stakes into goods and services. (21)

There is though a key debate in the literature surrounding stake-holder theory. On the one hand there is a view which downplays the privileging of any particular stake-holder group (especially share-holders). For example,

> The notion that boards of directors are the trustees of the tangible and intangible assets of the corporation rather than the agents of the share-holders is one, which the executives of most German and Japanese companies and of many British firms would immediately recognise. The duty of the trustee is to preserve and enhance the value of the assets under his control, responsibility of the trustees is to sustain the corporation's assets. This differs from the value of the corporation's shares. The difference comes not only because the stock market may value these assets incorrectly. It also arises because the assets of the corporation for these purposes includes the skills of its employees, the expectation of customers and suppliers and the company's reputation in the community. The objectives of managers as trustees therefore relate to the broader purposes of the corporation and not simply the financial interests of the shareholders. Thus the trusteeship model demands, as the agency model does not, the evolutionary development of the corporation around its core skills and activities because it is those skills and activities rather than a set of financial claims which are the essence of the company. (22)

Support for this view was given by the Royal Society of Arts in the mid 1990s, stating that '[A company] should balance and trade off the competing claims of customers, suppliers, employees, investors and communities in which it operates' (RSA 1995). Other interpretations of stake-holder theory, broadly supportive, suggest that stake-holder linkages are relational not transactional and that all relationships matter: ' the foundation for stake-holder management for the twenty first century is a humanistic commitment to the integrity of individuals, groups, other organisations and the general public. Successful stakeholder management also involves learning because stake-holder characteristics change over time' (Post, Preston and Sachs 2002).

On the other hand there are perspectives which tend to privilege share-holder interests, arguing that predominant stake-holder management concerns are usually justified in the general interests of the 'business case' (Craig Smith 2003). Other views range from those which privilege share-holders more directly, arguing from a share-holder dominance perspective per se (Sternberg 1999) to those arguing from a stake-holder management-agency view, which although broader in its definition of stake-holder still prioritises the shareholder (Jones 1995; Jones and Wicks 1999).

However, although stake-holder views of the firm legitimised wider societal engagement of managers, there were two areas of contention. The first was that the business-societal relationship was an uneasy one, with the involvement of business managers in the public policy arena leading to areas of questionable accountability and democratic deficit. The second was that the corporate governance framework in Britain did not yet formally recognise stake-holder interests among the duties of company directors. The Hampel Committee on Corporate Governance in the UK:

> A company must develop relationships relevant to its success---they will include those with employees, customers, suppliers, credit providers, local communities and governments. It is management's responsibility to develop policies which address these matters; in doing so, they must have regard to the overriding objective of preserving and enhancing shareholder investment over time---this recognises the directors' relationship with shareholders is different in kind from their relationship with other stakeholder interests---the directors are *responsible for* relations with stakeholders; but they are *accountable to* shareholders. (23)

Interestingly, Derek Higgs, the author of the Higgs Report (Higgs 2003) has written,

> In our work on reporting-- we make a distinction between those that directly affect share-holders and those that are indirect i.e., impact on influential stake-holder groups like employees, customers or local communities. The challenge is to ensure processes companies can adopt take account of these indirect influences on share-holder value. (24)

This lack of formal recognition (which some authors say is symptomatic of an Anglo-American approach to stakeholder theory, Lindsay and Hems 2003), may inhibit communication with stake-holder groups, decisions on the nature of responsibilities and performance measures relating to stake-holder concerns, though research and survey work has indicated an increasing number of firms (at least 'enlightened' ones, but by no means all large companies) doing this (Wheeler and Silanpaa 1997; Scholes and Clutterbuck; RSA 1995). It should also be noted that while there appears to be a growing realisation of the need to recognise wider social and community relationships of business management, there is some caution expressed about the effectiveness of the measurements likely to be used to assess the social, community, environmental relationships and their impacts (see chapter 12). The experience of a company in the films packaging sector is outlined in case study 2.

Summary and Conclusion

Externalisation of business management has been analysed through the organisation of commercial activities (the business dimension) and through the relationship of business to societal structures (the societal dimension).

Externalisation strategies were apparent in large swathes of British business both internationally and domestically even in the 'heyday' of the internally integrated multidivisional firm. A general trend away from the internally integrated firm to one employing a greater range of externalisation strategies and practices was observed from the 1970s, explained partly by transaction costs, the move from regional integration to globalisation and the resulting increase in intra firm trade by leading multinational companies, the exploitation of economies of scale, and new technology and product development. An economic perspective on its own did not provide a comprehensive explanation of the degree, nature and extent of externalisation in specific instances. It was also seen that while managerial roles and practices in M and post-M form environments were substantially different, the latter still prioritised the integration of management activities (now much more dispersed), rather than internalisation, a key feature of the M form.

Prior to 1930, the external-social engagement of business ranged from philanthropy to self-interest to the growth of varying types of engagement with the body politic in the pursuit of business goals, as well as the display of personal political influence. It was seen that government itself had a limited impact on the regulation of business organisation: at key periods in the inter-war years and from the late 1940s to the mid 1950s, government aims and enactment in the fields of cartelisation, monopolistic and restrictive practices appeared to support or even reinforce leading business practice.

While the attempt by government in the immediate post-war years to establish an early corporatist approach to improve productivity and efficiency had very limited impact on business management, there was a growing empathy (or perhaps 'softening') of some leading business figures to state-industry links; yet the machinery of corporatism had little influence on managerial practices at company level. The decline in corporatist approaches in the post-1970s political environment did not see an end to formal socio-political engagement by business. Instead, in some cases business and managerial practice extended its domain not only in terms of transferring business practice to the public sector, but in giving business managers a role in running a range of quasi-governmental and other public funded bodies. This was legitimised by stake-holder theory, though some key aspects of stake-holder company practice were inhibited by Britain's corporate governance framework.

Both cases in this section research and analyse externalisation themes. The external management of value chain activities is significant in both, and the contemporary case in particular indicates the function played by managerial roles in achieving integration of dispersed activities. The societal dimension is also important. In shipbuilding, the management of this is researched from the years when the sector had close links to the state due to the industry's strategic importance, to later corporatist style attempts to modernise and rationalise. In X Films plc, the current societal dimension of the firm's activities is examined.

Notes

1.   DC 96 28/12. The Weir Bulletin No. 77, 1953.
2.   Percy Barnevik of Swedish owned multinational engineering group ABB has spoken and written of the M form's demise, but at the same time the development of mechanisms and structures to integrate the activities of the corporation. See Bartlett and Ghoshal (1993); Micklethwaite and Wooldridge (1996).

3. Middlemass, K (1979), *Politics in Industrial Society. The Experience of the British System Since 1911*, London pp. 150-151.

4. Roberts, R (1984) ' The administrative origins of industrial diplomacy: an aspect of government-industry relations 1929-1935', in J. Turner (ed) *Businessmen and Politics. Studies of Business Activity in British Politics 1900- 1945*, London: Heinemann p. 32.

5. DC 96 1/251 File 1 Letter from W Weir to Winston Churchill, 'private and confidential' 5 September 1928. However, the pre formative nature of 'corporatism' dominated more by the individual business interest perspective in the inter war period is worth stressing. Industry's preference for self regulation, the pre-eminence of traditional free market views in government (dominated by the Treasury, though with alternative perspectives elsewhere in government) all indicate that the inter war years right up to the outbreak of war were not years of corporatism. See Ritschel (1991) and Rollings (2001).

6. DC 96 1/251 File 111 Letter from W Weir to Monroe of Sargent Lundy Chicago 25 June 1925.

7. DC 96 1/251 File 111 Letter from W Weir to Monroe of Sargent Lundy Chicago 11 Februarry1925.

8. DC 96 1/251 File 111 Letter from W Weir to Lord Stonehouse 21 October 1925.

9. DC 96 1/251 File 111 Letter from W Weir to Lord Stonehouse 18 November 1925.

10. DC 96 1/251 File 111 Letter from W (Lord) Weir to Comite des Forges de France 6 September 1928.

11. Mercer, H (1991), 'The Monopolies and Restrictive Practice Commission 1949-1956: A study in regulatory failure' in G. Jones and M.W. Kirby (eds), *Competitiveness and the State: Government and Business in Twentieth Century Britain*, Manchester: Manchester University Press p. 79.

12. DC 96 23/24 Memorandum submitted to Sir Harry Brand by Sir Ralph Wedgwood and Basil Sanderson on Reconstruction Policy (Labour) No date.

13. DC 96 23/24 Personal Paper on the Future Policy of the British Employers Confederation from Basil Sanderson 2 June 1942.

14. DC 96 32/24 Letter from Sir James Lithgow to Lord Dudley Gordon Chairman of J and E Hall and Co. 23 September 1942.

15. See McKinlay, Mercer and Rollings (2000). Their research on the FBI's approach to European integration from 1945 has indicated that for almost a decade before the 'Federation's serious exchanges with government' it built links with continental business federations and played a key role in government policy making. Employer organisations like the FBI were not only representatives of business but contained key figures (like Sanderson, Lithgow, Wedgewood and Brand) that helped shape business opinion and were part of a key network influencing the policy process. This changes the rather dated debate about whether pluralist or corporatist perspectives best explain the position of employers' representatives in Britain in the post war decades (Finer 1956; Middlemas 1979; Grant 1993).

16. Recent writing is rather sceptical about the government of the day's commitment to NEDC as a basis for providing long term growth. Booth (2000) indicates that government's immediate concerns were about inflation, pay and competitiveness rather than growth – the context being that pressure on pay, inflation and public spending (elements of the post war settlement) was inevitable given the over riding aim of macro economic policy, sterling convertibility and the manifest failure of monetary policy instruments alone achieving this.

17. Jones, B and Keating, M (1985), *Labour and the British State*, Oxford: Clarendon Press p. 88.

18. There was though successful rationalisation in the aerospace industry through the formation of British Aerospace.
19. Friedman, M (1962) *Capitalism and Freedom*, Chicago: University of Chicago Press p. 44.
20. Margaret Thatcher's 'Companies Committed to the Community' speech to the One per cent Club, Annual Meeting, RSA, cited in T Cannon (1999*), Corporate Responsibility*, London: Pitman p. 132.
21. Clarkson, M (1995) ' A stakeholder framework for analysing and evaluating corporate social performance' *Academy of Management Review,* 20 (1), p. 21.
22. Kay, J (1997) ' The stakeholder corporation' in G. Kelly, D. Kelly. and A Gamble, *Stakeholder Capitalism*, Basingstoke: Macmillan p. 135.
23. Hampel Report (1998), *Corporate Governance*, London: Committee on Corporate Governance, paras. 1.16 and 1.17.
24. Higgs, 'New Tone at the Top' , Guardian Nov. 17, 2003.

Chapter 4

Case Study 1: Clydeside Shipbuilding 1900-1965

The crowds felt somewhat awed; cheering was restrained, but there was wonder writ on every face at the masterpiece which has been fashioned by Clyde craftsmen (Glasgow Herald 25 March 1936 on the launch of the Queen Mary at John Browns).

There is a great shortage of managerial ability. Most managers lack commercial and business skills and there is a lack of general management skills (Booz-Allen Report on Shipbuilding 1973). (1)

The present organisation of shipyard labour so far as skilled trades are concerned is largely based on the pattern set when iron and steel ships were first built in this country (Shipbuilding Employers Federation referring to the late 1960s and early 1970s). (2)

Synopsis

External management in the case companies was viewed first in the context of business activities and second in the wider societal dimension. In business activity, much of the value chain in shipbuilding was externally managed. In the case of steel supply a range of agreements and cross ownership arrangements existed, and these were subject to extreme fluctuation, especially in the post first war years; initiation of the contract for the product itself, the ship, was often externalised through the creation of shipbuilding/naval industrial clusters; the marketing effort in the companies studied, common throughout the industry, was externalised and personalised. These approaches were later seen as barriers to change and modernisation. The second aspect of external management, business societal relationships, indicated in the period up to 1930 philanthropic giving, but also a considerable degree of business-government interaction with very specific pay offs for the companies studied. Government policy towards organisation of the industry showed a greater congruity between government intention and companies' desires between the wars than in the 1960s. The corporatist support framework for the shipbuilding industry after 1945 was, by international comparison minimal with little impact on managerial practices within the companies studied.

Internal management was highly personalised until 1945 with little in the way of managerial hierarchies beyond very basic departmental and personal control: this changed little by the end of the period under study. The key to understanding internal management was the craft system's advantages to employers in an environment of abundant labour supply in a cyclical industry thereby obviating the need for heavy fixed capital investment. This system came under stress given its own rigidities, accentuated by scarcity of craft labour exacerbated by alternative employment opportunities after the 1940s. Other internal management instruments including managerial training were under-developed. Finally, the role of the foreman in internal management was analysed. His key role in management control was identified, but so too the ambiguities of the role (in terms of managerial vis a vis craft employee identity) and the limited scope in managerial development and upward mobility from the 'craft leader'.

- Externalisation of management: an overview; managing throughput and the value chain; the societal dimension
- Development and strengthening of internal management?

The Externalisation of Management: An Overview

An analysis of the shipbuilding industry macro market can be viewed against the essentially 'modernist' paradigm, associating integration of activities, business growth and modernisation. As early as 1918 (even though at the start of hostilities Britain accounted for 60% of world output, 40% of this attributable to the Clyde) (Peebles 1987;Lorenz 1991), the fragmentation of the industry was noted as a matter of some concern:

> The tendency of the world appears to be in the direction of larger economic organisations and unless analogous steps are taken by shipbuilders and marine engineers [in Britain] to meet the new situation, it is to be feared that the industries may suffer needlessly to the detriment of the nation. (3)

This still caused concern over four decades later. In the mid 1960s, the Geddes Report (1966) highlighted the fragmentation and lack of economic scale leading to a dangerous under recovery of overheads:

> Yards are not able to earn a sufficient surplus over current outgoings to meet capital costs on the scale required for a modern and prosperous industry. (4)

But while there is much evidence of Britain's lack of modernisation underpinned by a considerable declinist post 1945 literature (e.g., Turner 1969; Coleman 1973; Locke 1984; Barnet 1986; Elbaum and Lazonick 1986), a valuable perspective can be gained from analysis at sector or company management level: there is evidence which questions the appropriateness of the integration-modernisation paradigm in this industry at least in the years prior to 1945 with externalisation seen as an effective management strategy.

The market environment in a cyclical industry could be managed either through a predominance of competitive strategies and the pursuit of cost efficiencies to gain market share; or through the pursuit of capacity/price regulation strategies with other firms in the sector. By all objective measures, the British shipbuilding industry's strategy for managing the market was successful up to the outbreak of war in 1914: between 1890 and 1914, the rate of growth of shipbuilding output exceeded that of the economy as a whole (Pollard and Robertson 1979). There was some indication of a collusive type of market regulation, though obviously evidence for this is slender. The motivation for such market regulation was there. The 'Shipbuilder' in 1907 thought there was too much competition and suggested a cartel of shipbuilders to regulate output (Pollard and Robertson 1979). On Clydeside, warship work appeared to be profitable: in the late 1890s, the Fairfield Company recorded a £505,188 profit on five contracts with an invoiced price of £2,334,787, a market then well worth nurturing. Of the 77 warships built for the Admiralty on the Clyde between 1909 and 1914, 52 were built by only four yards, and there was some evidence of collusive tendering by Browns and Fairfield for Admiralty work (Peebles 1987). This is obviously not liberally documented in company archives.

Certainly, the economic difficulties which faced the industry after the post first war boom, led to shipbuilders' attempts to bring order to a severe market environment through capacity regulation. This strategy was pursued through the instruments of the Warship Builders Committee, the Shipbuilding Conference and National Shipbuilders Security. The Shipbuilding Conference operated existing work through 'segregation schemes' where particular groups of companies would confine their bids to specific categories of vessels, with a surcharge placed on any company bidding outwith the designated sector. These schemes were described as a co-operative defensive reaction by the shipbuilders in conditions of severely depressed trade (Slaven 1980). But the important point to note was that given the pre-existing structure of the industry, when all market and profit signals had been highly positive, the inter-war behaviour was rational enough, explained by depressed markets rather than failure to adopt modernistic approaches to management from yard integration to production planning: the limits of such modernising approaches to management in the severe circumstances (particularly in the 1930s) has been highlighted (Slaven 1977).

However, the traditional managerial paradigm could be a barrier to modernisation after the second war when markets were no longer depressed as they had been in the 1930s.The post-1945 industry was a victim of its structure and past, illustrated vividly in the way that British shipbuilding did not respond to the changed market environment with a strategy of business growth. Managerial action was explained, and is analysed in some detail below, by the industry's commitment to low capital investment (by international comparison) linked to traditional craft based production, a process that imploded by the mid 1960s. Of all the shipbuilding countries, Britain alone chose not to embark on a growth strategy. Capacity grew hardly at all, with output in 1965 remarkably close to the 1948 figure (1965, 1,073,000 tons, 1948, 1,176,000 tons) with a peak of 1,474,000 tons reached in 1955 (Lorenz 1991). Britain's percentage of world tonnage in 1948 was 51.1% and in 1965, 8.8%. Clearly, changes in the international environment made a decline in Britain's share of world output inevitable: there were market entrants from the Far East as well as the revived industrial countries of Continental Europe;

there was also a decoupling of national shipowners and builders with the rise of flags of convenience such as Liberia and Panama. Nonetheless, company practice seemed to indicate a deliberate no growth managerial strategy. Various government led marketing and export initiatives (with their obvious aim of growth) were treated with half-hearted enthusiasm by the industry (Slaven 1980).

However, is the charge of 'backward thinking' sustainable? It can be well argued that a growth, 'think big' philosophy was very difficult given the well documented fragmented nature of the British shipbuilding industry, fragmentation both in terms of scale and vertical deintegration. There was no integration with the industry's major supplier (steel). Steel itself in Scotland was not vertically integrated and consequently suffered cost disadvantages when matched against the world leaders (Payne 1979). The benefits of horizontal integration, which could have included the possibility of synergistic strategies by combining yards and arranging optimal product mix were never realised. In 1965, the key companies and yards on the Clyde were basically the same as before the second war. The economic logic of greater scale and integration was obvious to some industry commentators and observers:

> In the present circumstances [writing of the 1950s] it is difficult to see how the distribution of orders can be improved without some changes in the organisation of shipbuilding and ship-owning. It appears unlikely that specialisation and standardisation will result unless ship owners and builders concert their efforts to concentrate demand and production on as limited a range of types and size of vessels as is consistent with the real requirements of various trades-- this could not however occur without some interference with normal marketing arrangements either by the establishment of some central agency governing the placing of orders amongst shipyards or by outright amalgamation. (5)

There were key indicators of a British lag in cost caused by this fragmentation (Lorenz1991). The cost consequences and the impact on international competitiveness were clear to some in the industry. Immediately after the war, Sir James Lithgow obviously felt the need to harangue 'traditional ' attitudes:

> Suggestions that foreign competition is of no great consequence and that British shipbuilding can flourish without foreign orders show ignorance of the facts. Unless we can obtain international business in large quantities in competition with our foreign rivals, our works and workmen cannot be fully employed and if we have to charge such of our home customers as may adhere to us higher prices than their competitors abroad have to pay for their ships, they, in turn, will have their business crippled. (6)

However, one must remember that UK shipbuilding operated in a free market environment, unlike some competitors whose environment was rather more statist/corporatist. As well as this, until the early 1960s market signals for British shipbuilding did not force radical re-organisation on to the agenda. Existing arrangements were producing healthy profit levels, giving, in a free market context, little incentive to change. (7) That these circumstances had an impact on managerial attitudes and culture within the industry can hardly be doubted (an impact ultimately terminal it may be argued). When the logic of integration and rationalisation (if not growth) was being well aired in the policy domain after the Geddes Report, there was a revealing comment from a Board of Directors meeting at Fairfield on August 2, 1965:

> Mr Wilson [Director] pointed out that after 4 years of discussion, Clyde shipbuilding and marine engineering companies had not rationalised and would not do so without compulsion from government. Regarding the future structure a likely grouping of Browns, Fairfields and Stephens with 1 engine works could of course reduce cost by rationalising the type of work to be carried out in each yard. (8)

The Externalisation of Management: Managing Throughput and the Value Chain

The case analysis will examine firstly the relationship with a key supplier to the industry (steel) and then a range of other important elements in the value chain.
Steel was crucial to the industry. Steel accounted for rarely less than 50% of the ship's total material costs (Patton Report 1962). In Britain, there was no vertical integration; so many international competitors had cost advantages. For example, in the United States, although the industry was not completely vertically integrated, it was reorganised early in the twentieth century by the Bethlehem Steel Company and had the advantages of the cheap steel which the company produced largely due to its own integration and scale (Pollard and Robertson 1979).

   The industry found it difficult to use buyer power (9) to influence this part of the supply chain. Even in the first two decades of the twentieth century, when 30% of national steel output was consumed by British shipyards (Lorenz 1991) and 60% of Scottish steel went to the shipyards (Payne 1979), Clydeside shipbuilders could be angered at the 'Scotch' Steelmasters' Association deferral of a rebate scheme where firms agreed to purchase only from Association members and received a discount at the end of each year. Although the anger led to a threat by the shipbuilders to resuscitate Clydebridge steelworks (closed down by the steelmasters to regulate competition and control prices in 1907), the steelmasters in fact purchased the works themselves, keeping them closed (Payne 1979). Though the high percentage of steel output consumed by shipyards (30% and 60%) declined, shipbuilding nonetheless continued to be an important customer of the steel industry after World War 2 (still accounting for over 10% of output) yet efficient control of this part of the supply/value chain proved illusory: shortages of steel and supplier control of pricing were commonplace until well into the late 1950s and beyond. The Patton Report in 1962 concluded:

> It is very difficult to secure supply of steel below the maximum price, or to obtain competitive tenders for steel from British mills. (10)

In 1964, the Directors at Fairfield noted the relationship between buyer and supplier to the disadvantage of the former:

> The Monopolies Commission's investigation has had little impact [there is] little chance of price reductions, in fact there has been a 5% increase. There is little point in threatening to obtain elsewhere when steel is in short supply. (11)

Nor apparently were group purchasing arrangements successful. In 1959, one of the Fairfield Directors raised the possibility,

> of endeavouring to get best possible terms from steel makers on a [Lithgow] group basis. (12)

This was some 25 years after Lithgow took control of the Fairfield yard.

It was clear that management or control of this important part of the value chain was not achieved by use of buyer power or production integration. The absence of value chain control by these strategies can be traced and illustrated in the important post-first world war environment. Coordination and control of steel supply was achieved by a strategy of externalisation through a complex of market coordination, interlocking ownership patterns and directorships, a pattern which was particularly marked after 1918 when there was a fear of steel shortage with the price of ship plates quadrupling 1918-1920 (Payne 1979). A range of shipbuilding-steel ownership clusters appeared. Harland and Wolff took the majority shareholding in Colvilles (95%) in 1920; Beardmore (along with Swan Hunter) took over the Glasgow Iron and Steel Company; Lithgow in 1920 acquired a controlling interest in James Dunlop and Company; a consortium of Clyde shipbuilders bought the Steel Company of Scotland (Stephens, Greenock Dockyard Company, Yarrow and Company, Ardrossan Shipbuilding Company, James Little and Company, Campbeltown Shipbuilding Company). The Fairfield ownership cluster was part of a much bigger initiative explained in some detail below. This involved Workman-Clark of Belfast purchasing the Lanarkshire Steel Company to bring it into the Sperling Group. Fairfield was brought into this group via the Northumberland Shipbuilding Company purchasing its shares. RA and WO Workman joined the board of Fairfield and a number of Fairfield directors joined the board of the Lanarkshire Steel Company. (13) The Lanarkshire Steel Company was then to provide Fairfield with much of its steel. The Northumberland Shipbuilding Company purchased a share of Baldwins in 1921 to secure its steel supplies (35,000 tons for two years). (14) Fairfield was involved in lending £100,000 to the Northumberland Shipbuilding Company to facilitate the sale. As well as ownership and inter-locking directorships the arrangements included sizeable contracts for steel from other suppliers, an arrangement that was costly for Fairfield. A similar pattern emerged in Browns: in 1920, steel supplies from the Steel Company of Scotland failed and an arrangement with Lord Pirrie of Harland and Wolff (who had cross shareholding interests in Browns) was agreed with Colville to supply Browns (Harland and Wolff had acquired Colville in 1919); but this too failed and Browns was required to purchase American steel. (15)

There was little evidence that these ownership changes were used in any way to lever economic efficiencies in the steel producing units, difficult anyway after the economic downturn of 1921.The Lanarkshire Steel Company, efficient enough in the early years of the twentieth century (due to tight cost control and aggressive marketing) was by 1921 failing to make any money largely due to under-investment and antiquated equipment. Nor was Baldwins leveraged into modernisation: Sir Montagu Norman, Governor of the Bank of England, considered Baldwins in 1926 in 'need of major economies---new blood--new management'. (Payne 1979). Although the alignment of interests altered somewhat by the 1930s, the separate ownership clusters persisted with regard to steel. Despite being a key protagonist of industry consolidation, Sir William Lithgow had to operate in the environment which existed rather than the one he wished. When his steel supplier (Dunlop) merged with Colvilles in 1931 although securing a 2 year exclusive supplier deal for his shipbuilding interests, Lithgow nonetheless bought the Steel Company of Scotland in 1934. Shortly after he purchased Fairfields, the company switched its main steel supply agreement to the Steel Company of Scotland. (16) Given the size of the Scottish steel industry's market, consolidation of the key interests was the only strategy, which made long term economic sense; Lithgow (and others) realised this but as a practical business entrepreneur he was required to play with the major interests to secure supplies of such a staple industrial commodity.

Even after the second war, continued resource shortage and government direction of the economy meant uninterrupted supplies of steel could not be guaranteed. (17) Quality continued to be a problem well into the 1960s and this was the subject of regular comment (so too was the price (18)), with complaints that there

> was a considerably better finish provided by steel firms on the North East coast than that being supplied by Scottish Steel makers. (19)

Externalisation rather than integration, easily understood in historical context, had become a cost barrier.

There was a range of important exteriorised business relationships in other parts of the value chain. In the case companies, these can be viewed through three distinct processes and relationships: the creation of shipbuilding/naval-military industrial complexes; the post-world war 1 attempt to create synergies through a shipbuilding, engineering and mercantile combine focused on Fairfield; the nature of marketing activity.

First, by 1910, the creation on Clydeside of armaments industries with shipbuilding companies at the core was a rather complex process, which involved ownership clusters and networks, obvious collaboration within these as well as competitive strategies with rival companies and clusters. John Brown and Company, the Sheffield based steel and armour plate manufacturers, took over the shipbuilding operation of Thomson in Clydebank to form what has been described as an armaments combine (Slaven 1980). Shortly after, Cammel Laird took a 50% interest in the ordinary shares of Fairfield - with this came one half of Cammel

Lairds shares in the Coventry Ordnance Works. Accordingly, Fairfield too became part of a vertically connected armaments industry (Peebles 1987). However, behind the fact of integration was a strategic mix of competition and collaboration. Prior to the Cammel Laird purchase of Fairfield shares there was clear evidence that Fairfield directors were in direct competition with the armaments interests of Beardmore (who formed a community of interest with Vickers) by requesting in 1903 that one of the company's agents operating in Japan (Brown, McFarlane and Company) refuse an agency for armour plating with Beardmore; the agent was then authorised to negotiate with Charles Connel and Company in Sheffield

> re. the supply of armoured plate that may be required for foreign warship work.

A director (Dr Elgar) was then

> [it was agreed] to go to Japan at once to negotiate with the Japanese government for warship work. (20)

Such competitive rivalry overturned the earlier relationship between the companies. In 1894 Beardmore was a major supplier of steel to Fairfield. (21) Beardmore in turn set up their own shipyard in Dalmuir in 1905, after having taken over Napiers in Govan in 1900.

The relationship between the Browns and Fairfield shipbuilding armaments groups indicated both competitive and collaborative strategies. Brown approached Fairfield unsuccessfully after the company had acquired Thomson's yard in Clydebank 'regarding an amalgamation of shipbuilding interests on the Clyde'. (22) The companies did however collaborate, but did so as two quite separate companies. The Coventry Ordnance Works from 1907 was owned 50% by John Brown, 25% by Camel Laird and 25% by Fairfield. Both companies also collaborated in the application of new technology: Fairfield in 1909 agreed a license with John Browns to manufacture under license Brown-Curtis turbines. Such competitive-collaborative strategies and the technology transfer between companies was a typical example of exteriorisation rather than integration of value chain management. Perhaps the most visible externalisation of value chain activities was the collaboration between Browns and Russian shipbuilders. Browns provided design and technical collaboration with the Baltic Works in St Petersburg on the construction of battleships, including supervision during construction, right up to the eve of the first war. (23)

Second, an important illustration of the management of external relationships and business linkages was in the post-1918 attempt to create a mercantile and engineering combine (which was UK wide) driven by a London based financial consortium, the Sperling Group. The strategy of this group appears to have been well thought out with the creation of significant business synergies in mind. There was no attempt, though, to create production integration. The combine was controlled not by internalised bureaucratic management structures, but externally by common and interlocking directorships, and the co-ordination of trading arrangements between the constituent parts of the combine.

Although Fairfield was not the lynchpin in this group (The Northumberland Shipbuilding Company in Tyneside was) it nonetheless played a very important part as a cash rich enterprise. By 1919, Fairfield was very vulnerable to predatory tactics. Lady Pearce's death in 1918 released a large parcel of Fairfield shares on to the market. Trinity College Cambridge (which had fallen heir to Sir William George Pearce's fortune) began to dissolve its holding in 1918. In 1919, Camel Laird chose to buy out Fairfield's interest in their joint ventures (English Electric Company and Coventry Ordnance Works) making the company highly liquid, with over £310,000 in cash at the beginning of 1920 (Peebles 1987). The post-war boom ensured that the mercantile sector was a lucrative one to be in. The Northumberland Shipbuilding Company was the vehicle used by the Sperling Group to gain control of Fairfields (owning 80% of the company's ordinary shares), Doxford Engines, Monmouth Shipbuilding Company, Blytheswood Shipbuilding Company the tanker specialists on Clydeside, Workman Clark and Company of Belfast and the Globe Shipping Company. As far as Fairfield goes, there was no evidence at all of production integration or economies being achieved by managerial action. Co-ordination of the group's business activities was achieved by changes at Board of Director level: in 1919, 4 new directors joined the Fairfield board, RA Workman, MacKay Edgar, William Workman and John Espley. (24) Both Workmans were from another part of the Sperling Group, Edgar and Espley too (The Globe Shipping Company). (25) The group undertook some joint tendering (e.g., for an order from the Argentine government). Internal trading occurred within the group too. For example, Fairfield received work for Doxford engines, machinery for oil tankers built at Chepstow, 4 tankers for the Globe Shipping Company. However, Fairfield suffered as the slump hit the combine, which by now was under financed and highly geared. Although Fairfield did not go down (parts of the group did, e.g. Northumberland Shipbuilding Company went into receivership in 1926) much of the group's liabilities fell on Fairfield: the group's orders for steel saw Fairfield lose £289,000, (26) and the company shifted from cash rich to cash starved in the mid 1920s.

Third, and from a wider perspective, Fairfield's approach to marketing illustrated the importance of external and personal relationships rather than the development of marketing through internally controlled management and functional hierarchies. Marketing was traditionally a personalised activity where the most senior figures in firms had long standing links with counterparts in shipping companies. The acrimony when these links were severed made the point: Fairfield's traditional link with Cunard ended in some bitterness over costs and contract specification changes which resulted in a senior executive of the company losing his position; it also led to the refusal to discuss fixed cost contracts with the company and Cunard changing to Browns as the favoured yard. (27) Also recorded in company archives was a serious conflict with Harland and Wolff over the division of work following the merger of Castle Line (a customer of Fairfield) with Union Line in 1900. The prizes for a successful relationship with a shipping company were evident. It was due to John Browns' long standing relationship with Cunard that the company was awarded the Queen Mary, when the payroll was down to 125 skilled men. Directors regularly journeyed overseas for sales purposes. Otherwise, overseas agents were used on a commission basis. Often these agents were Scottish or British, and known to the directors. Overall selling and marketing activity was personalised and required little investment in managerial infrastructure in the Chandlerian sense. Significantly, the industry's own investigation in the early 1960s (The Patton Report) did not even address marketing as an issue.

Nonetheless, external environmental change fundamentally undermined these traditional personalised market relationships. The fracturing of ship owner-shipbuilder links with the flag of convenience and the increase in shipbuilding capacity world-wide led to customer global mobility, and in this context, personalised approaches to marketing were of decreasing relevance. More than ever it was obvious that demand for British or Clyde built ships would be strongly dependent not only on fluctuations in international trade but other nations' (as well as other UK producers') efficiencies and the extent to which national governments chose to support their indigenous industries. It is doubtful if investment in marketing infrastructure would have made much difference on its own to competitiveness. (28) For example it was almost at the stage of desperation (in 1961) when Browns established a commercial organisation and sales function: it was to address declining orders for the engine works that a commercial organisation was established; John Browns had to actively seek work, a profound cultural change from a preceding era when the client came to Browns. (29) The company appointed its first commercial director in 1964 (Johnston 2000).

Undoubtedly the traditional market customer relationship had an adverse impact on cost efficiencies. Fairfield directors for example were aware of the inefficiencies of the relatively personalised bespoke approach to customer relationships, but seemed unable to do much about it. A Directors' meeting discussed Japanese methods in 1964:

> [In Japan] all specification points are agreed before signing a contract with no alterations thereafter. To achieve agreement of a contract the Japanese are prepared to sit up to 5 weeks with a team of 30. Mr Kimber [shipyard manager] pointed out that a large Japanese organisation could do this, but not Fairfield-- but Mr Kimber hoped to standardise sections of specification particularly for outfit. (30)

Other Directors' discussions outlined the problems in the construction of a vessel (The Nili) for the Israeli Navy:

> unnecessary alterations due to being pushed around by these owners for the past 18 months.

The same minute went on to note that this was exacerbated by:

> poor information supplied too late from the drawing office.

A possible solution was later suggested:

> A possible improvement would be the American system of having a firm of design agents to prepare a fully detailed specification and design on which quotations were submitted. (31)

Within six months, a Receiver had been appointed.

The value chain and value adding processes were historically both externalised and in many instances personalised. The corollary of such an approach was an inevitable fragmentation both in terms of scale and de-integration. The antithesis of the traditionalistic externalised management included vertical and horizontal integration and the consequent synergistic strategies achieved in terms of planning and optimal product mix. Yet in 1965, the main players on the Clyde (though rather fewer of them) were much the same as in 1939. The institutional barriers to change were clear enough to some at the time:

> In the present circumstances it is difficult to see how the distribution of orders can be improved without some changes in the organisation of shipbuilding and ship-owning. It appears unlikely that specialisation and standardisation will result unless ship owners and builders concert their efforts to concentrate demand and production on as limited a range of types and size of vessels as is consistent with the real requirements of various trades. This could not occur however without some interference with normal marketing arrangements either by the establishment of some central agency governing the placing of orders amongst shipyards or by outright amalgamation. (32)

External Management: The Societal Dimension

1900-1930s In the first three decades of the twentieth century, the relationship between the shipbuilding industry and wider society as represented in the case can be seen in terms of philanthropy, self interest and perhaps evidence of evolving neo-corporatism. It is often difficult to distinguish these motivations. Fairfield's (and its predecessor's) munificence to the local community (of Govan) was manifested in the donation of land for a public park, various buildings for civic and community use and donations to hospitals in other parts of Glasgow, most notably the Western Infirmary. There is evidence that use was made of this to help create a cohesive civic identity, but largely driven by the civic authorities rather than the company (Mavor 2000); this contrasted with research undertaken in other communities where a much stronger role was taken by employers in this respect (e.g., Macdonald 2000; Johnston, R, 2000).

Other societal relationships displayed combinations of company self interest and philanthropy. Fairfield's formal support of a chair in naval architecture at Glasgow University was civic minded, public spirited and self-interested: there was movement of people at senior level in the company into academic positions, giving access to and supporting leading thinking in a vocational discipline of vital importance to the company.

Use of political connection and influence to advance company interest was evident. Sir Alexander Gracie, Fairfield's engineering director, was one of the experts consulted by Fisher in developing the idea of the Dreadnought before the first war. Sir William Pearce, who became the dominating influence at the company after Elder's death, was MP for Govan and an Admiralty trained naval architect who used his former connections to secure orders for Fairfield (Slaven 1986). Indeed up to the end of the second war, there was rarely a year when the board of Fairfield did not include an admiral, presumably there for his market, technical and insider knowledge.

The continuation of work on the Cunard liner (No. 534, Queen Mary) in Browns yard in 1934, after several years' interruption, was the result of relationships and manoeuvring between key Clydeside (if not necessarily shipbuilding) figures and government. In October 1932, government requested Lord Weir to examine British shipping lines operating the north Atlantic, and to consider the level of subsidy foreign lines received from their government. Weir's report in 1933 recommended that Cunard take over White Star. After initial reluctance by the latter, Weir's arbitration agreed an amalgamation in proportion of 62:38 in favour of Cunard. This enabled Neville Chamberlain to state in the House of Commons, 13 December 1933:

> It is the intention of the government in that event [i.e. the amalgamation] shortly to lay before the House proposals for furnishing the necessary financial facilities for the completion of the new Cunard liner known as No. 534. (33)

The new company Cunard White Star Ltd. received loans from the Treasury of £3m to be repaid in1975, to cover the cost of completion of 534; further £5m for the cost of a second ship and £1.5m working capital for the new company. This took effect with the passage of the North Atlantic Shipping (Advances) Bill on 27 March 1934.

The difficulty distinguishing business-government relationships for state purposes on the one hand and company (or individual) self-interest on the other was apparent when Lithgow purchased Fairfield in 1935: he saved the yard from certain closure by purchasing the majority of ordinary shares and assuming responsibility for the company's overdraft as well as guaranteeing to meet the calls of bill-holders when the Anchor Line (a major customer of Fairfield) went into receivership. Lithgow had very strong personal and institutional links with the government, being a member of the Industrial Panel set up in 1934 to assist the government's Principal Supply Officer Committee in preparing contingency plans for re-armament. One author has written:

> It can be safely assumed that he did not act without the government's tacit blessing if not at its behest. (34)

The importance of Fairfield's to the war effort, and its profitability in the process, is well known. During hostilities 1939-1945, Lithgow was absented from Fairfield company business due to his commitments in government. The family business interest remained in-situ with Sir William's brother Henry.

Government and industry organisation In terms of government influence on the organisation and re-organisation of the industry, two key phases were predominant: the 1930s typified by the Shipbuilding Conference and National Shipbuilders Security scheme and the post-Geddes reorganisation. The Shipbuilding Conference operated existing work through segregation schemes, but government was more obviously involved in National Shipbuilders Security. This body was headed by Lithgow and was funded by the Bank of England to buy up and close down capacity. Although the organisation of shipyards altered little in the 1930s (Buxton 1968), it was nonetheless the case that government was quite in tune with the leading players in the industry: defensively in the sense that co-operative defensive reaction by the shipbuilders in conditions of severely depressed trade (Slaven 1980) was re-inforced; but offensively too in that it supported the control and rationalisation strategy thought necessary at the time to help re-establish overseas competitiveness through control of labour costs. (35) Lithgow, as owner of Fairfields, symbolised this strategy in that he outbuilt any other Clydeside shipbuilder by a factor of 2 to 1; Lithgow produced (in Fairfields and the other yards the family owned) over 20% of inter war tonnage launched on the river (Campbell 1980). There was indeed a congruity of government and business aims:

> Lithgow was not so much acting for himself as for a strategic vision shared by the leading families of Clydeside and firmly backed by the government and the Bank of England. (36)

There is considerable circumstantial evidence that government led approaches to organisation of the industry were not as closely synchronised with the aims of the key industry leaders on Clydeside in the post-Geddes era. Geddes (1966) recommended that government money be used to consolidate shipbuilding into estuary based groups, one on the lower and one on the upper Clyde. There was considerable wrangling amongst the shipbuilders, with Yarrow in particular hostile to inclusion in the upper Clyde consortium, and considerable effort and energy was made to dismantle the management structure put in place in Fairfields (during the 'Fairfield experiment' period), when Upper Clyde Shipbuilders was eventually established. There was a relatively easier path on the lower Clyde, with the merger in 1967 of Scotts and Lithgow. But although the consortia were eventually achieved, government funding was not used as government intended: the intention was for funds to be applied to the build-up of capital equipment and the elimination of technical weakness, but instead they subsidised contract losses (Payne 1985). There was also evidence that the Lithgow grouping on the lower Clyde was in fact part of a much wider perspective on Lithgow's part and not always synchronised with central government. (37)

Corporatism post-1945 Despite the war-time links between state and shipbuilding industry, the subsequent government led and financed reorganisation after the Geddes Report and the later nationalisation of the industry, the evolution to corporatism (which in the politico-economic environment of Britain generally accelerated from the late 1950s) should not be overstated in its impact on shipbuilding. Compared to competitor nations, the formal state-industry corporate support instruments were minimal. State involvement did not amount to much in comparative terms:

> German yards benefited from special taxation relief and low interest rates; Holland and Sweden enjoyed long term credit arrangements backed by either the government or local municipalities. In Japan the industry was officially controlled under a system of indirect subsidies on raw materials, low interest on loans and reduced taxation. In Britain, the Ship Mortgage Finance Company and the Export Credit Guarantee Department were weak supports compared with the range of subsidies and allowances available to builder and purchaser in foreign yards. The latter were frequently enabled to quote fixed prices and early delivery dates which Clyde and British yards could not meet, and orders were redirected to the recovering yards in Europe and Japan. (38)

Nevertheless, it was important to see shipbuilding as a key element in the heavy engineering sector, particularly significant in the west of Scotland. This sector played hard to maintain influence on the instruments of state industrial policy after 1945. For some time the Industrial and Commercial Financial Corporation's attempts to promote light industry were opposed by two Glasgow banks, the Union and Clydesdale (though supported by the Edinburgh based Commercial), which had close links with Murray Johnstone Investment Trust and drew most of their funds from Clydeside heavy industry. The Glasgow banks proposed a different structure for the Corporation that would include representatives from iron, steel and shipbuilding. The government actually depended on new management in the Bank of England to outflank them (Checkland, 1975). But like experience in other sectors, corporatist styled links between business and state had little impact at the level of business management practice: the war-time and post-war workplace based Joint Production Committees designed to involve unions and management in production matters may have implanted ideas (if little else) in some sectors, but there is no evidence of such an occurrence in shipbuilding or indeed in Scotland as a whole (Wigham 1973); research in the engineering sector on Clydeside revealed 'traditional' labour management relations rather than more participative or consensual approaches. (39)

Finally, a piece of corporatist history pertinent to the case, the Fairfield experiment and the subsequent designation of the Fairfield yard as a constituent part of Upper Clyde Shipbuilders, was the exception to prove the general rule that corporatist approaches had minimal impact on managerial practice. The experiment, though restricted to one yard, was corporatism in microcosm: a failing shipyard, technically insolvent, received government funding in addition to some bank funding and financial support from trade unions. In return joint management was installed drawn from government, unions and business; considerable micro-management changes were introduced including productivity bargaining, the introduction of production and work scheduling systems and labour flexibility (Alexander 1970). Events (with the post-Geddes creation of Upper Clyde Shipbuilders) overtook the experiment. Yet the negotiations prior to the creation of UCS made the point. Sir Iain Stewart of Fairfields proposed a merger with Browns where his 'new' methods would be implemented; Rannie (of Browns) resisted the idea in the belief that these methods of work study and work measurement would interfere with Browns' own. Fairfield was unhappy with a merger which could not embrace its radical approach (Pauldin and Hawkins 1969). However, although the eventual creation of UCS had Browns and Fairfields at the core, government funding to support the restructuring failed to alter management or production practices much on Clydeside (40) (or elsewhere) (DTI 1973; Sawyer 1991). Furthermore, the newly created UCS deliberately dismantled the management structures and many of the practices which government had previously made a condition of support to Fairfield. This led to the early resignation of Sir Iain Stewart from the new UCS board (Foster and Wolfson 1986).

The Development and Strengthening of Internal Management?

Structures and control Both case study firms saw the early dilution of family control. By 1896 when Thomson's Shipyard in Clydebank changed its name to Clydebank Engineering and Shipbuilding Company, the Thomson family interest was negligible. After the death of Sir William Pearce in 1888, Fairfield became public (1889) to realise some of the family fortune while still retaining (though much diluted) family control. When Cammel Laird took a 50% interest eight years later, the Pearce dominance was gone. Ownership and management were distinct. Although directors in both companies retained equity, Board responsibilities were by no means correlated with equity holding. Despite this, it was personalised management and control rather than formal or hierarchical bureaucracies which typified management.

Systems of managerial accountability and control were individualised and overlaid with a very basic form of organisational departmentalism. Early records indicated the payment of bonuses to the managers of the engine and shipbuilding departments based on the respective profit levels in the departments. Directors' remuneration was based on a salary and bonus, the latter related to profit level (usually 4% of profit). There was no evidence of a similar form of incentivisation embedded further in the companies to cover other employees.

A major consequence of an individualised system of control and accountability was its dependence to an overwhelming extent on the qualities of key individuals. The dispute between one director and the board at Fairfield in the mid 1890s illustrated this: board member and shipyard manager (Mr White) was forced to resign when cost over-runs on a ship being built for Cunard caused difficulty and embarrassment to the company. It was also apparent that there was no robust system of allocating materials (mainly steel) against specific contracts when concurrent building programmes were underway, (41) and no proper system for comparing estimated and actual building costs. His replacement (from out-with the company) immediately introduced an estimated versus actual build cost framework of accountability.

The system of individualised accountability seemed to work. The most senior individuals were made directly accountable through the devise of five year service contracts and a fairly ruthless approach to transgression or performance failure. Difficulties in the shipbuilding department of Fairfield in the years immediately prior to the first war led first to the dismissal of two shipyard managers (42) and then the 'requested' resignation of the shipyard manager, also designated a director. The Board justified its action in the context of:

> reported losses in the shipbuilding department 1911-1914 notwithstanding repeated references by the management, no change had been made in any section of the ship department with a view to improving matters.

The individual then offered to leave the Board,

> but to continue in the company's service and devote all his time to duties of shipyard manager. (43)

The Board promptly declined the offer.

Evidence that parameters of control were in place is found in the fact that cost control systems (and the managerial accountability that went with this) were in place and operating effectively enough in both Fairfields and Browns beyond the post first war years. This of course was not to say that production volumes were satisfactory-quite another matter.

Hierarchies for control and co-ordination were very rudimentary, going little beyond basic departmentalism. Unsurprisingly, such hierarchy and co-ordination which did exist, was product dominated with little investment in marketing or commercial infrastructures. A dispute over reporting lines between the naval architect and production directors and the managing director in Fairfield saw a very dim view taken of the attempt to have a control/co-ordination role given to the company's naval architect. A statement from the managing director resolved this:

> The departments are responsible to the Managing Director and through him to the Board---it is necessary that information of a technical nature be supplied to Dr Elgar [the company's naval architect]. (44)

A similar rudimentary system was in place in Browns as indicated in figure 4.1. Such a basic production oriented system, rudimentary though it was, appeared to provide adequate control for the market and commercial conditions of the time. Beneath the Managing Director there were basically two levels above the front line supervision role undertaken by craft supervisors. Immediately reporting to the Managing Director were a Naval Architect, Shipyard Director, Engine Works Director and Company Secretary; beneath those were two Chief Draughtsman (one reporting to the Naval Architect the other to the Engine Works Director) an Estimator, two Head Foreman and an Accountant; under this level were the Foremen.

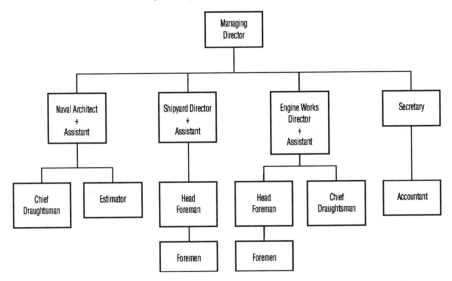

**Figure 4.1 John Brown, Management Structure at Clydebank Shipyard
1924 (adapted from Johnston 2000)**

In the post-second war boom years and beyond, managerial and organisational structures were more problematic. It has been argued that structural problems were already evident in the industry well before the second war (Pollard and Robertson 1979; Lorenz and Wilkinson 1986; Peebles 1987;), but a lack of awareness of the long-term seriousness of the industry's underlying competitiveness was not difficult to understand. Britain still had the world's largest navy and the naval rebuilding programme in the 1930s saw 'good times' return to the industry. Despite world trade disruption, in the period 1934 - 1939, British yards' share of world tonnage averaged 40%, with the Clyde's share of this fairly consistent with pre-1914 figures. Though the British percentage was below pre first war levels, capacity utilisation in British yards was high. The years after 1945 were different. British output was relatively stable, but world output rocketed, leaving the British share declining from 37.9 % in 1950 to 16 % in 1960 to 8.2 % in 1967 (Lorenz 1991). This international competition meant more competitive costing, increased speed and reduced build times with the consequent need for managerial and cost efficiencies. How did managerial structures respond to this?

An examination of the private salaries books of Fairfields in 1948 indicated an organisation structure as follows:

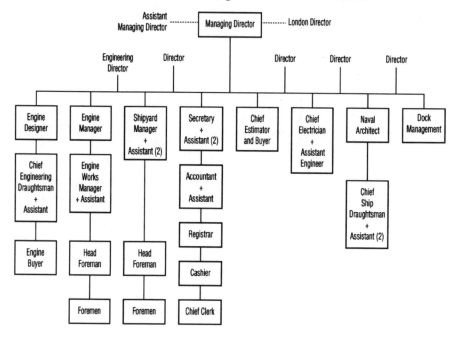

Figure 4.2. Management Structure, Fairfields 1948
Source: private salaries book UCS 2/29/1).

This structure was rudimentary, in effect a very basic departmentalist organisation with no general management, marketing or management support services. Including directors there were three, at most four, layers of management. In effect the only difference with Browns structure some 25 years earlier was the creation of another level, in reality five directors on top of a very similar pre-existing departmental structure.

Over the next decade, there was some incremental growth but little deepening in the organisational hierarchy or other co-ordinating mechanisms. For example, in 1951 an additional shipbuilding manager was added as was a deputy managing director and in addition to these changes an existing director's post was designated 'shipbuilding director'. It was obvious there was no clear division between the strategic responsibilities of the board and day-to-day operational management. This could clearly create workload problems for the directors affected. A Board discussion of Mr George Strachan's 'onerous responsibilities' resolved that

> as a result, Mr AW Davies be appointed Engineering Manager in control of the Engineering Department responsible to Mr Strachan.

However, the same Engineering Manager was two years later appointed to the Board under the conditions:

that he continues responsibility of managing the Engineering Department. (45)

The most significant change in management and organisation structure occurred in the early 1950s in Browns and this was for business-political reasons rather than management efficiency:

> In 1953 the corporate structure of John Brown and Co Ltd was changed. The divisions, of which Clydebank was the major one were spun off into separate companies under the overall control of the parent which then became a holding company. This was more prompted by the desire to limit the impact of the Labour government's commitment to nationalisation of the steel industry. (46)

There was little change up to the mid-1960s (Alexander 1970). Yet managerial resource and investment was needed. The high post war growth in competition and the increased speed in production cycles required a managerial co-ordination and control which was lacking. A key area of activity where managerial capability was required was the linkage and co-ordination between design, drawing office and ship production. Some investments were made in these critical functions: a Programme Planning Department was brought into existence in Fairfield and investment was made in key new technologies. For example, in 1964 a De la Rue Gamma 10 computer using network analysis to co-ordinate the various drawing office activities and production scheduling was installed at an annual leasing cost of £10000. (47) Nonetheless, throughout the 1960s references like 'contracts suffering from poor information supplied too late from the drawing office' (48) were commonplace.

Quality assurance was not part of the managerial resource or structure: the quality problems in the QE 2 contract at John Browns, which became apparent at the contract commissioning stage, have been well documented; Fairfield had a quality control department set up in the mid 1960s but only 'to meet the navy's stringent requirements in connection with ship no. 833' (49) but it had little impact throughout the company's operations, 75 % of welders failing to meet commercial standards on trade tests and only 20 % of welding passing Admiralty tests first time (the comparable figure for Dutch yards was 98% (Alexander 1970).

There were also problems co-ordinating various production activities with cost control. The traditional nature of individual relationships with customers (which persisted) made cost control difficult due to changes in specification after commencement of the build programme. Cost control was not robust or well co-ordinated. Fairfield Production Planning Department was regularly requested to revise costings against estimates, not (it is obvious from board records) as an ongoing time sensitive or iterative management process but because costs were running out of control. As late as 1962, statements provided to the board for discussion did not illustrate the value of steel purchased against existing contracts, much to the annoyance of some board members. (50) Attempts were then made to introduce a form of budgetary control. Subsequently, one director stated 'that while a form of budgetary control was in place, he felt that the system could be much improved'. (51) Less than three years later there appeared to be a complete absence of monthly departmental budgets, proper capital expenditure procedures and up to date store records (Alexander 1970). With reference to this shipbuilding case, it is difficult to escape the views of Elbaum and Lazonick (1986) and others who have linked lack of competitive performance in many of Britain's industries to the lack of development of bureaucratic procedures, hierarchies and other modernising processes.

Managing human resource and management control. Management bounded by the craft system? There were certain efficiencies and advantages inherent in the craft system. First, labour markets for craft workers were internal to the shipbuilding district with movement between yards according to phases of yards' building cycle. There is considerable evidence of this occurring well after the second war in the records of both Fairfield and Browns (see also Johnston, I, 2000); the persistence of the practice was much bemoaned by a director of Fairfield who as late as 1964 commented on the demise of the shipbuilding district labour market for craft workers, seen by him as a relatively recent event. (52) However as will be shown later, this internal (to the district) labour market was under considerable pressure much earlier. Second, the craft apprenticeship system provided a means of internal training within shipbuilding firms. Some of this was more formalised and systematic than previously supposed. John Browns in the early 1920s ran evening classes in a dedicated area of the yard for the various trades: classes were run for platers, sheet iron workers, joiners, shipwrights, boilermakers, moulders and patternmakers; conducted by a leading hand, foreman or journeyman; designed and programmed in a systematic way,

> open to all apprentices 18 years and any young journeyman desirous of improving himself. (53)

The records of Fairfield also show that training in new craft technologies was undertaken. Allowances were paid to boilermakers and other trades while undergoing training in welding techniques. Such allowances were (inevitably) negotiated and it is in the negotiation process that research and writing has concentrated (Lorenz and Wilkinson 1986; McKinlay 1989). It is certainly the case that the craft worker was able to appropriate technology and this was the key to exploring the rate of uptake of new technology from the multiple punch in the 1920s to the introduction of welding in the 1930s (Knox 1999). Nonetheless, training occurred largely organised through the craft system. (54) Third, the piece rate/squad system, especially in many of the metal working trades, was self-managing. The skilled metal workers were organised on the squad system: a group of skilled workers contracted for tasks such as a row of plates; the squads took responsibility for co-ordinating the production process on the shop floor and for supervising (and often paying) their semi skilled assistants. This reduced the need for managerial planning of production and for supervision of the manual workforce. However, after the first decade of the twentieth century the tensions in this system led to its gradual demise (Littler 1982). In shipbuilding, the gang system with the increasing throughput and bureaucratisation of production failed to enable managerial control. Thomas Bell, managing director of Browns, outlined the situation to the Board of Trade Committee in Shipping and Shipbuilding in 1916:

> In shipyards it was thought that by giving the work out to squads you reduced the general charges and did the work more economically, forgetting that these squads were a number of men banded together who in time got worse and worse. By having only squads like that you play into their hands. If a squad refused to do a job you were at your wits' end if you did not give way to them. Even if you offered some sum, no other squad in the shipyard would take their job up. You were in the hands of the squads instead of having proper discipline. (55)

More favoured was directed control by a craft trained foreman and this is analysed below. Some of the initiative to change also came from the craft squad workers themselves who became less enthusiastic for a management and control role over fellow, semi-skilled, employees (Knox 1999).

A fourth advantage of the craft system was that a plentiful and relatively cheap supply of this key factor meant that the labour to capital cost ratio obviated the need for large fixed capital investments. Although particularly attractive in the cyclical and uncertain environment of shipbuilding in the inter-war years (McKinlay 1989; Lorenz 1991), it also explained the light capital investment intensity of UK builders in the post-war years, leading ultimately to cost and efficiency disadvantages compared with other nations.

If the shipbuilding employers 'Programme for Action' in the period 1902-1906 did not quite amount to an assault on the craft system, it certainly was an attempt at rationalisation and the injection of some managerial control. A memorandum on behalf of the Shipbuilding Employers Federation for the opinion of Counsel in 1903 stated:

> Where so many different trades are employed it is difficult to preserve a uniform set of working conditions; some of the more aggressive trades have secured greater privileges for their members and in some trades workmen are compelled to submit to restrictions, which other trades, do not impose. It is felt that all trades employed in one industry should as nearly as may be, be subject to the same conditions. (56)

While the employers were successful in establishing a nationwide disputes procedure, the craft system at local level and certainly in the two companies studied remained intact. Although it is difficult to determine the attitudes of Browns and Fairfield management per se through the Employers Federation records, it is clear that not all Clydeside employers wished to take a hard line against the craft union system: D & W Henderson certainly did, but Barclay Curle and Alexander Stephen were either unenthusiastic for this challenge or thought 'the time not appropriate'. (57)

A plethora of piece-rate arrangements and allowances continued to exist and (until the early 1960s) remained the norm in shipbuilding. (58) The contrast with the system introduced by D Rowan and Company a Clydeside engineering company and a supplier of Fairfield, after the major strike in 1898 could hardly be starker. The system, if not quite Tayloristic in detail, was influenced by current ideas on managerial control, work measurement and throughput management:

> Time allowed for the job will be fixed by management. Time allowance will only be changed if the method or means of manufacture change, each workman will be given a 'job ticket' with a description of the job, the time started and time allowed. When finished, the ticket is returned to the foreman who will mark his name and time on it if satisfied with the job, and the finishing time of the job. (59)

The Rowan system of payment (and also the Rowan-Halsey system) became an internationally recognised efficiency practice (Wren 1994) and the Rowan system was proudly presented at a meeting of the Royal Philosophical Society of Glasgow in 1917. In one of the rich ironies of history, Rowan was taken over by Fairfields some 60 years later and the early losses of the Fairfield Rowan company were attributed to inefficient practices in the building of Sulzer engines before the takeover. (60)

However, the reliance on the craft system in shipbuilding did seem to develop a certain rigidity of thinking, which inhibited internal labour movement and mobility. Craft workers were rarely seen as a potential managerial resource beyond the level of foreman. A 'cloth cap ceiling' seemed to exist. This was in contrast to other sectors, especially those less cyclical in nature where the value of investing in human resource to ensure a continuous flow of managerial personnel was more obvious. Consequently, shipbuilding was not well equipped to meet managerial resource requirements in tight labour markets, which appeared towards the end of the case period. The contrasting approaches to developing managerial resource were highlighted by the differing views of a leading engineering employer in the west of Scotland (like shipbuilding, craft dominated) and shipbuilders. The former indicated a view of craft to management mobility: Mr Sam Mavor, Managing Director of Mavor and Coulson Engineers, Glasgow, writing of his own company's practices, argued that

> There is a need for two types of operative, semi skilled grade and skilled craftsman. Of the latter, there are two types. Engineering apprentices whose technical and scientific education is continued during apprenticeship, becoming foremen or gaining supervisory and managerial appointments----at the beginning of the apprenticeship it is open to every boy of superior capacity and industry and if he has the requisite education to qualify himself for the advantages of the engineering apprenticeship training the special feature of which is that opportunities are given for gaining experience in different departments of the works {and to attend] technical college evening classes or university classes with work experience. The problem that remains is with the education and training of craft apprentices-about 80% of the whole-the proportion of which has a grasp of the principles of their trade is lamentably small. The urgent need is to raise the level of technical intelligence and to develop initiatives in the general mass of our

operatives. The present system fails to assure the continuity of the boys' education. (61)

This was different to the view of the Shipbuilding Employers Federation:

> There is a shortage of men in the industry capable of filling managerial posts. Various reasons have contributed to this shortage. The years of depression since the last war reduced the attractiveness of the industry, other industries promising more stable and better immediate prospects. Changes have had their effect in curtailing entry of shipbuilding families to the same extent as occurred when the family type of business was more common. The increased intricacies of modern business also has had an influence in rendering recruits from the drawing office. (62)

Perceptive though this was in many respects, their solution was not to be found by a process of selection and continued education and training of internal craft based resources in a way similar to Mavor. Instead it was thought the best way forward was to recruit nationally, with applicants attending technical college or university after recruitment.

The craft system under stress What can now be analysed was the stress which led eventually to, in effect, an implosion of production organisation as organised around the craft system. A system, which was labour intensive and employed relatively low levels of fixed capital investment was placed under severe pressure when economic development and diversification in the economy led to other points of demand for scarce labour resources. Added to which, foreign competitors had better equipped and more highly capitalised companies with strong growth ambitions, in some cases lower labour costs and better arrangements for the efficient management of throughput (Payne 1992; Slaven 1980). When researching Fairfields and Browns archives from the late 1950s one is painfully aware of companies bravely attempting to continue and survive but gradually being overwhelmed by the harsh realities of building ships in the last four decades of the twentieth century.

The key advantage of traditional craft production was the availability of labour within the shipbuilding district. In its key years, shipbuilding, due to its size, had a major call on labour resource in the west of Scotland. This was buttressed by an apprenticeship system, which involved community, and family ties to a working life in shipbuilding. The inevitable growth and diversification of the west of Scotland economy added an alternative demand for labour and an additional employment outlet for the workforce. As early as the 1920s, it was realised in the industry that alternative sectors of economic activity made apprentice recruitment difficult, though the tone of the employers' analysis suggested an assumption that shipbuilding needs should be uppermost in policy makers' and others' minds. A letter from the Engineering and Allied Employers National Federation to the Secretary of the Regional Committee for Scotland referred to apprentice recruitment difficulties in the industry in the 1920s:

The difficulty is caused by higher rates paid to apprentices in other industries, also the high wages paid to unskilled classes in sheltered employment retarded youths from entering the skilled trades. High wages are also paid by municipalities and such bodies in the building trades. If government subsidies to municipal and other bodies in connection with housing schemes etc were stopped, it would largely help towards the wages in the building trade being brought to a proper economic level. (63)

After the depression of the 1930s and the passing of the wartime demand for ships, this was indeed a long term structural problem for the industry. Post-war governments had industrial distribution policies with the use of Industrial Development Certificates as instruments to boost and diversify economic growth, especially in areas like the west of Scotland. This led to recruitment difficulties in the peak years of ship build cycles which records of Fairfield allude to in the 1950s on a very regular basis. Browns records indicate this too. For example, papers relating to the sale of the Royal Ordnance factory in Dalmuir to Babcock and Wilcox boilermakers in Renfrew, showed a fear that this would create labour supply problems. (64) The length of apprenticeship and demarcation between the trades (caused by job insecurity, for despite near full employment in the economy as a whole, shipbuilding still experienced peaks and troughs) inherent in the craft system only exacerbated these labour supply problems. But even despite earlier advantages of the craft system at least some in the industry in the 1920s had a deeper perception of the problems than the quotation above suggested.

> every member [of the Clyde Shipbuilders Association] should be encouraged and urged to adopt a definite and long sighted policy in the matter of training rather than the pre war employment of apprentices. This policy should include an obligation to give a proper training and continuous employment. To my mind the present shortage [of skilled labour and supply of apprentices] is largely due to the failure on the part of most firms to adopt the foregoing, a perfectly understandable attitude during the past years of extreme uncertainty, but to my mind an attitude for which there is no longer any excuse in view of the present situation. (65)

Four decades later in 1965, Fairfield directors identified the lack of joint employer action and demarcation against a context of employment insecurity as a major problem. A directors' meeting of 25 January 1965 referred to

> labour shortage and demarcation between shipwrights and platers. There is no joint planning by employers to tackle this, each firm looking after its own interests. A guarantee of employment could solve this problem, such a guarantee would have to be on a selected basis excluding outfit workers and would not suit the unions. It might be possible to guarantee employment even for the outfit workers in conjunction with another yard, say Browns. (66)

The front line supervision system, articulated through the foreman was also under pressure. There was a shortage of foremen in Fairfield, inevitable given the recruitment difficulties and supply problems of craft labour, the main source of foremen recruitment; there was no recognised training system for foremen, the vast majority in Fairfields in 1967 having gone through a craft apprenticeship. Only one third had gone through further education evening classes with 90% having received no training, managerial or technical, before taking up their post (Alexander 1970). There appeared to have been little improvement since the Government Minister's observation of the industry's lack of enthusiasm for Training Within Industry (TWI) programmes some 24 years earlier:

> It was reported that the Minister of Labour at a recent interview with representatives of the industry had referred to the Government Training Centres which had been set up for supervisors and had expressed the view that the shipbuilding and shiprepairing industry was not taking advantage of these courses as other industries. (67)

Training and development of managers It would be wrong to suggest that no attention was paid to the development and training of managers. There is ample evidence that at least until the industry peaked at the outset of the first war there were no major difficulties in meeting the required levels of managerial capability. Evidence from both Browns and Fairfield indicate that Admiralty trained personnel were a source of recruitment not only for the most senior positions in the companies, but as a source of naval architects. There was also movement from the drawing office, with encouragement given to individuals to attain qualifications in various branches of engineering and naval architecture, into production management. (68) Naval architects trained at Glasgow University also found their way into the companies - Fairfield in particular: it was this company which initially supported the chair in naval architecture at that university. The evidence also suggested that production management positions were accorded equal status with the specialist naval architects. From 1899-1904, the managers and assistant managers of the shipbuilding and engine works departments in Browns were paid a basic salary similar to the company's naval architect, but the latter's was inflated due to 'compensation for loss of pension' (he had worked in the Admiralty) and the formers' supplemented by 1.5% of the department's net profit but with an additional 25% minimum guaranteed whatever the profit. Between 1900 and 1920 in Browns, the chief electrician was paid a salary similar to the estimating naval architect. (69)

Although the limitations of the shipbuilding employers scheme for manager recruitment and development for the post-second war years have been outlined, it should not be ignored that their scheme did show an awareness that some action was required to address the industry's management needs, or at any rate its senior management needs. The Shipbuilding Employers Federation had in mind a scheme that would identify applicants and provide tailor made training for the industry on a national basis. Applicants were required,

> to have the capacity to acquire the necessary scientific, technical, economic and psychological knowledge involved in successful shipyard management--- [the scheme would involve] attendance at university or technical college, and will have an initial intake of 30. (70)

The indication was that some non traditional sources were envisaged as worthwhile recruitment possibilities. Applicants came from some unexpected sources: the careers master at Rugby School was particularly interested, though it is unknown if he took employment in a shipyard on Clydeside or elsewhere.

The scheme in fact never even reached its modest initial recruitment targets and was not fully supported by many of the bigger yards on the Clyde or elsewhere. Throughout the 1950s the case evidence suggested growth in the education and training of managers in both companies, but in traditional ways supporting employees through evening class attendance; some ambitious attempts were made by companies to improve technician (as well as craft) training in the early 1960s. (71) There was also some apparent development in the training of managers. The Shipbuilding Industry Training Board had what appeared to be a widely supported scheme for the training of existing managers in the industry, (72) while the Shipbuilding and Shiprepairers National Association set up a scheme in 1967 for the recruitment and training of new managers:

> We are agreed that a wider range of disciplines than has hitherto been regarded as appropriate for management trainees in the industry should be encouraged—there is a continuing demand for naval architects but a growing need for other professional skills—mechanical, marine or electrical engineering, economics and degrees in business management could bee appropriate. (73)

But the managerial shortage, especially in general management was significant. In 1972, the Booz Allen Report indicated

> there is a major shortage of managerial ability particularly in non technical areas. Most managers have good technical backgrounds but lack commercial and business skills. As a result, company organisational structures are often unbalanced and some major functions such as management services are under represented. There is a lack of general management skills. (74)

Use of the word 'lack' rather than 'shortage' was perhaps revealing. Booz Allen noted the previously noted ceiling of attainment for the craft trained foreman:

> Training and development of supervisors is largely neglected. (75)

This appeared to be entrenched in industry thinking. A joint commitment in 1963 by the TUC and the British Employers Confederation on craft supervisor and shop steward training was enthusiastically welcomed in some quarters, for example the broadsheet press in Glasgow:

> Employers have everything to gain from having men who can command sufficient knowledge to dispel these irrational fears that characterise many workers reaction to technical change. (76)

The Shipbuilding Employers Federation, on which the case companies were represented, took a rather different view:

> [there is] some scepticism as to the likely benefit to the industry from such course since it was anticipated that trade unions would have the major say in running these courses, but since the Business Education Council and the employers [i.e., the British Employers Confederation] had given their blessing it would be somewhat invidious for the shipbuilding industry to remain completely aloof. (77)

In fact, programmes for the courses (the records show one in Glasgow and one in Aberdeen) indicated the following subject areas: work study; method study; work measurement; job evaluation; payment by results; safety at work; employment and legal aspects; structures and functions of management; aims of collective bargaining. Yet such efficiency and managerial topics caused employer scepticism.

Management control; the role of the foreman   Some of the practices targeted at aspects of management control outlined in chapter 2 had minimal bearing in this case. There was no evidence at all of practices influenced by 'human relations' thinking, even though the leading work in Britain was carried out in a craft environment, in Glacier Metals Company. While there was a range of personnel and welfare schemes developed, these were targeted at white collar workers only. For instance, Lithgow introduced a staff pension scheme into Fairfield in the late 1930s, and housing was provided for foremen in Browns before the first war. Though these may be important elements of a control agenda (especially in the case of foremens' housing as indicated below), research has shown that in some other sectors these non wage items could be a relatively significant part of the remuneration package for hourly paid staff and were sometimes used by companies in response to increased union recruitment and activity. The management of the craft system, and in particular the role of the foreman, is vital to understanding management control. While this does not challenge the Gospel thesis (Gospel 1992) about the product-market mix in sectors like shipbuilding preventing the establishment of internal labour control systems, the internal management control role of the foreman in certain periods leads to some qualification of that thesis.

Despite various 'assaults on the craft system' in the early years of the twentieth century (Lovell 1992), the industry actually increased the numbers of craft employees in the decades prior to 1914. Modern management thinking at the time, e.g. Taylorism and 'scientific management', emphasised managerial control and a scientifically designed, timed and calibrated 'one way' approach to the job. Although it has been pointed out that employers' support for such efficiencies in Britain was often partial and meant in actuality cost cutting and work intensification rather than the full Taylorist package (Zeitlin 1983), the shipbuilding employers' view during the 'assault on the craft system' was even further removed from pure Taylorist approaches: A Report of the Shipbuilding Employer's Federation in 1902 suggested that:

a workman of average efficiency should [be able to] earn at least his time rate of wages plus increased earnings in respect of increased production due to such additional exertions or ingenuity or improved methods which he may devise to adopt. (78)

For Taylorists, ingenuity or devising improved methods was management's, not the worker's role. (79)

Fundamental to the craft system was front-line supervision, carried out by a craft trained foreman. This was particularly important with the decline of the internal sub-contracting gang system. Given the lack of managerial hierarchies in shipbuilding, his importance was accentuated. His role in the management of the production-craft system was interesting and complex. Those wishing to rationalise or even attack the craft system - for lack of a better phrase the 'management control school' - saw the foremen not so much in production terms but in management control terms. He was viewed as an agent of management and as such was discouraged from trade union membership and encouraged to join the Foreman's' Mutual Benefit Society. (80) Clydeside yards were not unanimous in this view, with some yards happy to have foremen as members of their appropriate craft union. Other strategies were used to tie the role and loyalty of this crucial first line manager to the employer's interest. When the build cycle reached the stage where less labour was required, foremen tended to be laid off last. The ratio of foremens' wages to the total wage bill in Fairfield Engine Department during the very bad year, 1931, indicated this. (81) Browns' foremen ledger also showed foremen laid off in the severe depression years re-engaged without loss of status. (82) Also in that company, strenuous efforts were made to ensure employment for foremen as long as possible in the depression years of the early 1930s (Johnston, I, 2000). Foremen were also paid bonuses during war time in Fairfields to ensure their earnings did not fall behind the tradesmen they supervised: this practice may have been adopted due to a fear of militant unionisation among foremen (Melling 1980a). Housing was provided for some foremen (Melling 1980b) and in some instances they were helped with house purchase. It was also felt necessary to gain and maintain the loyalty of under-foremen as the following statement of a shipyard manager in John Browns highlighted:

> a question which is causing us grave concern is that of our Ironworker, Carpenter and Joiner Under-foremen. Owing to the great fluctuations in the amount of our work in the last ten or twelve years, the larger number of these men seem reluctant to throw themselves heartily on the side of their employers on account of not knowing when they may be disrated and have to work as mates with the men at present under them and with whom they live in adjacent flats. These men are our non commissioned officers and our economical production is largely dependent especially in the shipyard on them. (83)

The memorandum then went on to recommend that the company provide housing for the under-foremen ' very near to the yard, but entirely devoted to cottages and separated by the railway from the working-mens' tenements'. The company, at the most senior levels, took this separation very seriously. The managing director of

John Browns told the government committee on shipping and shipbuilding in 1916 that the construction of company housing,

> was not all philanthropy, but hard-headed business to separate foremen from the men. (84)

If relative security of employment and in some instances provision of housing (in an environment, it must be remembered, of desperately inadequate housing) were means of creating managerial loyalty and identification from foremen, then it is worth exploring the extent to which the movement of skilled tradesmen into foremens' positions helped reinforce identification with managerial, organisational and company norms as distinct from a craft, collective trade identity. A similar set of questions has recently been posed with regard to the changing nature of discipline (using for example the Great Western Railway as a case study, Savage 1998) with the increasing use of the 'career' as an instrument to gain loyalty. The career was seen as 'a means of working on the soul' as distinct from more punishment based forms of discipline and has been conceptually linked to a debate on the balance between traditional managerial discipline and self regulation and commitment (McKinlay and Taylor 1998; Findlay and Newton 1998).

A detailed examination of the available John Brown's apprentice registers in the early 1900s (in various trades) along with Foremens' ledgers from 1920 to 1934 indicated a degree of upward mobility, or at least a progression pathway up to foreman level. As Table 4.1indicates, 85% of angle iron smith apprentices recruited between 1888 and 1907 completed their apprenticeship; of those, around 14% ended up as foremen, sometime between 1920 and 1934. For carpenters and boatbuilders recruited as apprentices from 1889 to 1906 the figures are 90% and 12%. A similar pattern is difficult to discern in the riveting trade. This trade was rather different, more prone to casualisation and this is addressed below.

While these figures help explain strong company as well as craft identities, (85) there was little indication of the use of the managerial career as a self discipline instrument or a means of gaining commitment to managerial norms-managerial hierarchies were not well enough developed in the shipbuilding industry (in contrast to other sectors); the immobility of craft workers beyond a certain level has previously been alluded to. From payroll numbers, Browns had less than 3% of the workforce in supervisory positions in the 'good years' of the 1920s and 1930s. In 1951 at 2.9%, the figure for the UK shipbuilding industry as a whole had barely changed (cited in Lorenz 1991). A pattern can be discerned: there was much movement of labour from yard to yard due to different build cycles as well as 'rate chasing' (well noted in Clyde Shipbuilders Association minutes of meetings). But there was a 10-14% chance of achieving foreman status; not high by contemporary standards but a very significant figure given the low numbers in supervisory or managerial positions, and this may explain strong company identification (low supervisory and management ratios were also noted by the Patton and Booz Allen Reports). But craft identities were certainly as strong as company identities: many foremen far from being career managers still 'worked the tools', a situation apparent in the late 1960s. The survey of Fairfield foremen in 1967 indicated almost 25% to be in this position. (86)

Table 4.1 Apprentice Progression to Foremen in John Brown Shipbuilders

	Apprentices Recruited	Number of Those Completing Apprenticeship	Number of Those completing apprenticeship and employed as Foremen between 1920 and 1934
Angle Iron Smiths /Fitters	(Years 1888 to 1907) **302**	➤ **257** (85%)	➤ **36** (14%)
Carpenters/Boatbuilders	(Years 1889 to 1906) **297**	➤ **273** (92%)	➤ **32** (12%)
Riveters	(Years 1888 to 1910) **131**	➤ No Figures Available	➤ **8** (6%)

Source: Compiled from John Browns Apprentice Register and Foremen's Pay Book
(UCS 1/65/1-3)
(UCS 1/49/10-11)

Perhaps the most convincing explanation of the foreman and his key position in the craft system was found in the ambiguity of the role. The position could be very powerful, indeed monarchical. Patternmakers when complaining of the spread of the Enquiry Note system in 1909 (in effect an employer-led attempt to gain intelligence on workers moving from one firm to another) were told 'that the signing of these notes by the firm would act as a protection to the workmen against vindictive foremen'. (87) The foreman's role and power seems to have been bound up with community based loyalties and networks often of a sectarian or quasi-religious nature; by its nature this is difficult to verify with hard fact, but fragmented evidence is there. (88) Foremen in many instances saw that their role as production co-ordinators required bargaining on behalf of their tradesmen (McKinlay 1980). This role was highlighted in the following extract from the proceedings of the Clyde Shipbuilders Association:

The incentive payment had been applied not on prices laid down by the Clyde Riveters Piece Work Price List of 1926, but an enhanced price which had previously been introduced by the foreman, this has led to difficulties. (89)

Finally, the ambiguity and complexity of the foreman's role was seen through the apparent degree of craft union (rather than managerial) identity. At the end of this case study period, the 1967 Fairfield survey indicated that around one third of foremen had held a position in a trade union (either shop steward or branch official); this possibly indicated the necessity of knowledge and experience of craft trade union job definitions in this highly unionised company and industry. The survey also indicated that when asked why they were union members, 'necessary to take up the job' ranked (unsurprisingly) 1, the necessity of union membership to fulfil the foreman's job was most noticeable in the steel trades; but 'belief in trade unionism' ranked 2, above 'expected to be a member' (ranked 3), and 'protection against possible injustices' (ranked 4).

Summary and Conclusion

Shipbuilding was an industry, which traditionally operated through a series of external and personalised management relationships and strategies. Key parts of the value chain (most notably steel supply) were managed not by integration but by shifting and dynamic relationships between alternative suppliers and cross ownership between shipbuilders and steel producers. The industry and the case companies were organised at key times (especially in the lead up to the first war) as constituent parts of industrial-military clusters forming communities of interest and ownership/managerial linkages. Fairfield's'participation in the Sperling Group after 1918 typified the externalisation of management with linkages between the group based on ownership patterns and management arrangements rather than internal production integration.

Personalised and externalised management was evident in other areas, most notably in marketing where there were personal links between ship owners and builders, and second, in the approaches to market regulation. In the former, such approaches were seen as particularly advantageous in harsh environments: for example in securing orders from shipping line owners. However, such advantages disappeared in the post-second war environment when shipping company and builder links were fractured with the flag of convenience and increased international competition. However, the legacy of traditional approaches may have prevented the creation of marketing and commercial structures and influenced approaches to market product relationships in the industry as a whole. Second, in the approaches to market regulation the inter-war period and especially the early to mid 1930s, saw externalisation strategies predominate; agreement and regulation between the big players aimed at capacity reduction rather than internally re-structuring and carrying out production integration or yard rationalisation. These externalisation approaches left the industry ill-placed for the long-term structural changes required in the post war years.

The broader societal aspects of external management indicated philanthropic and individual company interest at play. As representatives of a key strategic industry, leading shipbuilding figures were at the heart of government policy making. In the 1930s, it seemed that government and industry aims for the sector's organisation were synchronised. This was articulated through the experience of the case companies, though less so in the post 1960 years when government and industry again required to address industry organisation and management. Corporatist engagement with government appeared to have little influence on management practices at company level: the brief Fairfield experiment proved exceptional in this respect.

The externalisation focus in shipbuilding clearly meant that there were few highly developed internal management structures and control systems. It is precisely this which made a study of internal management interesting. Managerial structures were personalised and rudimentary, but successful in an era of British shipbuilding dominance. While some developments occurred and investments in internal systems were made, these were clearly inadequate to support the companies in the competitive higher speed production cycles of the 1960s. Did the internal management of human resources contribute to the development and strengthening of management in any sense? The craft system, of considerable advantage to the employers in the management of their companies in training and maintaining control and discipline certainly up to 1945, appeared to lead to rigidities of thinking with regard to mobility of craft employees into managerial positions. Combined with difficulties caused by craft labour shortages, the resulting production and quality problems appeared to overwhelm company management by the close of the case study. In addition, although the training and education of the most senior managers in the companies was traditionally high, the lack of depth of managerial capability and competence (commented upon by the Booz Allan Report in 1972) indicated that managerial training, education and development did not occur at a rate sufficient to strengthen company management, even though there were some progressive initiatives in the 1950s and 1960s. Finally, the traditional instrument of management control in shipbuilding companies, the foreman, could at key times be considered as playing an important role in developing and strengthening internal management; this was limited in the longer term given the duality and ambiguities of his position.

Notes

1. Booz-Allan and Hamilton Report (1973), *British Shipbuilding*, London: Department of Trade and Industry p. 144.
2. McGoldrick, J (1983) 'Industrial Relations and the division of labour in the shipbuilding industry since the war' *British Industrial Relations Journal* XX1, p. 203.
3. Booth Committee 1918, *Report on Shipping and Shipbuilding after the War*, Cmnd. 9092, pp. 30-31.
4. *Shipbuilding Enquiry Committee (Geddes Committee)* 1965-66, Paper 108, Cmnd. 2937(1966).

5. Parkinson, J.R (1960), *The Economics of Shipbuilding in the UK*, Glasgow: University of Glasgow Department of Economic and Social Research, p. 150.

6. Reid, J.M. (1964), *James Lithgow. Master of Work*, London: Hutchinson p. 83.

7. This was indicated in a report by Hoare and Company, cited in Slaven, A. (1980) 'Growth and stagnation in British/Scottish shipbuilding 1913-1977' in Kuuse and Slaven, *Scottish and Scandinavian Shipbuilding Seminar*, Glasgow; also in Lorenz, E (1991), *Economic Decline in Britain: The Shipbuilding Industry 1890-1970*, Oxford: Clarendon Press.

8. UCS 2/1/8. Minute of Board of Directors meting August 2, 1965.

9. Michael Porter's (1980) analysis of competitive advantage discussed the five forces, which determine the attractiveness-and by implication the success- of an industry and the firm's positioning within this environment. One of these forces, the power of buyers, should have been in theory manipulable in favour of the shipbuilders vis a vis steel producers.

10. Patton Report (1962) *Productivity and Research in Shipbuilding*. Report Prepared under the Chairmanship of the Joint Committee of the Shipbuilding Conference, The Shipbuilding Employers Association and the British Shipbuilding Research Association p. 61.

11. UCS 2/1/8. Minute of Board of Directors meeting 12 February 1959.

12. UCS 2/1/8. Minute of Board of Directors meeting 12 February 1959.

13. UCS 2/1/5. Minute book of Board of Directors meetings 12 April, 18 May 1921.

14. UCS 2/1/5. Minute of Board of Directors Sub Committee meeting 22 May 1921.

15. UCS 1/5/19. Report to Board of Directors 20 May and 29 June 1920.

16. UCS 2/1/6. Memorandum presented to Board of Directors 20 March 1935.

17. UCS 2/1/7. Minute of Board of Directors meeting 24 Nov 1947.

18. UCS 2/1/8 Memorandum presented to Board of Directors meeting 18 March 1963.

19. UCS 2/1/8 Minute of Board of Directors meeting 28 November 1963.

20. UCS 2/1/3 Minute of Board of Directors meeting 3 February 1903.

21. UCS 2/1/1 Minute of Board of directors meeting 27 December 1894.

22. UCS 2/1/3 Minute of Board of Directors meeting 29 November 1901.

23. UCS 1/1/13 Minute of Board of Directors meetings 20 January, 25 February; UCS 1/1/1 Minute of Board of Directors meeting 28 August, 16 September 1913.

24. UCS 2/1/5 Minute of Board of Directors meeting 9 December 1919.

25. UCS 2/1/5 Minute of Board of Directors meeting 18 May 1921.

26. UCS 2/1/5 Minute of Board of Directors meeting 16 October 1928.

27. Board minutes prior to 1902 indicate Fairfields building for Cunard. There was however a protracted dispute in 1901 over the final cost of contract, and this led to a rather acrimonious tendering procedure in 1902 when a tender to Cunard refused to state a maximum price agreeing to build on the basis of time, material plus 20% for charges and profit, with payments to be paid monthly UCS 2/1/3 Directors meeting 18 November 1902. Subsequently the relationship was not quite as unequivocal between yard and shipping owner, and certainly not as close as that between John Brown's and the Royal Mail Group of shipping companies, which included interlocking directorships as portrayed by Slaven (1977).

28. Significantly, the Fairfields 'experiment' which was not diffident about establishing hierarchies and support structures did not do so in marketing. Marketing was not specifically addressed by a designated director at board level (Alexander 1970).

29. UCS 1/5/90 Report to Board of Directors 14 November 1961.

30. UCS 2/1/8 Minute of Board of Directors meeting 23 October 1964.

31. UCS 2/1/8/3 Paper presented to Board of Directors meeting May 1965.

32. Parkinson, JR (1960) *The Economics of Shipbuilding in the UK,* Glasgow: University of Glasgow Department of Social and Economic Research p. 150.

33. Johnston, I (2000), *Ships for a Nation. John Brown and Company Clydebank,* Glasgow: West Dumbartonshire Libraries and Museums, p. 198.

34. Peebles, HB (1987), *Warship Building on the Clyde: Naval Orders and the Prosperity of the Clyde Shipbuilding Industry,* Edinburgh: John Donald p. 143.

35. Close interest was taken by Lord Norman and the Court of the Bank of England in ensuring a satisfactory reduction in industrial capacity on Clydeside: Clay, H. (1957*),* *Lord Norman,* London: Macmillan; see also Foster and Woolfson (1986) Ibid.

36. Foster, J and Woolfson, C (1986) *The Politics of the UCS Work In,* London: Lawrence and Wishart p. 87.

37. From the mid 1960s to 1970, Lithgow was a powerful figure in the Scottish Council Development and Industry and was instrumental in the Oceanspan project (Scottish Council 1970), at the time integral to his shipbuilding interests on lower Clyde: *'the ocean terminal on the west will be used to feed local manufacturers as well as existing industrial ports by means of a transhipment system---an export oriented conversion economy will have the advantage of low cost materials and good services to its principal markets---an industrial corridor will be created to supply capital equipment and services on the one hand to obtain raw materials at the lowest possible cost---- central Scotland with its narrow waistline has the potential to become a new industrial doorway to Europe'* (SCDI 1970 Section 1.14 and 1.26). This initiative had a vision of the redevelopment of Scottish based metal using industries and was premised on cheap steel, the result of plans for an advanced steel smelter at Hunterston. This however ran counter to the UK steel industry and government intention: British Steel Corporation headquarters opposed the initiative (which had come from BSC's Scottish and North Western division) and soon thereafter dissolved its entire regional structure (Payne 1979; Foster and Woolfson 1986).

38. Slaven, A (1975) *The Development of the West of Scotland 1750-1960,* London: Routledge and Kegan Paul p. 218-219.

39. A McKinlay, Seminar paper delivered at Glasgow University 20 March 1997.

40. UCS 5/2/15 *Report by PA Management Consultants Ltd on Possible uses for Clydebank Yard.* No date.

41. UCS 2/1/1 Minutes of Directors meetings 10 march 1892, 23 November 1892, 9 December 1892, 6 June 1893.

42. UCS 2/1/4 Minutes of Board of Directors meeting 15 March 1912, 19 April 1912.

43. UCS 2/1/4 Minute of Board of Directors meeting 14 May 1914.

44. UCS 2/1/1 Minute of Board of Directors meeting 23 November 1892.

45. Johnston, I. (2000), *Ships for a Nation. John Brown and Company Clydebank,* Glasgow: West Dumbartonshire Libraries and Museums p. 243-244.

46. UCS 2/1/7 Minutes of Board of Directors meeting 3 June 1948, 24 May 1950.

47. UCS 2/1/8 Information presented to the Board of Directors meeting 29 May 1964.

48. UCS 2/1/8 Information presented to Board of Directors meeting 31 May 1965.

49. UCS 2/1/8 Minute of Board of Directors meeting 25 January 1965.

50. UCS 2/1/8 Minute of Board of Directors meeting 16 April 1962.

51. UCS 2/1/8 Minute of Board of Directors meeting 18 June 1962.

52. UCS 2/1/8 Minute of Board of Directors meeting 6 March 1961.

53. UCS 1/58/6b Committee on the Education and Training of Apprentices 14 December 1926.

54. TD 241/9/179 Summary of Items in respect of Continuity and Interchangeability of Work within the Boilermakers Society 1931;TD 241 Clyde Shipbuilders Association. Circular Letter 43-181, 26 May 1943 – reference to agreement of December 1937

55. Knox. W.W. (1999) *Industrial Nation. Work Culture and Society in Scotland 1800-Present*, Edinburgh: Edinburgh University Press p. 213.

56. TD 241/12/1 Memorandum on behalf of the Shipbuilding Employers Federation for the opinion of Counsel 1903.

57. TD 241/12/1 Letter from FJ Stephen of Stephen of Linthouse to Thomas Biggart, Secretary of the Clyde Shipbuilders Association 28 November 1902; Letter from Alexander MacLean, Director of Barclay Curle Ltd to Thomas Briggart 29 November 1902.

58. The cost effectiveness of the piece rate system was apparently considered by Fairfields as early as the 1880s. Comparative costs of piece work and time payments for certain trades were considered (UCS 2/53/4). The continuation of piece rates and the integral link with the craft system attests to the advantages to the employer until well into the twentieth century.

59. UCS 1/55/16 Rowan Premium Bonus System of Remunerating Labour. Memorandum of an Arrangement made by D Rowan and Company with their Engine Shop Workmen, 2 February 1898.

60. UCS 2/1/8 Minute of Board of Directors meeting 24 January 1964.

61. UCS 1/58/6g Committee of Enquiry on Education and Industry in Scotland. Evidence by Mr Sam Mavor Managing Director of Mavor and Coulson Engineers Glasgow.

62. TD 241/12/5/549 Recruitment and Training of Management Personnel. Shipbuilding Industry Apprentice Scheme. Paper presented to the shipbuilding Employers Federation Executive Committee 1 October 1943.

63. TD 1059/21/1 Letter from Engineering and Allied Employers National Federation to Regional Committee for Scotland 21 November 1924.

64. UCS 1/22/31 Papers relating to sale of Dalmuir Ordnance Factory.

65. TD 241/108 a. Letter from Sir James Lithgow to D Higgins Secretary of the Clyde Shipbuilders Association 22 January 1925.

66. UCS 2/1/8 Minute of Board of Directors meeting 25 January 1965.

67. TD 241/12/549. Federation of Shipbuilding Employers Executive Committee 1 October 1943.

68. John Browns records make it clear that support was given to capable drawing office recruits to train at university for naval architecture qualifications and other related disciplines. UCS 1/58/6f.

69. UCS 1/4/1 Service Agreements with Personnel.

70. TD 241/12/12/5/549 Management Recruitment Scheme.

71. A training centre was established in Stephens shipyard in joint venture with Stow College Glasgow. There was also significant growth in further education provision at the time, much of this focused on day release training for craft apprentices. At least one further education college in Glasgow (Anniesland) was partly justified on the basis if its support to the shipbuilding industry.

72. TD 241/12/1193 Shipbuilding and Shiprepairers National Association Management Training Scheme, 1967 para. 2.

73. TD241/12/1193 Shipbuilding and Shiprepairers National Association Management Training Scheme. Report of Working Party June 1967.

74. Booz Allan Report (1973) *British Shipbuilding*, London: Department of Trade and Industry p. 144.

75. Ibid p. 143.

76. *Glasgow Herald* 20 June 1963.

77. TD 241/12/402 Shipbuilding Employers Federation. Report to the Central Board of the Shipbuilding Employers Federation 14 November 1963.

78. TD241/12/1Shipbuilding Employers Federation. Management in Shipyards: Yard Management, Discipline, 1902-1908.
79. Taylor believed in functional foremen. For example one to chase the job, one to check time, one to check methods etc (Taylor 1903).
80. TD 241/12/1 Clyde Shipbuilders Association. Unattributed Memo: 'Management and Discipline in Yards' 9 October 1902.
81. UCS 2/90/1 Engine Department Pay Book 1930-31.
82. UCS 1/49/11Foremens Pay Books 1930-31; 1934-35.
83. UCS 1/23/3 Memorandum on the Shortage of Ironworkers 1913-14.
84. See Knox, W.W. (1999), *Industrial Nation. Work Culture and Society in Scotland 1800 – Present*, Edinburgh: Edinburgh University Press p 152. Significantly perhaps by the late 1940s, in contrast to the situation in Browns around the time of the first war, when Fairfields decided to provide some housing for their foreman and other staff, there was little discussion of the separation of foremen from others: ' [re the purchase of dwelling houses-tenemental property]---with a view to providing houses for foremen who are unable to obtain suitable accommodation' – UCS 2/1/7 Minute of Board of Directors meeting 30 May 1949. In the long term, any separation of foremen/craft worker identity disappeared from the industry. While Fairfields survey of foremen in 1967 indicated very strong company identity, a strong belief in trade unionism was more important than managerial identity (Alexander 1970).
85. This appeared to be a strong feature of the shipbuilding industry as indicted by Alexander (1970).
86. Fairfields Survey of Foremen. Alexander (1970).
87. Melling, J (1980), 'Non commissioned officers: British employers and their supervisory workers 1880-1920' *Social History* 5, No. 2 p. 204.
88. McShane and Smith (1978); Melling (oral history transcripts 1978, cited in Melling 1980). Brown's apprentice registers and Foremens ledgers for riveters (UCS 1/65/2; 1/65/15; 1/65/23; 1/65/30) show a preponderance of Irish origin surnames. Such names are almost totally absent in the registers/foremens ledgers for other trades. It is known that riveters pay was subject to wilder fluctuations than other trades, more prone to extended lay off and casualisation. A concentration of such names in this trade alone appears to indicate some form of ethnic religious element in apprentice and foreman selection. Devine (1999) has indicated the historic flow of skilled working class protestants into shipbuilding on Clydeside; the same author has indicated that there was a branch of the Orange Lodge inside Brown/s shipyard in Clydebank. According to Foster and Woolfson (1986) some shipyards on the Clyde operated a policy of ethnic discrimination and core yard workers tended to be Freemasons and members of the Orange Order. Confidential information given to me verbally during this study indicated quasi sectarian foremen recruitment practices for many trades persisted into the early 1960s on Clydeside.
89. TD 241/12/549 Clyde Shipbuilders Association Executive Committee, Minute of Meeting 30 May 1955.

Chapter 5

Case Study 2: X Films plc

Synopsis

The company studied in the case (X) is part of a Belgian multi-national group (the Group). X is the headquarters of the films sector of the Group and manufactures film in the two broad product technology areas of bioriented polypropylene (OPP) and cellulose (Cello): the latter is in a maturing-declining market. X is a company where the international competitive environment has provided an engine for change and modernisation.

X has not managed throughput by integration, rather by managing external linkages in the supply chain, but by methods other than Just in Time (JIT) practices. The company does however have a strong engineering and technical resource internally managed, though until recently not matched by the strengthening of company capabilities through managerial education and development. HRM approaches to internal management were patchy though significant developments have occurred in the attempt to align managerial development to the increasing globalisation of business.

External management was important in explaining company operations. Two aspects of the business dimension of external management were examined. First, the external out-sourcing of key activities. Industry definitions of asset specificity were problematic and at least some externalisation in X could be explained by individual managerial/personal decision. Second, the relationship between the company and the Group in Belgium was certainly not explained by the model of internal integration typified in the M form; yet the decentring and localisation of decision making while strong in some areas was not as distanced from the corporate headquarters as the archetypal post M form. Managerial roles and practices were analysed using the post-M model of Bartlett and Ghoshal and while some aspects of the model applied in X, others did not. The current relationship between X and the Group is likely to change in the context of strategic shifts in the global scope of business activities. The societal dimension of external management practice was analysed. A combination of traditional civic mindedness and new right ideological thinking explained the motivation behind managers engaging in public and quasi-public sector bodies. The company also displayed features of the stake-holder company; but key aspects of this were framed by national governmental structures rather than corporate initiation.

- Internal and External Management: the supply chain, managing throughput Overview of the Business Competitive Environment
- and internal management of human resource
- Externalisation of Management?

Introduction to X Films plc

This company ('X') is responsible for the films sector of a major European multinational (the 'Group'). Located in the north west of England, it employs around 1200, produces and sells flexible films for the food industry packaging sector, various industrial applications such as films for self adhesive labels and security coatings for bank notes; X is responsible for the Group's film sector operations in the UK, Spain, Italy, Belgium, Australia, the United States and Mexico. The Films sector's turnover was 360m euros (£252m) in 1999. The Group, which is Belgian based, has two other sectors: Pharma in the pharmaceuticals sector with a turnover in 1999 of 903m euros (£632m) involved in the research, production and marketing of prescription medicines in the fields of the central nervous system, the cardiovascular system and immuno-allergology and Chemicals with a turnover in 1999 of 583m euros (£408m) manufacturing intermediate, fine and speciality chemicals including resins for adhesives and for coating paper, wood, glass, metal and plastics. In 2000 the Group was positioned as Europe's 264th company by market capitalisation and 388th by profit (European Business Database 2000).

The films sector is structured in 2 business units, cellulose films ('cello', cellophane) and bioriented polypropylene films ('OPP', propafilm).

X Films. The Business-Competitive Market

The market/sector environment which provided the context for an analysis of the internal and external management of X plc was a significant long term decline in global cellophane film sales since 1984 (see table. 5.1).

This was allied to world wide over-capacity, despite company and plant consolidation in the 1990s. Changes in market structure added to the difficulties in the cello sector. The substantial increase in demand from the food packaging sector from the 1970s was the key factor responsible for the growth in cello production, yet the steady growth in the power of buyers in food packaging (closely correlated with the growth in market share of supermarkets-Winstanley 1994) pressurised margins and profit levels. (1)

Table 5.1 Global Demand for Cellophane Film 1988-2000
('000 tonnes)

	1988	1994	2000
United Kingdom	26	14	10
Western Europe	72	36	25
U.S.A. / Canada	52	49	36
Australia / New Zealand / South Africa	11	9	7
Japan	38	40	30
Rest of the world	150	98	46
Total	349	247	154

Source: X Films plc Business Plan 2000).

The strategy of X (and its predecessor in the 1980s, a joint venture between the Belgian Group and Britain's ICI) was to reduce reliance on food packaging, and more recently, an acquisition strategy to consolidate and protect and build (Ansoff 1988) its position in cellophane production. (2) The company in 1996 purchased the UK cellulose manufacturing plant of Courtaulds; the following year the purchase of a cellulose manufacturer in Tecumseh, Kansas was completed. More recently, manufacturing capacity in Burgos (Spain) and in Mexico has been acquired. The second related strategy was to develop niche markets in cellophane and OPP based products through a process of research, development and commercialisation of product innovation focused largely in the UK. (3) This twin strategy was re-inforced when the Belgian owned multi-national terminated its joint venture with ICI for the production of polypropylene film in the UK, instead taking full ownership of the British end of the venture (Sidex Ltd).

To implement and manage the strategy, in 1997 the Group structured the films sector around two business units (Cello; OPP) rather than the previous arrangement of functional/departmental divisions covering all product areas. What was created was a global business product division responsible for two business units (Birkinshaw and Toulan 2000), with the chief executive/director general of the films sector based in the north west of England. The experience of X plc in the 1990s (as the British component of a Belgian owned multinational company) has significance in the debate surrounding the management of British firms in the international global competitive environment of the last two decades of the twentieth century. First, the non British ownership of the firm was consolidated. Second, X was positioned to lead production, research and development, distribution and sales of film products as part of the multinational company's global strategy. This has resulted in capital investment and other transmission effects to X. From 1997-1999, a significant period for the development of the Group's films business, turnover increased from 305m to 356m euros; ordinary profits rose by 17% from 21m-23m euros; capital expenditure was up 75% from 35m-61m euros; research expenditure doubled from 7m-14m euros. The resultant changes and improvements in production and infrastructure in X's facility in north west England lends support to the research literature on the positive transmission effects of much inward investment (Barrel and Pain 1997; DTI 1998; Hubert and Pain 2001), though it is out-with the scope of this case research to assess the wider transmission impact on supplier and other related companies.

Internal and External Management

Supply chain and managing throughput X plc did not evolve as a company through growth predicated on the integration and internalisation of management and business processes. The predecessor firm (located on the current site) was in fact a joint venture established in 1971, with ICI holding 49% of the shareholding; the company was seen purely as a manufacturing facility with ICI providing marketing, research and development. Most but not all production was undertaken on site, and research, development and marketing activities were fragmented: these functions were undertaken by ICI's own organisation split over various locations. Although the Belgian multinational bought X four years after the establishment of the joint venture with ICI, it was not until 1987 that ICI's interest was bought out. (4). And it was only from then that integrated marketing, research and development was put in place housed on the one site and staffed largely by ex ICI employees. However, despite the integration and internalisation which this represented, the company later undertook a de-integration process of its own in the 1990s. It separated film production and conversion (i.e. the conversion of film based packaging, adhesive, display and other material to the final end use product). Presently, similar to many leading manufacturers, co-ordination of large parts of the supply chain is achieved through supplier and contractor linkages, lean and flexible production systems rather than supply chain vertical integration (Womack, Jones and Roos 1990; Sandkull 1996).

X's links with suppliers (and many customers) were long term and stable. (5) This was highly significant, since the relatively remote geographical location of the company could lead to competitive disadvantages. This is due to the fact that local embeddedness and untraded interdependencies are presumed to build up between industrialists in the supply chain located in the same region (Pyke and Sengenberger 1992; Cooke and Morgan 1993; Storper 1995). X plc could therefore (it is presumed) be excluded from proximity benefits. However, such advantages expected of proximity and integration appeared to be achieved in other ways: through formal supplier approved procedures (e.g., conformance to ISO 9002 standards), collaboration and joint innovation apparently focused on long term obligational contracts (rather than adversarial ones) based on trust (Sako 1992). (6) X's experience was consistent with a range of research carried out on inter-firm networks and regional economies indicating that for companies at a distance from other related producers, a spatially dispersed supply system was not a disadvantage, if 'supply chain learning' took place in other ways (Durnin and Peck 1999; Peck, Durnin and Connolly 1999; Peck, Holme and Durnin 1999).

Nonetheless, it is clear that supplier links were not integrated to the extent required by Just in Time (JIT) production systems. Although the development of such systems in collaboration with suppliers is apparently being seriously considered at senior management level, any move to JIT was some way off: information systems in ordering, production, stock and accounting systems were not all compatible with each other, making progress to a JIT system almost impossible in the near future. It should also be noted that adoption of JIT would not necessarily support the current integration which has a strong relational basis: the intention of JIT is that joint effort should reduce total inventory in the supply chain, yet studies have shown that companies implementing the principles of JIT will move to lower their inventory levels by simply pushing stockholding responsibility down the supply chain towards suppliers; this does not result in a reduction in overall inventory levels in the chain; there is no sustainable benefit and the obligational, collaborative relationship with suppliers can become adversarial (Christopher 1998). In the short-medium term, there is likely to be some disruption to the current supplier integration and relationship nexus. With the implementation of the global product division structure, the company was aware that it must actively operate in a global supply environment. This was particularly significant in OPP production: current suppliers were predominantly European and X was attempting to shift from this, a move given some urgency for two reasons: first, the consolidation currently taking place between suppliers and second, the fact that key suppliers operated in two of the key global trading areas, Europe and the USA. To prevent possible marginalisation, X may require to develop and manage different players in the supply chain, necessitating the creation of new supplier relationships. Management of the supply chain, then, is typified by external management but certainly not to the degree or extent typical of JIT systems.

The management of the production operation indicated a rather tentative move to make the system more sensitive to external customers and to design external customer management into production activities. The company made an attempt in early 2002 to move its production throughput process from one based on narrow delineation of task (resembling a production flow line in that film passed through one departmental process or task before moving on to the next) to one designed on team-based flexible production with multi-tasked teams operating on specific customer lines or production runs. External management was designed and structured into organisational procedures and practices: a defined customer liaison function was 'engineered' into team operations with a production manager (not a team leader) given overall responsibility (and reporting directly to a senior manager) for this aspect of team operation. Discussions with the two operations directors in the middle of 2002 indicated their belief that this was a more flexible and efficient way to run operations: small multi-skilled teams (by-passing traditional departmental/functional lines) dedicated to specific customer product lines would be able to respond more quickly to market led product changes or innovations. Such changes were to be implemented in each functional department leading to cross functional/departmental working. This resulted in a role change for first line supervisory management (foremen) from functional foreman to team leader, with responsibility for encouraging team responsibility in quality and subsequently for other production issues relevant to customer requirements. This change, encouraged by senior managers both in England and in Brussels was introduced early in 2002 for a 6 month trial in one of X's two production facilities and there appeared, during this trial period, to be some resistance based on the payment status (hourly paid though with increased earnings, previously salary status) for team leaders. The autonomy given to teams appeared relatively minimal (currently restricted to a narrow range of product quality issues), though this was intended to increase as experience was gained. The external customer management role appears as yet (towards the end of the trial period) not to be part of the team's main function, though production managers who in turn liaise with the team increasingly undertake the role. There did not appear to be any significant degree of work intensification or strengthening of internal control, unlike experiences recorded in other firms (Green 2001): overall the workforce numbers were stable in the three year period to 2003, with output, productivity levels and work processes at plant level changed only incrementally.

Internal management of the human resource   Internal management practices, in particular those relating to managing the human resource, were assessed in four areas. First, the management of the craft and technical resource; second, the education and training of managers, and third, the adoption of specific human resource management (HRM) approaches. Fourth, specific practices framed by the company's global business scope were identified. The first two analyses outlined the scope of internal management of the craft and technical resource. The second gave an indication of training and educational capability of managers. The third and fourth, by indicating the extent to which human resource management practices were aligned with and contributed to business goals, gave signs of the position and strength of internal management.

The engineering craft resource was traditionally a strength of X (this is also considered below). The company, unusual in the industry, manufactured much of its own plant and provided on occasion engineering services to other firms in this and related sectors. The engineering workforce was unionised and there was no history of industrial relations disputes or of disputed areas of managerial control. (7) On the other hand, out-with the engineering craft area, accessing the appropriate technological (especially scientific-technological) resource presented a challenge given the geographical location of the company. This has been combated in various ways, particularly through close relationships with local schools and the support of students through science based degree and other programmes; in addition, the existence of a research and development facility with recent capital investment from the Group brought increases in the total research and development employment to a planned total of 150 scientists and technicians. This investment helped attract appropriate levels of scientifically and technologically qualified personnel. (8)

According to some senior managers, the scientific and technological resource in the company had not been matched by the strengthening of management through managerial training and education. A recent 'Investors in People' report heavily criticised the company for its lack of management training; X subsequently attempted to address this and established a relationship with a local university to provide management education for a number of managers in the medium-long term. (9)

As indicated in chapter 1, HRM was categorised as the attempt to identify human resource practices closely with business organisational and management goals (Storey 1989; Legge 1995). To achieve these objectives, two broad approaches were identified, 'hard' and 'soft' (Sisson 1994, but see also footnote 12 chapter 1). The former was focused very deliberately on business goals and rooted in the efficiency and economy concerns of management; the latter emphasised integration, socialisation and commitment showing concerns for 'empowering' teams, devolving managerial responsibility and seeking commitment rather than compliance. In 2000, the company failed in its attempt to achieve Investors in People (IIP) accreditation. The aim of IIP, a government led initiative, is to align training and development opportunities for individual employees with companies' business, strategic and operational objectives. In aim therefore it was at the core an HRM initiative. X's failure was due to its unsystematic and patchy approach to identifying employees' training and development needs. The company subsequently gained recognition after conducting a comprehensive employee survey and instituting a methodology and structure throughout the plant to address training and development needs on an on-going basis. (10) There were practices which did not fit well with HRM philosophy. (11) There was also considerable evidence that the appropriate measures used in the recruitment of operations workers was better explained by reference to locality and network based approaches, rather than adherence to HRM principles and practices: process trainees were recruited from the local comprehensive school at age 16; alternatively, individuals (mainly male) in their mid-late 20s were recruited from the local agricultural workforce; 86% of the workforce lived within 3 miles of the factory; there was no advertising of process worker vacancies with potential employees enquiring speculatively and local family networks often employed. (12)

Performance appraisals for all salaried staff were embedded into the company's procedures. However, the direct linkage to business and individual objectives was patchy and only at the most senior levels was there a systematic attempt to couple individual and business goals, through a system of management by objectives (MBO). A performance based bonus system (and a share option scheme) operated only for the top 5 senior managers, and though there was an intention to cascade this, the management survey found that below the top two levels of management, salary was based entirely on an incremental scale. Quality led managerial initiatives with apparently strong HRM underpinning have been implemented in one of the company's production lines; this initiative involved the alteration of traditional production/departmental functions (e.g., slitting, viscose coating etc) to multi-skilled team operations led by a team leader, and was currently undergoing a trial period, though implementation encountered some resistance. There was very little indication of a 'soft' HRM contextual underpinning. The company undertook very little investment in the training or development of team members in either normative (gaining commitment through socialisation) or governance (increased responsibility and decision making) dimensions of team-working (Findlay, McKinlay, Marks and Thompson 2000), though it was recognised by senior management that this would require to be addressed if the team-working initiative was extended and rolled out. HRM initiatives though are in place to ensure that there are opportunities for movement of production operatives into first line supervisory roles and beyond, thereby attempting to integrate individual career development and company needs. X's experience was not out of step with practice in many other companies in the UK: research in the use of HRM in Britain undertaken in the mid 1990s in 100 medium-large companies in six sectors (food processing, plastics, steel, textiles, pharmaceuticals, footwear) found companies practicing a relatively low level of devolvement in comparison to the integration function (Budhwar 2000a).

Finally, there was a human resource response to the globalisation (global product division) dimension of X's business. The ten or so most senior managers had well defined global roles. The chief executive/director general was head of the Group's films sector with responsibilities for the development and production of films in all locations including Britain, Belgium, Spain, Australia, Mexico and USA. 57% of turnover was from Europe (with almost 70% of this from the UK). The operations directors (2 in number) and business unit managers (2 in number) had overall responsibility for their businesses and operations in all these locations. The sales director had responsibility for a number of country managers. The research and marketing director's responsibilities included two roles: marketing, which was global in scope, and research and development, which though based largely in Britain, increasingly developed linkages with research institutions and universities internationally. These post-holders, all UK based, spent a considerable proportion of their working time (up to 70%) out-with the UK. It was anticipated that an increasing number of managers would be required to have global roles, with stated Group policy to increase globalisation of management through an increase in expatriation of senior and middle managers. (13) A 'global leadership programme' had in the last two years been initiated at Group headquarters and participation from all three sectors (films, pharma, chemicals) expected. In X, two career development groups have formed (one research and development, the other business-commercial) with the aim of identifying individuals with particular career development potential. A significant part of the development programme involved engagement with the international-global aspects of the business, including relocation outwith the home country for a period.

Analysis of the value chain and throughput management highlighted a varied and diverse picture of internal and external management. Elements of externalisation were observed in supply chain management; attempts to introduce external customer based management into production were tentative and at a very early stage of development. Aspects of value chain management within the company were observed through analysing management of the human resource. This gave a picture of the company's internal management: the craft/technical resource was strongly internalised. Internal management strength was not so clearly manifested in other areas, with 'patchy' HRM approaches, though more recent development in management training and in training for the company's global objectives indicated a stronger internal management, HRM influenced approach.

Externalisation of Management?

The analysis of internal and external management of the supply chain and throughput is extended to pose the question, externalisation of management? Analysis of the business dimension will focus on: external and internal management of a range of value chain activities, structures and controls within the firm's boundaries, and the nature of management roles and links between X and the Belgian based Group. The societal dimension of external management will also be researched.

The Business Dimension

The two value chain activities to be analysed are engineering and transport, the former because this was often externalised in the films sector and the latter due to the mix of internal and external provision, which the company adopted. (14)

X built a reputation renowned in the industry for expertise in engineering services, which is interesting in terms of the debate on externalisation and transaction costs. Since most players in this sector externalised their engineering services, X's experience suggested no general agreement or consensus regarding the asset specificity of engineering (Williamson 1975). There may be some evidence to support Coase's (1937) original argument that a large enough volume of transactions would encourage a company to conduct these activities in house: since other firms in the sector (and related sectors) did not manage their own engineering services, X could carry out some of this work on a contractual basis, which support the volume argument. (15) Managers certainly believed that in-house provision had cost advantages: many of those surveyed felt that some of the out-sourced engineering had to be closely monitored due to the 'automatic' (to use the words of one manager) tendency for cost escalation by external contractors. Yet this did little to explain why X traditionally conducted most engineering in-house and other firms did not. One explanation, supported by a number of senior managers was personality and personal commitment: the chief executive/director general had an engineering background, started his early career in engineering with X's predecessor on the current site and was employed with this and predecessor companies his entire working career. He was personally involved in setting up arrangements with the local comprehensive school for the recruitment of engineering apprentices regularly recruited (albeit in small numbers) to the company. The internalisation of this key company activity is explained, in large measure, by managerial/entrepreneurial initiative and personal decision.

In transportation, the company operated its own fleet of vehicles responsible for about 60% of transported goods (by value), the remaining 40% being externally contracted. X recently undertook a detailed examination to consider externalisation of transport and determined to maintain a mix of internal and external transport capacity. Like engineering, there appears to be no industry consensus over the importance of maintaining this asset in house. Cost alone would suggest that transport be largely externalised. (16) Low entry costs and increased competitive activity have driven down costs in the road transportation sector, below the cost level, which the company can maintain in house. However, senior managers believed that for strategic reasons it required to maintain some internal capacity (it has reduced this from 60-50% of the annual transport spend), believing this particularly important given the relative geographical isolation of the main plant. Asset specificity appeared partly to explain the pattern of external/internal management of transport.

Structures and control beyond the M form: externalisation or the management of dispersed activities? The manner in which the company structured itself and organised relationships within the scope of its own boundaries indicated the configuration of external and internal management. The relationship between the Group headquarters and X was clearly not that of the integrated multi-national typified by the M form (figure. 5.1).

As seen in figure 5.1, there was no layer of control between the Executive Committee in Brussels and X. The advisory and strategic functions at the centre were minimal (e.g., human resource management undertaken at sector level). Although the legal capacity in Brussels was significant, this was dedicated almost entirely to the pharmaceutical sector, underlining the importance of patents, intellectual property rights, proprietary branding and regulatory procedures to that sector. Control and integration with the centre was actioned through the finance function. The only non UK based member of X's board was a Brussels located comptroller. It was clear from the survey and discussion with managers that the main control operated was financial, to ensure expenditure kept within agreed budgets. This led to a perception (held by some in the company) that the nature of the relationship with Brussels headquarters was like a holding company (H form). In fact integration between X and the Group was much closer than that, with the chief executive/director general of the films sector also a member of the main executive committee: he was one of the five members of that committee (the only non Belgian) which included the depute chairman and one other director from the Group board along with the directors general of the other two sectors. Integration was also evident in aspects of the governance structure. Unlike the highly decentralised federal style model outlined in the preceding chapter, exemplified by the archetypal 'post-M' form structure (Bartlett and Ghoshal 1998), there was no notion in X of a   percentage of profits or revenues ring fenced for exclusive and discretionary use by X. In addition all the constituent companies in the films sector, which came under the control of X, were, with one exception, wholly owned companies rather than joint ventures, a decreasingly common pattern for multi-national activity (Shaw and Kauser 2000). (17)

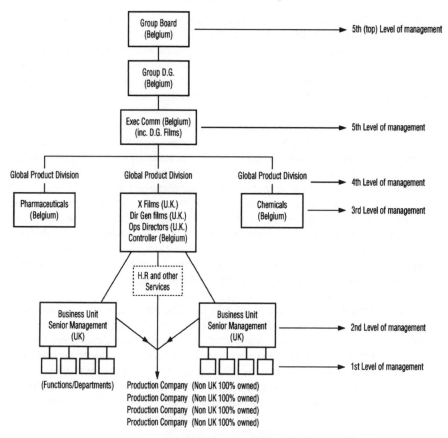

Figure 5.1 The Relationship Between X Films plc and Multinational Group 2001

On the other hand, there was much evidence of decentralisation in the sense of 'loose control' from the centre, with considerable initiative, development and maintenance of supplier, customer and other linkages in Britain with little reference to Brussels: in fact for supply contracts only those over 12 months duration were referred to Brussels for approval. X too could if desired purchase considerably more of its raw materials (especially in chemical coatings) from the chemicals sector of the Group, but chose not to do so, preferring its own supplier arrangements. There appeared to be no pressure to alter this arrangement.

While there was integration with the centre in research and development, this proceeded in tandem with considerable local initiative in the associated product innovation and commercialisation of research and development. As a research and development led company the Group's director general took strong steps to integrate all three sectors' research activity as well as increasing expenditure, from

128m euros (£90m) in 1998 to 173m euros (£121m) in 1999 an increase of 35% (Group Annual Report 1999); and in the films sector, a doubling of expenditure to 14 m. euros (£10m). The Group director general's background in research chemistry no doubt influenced the initiation of a cross sector global research and development group. In place now for one year, this group contained five key individuals (1 at director level) who were based in the UK.

Managerial practices and roles: externalisation and integration; organisation structure and integration   Managerial roles were analysed in the context of dominant external and internal management practices. In the post-M model outlined by Bartlett and Ghoshal (1998) this was seen as a very significant feature of managerial practice. In this model, front line managers (e.g., at business unit level) were in large measure the strategic initiators who developed strategy and initiated external relationships to implement strategy. Mid level managers (those between business unit and corporate executive level, for example, global division or area executive) played a key integrative role through resource winning for strategy implementation where previously in the M form their role had been planning and co-ordination. The corporate level set the agenda and helped provide resourcing. Control therefore was relatively decentralised.

In some respects, X was less clearly defined than this, and rather more complex. Parts of Bartlett and Goshal's typology did not fit this case: the distinction between business unit and global division was less clear, given that the head of the films sector was a main member of the corporate executive and there was no intervening layer between the films sector and corporate executive; it was also clear that within the films sector global division there were three levels of management. Given these nuances, the conceptual framework was nonetheless useful in determining managerial roles and practices and the significance of such for internal and external management of the business.

Level 1 managers were those located below the business unit line in fig. 5.2. It would not be accurate to suggest this level of management was involved per se in strategic innovation or initiation. In production, the role was best described as operational control and co-ordination. However, in the research and development area (and for a small number of individuals in production), the management survey indicated a very different picture indeed: many research and development staff spent a considerable amount of time with customers and suppliers working on product innovation. These external relationships were re-inforced at more senior levels in the research and development function of the company, (18) but it was clear that most of the initiation came from relatively junior levels in the organisation. Given the differentiation strategy based on product development and innovation this was not surprising (Porter 1985).

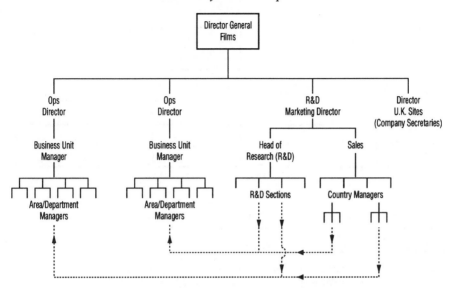

Figure 5.2 X Films plc, Internal Organisation 2001

Level 2 managers (business unit managers represented on figure 5.2) also formed external linkages as part of their remit, but the individuals interviewed stressed a dual role of internal control and strategic co-ordination. Their role was critical: the business units in the UK controlled all global relationships in the Group's films sector.

Level 3 managers (the films sector board) also played a dual role, with functions clearly attached to named individuals. In particular, operations directors had a strong production co-ordination and control role. The director general of the films sector came closest to Bartlett and Ghoshal's mid level managerial role of resource winning: it was widely acknowledged within the company that he had been responsible for the investment and development in the films sector; independent sources outwith the company also attested to this. (19)

However, it was likely that future developments would alter the current organisational configuration of films sector operations with the Group. With growth and further globalisation, particularly global sourcing of raw materials and the globalisation of logistics and distribution, pressure would likely be exerted on the present managerial infrastructure within the films sector. There were currently discussions at the most senior levels in X and in the Group on the best means of achieving the integration which such developments will bring, an option being the creation of an area management level combined with the existing global product division. Of the two versions currently under discussion: figure 5.3a would be likely to consolidate X's existing management of external relationships and internal integration with the Group, while figure 5.3b could lead to greater uncertainty regarding respective roles of area and product divisional management. (20)

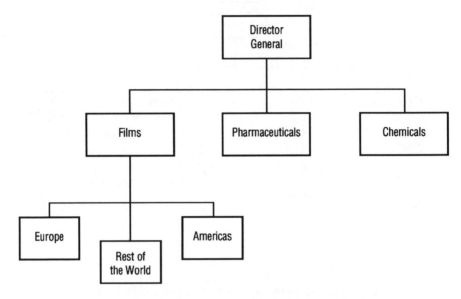

Figure 5.3a Possible Structure to Introduce Area Management into Global Product Divisional Organisation at 2001

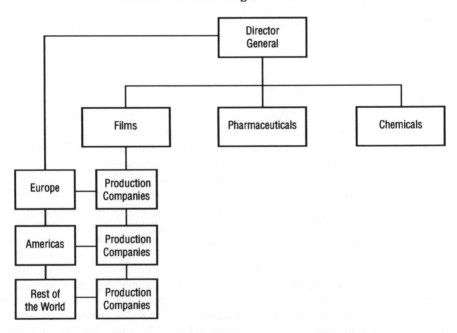

Figure 5.3b Possible Structure to Introduce Area Management into Global Product Divisional Organisation, at 2001

The Societal Dimension

The post corporatist era was typified in the preceding chapter by two key trends. First, an increase in the breadth and depth of business managers participating in aspects of the public policy process, including membership of local public spending bodies (LPSBs), national and local economic development agencies and other public sector funded bodies. Second, a growing debate about stake-holding views of the firm and evidence of this having an impact on company management practices was noted.

There were a number of managers in X with membership of public funded and public-private partnership bodies. The chief executive/director general was an active member of the local economic development agency and more recently the county wide inward investment organisation. Other managers were represented on the board of management of further education colleges. Interviews with four of the individuals involved (including the chief executive/director general) did not indicate on their part a new public service ethos ideology as outlined by Brereton and Temple (1999,see preceding chapter 2), but a combination of local civic mindedness and a desire to introduce

some private sector business thinking into bureaucratic organisation. (21)

There appeared to be, without much question, at both company (X) and Group levels, subscription to stake-holder views of the firm. According to Kay, this view

arises because the assets of the corporation---include the skills of its employees, the expectations of customers and suppliers and the company's reputation in the community---the objectives of managers---therefore relate to the broader purposes of the corporation and not simply the financial interests of the shareholders—. (22)

Such a perspective was represented in the Group's mission and strategy statement:

[the Group] aims to be a pharmaceutical, chemical and films group which operates on a global scale. Its sphere of activities cover three industrial sectors: pharmaceuticals, speciality chemicals and flexible films.
Whilst [the Group's] first objective is to satisfy the needs of its customers and its target population, it also seeks to improve the environment and the welfare of mankind. Towards its personnel, [the Group] is developing a policy of training and internal movement, which will enable each person to develop his respective talents and to adapt skills to the [group's] international dimension. For its share-holders [the Group] seeks to offer an optimal return to those who have put their confidence in its shares. (23)

To take the stake-holding perspective further, strongly implied in this mission statement is a view of the company which seems rather different from an Anglo-American approach to stake-holder legitimacy (hardly surprising since X is a Belgian based multi-national): the Anglo-American approach has been typified by the over privileging of share-holder interests and the instrumentality of stake-holder management towards this end (Friedman and Miles 2002; Lindsay and Hems 2003), a view not obviously identified from the above mission statement. Whether X's views of stake-holding can be categorised as belonging to a conceptually formed 'European model', that is a model more integrationist and pluralist in nature (now appearing in the developing research and literature base - see Lindsay and Hems 2003) cannot be determined without further research beyond the scope of this case study.

Beyond the words of the mission statement can be seen activities which confirmed the company's approach to stake-holders. X was active in fulfilling commitments to a European wide system of audit and environmental management (known as EMAs); verifiable attempts made in the area of liquid effluent, waste and atmospheric emissions. In the films sector in Britain a new coatings installation enabled loss and thus waste to be reduced at each change of the film reel. Considerable efforts were made to communicate with the local community: the chief executive was the chairman of the local school board of governors. The company funded language laboratories in the school and was active in school-industry projects of mutual benefit to school and company. Local students were sponsored through programmes of further and higher education. X would appear to be one of the increasing number of firms communicating actively with stake-holder groups (Wheeler and Silanpa 1997; Scholes and Clutterbuck, RSA 1995). However, although the mission statement may give some indication of an approach to stake-holders broader than the Anglo-American model, actual practices in X and in the Group (and other sectors based in Belgium) indicated that stakeholder views may well be framed more by the national governmental legislative framework on corporate governance than by proactivity of organisations or corporate thinking per se. According to Hampel, in the UK,

> directors are *responsible for* relations with stakeholders; but they *are accountable to* shareholders--. (24) [italicised in the original report]

These accountabilities differed in the various parts of the multi-national Group. In Belgium, the different governance framework saw the headquarters and Brussels based employees consulted on a range of issues (including remuneration) through a works council, training for which (with paid time off work for employees) was included in collective agreements in Belgium (Miller and Stirling 1998). In Britain, there were rather different stake-holder accountabilities. Here there was no such employee communication, training or representation, nor any plan to alter this situation. (25)

Summary and Conclusion

In broad terms, X appeared to provide evidence of a company where engagement in the international competitive environment provided an engine for modernisation and growth. In greater detail, several factors in the business-market environment were of particular importance in analysing this case. A key factor was the location of X: situated in the far north west of England, although well enough served by transportation links, its relative isolation from main industrial and supplier infrastructure helped explain various aspects of company management: the difficulty of developing JIT links with suppliers, links which often require geographical proximity to suppliers, led to the development of alternative means of controlling key parts of the supply chain. Aspects of recruitment were also heavily contextualised by location. The market environment was similarly important in understanding company management and strategy. Overcapacity and structural changes in the market led directly to a consolidation strategy, which was global in scope; and along with this, a differentiation/niche product strategy. These factors underpinned relationships between X and the Group, and managerial roles within X.

Given this business-market context, two broad aspects of internal management were analysed. First, management of throughput along the supply and value chain was inspected. X, and its predecessor were not traditionally integrated companies. Important functions like marketing and research and development were carried out elsewhere, though this was not the case currently; more recently de-integration took place with the conversion process split from production. Significant elements of the value chain were controlled not by vertical or related integration, but through a series of linkages with suppliers and others. The use of long term trust based obligational relationships (rather than short term adversarial ones) was widespread and this was mirrored in some recent research and literature on regional economic and business development, though further globalisation was likely to disrupt aspects of existing supply chain management. Relationships were clearly not of a JIT nature. The company was currently piloting changes in the organisation of production throughput within the plant from a departmental flow to a team-based system, with external customer/product relationship designed into the initiative.

Second, management of human resource within X was analysed. The craft resource, traditionally considered a strength, was internally managed without any apparent difficulties or conflicts over managerial control. There was no background of industrial dispute or challenges to management operation; this pacific stability was in contrast to the situation highlighted by research on foreign (mainly US) inward investment in other parts of the UK. The scientific and technological resource, though given the difficult geographical location, was developed and sustained through investment in research and development capacity and in other ways. This competence building was not matched or complemented, until recently, by attention to managerial training, education and development. The extent to which internal management practices grounded themselves in HRM approaches can be an indication of the strength of management, since by definition HRM aligns people management practices to business and managerial goals. Such practices were seen to be far from comprehensive though a key (recent) aim to move in this direction was envisaged for the company's training and development effort, in particular by helping to support the increased global focus required by managers. Current evidence though did suggest that for the recruitment of certain grades of employee, more traditional approaches rooted in locality and tradition held sway.

External management and the configuration of managerial boundaries between X and the Group were explored. The externalisation of some key value chain activities was explained partly by asset specificity, but in one very significant area, engineering, by circumstances very particular to the company. The integration of X and Group management was not of a multi-national headquarters/division nature akin to that displayed in the M form. There were, though, areas of relatively strong integration with the centre but also areas of substantial local initiative and discretion, reflected in the practices and managerial roles displayed at various levels in the company. Bartlett and Ghoshal's post-M form model provided a good reference point, though X diverged from the model in some respects. The current drive towards further globalisation was likely to alter the existing structural relationship between global product division and Group headquarters.

Finally, the societal dimension of external management was briefly analysed. In the post-corporate environment, it was seen that a number of managers were represented on a range of public funded organisations charged with implementing aspects of government and public policy. The motivations of the individuals interviewed ranged from 'traditional' (in the sense of a perception of responsibility to the local community) to a belief that private sector managerial approaches were 'needed' in public organisations, a view that is analysed in Part B in the context of 'new right' or new managerial ideology. It was also found that while both X and the Group displayed practices typical of the stake-holder company, such approaches were influenced by national legislative frameworks.

Notes

1.   Information from Mr D. Dewis, Operations Director.
2.   According to Mr Brian Tomkins, Business Unit Manager, X is now involved in an 'end game war of attrition in the cello sector'.
3.   These product innovations for differentiated niche markets include cellulosic film (with osmotic properties) used for water filtration in developing countries and an OPP based security coating for bank notes and credit cards. These products are referred to in the Group's 1999 Annual Report; more detailed market development plans for these products were shown to me (confidentially) in X's business plan 2000-2003.
4.   ICI took a decision to cease film production on the basis that the main product base at this time was cellophane packaging, not considered part of ICI's core business.
5.   The survey of managers indicated that major suppliers had been supplying to the company for about 10 years.
6.   Mohr and Spekman's (1994) study into whether high levels were an attribute of successful supplier and customer relationships concluded that trust, the willingness to co-ordinate activities and the ability to convey a sense of commitment were key attributes. There is considerable evidence of this in X: there is constant interchange of personnel with supplier and customer firms especially in the research and development area; many supplier companies have key staff dedicated 100% of their time to the development and maintenance of products for X's portfolio.

7. The pattern here is rather different to that outlined by Knox and McKinlay in US inward investing companies in Scotland. Their research has indicated a firm establishment of workplace trade unionism in most US subsidiaries by the 1970s, only after many US companies toned down anti union strategies, though in some instances there was still a background of adversarial collective bargaining climates. Very little –if any – disruption to existing trade union collective bargaining occurred with Belgian investment in X due partly to the pre existing joint venture with ICI, enabling acclimatising to the environment in X, and partly to the lower density of trade union membership and activity: while engineering workers were 100% unionised, process workers (75-80% of the workforce) had union membership rates of c. 50%. Conversely, Knox and McKinlay's research showing a dramatic change post 1970s with shop steward acceptance of corporate employee involvement schemes underwriting plant management business (often survival) strategies, is unsurprisingly not reflected in X. Such corporate involvement survival initiatives have not (to date) been necessary, and managerially led HRM initiatives have not been comprehensively attempted or applied (Knox and McKinlay 1999). Information in chapter 1 gives further support to this: since X's workforce was less 'regulated' than many areas of industry in the post 1945 decades, then the 1980s and 1990s de-regulation has had less impact and been less traumatic.

8. This investment programme has enabled the company to recruit Professor Peter Mills, an international authority on surface chemistry, from the University of Sheffield to lead the company's research and development effort and establish links with universities in Britain and USA.

9. An interview with the Investors in People (IIP) advisor/consultant to the company indicated that this and other initiatives (mainly in collaboration with the Institute of Management) would be likely to lead to substantial improvement and the likely granting of IIP status in 2001.

10. Training and development was until recently the responsibility of the Human Resources Department. After failure to gain IIP recognition a training and development group was established in the company under the leadership of one of the business unit managers (that is the level immediately below the chief executive/director general of the film sector). The managers in each department and area are now responsible for constructing a training and development plan reported to the training and development group.

11. In some areas of the company, the recruitment process involves a 'notification of vacancy' or request to the Human Resources Department, and only after a period of time and negotiation between that department, the business unit manager and in some cases the chief executive/director general, is approval given. As one manager stated: 'the link between business need and resource requirement is blunted due to an over bureaucratic process and involvement of some with little knowledge of business needs'.

12. Information given by the company's human resources manager.

13. Confidential information from the films sector's business plan 2000-2003 shows that the Group plans to increase the number of expatriates to 150 with approximately 25% of these in the films sector. Managers interviewed clearly believe this trend will take place even if precise numbers are apparently not widely known outwith a very small group of senior managers. As one manager said, 'my career path [i.e. first class degree in chemistry from Durham, working with X and predecessors in this location for 25 years] will certainly not be repeated. Scientists and managers in this company above a certain level will be expected to work at an international, at least a European level. This is already happening'.

14. There are other areas of activity, which are externalised but relatively unimportant in terms of expenditure and importance to the firm's core activities. These include elements of public relations, cleaning, ground maintenance and catering.

15. The validity of this argument is difficult to determine. X's engineering department does carry out work for other companies, but the volume of this is confidential. Senior managers claim that 'engineering runs at a profit'.

16. I was given the opportunity of observing parts of the tendering process for the provision of transport services. This included hearing and reading presentations from rival bidders.

17. Shaw and Kauser's (2000) research indicates that the dominant pattern of alliances in the 1980s was for part or complete ownership with the key purpose being the exploitation of research, product development and innovation; in the 1990s the pattern has been for a minimal degree of share ownership, the main purpose of alliances being related to market development.

18. X is represented on the Northern Universities Product Research and Innovation Group.

19. Interview with Tim Knowles, Chief Executive of Westlakes Research Park and formerly chairman, Confederation of British Industry North West Region.

20. Figure 5.4b (the global matrix) has had a rather turbulent history. This structure and configuration emerged in the defence industry as a way of structuring cross functional teams, and was adopted in the late 1970s by global companies attempting to reconcile tensions between product divisions and countries. However, most found it unworkable because of decision making gridlock. In the 1990s others claimed to have found ways to make it work and current think claims that it can only really be effective if the matrix is 'unbalanced'. That is, to ensure that the reporting lines to global divisions and the chief executive officer are not equal: for example, a manager reporting directly to the product division with a 'dotted line' relationship to the country manager (Bartlett and Ghoshal 1990; Birkinshaw 2000).

21. A verbatim quotation from a manager who is a member of a further education college board of management.

22. Kay, J. (1997), 'The stakeholder corporation' in G. Kelly. D. Kelly and A. Gamble (eds) *Stakeholder Capitalism*, Basingstoke: Macmillan p. 135.

23. *UCB (1999) Annual Report*, Brussels: UCB SA.

24. *Hampel Report (1998), Corporate Governance:* Committee on Corporate Governance and Gee Publishing, para. 1.16.

25. The European Union legislative environment has some bearing on this. The EU Directive on European Works Councils (Council Directive 94/95/EC) took effect in 1996. The UK opted out of the Social Protocol annexed to the Treaty of Maastricht, therefore the Directive did not apply in Britain, though UK multinationals whose employment in the EU countries met the threshold had to observe it (European Journal of Industrial Relations Vol 4. No. 1 1998).

Part B
Management of the Public Sector
1945-2003

Overview

Pre-existing structures and practices in the public sector were important determinants in the key developments after 1945. Traditional civil service, treasury driven, approaches to the supervision of moneys voted by Parliament, allied to the generalist policy advice giving ethos in the senior reaches of the service, provided the background to post-1945 expansion in the public sector. In health care, a growing consensus in the inter-war years on the desirability of some form of national service as well as a strongly influential medical profession (despite a variety of funding for health including state, charity and local government), set the context for the creation of the NHS post-war. In local government-the governance machinery through which much of the growth in public spending was delivered-there was the firm establishment of the elective principle and a considerable responsibility for the provision of services to the local community.

As chapter 7 illustrates, the growth in these three parts of the public sector after 1945 displayed a strong concern for resource efficiency; management arrangements to handle this growth were particular to each part of the public sector. Civil service management was understood by reference to the supervision of the appropriate use of government money and the division of governmental functions by departments of state; hospital service management by the twin foci of professional-executive control and clinical autonomy (the general/family practitioner service was organised separately with GPs as self employed contractors to the NHS); management in local authorities by the need to provide a service to a local community within an elected member framework. Each was managed by approaches and practices explained by their particularistic frameworks. This has been termed internal management, though attempts to change from the 1960s saw a degree of interplay between the internal management arrangements and external influences (termed external management).

Chapter 8 outlines how the political and economic environment altered significantly in the late 1970s with externalisation introduced in all parts of the public sector often under a new managerial agenda. Internal management requirements of this agenda often appeared in sharp distinction to traditional internal approaches and practices and in fact often challenged these.

Case study 3 explores in some depth the themes through research of the hospital service in Greater Glasgow 1947-1987. The case highlights the way in which professional control of hospital resources was established; the attempt of central government in the early 1970s to externally introduce change and support rational planned approaches to management, with some differences noted in Scottish and English experience; the systematic attempt to alter prevailing internal management arrangements underpinned by clinician autonomy after 1980.

Case 4, Management of Education in Glasgow and Strathclyde 1955-1992, indicates how internal management of education was developed within the local government framework. Internal management of the department was often in conflict with the corporate centre of the council in the period 1976-1989: there was an external dimension to this, but often defined by education departmental management rather than council management external to the department. Of particular significance in the period after 1989 was the attempt by the local authority to retain control of education in the full force of the new managerial externalisation agenda.

Case 5, a contemporary case also explores the themes of internal and external management and complements the more historically grounded cases. As an organisation which was removed from internal local authority management control by legislation and given responsibility for its own internal institutional management (like all further education colleges), Y College displays key aspects of management typical of new managerial institutions. The case researches first, the extent to which institutional management has replaced 'traditional educational' college management with a robust managerial agenda; second, the management of external relationships previously undertaken by local authorities; third, how the new managerial relationship between the centre (central government) and the college operates. Also researched is the proposition that the changed configuration in institutional and external management brought about by the removal of colleges from local government led to the migration of public policy discussion and values from service delivery.

Chapter 6

Context and Overview of Public Sector Management from 1945 to Present

'Administrative systems traditionally dominated public organisations because historically the public services emerged as administrative bodies supporting political policy makers and law makers and ensuring that the law is implemented. The expertise of public managers has traditionally derived from their skills as either generalist administrators or specialist professionals---public management is traditionally particularist---the civil service has always been dominated by the administrative generalist whose expertise has been rooted in understanding the machinery of government and the political process---local government managers have tended to be specialist professionals with chief officers drawn from the professional groups they manage. In the NHS it has traditionally been the professionals especially doctors who have dominated the managerial processes' (Farnham and Horton 1999). (1)

'Efficient management is the key to the national revival---And the management ethos must run right through our national life-private and public companies, nationalised industries, local government, the National Health Service' (Michael Heseltine 1980). (2)

'Another managerial revolution is not waiting to happen. It is more likely that a 'hard' form of managerialism will persist in the public services under New Labour underpinned by a softer ethic based on cooperation, partnership with professionals and others and greater democratic participation' (Horton and Farnham 1999). (3)

1945-1970s

There is a rich pre-1945 public sector management history. Much of this indicates the difficulty of appreciating the management practices and strategies adopted in the public sector in the second half of the twentieth century without an understanding of the decades preceding the end of World War 2. This is true for the civil service (Fry 1969; Drewry and Butcher 1994; Theakston 1999), local government (Wilson and Game 1998), the health care sector (Eckstein 1955; Webster 1988) and what were to become the nationalised industries (Foreman-Peck and Milward 1994; Chick 1994; Milward 1997).

However, just as the turn of the nineteenth century was a watershed for the study of business management due to the increase in scale and throughput management needs of firms, then 1945 was similarly significant for the study of public sector management. From 1945, resources allocated to the public sector grew substantially and consequently the management of these resources and management practice assumed immense importance. At governmental-policy level, this was underpinned by the 'post war settlement' based on Keynesian economics, a mixed economy, a welfare state and broad political consensus on the acceptability of a significant public sector. The nationalisation programme alone added over 1 million employees to the public payroll. The civil service grew from 387,000 in 1939 to over 1 million in 1951, with about 675,000 of these non industrial civil servants and 400,000 industrial, though by 1980 civil service employment had fallen to about 700,000. Local government grew at an even faster rate. It was the key provider of the new and expanded services in housing, education, personal and social services: it employed over 100,000 by the late 1940s and over 3 million by 1979. The creation of the National Health Service also brought private hospitals, doctors and health practitioners into the public sector. By 1979, 7 million were employed in the public sector. In the 50 year period to 2001, general government expenditure as a percentage of G.D.P. increased from 36 % to 40%. This was very substantial given GDP growth in these years (Farnham and Horton 1996; Horton and Farnham 1999). Yet, as seen in Section 2 of this chapter, despite the environment of growth and the idea of post-war settlement, the emphasis on resource usage efficiencies was extremely important within governments' macro-economic policy of the 1950s. This policy focused on extending sterling convertibility, and the apparent limitation of monetary policy after 1951 led to governmental pressure on pay bargaining and public expenditure: this has led some to suggest that actual government policy and action sits uneasily with the idea of a consensual post-war settlement (Booth 2000).

The immediate post-war years were also important for public sector management because of a range of foundation laying decisions taken regarding the operating parameters of the public sector. Nationalised industries were to be managed by the 'Morrisonian' model, effectively eliminating direct employee or political involvement in operational management. In the main, the NHS (the GP and hospital service) was deliberately kept out of local authority control, a decision not universally welcomed (Klein 1995; Fry 1999); work on 'business efficiency and organisation' of the civil service machinery of government was attenuated, a lost opportunity according to some commentators (Hennessy 1989).

Particularistic Approaches to Public Sector Management: Civil Service 'Constitutionalism' and Generalism; Local Authority, Local Accountability and Service Provision; NHS and Professional Executive Control

Management in the three main parts of the public sector-local government, civil service, National Health Service-is viewed particularistically rather than generically, given the differing historical background of each. The civil service traditionally held a unique constitutional position at the very heart of government. The notion of commitment to 'public service', in particular the trusteeship of public finances voted by government, was embedded not only in treasury tradition, but also throughout the civil service in the before 1945 (Theakston 1999). Also ingrained in the practices of the senior civil service was the policy advice role, gained it was believed through 'constitutional expertise' built up on the job. The significance of this for management practice was the belief that such expertise came from an 'all round' experience which was generalist not specialist (Chapman and Greenaway 1980; Theakston 1999). This dominance of generalism vis a vis specialist or technical expertise influenced practice considerably. Warren Fisher, the dominant figure in inter war Whitehall who served as Permanent Secretary to the Treasury and Head of the Civil Service for 20 years suggested that:

> The expert is a good servant, but the last person to have the final word. Administration is a question of 'sound judgement' and a good fighting case-- rather than technical knowledge. (4)

The notion of public service also reflected attitudes to management of people and other employment practices. Evidence to the Tomlin Royal Commission on the Civil Service in 1929 from the Senior Civil Service Association saw government's role as being a 'model' and 'good practice' employer to provide terms and conditions necessary to attract, retain and motivate staff; to ensure harmonious and equitable practices across the public sector and to promote stable employment relations (White 1933; Farnham and Giles 1996; Theakston 1999). Whitleyism (consultation and in some cases participation on a range of issues including wage negotiations) was widely practiced in civil service departments from the 1920s.

The context of local government evolution was the extension of the elective principle, extended to parish and town councils in 1894 and burgh councils in 1900, and the development of local services. From the late Victorian era, services like education, public health and (more slowly) housing were increasingly assumed by local councils (Wilson and Game 1998). Though there were examples of municipal service provision, 'municipalisation' was a less compelling explanation of growth than a crisis of private enterprise and the failure to provide the required amenity for an urban industrial infrastructure (Adams 1978; Lynch 1991). This should not under-estimate the role played by some leading municipalities in the development of amenities and services from the late nineteenth and early twentieth centuries (Maver 2000). The period up to the early 1930s was termed the golden age of British local government, (5) which progressed from the previous tangle of services (Hollis 1987). The ambitious scope of local government's role was evident from the Government's White Paper on modernising local government in Scotland in the late 1920s.

> [local government in Scotland] the services for which there is a clear case for modification are Poor Law, public health and highway administration-- duties should be entrusted to local authorities and that this area of change should be as wide as is compatible with scope for effective local interest. (6)

Since much of Byrne's (1994) thesis was premised on the Local Government Act of 1929 which saw the functions of Poor Law administration pass to local government, the golden age was short lived: the creation of the Unemployment Assistance Board in 1934 signalled a central government role for unemployment relief. Nonetheless the pre-war years did see a significant increase in the scale and scope of service provision. The development of local authority housing in Glasgow provided an interesting case. The city by 1914 had built 2000 houses through the City Improvement Trust, was landlord to 2% of the population at this time and had undertaken slum clearance work (Damer 1980; Lynch 1991). The importance of housing grew rapidly in the 1920s and 1930s: from 1920 to 1947 59,734 houses were built by the Corporation Housing Department. (7) This situation was not unique to Glasgow: between 1919 and 1941 70% of new homes in Scotland were built at the behest of local authorities, though the English/Welsh figure was 28% (Rodger 1996).

Fundamental to the local government role in service provision was the local dimension, the direct supply of services to local inhabitants. This was felt to be the defining feature of local, in contrast to central, government. For instance, the director of education of Glasgow took a dim view of an internal council investigation of his department, when a comparison was made with a civil service department:

> There is a fundamental difference between the civil service work of a central government department and that of a local authority education office---we deal with individual members of the public, parents, teachers and children to provide a service. A central government department can be remote. If we were, it would lead inevitably to deterioration in quality and expedition of the service. (8)

The NHS was created in 1947, though there had been a growing consensus in favour of some form of national health service from the 1930s or before (Klein 1995), perhaps accelerated by wartime experience. As part of the UK wide Emergency Hospital Programme to meet the threat of civilian air raid casualties, the Scottish Department of Health built and directly administered 7 new general hospitals supplying 7000 beds (Webster 1988). When Gleneagles hotel was not required for emergency hospital facilities it was diverted to an initiative involving the rehabilitation of workers from Clydeside (Dept of Health in Scotland 1943). Thomas Johnston, the wartime Secretary of State for Scotland concluded that this initiative, unique in the UK blazed the trail for the NHS. (9)

A significant feature of the health care pre and post-NHS creation was the power and prestige of the medical profession, especially the important Royal Colleges. Although the position of general practitioners has been considered less favourably (with the notion that the profession was 'overstocked' on the eve of the NHS-Digby 2000), nonetheless special contractor status was guaranteed to GPs, to their satisfaction, in the NHS settlement.

The specific settlement between government, medical profession and others is the key to understanding the context of NHS management in the 1950s and beyond. First, the service was to be funded overwhelmingly and directly by the Exchequer. This was not a decision taken without discussion of alternatives; (10) it did however put central government at the heart of the NHS, and in most periods since its creation the NHS has rarely been excluded from the political agenda. Secondly, the medical profession (or at least key parts of it) had to be brought on board. Bevan's strategy of allying the Royal Colleges with government plans in opposition to the BMA (Klein 1995) was influenced by this necessity. The settlement with the medical profession institutionalised the employment of hospital consultants on a sessional basis with no contractual restriction on private patients; private pay-beds existed in NHS hospitals. General practitioners were self employed, contracting with the NHS for the provision of services to patients. Third, the hospital service was to be run by regional hospital boards (RHBs), with members appointed by the Secretary of State for Health and in Scotland the Secretary of State for Scotland. The medical profession had strong representation on these RHBs, which were responsible for the control and funding of hospitals within their areas. A management board heavily influenced by professional representation managed the hospitals themselves. In a very real sense this localisation strategy gave the medical profession hold of the levers of power; it also made them gate-keepers and controllers of resources. Finally, this governance structure was underpinned by individual clinician autonomy, which in effect meant that the key medical resourcing decisions were taken by individual clinicians who performed treatment and provided care based on their professional judgement.

1970s-Present

By the early 1960s, the post war growth in public sector expenditure was perceived to be responsible for generating pressures in the public finances. Studies of key Whitehall insiders indicate that seminal initiatives like the Plowden exercise and Public Expenditure Survey Committee (PESC) reviews were largely influenced by a fear of public spending, particularly welfare spending, outstripping growth in national income (Theakston 1999). Much of the 'rational' approach recommended by Plowden and the PESC system had this backdrop. Central to Plowden's report (1961) in particular were not only radical changes in the planning and control of public expenditure (in organisational terms meaning bringing together of public expenditure and resources under the unified control of a Permanent Secretary) (Heclo and Wildavsky 1981), but the notion of management as a central activity placed responsibility for managerial efficiency with top administrators (Horton 1996). Management arrangements, proposed and actual, in the civil service, NHS and local government from the 1960s had efficiency and often rationalistic (and in the case of the civil service 'modernising') practices as key premises. Significantly, these concerns occurred in the 'post-war settlement' era. However, it was the questioning of that settlement which gave even greater concern and focus to the management of public sector resources.

The post-war settlement was undermined from the early 1970s by a sustained slowing down of economic growth triggered by the sharp rise in oil prices after 1973. Kreiger (1986) estimated that compared with the previous 10 year period,

1973-1981 saw a significant reduction in the average increase of world trade from 9-3%. Britain, less efficient than most of its industrial competitors, was badly hit by the recession and the slow down in economic growth placed great stress on the ideas and political consensus underpinning the post-war settlement (Gough 1979). Of special importance was the impact on the public sector: the expanding role of the state, especially in the non market sector, was seen as largely responsible for Britain's economic problems as the 'wealth consumed' by the public sector crowded out investment in the 'wealth creating' private sector (Bacon and Eltis 1976). This is a view now largely discredited, but which had some force in policy communities in the 1970s and 1980s.

'New right' thinking (particularly influential with the 1980s and 1990s Conservative governments) de-emphasised the role of the state and applied the principles of economic liberalism and the market drawing on the theoretical perspectives of economists like Friedman (1962) and Hayek (1979) and political economists such as Lindblom. The impact on public sector management was significant. There was clearly an ideological and policy preference for the public's resources to be managed according to the best managerial practices available, inevitably found, it was believed, in the private sector. This was defined as 'managerialism' identified by Pollitt 'as a set of beliefs and practices, at the core of which burns the seldom tested assumption that better management will prove an effective solvent for a wide range of economic and social ills'. (11) The Secretary of State for the Environment in 1980, with a degree of evangelical zeal, put it thus:

> Efficient management is the key to the national revival-- and the management ethos must run through our national life-- civil service, nationalised industries, local government, the NHS. (12)

Management was therefore viewed as an over-arching concept quite irrespective of the specific part of the public sector in question. The contrast in emphasis with the environment in the post-1945 decades was marked: in these years the growth in the public sector was to occur largely within existing internal institutional administrative and professional arrangements.

These generic styled approaches were applied in the parts of the public sector under study. The Financial Management Initiative (FMI) was introduced in 1982 in central government. It was an attempt to achieve managerial performance and accountability in government departments by forcing managers to carry out tasks according to agreed criteria for performance (Day and Klein 1985). The Resource Management Initiative introduced in 1986 into the NHS emphasised the importance of developing proper accounting and management information systems, which related financial information to activities and outputs rather than inputs. The work of the Audit Commission (established in 1982) in local government was premised on a similar managerial approach (Rouse 1997).

The 'new managerialism' then was seen as a generic management approach in the public sector as a whole. It emphasised injecting market forces into government and attempted to bring managers closer and more accountable to their 'customers' or marketplace, 'reorganising public sector bodies to bring their management, reporting and accounting closer to (a particular perception of) business methods'. (13) It also centralised the making of policy and strategy and separated 'steering from rowing', leaving the centre to steer (14). Activities were in effect operationally devolved and strategically centralised. Finally, the delivery of public policy was decentralised to a plethora of local agencies, quangos and private contractors that exercised discretion within the limits of policy set from the centre, possessing 'freedom within boundaries'. (15)

Generic new managerialism provided the contextual backdrop for an analysis of an internal-institution focused approach to management vis-à-vis external influences of.

Summary, Conclusion and Preview of Chapters 7-11

There was a substantial increase in resources devoted to the public sector in the decades after 1945. The management of these resources necessitated and led to developments in managerial structures and practices, though approaches adopted were particularistic rather than generic: civil service management was predicated upon traditional departmentalism, 'constitutionalism' and the generalist principle; local government on the elective principle and the delivery of service to local citizens; NHS management was founded on a settlement between the medical profession and government which gave substantial executive powers to the profession, surrounded by the principle of individual clinician autonomy.

From the 1970s there were considerable ideological, political and economic pressures on large areas of public sector spending, though significantly some of these pressures had surfaced long before the mid 1970s. These pressures gave rise to a belief that generically styled managerial approaches, specifically the 'new managerialism', were appropriate to management of the public sector, and that many public management functions should be devolved to local agencies, the private sector and other bodies.

In the following chapters, the themes of internal and external management are developed. Chapter 7 outlines how the quest for efficiency and the growth of departments and hierarchies, though taking different forms in the main parts of the public sector, represented a development and strengthening of internal management in the three decades or so after 1945. In contrast, Chapter 8 examines the extent to which the period from the late 1970s can be better explained by the introduction of external influences and management practices – an externalisation of management in the public sector? Case studies 3-5 in chapters 9-11 research these themes through the appropriate time periods: case study 3, the 1947-1987 period; case study 4, 1955-1992. Case study 5 is a contemporary study.

Notes

1. Farnham, D. and Horton, S. (1999), 'Managing Public and Private Organisations' in S. Horton and D. Farnham (eds*) Public Management in Britain,* London: Macmillan, p. 41.
2. Heseltine, M. (1980), 'Ministers and Management in Whitehall'*, Management Services in Government*, 35, p. 15.
3. Horton, S. and Farnham, D. (1999), 'New Labour and the management of public services: legacies, impact and prospects' in S. Horton and D. Farnham (eds) *Public Management in Britain,* London: Macmillan p. 257.
4. Public Accounts Committee, PP 1920 Vol. V1, q 2175 cited in Theakston, K. (1999), *Leadership in Whitehall,* London: Macmillan.
5. Byrne, T. (1994) *Local Government in Britain,* London: Penguin p. 22.
6. *Modernisation of Local Government in Scotland* 1928, Cmnd. 3135, Edinburgh: HMSO, para. 8.
7. DTC 7.12.2.3. Glasgow Corporation Housing Department Review of Operations 1919-1947.
8. D-ED 8/1/1 Report by Director of Education on Review p. 8 Feb-March 1955.
9. Johnston, T (1952), *Memories,* Glasgow: Collins p. 49.
10. Klein, R. (1995), *The New Politics of the NHS,* third edition, London: Longman) has shown that various options were seriously considered in the policy community including some form of local funding through local authorities.
11. Pollitt, C. (1990), *Managerialism and the Public Services,* first edition, Oxford: Blackwell, p. 8.
12. Heseltine, M. (1980), 'Ministers and Management in Whitehall'*, Management Services in Government,* 35, p. 15.
13. Dunleavy, P. and Hood, C. (1994), 'From old public administration to new public management'*, Public Money and Management,* 14 (3), p. 9.
14. Osborne, D. and Gaebler, T. (1992), *Reinventing Government,* Reading MA: Addison Wesley, p. 34.
15. Hoggett, P. (1991), 'A new management in the public sector', *Public Policy and Administration,* 69 (4), p. 251.

Chapter 7

Management of the Public Sector from 1945 to the 1970s

Synopsis

It was inevitable that the substantial growth in public sector expenditure after 1945 would lead to concern for the control and management of resources. However, the differing functions and operations of civil service, local government and the hospital sector of the NHS indicate that management occurred within quite different traditions and contexts in each of these distinct parts of the public sector. In local authorities, the pursuit of efficiency was framed, not only by expenditure control, but also by practices needed to maximise input-output efficiencies in the management of a service. In the civil service, the constitutional public service ethos saw practices influenced by the governance and regulated control of public money but within traditional departmental grades and structures rather than functional hierarchies. The newly created NHS operated at central government level through the Department of Health, with civil service style resource control of moneys voted by Parliament; the hospital service executive authority was in the hands of local hospital boards heavily dominated by medical professional interests. Management in hospitals, like local authorities, addressed the input-output requirements of service provision, and professional and clinical administrative hierarchies were created. The pressures for change which occurred in all three sectors from the late 1960s illustrated an inter-play of internal and external management: in local government, change was influenced by both internal local authority management concerns as well as central government, though the creation of new corporate structures left local council activity largely contained within the council's own management. However, research indicates that the success of these structures and attempts to strengthen internal management were limited. In the civil service, post-Fulton reforms were largely internally driven, and in the hospital service existing management arrangements continued to be controlled by professional and executive practices particular to the health service.

- Development of internal management strategies and practices
- Hierarchies and professional control
- Externalisation of management: management and change in the public sector

The Development of Internal Management Strategies and Practices: The Quest for Efficiency; Growth of Departmentalism and Hierarchy

The Quest for Efficiency

Local Government The management of resource efficiency in local government was particularly important in the years after 1945. Local authorities were the key providers of the new and expanded services in housing, education, personal and social services, and employment grew from 1 million in the late 1940s to 3 million some 50 years later. The accepted view is that conventional committee and departmental structures took the strain of this expansion, but by the early 1960s were giving growing concern about the inefficient use of resources (Greenwood and Stewart 1974; Elcock 1994). A study of the departmental archives of Glasgow Corporation reveals a more complex picture. There is evidence, for example, of comparisons made between local authorities to determine levels of efficient resource usage within departmental spending programmes. A detailed comparative study of supervision and management costs of housing in Aberdeen, Edinburgh, Dundee and Glasgow was undertaken by the Institute of Municipal Treasurers in 1958. (1) There were, on the other hand, instances of inefficient resource usage. A review of the City's Water Department in 1964 found that,

> Much of the engineer's post now was really the supervisory maintenance of pumping stations which are now automatic-- inspectors spend too little time in the field, too much in the office, only about three hours per day on inspection-- more than half of [the time of] the post of Chief Inspector of Waste Prevention is absorbed with clerical duties. (2)

Other council departments appeared to be very aware of resource efficiency. The reviewers of the markets department in 1955,

> could not fail to be impressed with the facility and orderliness and efficiency with which this huge undertaking provides a population of over half a million with its meat, fish, fruit etc.-- the team spirit of the employees and the readiness with which they interchanged duties one with another and were switched from job to job according to departmental exigencies. (3)

Other areas of council activity indicated joint management and workforce attempts to improve efficiency. A study of the Office of Public Works Tarmacadam Section in 1955 concluded that it was

> Clear that the section was overstaffed and labour was not utilised. For example, a 6 man squad excavating and infilling an opening which could only be done by 2 men at a time, while outside squads maintained constant maximum manning irrespective of the size of the job. The chief foreman and his assistants are unable to control this because it was physically impossible to spend more than a limited time with each squad and they found difficulty in assessing what constituted a fair day's work. (4)

A reduction of 45 men was recommended, though this was reduced to 40 after local negotiation with the union. This was implemented, along with a performance bonus based on a measured day calculation, gaining union and management agreement without matters going to a council committee. Clearly, efficient use of resources was an issue which concerned and exercised local authority management in Glasgow.

The Civil Service Prevailing civil service views on its 'public service' role, and in particular its custodianship of public finances voted by the legislature, ensured that efficiency (defined in the broadest sense as control of input resources) was prioritised. This was often achieved through treasury control. Warren Fisher's appointment to the treasury in 1919 saw that department re-organised into three functional departments - finance, supply and establishment; the requirement of prime ministerial consent over all senior appointments, and the authority of the Treasury to issue regulations controlling the conduct of departments and civil service conditions of service (Theakston 1999). This large-scale review, however, was not matched by attention to micro-issues of efficiency involving studies of improvement in the management of resources, organisation and methods of work etc 'as a damning Parliamentary Report argued in 1942'. (5) In fact, some commentators indicated that the immediate post-second war concerns for efficiency and business like approaches in government and business in Britain presented an opportunity to tackle inefficiency in government's administrative machinery, but an opportunity which was lost (Hennessy 1989); others that an agenda for such initiatives was not there, since the civil service appeared to have 'had a good war'. (6) Even later attempts in the 1960s to introduce greater sophistication and planning into public expenditure like the Plowden influenced Public Expenditure Planning and Control (PESC) system five year rolling programmes did not fully tackle resource usage within departments. The key inspiration behind the PESC system, 'Otto' Clarke (senior Treasury official at the time and later Permanent Secretary at the Ministry of Technology) admitted that a deficiency of the system was that PESC focused on the division of resources between departments rather than on examining departmental objectives, priorities and resource use required to achieve these (Fulton 1968; Clarke, 1971).

National Health Service Concern for resource allocation efficiency was from the outset of the NHS a consideration for management. It was never considered that this would become a resource hungry service, (7) a view difficult to conceptualise now, and overall financial resource (like other parts of the public sector) was allocated and controlled through the public accounting system. Overall public spending was controlled by central government, sometimes to the annoyance of RHBs. For example, the financial difficulties faced by the government in 1951 (Aldcroft 1986) led to pressure on public spending, and an across the board cut of 7% was faced by the Western Regional Hospital Board (WRHB) in its allocation to the Glasgow South Western Hospitals Group. The cut was protested by the WRHB in its representation to the Scottish Office, a protest that was only partially successful. (8) There was ample evidence of central government pro-activity to ensure control of resource usage in this new service (Klein 1995).

It is important to assess whether concern for the efficient management of the service was embedded at levels beyond crude control by government of financial inputs. There is an implication in the literature (with regard to the public sector generally) of little beyond this until well into the 1960s. Although the ministry of health set up an advisory committee for management efficiency in 1960, in 1963 efficiency studies amounting to only £18000 were carried out, though this rose dramatically to £250000 in 1967 (Klein 1995). However, as research at the executive delivery level indicated, there was concern for efficiency management close to day to day operations (see case study 3).

The Development of Internal Management Strategies and Practices: The Growth of Departmentalism and Hierarchies

Local Government Management in local government in the period up to the late 1960s was grounded in the departmental-committee system. Relatively autonomous departments carried out policy decided by elected members, though some departments (e.g., education) were also bounded by strong central government and/or professional guidance.

Unsurprisingly, there was a wide variety of practice in the detailed management of departmental structures. This much was indicated in evidence to both the Redcliffe Maude and Wheatley Royal Commissions on Local Government in England and Wales and Scotland respectively. Service provision within local authorities was in general fragmented with little notion of a corporate or policy centre. The statutory/administrative head of the local authority was often the Town Clerk, who typically had a small department but no strategic function. For example, Glasgow Corporation town clerk's department prior to local government reorganisation in 1974 employed 160 staff, with the bulk of these in legislative/ administrative roles. (9)

It is clear however that even within a single council, there existed different approaches to departmental management. Glasgow's burgeoning housing department's growth appeared to have been achieved with minimal hierarchical organisation or investment in human capital. Analysis of staffing lists at the city's housing offices indicated little in the way of hierarchical structure apart from the designation of 'chief bookkeeper' and 'senior letting officer'. There was a lack of educational or other formal qualifications among the increasing numbers of employees in the city's housing offices. In 1959, none of the staff in the Anniesland district office (including 4 bookkeepers) had qualifications of any sort. The same applied in Drumchapel and in Gallowgate (29 employees); the only imminent qualification was one individual studying for the Certificate of the Institute of Housing. (10) However, this was not a reflection of diminished status of that department within the council generally. There was evidence that the housing department consistently achieved release of the best land sites for house building at the expense of the education department for its school building programme. (11)

On the other hand, the Council's works department had a well defined hierarchy for administrative technical and clerical posts. A proposal to reduce numbers in this hierarchy by around 20% provoked staff opposition:

> The staff protest most vigorously against the procedures adopted by the management-- the remoteness of management from the individual work done by staff most obviously entail a lack of detailed knowledge of the jobs concerned and for that reason they deprecate strongly the lack of consultation given to the sectional chiefs. (12)

Finally, the education department experienced the development of professional hierarchies in a key growth area, further education. Expansion was significant. From 1960 to 1966 the number of full time students grew from 2025 to 4061, part-time day students from 9,123 to 17,925. Full time teachers increased from 313 to 740 and in 1966 plans were approved for 4 new further education colleges in the city to service 31,250 day release places. A promotional hierarchy was created within the colleges on the basis of '1 promoted to 4 unpromoted'. (13) The department also adopted a policy, which systematically protected its (and its senior staffs') position within the Council, as the case study analysis indicates.

Civil Service   The growth in the civil service was based on 'traditional' departmental lines within the existing departments of state and territorial departments, given the absence of reform and disbanding of 'machinery of government' work after the post-war Labour government. Management in the civil service in this period has been well recorded by the Fulton Royal Commission. Most of the subsequent writing on the civil service has been guided by Fulton's analysis of the culture of generalism in the service, and the senior civil service role of policy advice and administration rather than management of budgets, resources and policy outcomes (Chapman and O'Toole 1995; Horton 1996).

Fulton, however, gave an indication of the complexity of traditional departmental arrangements. Growth had occurred within the traditionally based structures. He believed that these administrative hierarchical structures were outdated, being based on the Northcote Trevelyan system:

> The present system of classes in the service seriously impedes its work. The service is divided into classes both horizontally and vertically. There are 47 general classes whose members work in most government departments and over 1400 departmental classes. (14)

He recommended change:

> We recommend that the divisions between higher and lower classes should be abolished and that a continuous grading system from bottom to top should be substituted in each occupational group. (15)

> Although this reform will bring the civil service into line with other large organisations in the country where division into higher and lower classes are rare, it will present a radical change for the service. (16)

Concomitantly, Fulton also indicated that the current system where the senior civil service saw its role as policy advisory and 'constitutional' rather than the management, execution and implementation of policy objectives could have 'damaging consequences'. (17) His remedy was to have a planning unit in each department and a senior policy advisor. (18) The desirability of hiving off executive activities to non-departmental organisations was also mentioned as worthy of further enquiry. The greater use of specialists was recommended. (19)

However, it is clear that Fulton, moderniser though he may have been, saw the department as the key management mechanism of government, in need of protection from centralising and controlling trends, from the Treasury in particular. Strategic structures above the departmental level (i.e. out-with cabinet and ministers) were not considered. The civil service department, which he recommended

> should be positively and creatively concerned with maintaining and improving standards of the civil service-- and should be in a position to fight and be seen fighting the Treasury on behalf of the service. (20)

There was little here to challenge the views of Edward Bridges who was head of the civil service until 1956:

> [a permanent civil service provided] a continuity of knowledge and experience-- departmental views shape the advice given to ministers and affect the implementation of policy. It is the duty of a civil servant to give his minister the fullest benefit of the storehouse of departmental experience; and to let the waves of the practical philosophy wash against ideas put forward by his ministerial master. (21)

National Health Service   Like parts of local government organisation, there was growth and development of management systems and hierarchies to deal with expansion in the 1950s and 1960s. The Institute of Hospital Administrators established classes and qualifications for the increased number of administrators the service required. New grades of staff were created e.g., domestic superintendents. In the WRHB area the structure and training systems in place sharply contrasted with the situation found in Glasgow's housing department. By the early 1960s, the appointment of clerical grade trainees in the WRHB's treasurers department was

> on the understanding that it be made a condition of appointment that a course of accountancy study with a view to obtaining a suitable qualification be undertaken. (22)

New specialisms and structures were introduced. For example, from the mid-late 1960s electronic computers were being introduced and WRHB seems to have led the way hosting the first symposium on the application of electronic and digital computers in the hospital service in 1965. (23) Four years later WRHB had a staff of 44 in its computer unit. By the late 1960s work study evaluation in the hospital service throughout Britain was commonplace and many local hospital boards built up specialist departments to carry out these studies. Specialist skills in capital project appraisal were also developed to address the rapid hospital build programme in the 1960s.

The picture portrayed for England and Wales is that administration in the hospital service was typified by a degree of conflict and 'jockeying' for position between medical administrators, lay administrators and financial administrators (Ham 1981). Administrative control of hospitals in Scotland was slanted noticeably in favour of medical administration, largely due to the post of medical superintendent in Scottish hospitals. This post-holder was seen as the chief officer in the hospital with responsibility for all staff; this was markedly different from the senior administrative medical officer post in England and Wales (Klein 1995).

A final feature of hierarchical and specialist growth in the hospital service was the development of professional career structures for clinicians within the NHS, institutionalising recruitment and selection, training, promotion and aspects of remuneration (e.g. the distribution of merit awards). In large measure, the specialist establishment committees of the regional hospital boards along with the medical professional bodies controlled this system. It is interesting to note though that this did not necessarily lead to improved financial reward for the medical profession per se: in the 1950s and early 1960s, the medical profession (and other NHS employees) did relatively badly in terms of income, compared to the rest of the population. (24)

Externalisation of Management? Management and Change in the Public Sector

The externalisation of management practice is defined in terms of the extent to which management within the NHS, civil service or local authority sectors responded to and engaged with influences and agencies external to their own organisational boundaries. In the public sector context, this in fact means that externalisation can be defined in two ways: influences and practices originating from the centre of government; or those bounded by relationships and agencies out-with the public sector, for example market-based or professionally regulated relationships.

Local Government

Major management and structural changes were suggested for local government from around the late 1960s. The Redcliffe Maud (1968) and Wheatley (1969)

Royal Commissions on Local Government recommended structural reform to create, amongst other things, larger and more effective strategic local authorities. These Commissions were complemented by reports which suggested the creation of management arrangements to give greater focus to policy co-ordination and strategic control functions of councils (Bains 1972; Paterson 1973). This led to a strong consensus in favour of the creation of corporate management structures, down-playing traditional local authority departmentalism in many of the newly formed local councils (Greenwood and Stewart 1974; Midwinter 1980; Elcock 1994).

In constitutional terms, the reforms and changes in management arrangements originated out-with local government, that is directly from central government. There was evidence that many of the appropriate central government departments with a locus on local government were strong protagonists, for example the Scottish Development Department within the Scottish Office [Midwinter, Keating and Mitchell 1991]. There was evidence too, which suggested strong internal management support for change. Many of the recommended changes were advocated by senior local authority figures. For instance, the author of the Paterson Report was the County Clerk of Lanark. Even local authorities opposed to the proposed structural reform were not, it seemed, opposed to corporate management practices and structures as such. A consultancy study commissioned by Glasgow Corporation, the main purpose of which was to support Glasgow's case in the post-reform era, indicated strength of support in the Corporation for a more corporate centrally controlled approach to management. (25) But the provision of local services was clearly defined and seen as a policy and management responsibility of local authorities, subject to the local authority's own internal management practice. Indeed, the key argument for re-organisation and strengthening of management structures was that it would enable local councils to organise these services better through their own internal structures. Primary source material from Strathclyde (Scotland's largest regional council in the re-shaped structure) indicated that the council intended to strengthen internal management in two ways. First, there was the establishment of a central policy co-ordinating facility (a chief executive with organisational resource, later developed to a full department), though this initiative was contested. Second, there was an attempt to strengthen the internal management and policy making of the council through integrating more closely senior council officials and elected members in a range of initiatives.

Creation of a Chief Executive's Department   Soon after its formation, Strathclyde responded to the corporate thinking behind the Paterson Report by creating a policy planning unit under the direct control of the chief executive, and constituting a management team consisting of departmental heads (Strathclyde Region 1977). The existence of these managerial arrangements appeared to frustrate the corporatist aims of a central policy co-ordinating facility by leaving considerable power to departments:

> Strategic issues are too far removed from the chief executive---too many things originate in Physical Planning without the centre knowing to be picked up later by Policy Planning. (26)

Other departments, not surprisingly, defended their own interests. According to the director of administration,

> co-ordination of policy making should lie in Administration-- once political policy is formed it should be input to Administration for the latter to co-ordinate with the input of other departments. I would accept Policy Planning should monitor but not co-ordinate. (27)

The outcome of course was the creation of a chief executive's department later in 1977, but the key point to note was that the ambitions of the maximalist centralisers were not fully realised in the eventual outcome. A policy review group,

> saw no real scope or part [to be played] by the management team [i.e., departmental heads] in the process of formal decision making-- the group might be loosely restyled chief officers meeting. (28)

More radically,

> Is there a case for involving Finance more closely within the boundaries of the Chief Executive's, since the department is involved through the policy process? It is 800 strong. (29)

However, the view, which prevailed and went before the council committee did

> endorse the principle of having a representative of major departments to arrive at a corporate view to mirror on the official side the role of the P and R [Policy and Resources] Committee. The concept of the small executive group-- thus achieving an essential check against over centralisation.

And, as regards the finance department 'being within the boundaries of the chief executive's' - this idea was substantially modified:

> to strengthen the links between Finance and the major service departments, it is desirable to have in each of the latter a clearly identifiable finance oriented middle management post. (30)

Nevertheless, a strong chief executive's department was created and it assumed an important role in the provision of committee services: the committee secretariat was rationalised and regrouped into three parts (personal services, technical and protective services, central support and resource services)

> each controlled by a qualified officer of third tier status and supported by a principal or senior non legal committee staff. (31)

The chief executive's department gained an establishment of three depute chiefs-later expanded to five-covering each of the three areas. (32) The clear loser was the administration department, later abolished. Other departments, however, remained apparently unscathed. For example, the education department was able to shun corporate services involvement in the activities of the department. In February 1977, the director (of education) wrote:

> It was agreed with the Chief Executive, Director of Administration and Head of Management Services that the appraisal officer (appraising school supplies) be withdrawn from the education sector-- we are perfectly capable within the education service of operating a coherent rational control over education supplies within our own department. (33)

The ambiguities of service departments' managerial accountabilities and the Chief Executive's policy co-ordination role were also indicated at this time (i.e. just prior to the establishment of the chief executive's department):

> If the co-ordinator [i.e., a new appointment] is responsible to the Chief Executive through the Department of Policy Planning, he would not be responsible to me in the field of education, [this will create] difficulties in line management and an increasing danger of too many chiefs and not enough Indians. (34)

Was corporatism actually implemented?   It seems apparent that corporate structures were about the internal strengthening of management in the council, but more targeted at cost control than the attainment of corporate objectives per se. There is much indication of this in the literature. Some doubt has been expressed in the literature and research as to how effective local authorities were in the late 1970s in instituting corporate management practices at all. Diversity of practice was more apparent than a proliferation of corporate management (Greenwood et al 1978; Elcock, Fenwick and Harrap 1988; Norris 1989; Isaac-Henry and Painter 1991); many councils continued to be predominantly role driven (and, it has been argued, by rigid and unnecessary rules-Crewe 1982; Parkinson 1987). Although much time and effort was devoted to structures and organisational configurations there was little evidence in Strathclyde's early years of costed options being presented as alternative ways of meeting given objectives, a vital aspect of corporate management (Midwinter 1980). All the evidence examined suggests that the use of options occurred in the budgetary process when the aim was to meet a desired level of expenditure rather than the accomplishment of specific desired ends - and this was accentuated during the periodic episodes of financial constraint from the late 1970s.

The director of education's dissatisfaction with such an approach is hardly surprising, since as one of the largest budget holders he was 'hit' on a regular basis. But his reflections on the policy options process 1983-1984 indicated an absence of policy direction for the education service:

> [referring to] the Chief Executives request for an appraisal of the likely consequences of a 6% volume reduction in the current level of service – taking

into account the required 6% cut, and the need to finance urban aid projects which are recommended for mainline funding, the department had to submit negative policy options amounting to £3,546,500. The education service in Strathclyde is losing 700-800 teachers each year through falling school rolls and the savings which should accrue from this huge reduction are absorbed by the Region before policy options are considered--

The most disturbing outcome of policy options and budgetary decisions over the past 7 years has been the emergence of Strathclyde as the Scottish education authority with the least favourable pupil teacher ratio and the most favourable non teacher establishment. It is not possible to justify this position. (35)

The integration of senior council officials and elected members A systematic attempt was made to deepen the policy management process through a series of officer-elected member groups. These groups, set up on a programmatic basis had a 'democratic validity' in their attempt to engage elected members directly in the formulation of council policy – but there was also a clear intention that this would be an instrument to strengthen the council's internal management and to focus it on achievement of policy objectives. The impact of this initiative was less than comprehensive. A senior official within the Chief Executive's Department wrote in 1982,

> The strategic heights of policy making and budgeting are strongly guided by the leader of the council and a small group of senior elected members-- this policy control is reflected in the organisational structure at the centre. (36)

This was consistent with information received in a private interview suggesting 'narrow' rather than 'broad' political in-put to policy. The same interview also indicated that some officer-member groups were very effective in achieving aims and implementing findings: those groups were strongly led by the most senior members of the council. (37) This of course may have represented internal strengthening in management of the policy process, but does not address the issue of accountability and participation of elected members in the process.

In addition, evidence from some specific areas of policy management suggest that the actual experience of elected member involvement in policy management and any subsequent strengthenening of internal management can be explained primarily in terms of the pursuit of official 'bureaucratic' interest rather than a deepening or strengthening of council policy management, giving some support to the view of the public choice theorists (Dunleavy 1991). For instance, one can clearly see the attempt by the chief executive's department to capture the policy management process there-by consolidating his or his department's management and hold on the policy process in relation to other council departments and elected members. This was reflected in a note written by the director of education to his senior management team on 21 July 1982:

Policy Options 1983 / 1984
Mr Calderwood [the chief executive] convened an emergency meeting and indicated that observance of government guidelines would necessitate 10%

reduction in expenditure in Strathclyde-- Mr Calderwood anticipates this will show such catastrophic consequences that members will recoil and that thereafter the real policy options exercise will begin around mid August on the basis of c. 5%. I make the following points-- this was stupid and meaningless and involved major departments in time consuming work and had the effect of baffling elected members with apparent science. (38)

Civil Service

A considerable momentum for changing management practices in the civil service came in the aftermath of the Fulton Commission and the subsequent pivotal role of William Armstrong who took over as Head of the Civil Service in 1968. Some, who claim that many internal practices were relatively unaltered in the aftermath of Fulton, have countered this. For example, change in the non unified 'class based' (to use Fulton's terminology) pay and grading structure was very patchy and spasmodic; Kellner and Crowther-Hunt (1980), the latter a member of the Fulton Commission, detailed Armstrong's 'rearguard action' in undermining key reforms to the civil service class structure; (39) Hugo Young wrote somewhat cynically that

> in anaesthetising Fulton, while retaining his reputation as a progressive minded man, Armstrong demonstrated perhaps the highest measure of his finesse as a public servant and private operator. (40)

Nonetheless, significant management changes took place as a result of Fulton. The development of a strategic approach to policy led to the civil service preparing plans for the 1970 Heath Government inspired Central Policy Review Staff. Significant changes in training and personnel management proposed by Fulton were implemented, culminating in the creation of a Civil Service Staff College. In terms of the externalisation of management in the civil service, the 1970s may have achieved little, but can be considered a watershed. The Royal Commission did recommend a split between small policy-making departments and large attached executive agencies. Ministers would remain responsible for major policy and forward thinking but management boards would have public accountability for service efficiency and delegated financial responsibility within the framework of an overall budget set by Ministers. Little came of this at the time, but it clearly foreshadowed 'Next Steps' reforms of the late 1980s and beyond, and coupled with marketisation clearly paved the way for externalisation of management. (41)

National Health Service

The NHS settlement, which saw executive responsibility given to local hospital boards along with the concept of clinical autonomy, institutionalised the position of the medical profession in the management of the hospital service of. Thinking in the 1960s and 1970s provided a conceptual (if not actual) challenge to these internal management arrangements. Apparent in all parts of the public sector and certainly influencing the Fulton, Redcliffe Maude and Wheatley Royal

Commissions, was a 'new rationalism' which believed that rational and technocratic practices could be introduced across public and private sectors (Heclo and Wildavsky 1974). Superficially at least there were three attempts to alter management arrangements. The various 'Cogwheel' and other reports addressed hierarchical and management structures for nurses (Salmon Report 1966), relationships between clinicians and organisational goals (Working Party on Organisation of Medical Work in Hospitals 1967), structures and hierarchies for scientists and technicians and pharmacists (Zuckerman and Hall Reports respectively). (42) This culminated in the 'Grey Book' (1972), which sought to introduce managerial goals and responsibilities into the key areas of resource management in the NHS. The Farquarson-Lang Report (1966) in Scotland called for the creation of chief executive posts, to give a unified management structure with a clear line of managerial accountability predating (the Thatcherite inspired) Griffiths Report by 20 years or so (Hunter 1986).

However despite the appearance of managerial ideas, (in England, particularly in the early 1970s, much was made of the attempt to introduce 'managerialism', especially during 1970-1974 when Sir Keith Joseph was Secretary of State for Health), (43) there was minimal disturbance to the prevailing practices and arrangements. Recent writing has strongly re-inforced the importance placed on professional specialisation, despite the other issues addressed by the Cogwheel Reports and the 'Grey Book' (Harrison and Wood 1999). Scotland, as the case study shows, was even less influenced by managerial ideas. The irony of course was that Farquarson-Lang was a senior employee of a hospital board in Scotland, yet the Scottish health boards (backed up by strong insider resistance) opposed his proposals. (44)

Summary and Conclusion: Internal Management in the Public Sector

Despite the substantial growth in public sector spending, resource allocation occurred in a macro-economic environment which from time to time pressurised public spending. Therefore resource efficiency was rarely far from the managerial agenda in each part of the public sector studied.

There were particularistic traditions of internal management in each sector and these traditions framed activity: the power of medical professionals given executive control of key parts of the NHS; service provision and elective accountability in local government; constitutionalism and generalism in the senior civil service. Growth occurred within these traditional paradigms, with practices aimed at local efficiencies and the evolution of departmental controls and hierarchies.

From the late 1960s, there appeared to be external influences attempting to alter the management arrangements. In the re-structuring of local authorities, although initiated by central government appointed Royal Commissions, the recommendations for the creation of corporate structures was seen as originating from within local government with the clear purpose of strengthening councils to help them achieve their aims. Analysis of one local authority in Scotland revealed such a motivation behind the creation of a council corporate structure; this same authority also attempted to strengthen its internal management and policy making through closer integration of elected members and senior officials. The success of these internal initiatives was limited. However, it is clear that the attempts were internally, and not externally, generated.

In the civil service, changes to the internal management were suggested as a result of an externally appointed Fulton Commission. The recommendations led to some changes for instance in personnel and training practices, but the actual extent of the change has been debated. The Royal Commission paved the way for external management after a key recommendation regarding the splitting of policy advice and executive responsibility, with the latter to be attached but external to the civil service through executive agencies. This did not occur in the wake of Fulton but re-surfaced in the late 1980s and 1990s.

In the NHS too, the government Grey Book in 1972 attempted to introduce managerial goals into the prevailing methods and practices of resource allocation. Use was made of management consultants, at least in England. Yet research and the literature has shown that the prevailing internal management arrangements were little altered at this time. The following chapters will analyse these issues in greater detail.

Notes

1. D-CF 9/2 Report by Institute of Municipal Treasurers on Supervision and Management Costs of Housing in Glasgow, Aberdeen Edinburgh and Dundee, 1958.
2. D-OM1 Review of Water Department, May 1964.
3. D-OM8 Review of Markets Department November 1955.
4. WS3 Comprehensive Work Study of the Office of Public Works Tarmacadam Section 1955.
5. Theakston, K. (1999), *Leadership in Whitehall*, London: Macmillan, p. 51.
6. Ibid p. 82.
7. There was a view that expenditure on health care in the long run would be self liquidating by providing a healthier population-see Klein (1995 p. 32).
8. HB 16 1 / 2 Minute of Meeting GSWH 24 April 1951.
9. O and M 35 Town Clerk's Department March 1973.
10. D-CF 9/2 District Housing Office Notes 1959.
11. McPherson, A and Raab, C.D. (1988), *Governing Education*, Edinburgh: Edinburgh University Press, p. 142 indicate that Glasgow Corporation's practice in this respect did not help Glasgow's status within the Scottish Education Department in the Scottish Office.
12. O and M 2 Review of Works Department. Letter from Margaret Robertson ('for staff') to TW Robb Manager 8 April 1954.
13. D-ED 12 1 / 47, 48 Review of Establishment of Teaching and Professional Staff Further Education. Report by the Director 8 August 1967.
14. Fulton Report (1968), *The Civil Service, Vol. 1*, Cmnd. 3638, London: HMSO, para. 16.
15. Ibid para. 215.
16. Ibid para. 216.

17. Ibid para. 15.
18. Ibid para. 14, 15.
19. Ibid para. 1.
20. Ibid para. 252.
21. Theakston, K (1999), *Leadership in Whitehall*, London: Macmillan, p. 86.
22. HB 28 2 / 15 Establishment Committee 3 May 1962.
23. HB 28 2 / 18 Minute WRHB. Paper on First Symposium on the Application of Electronic and Digital computers in the Hospital Service 7 May 1965.
24. In 1957 a Royal Commission on Doctors and Dentists Remuneration found that medical salaries had continued to fall behind earnings in comparable occupations; in addition they did no better or rose than other NHS employees in this respect. *Royal Commission on Doctors and Dentists Remuneration*, Report (1960).
25. SR 1 /3 /1 Local Government Reform in the West of Scotland. A Report Prepared by PA Management Consultants for Glasgow Corporation 1971.
26. SR3 PRG-Exec Dept, September 1977. Comment from Iain McFarlane Policy Programme Director.
27. SR3 PRG September 1977. Submission from Director of Administration.
28. SR3 PRG, Executive Office n.d.
29. SR3 Executive Department, JT/GEB 14 September 1977.
30. SR3 Policy Review Group-Departmental Structures. Executive Office Department, PRG 1-6, 7, August 1977.
31. Ibid.
32. SR 3 Policy Planning Improvement and C-ordination G McG/GEB 14 November 1977.
33. CII25, Box 4 6336. Memo. from E Miller Director to JC Sibbald 23 February 1977.
34. C1125, Box 4 6331 E Miller, Director of Education to Iain McFarlane.
35. SR 10.9.130. Policy Options Statement 1983/84, E Miller Director of Education, September 1982.
36. Black, R. (1982), *Local Government Policy Making*, Birmingham: Inlogov.
37. The key member-officer groups were led by the most senior councillors and supported by 'project champions' within the Chief Executive's Department. The groups were used to generate policy and eventually (by the early to mid 1980s) two of the most important groups generated the key planks of the council's stated strategy. These were: community development; area based approaches to the alleviation of social deprivation. Both were led by two of the council's most senior members: Councillor Tony Worthington (who subsequently chaired the council's finance committee and became a member of parliament serving as a junior minister in the Northern Ireland Office); Councillor Ron Young, chair of the powerful Social Strategy Sub Committee of the council and Labour group secretary. These member-officer groups contributed to the thinking behind the 'Social Strategy for the Eighties', the key components of which were the targeting of additional resource in 'areas of priority treatment' and a range of community development activities mainly focused in these same areas. This information was provided in a private interview with Laurie Russell, personal assistant to the chief executive at the time.
38. C 1125, Box 5, 6337. E miller, Director to the Senior Management Team 21 July 1982.
39. Theakston, K. (1999), *Leadership in Whitehall*, London: Macmillan p. 186.
40. This view is elaborated in Kellner and Crowther-Hunt (1980), but more stridently in newspaper and television: articles by Kellner and Crowther-Hunt in the Sunday Times (13 July 1980) and in a transcript of BBC 2 'Man Alive' 9 May 1978 – all cited in Theakston 1999 p. 199.

41. William Armstrong in his evidence to the Fulton Commission advocated a radical transformation in the administrative machine with a split between small policy making departments and large attached executive agencies (Barberis 1996).
42. Excellent source material for these and other NHS Reports can be found in Watkins (1975).
43. For example the Secretary of State for Health Sir Keith Joseph appointed a series of management consultants including Elliot Jacques then of Brunel University to introduce his time span management system (see chapter 1) into the NHS. This information was given to me by Dr Martyn Dyer-Smith University of Northumbria. See also Webster (1988).
44. Confidential information given to me indicated that the failure to implement the Farquarson Lang Report recommendations was due in no small part to Sir John Brotherston, Chief Medical Officer for Scotland 'vetoing' behind the scenes any movement towards implementation.

Chapter 8

Public Sector Management 1970s-2003

Synopsis

Although the control of resources devoted to the public sector was a constant concern throughout the period of this study, the unsettling of the post-war consensus from the mid-1970s focused much more attention on management of these resources and the promotion of managerial practices in the public sector generally. In each service studied, both external and internal managerial practices were displayed. In the civil service, marketisation and agencification exteriorised much traditional civil service and central government management and practice, though some research indicated change occurring in the external agencies at delivery level rather than in the departments of central government; institutional management has though, to an extent, been strengthened by changes in labour market and labour negotiation and HRM practices and this may continue in the operation of emerging 'post-new public management' approaches and practices. In local authorities, private tendering of services and the growth of local public spending bodies (LPSBs) fragmented and externalised many traditional council activities; localisation of management in education provision to individual schools and colleges was particularly symptomatic of these trends, though there were key differences between Scotland and England/Wales. In the NHS from the late 1970s there were sustained attempts, driven externally from central government, to strengthen internal management's control over resourcing decisions vis-à-vis control by the medical and allied professions; this was intensified by the creation of an internal market. Such a challenge addressed the very core of clinical autonomy. Despite some hostility and difficulty in reconciling managerial and professional claims to control, there was evidence of an accommodation between professional bodies and the external governmental driver, thereby enabling professional retention of control over key parts of the NHS.

- Externalisation of Management in the Public Sector? Civil Service; Local Authority; NHS.

Externalisation of Management in the Public Sector?

Civil Service

There is a general consensus that a revolution took place in the management of the civil service during the Conservative governments of 1979-97 (Butler 1994; Cabinet Office 1997), though less agreement over whether this was achieved pragmatically and incrementally (Barberis 1995) or planned strategically (Fry 1984). Much of the change was driven by externalisation strategies and approaches to management. The creation of 'Next Steps' agencies required all candidates for agency status to be subjected to a series of tests, including the feasibility of the activity being conducted externally by the private sector; if unsuitable for private sector management then agency status was considered. However, key to the process was a re-visitation of agency status every three (and after 1995 every five) years. Consequently, agency status was always seen as a possible interim stage to the next step of transfer out of the civil service (Jordan 1993). By 1998, there were 11 Next Steps Agencies, which had been privatised, 3 wholly contracted out, 11 merged or amalgamated, 1 abolished, 1 transferred to non-departmental status and 1 transferred back to a central department (Horton 1999). The main theme of the Citizen's Charter (1991) was responsive and high quality public services, and privatisation and competition were seen as the means of achieving this. The Government's Guide to Market Testing (Cabinet Office 1991) imposed market testing targets upon departments and agencies. Most departments set up their own market testing units and market tested selected activities. The second report of the Citizen's Charter Unit (1994) indicated that 389 market tests had resulted in 195 contracts being awarded externally and 147 internally. 'By 1997 market testing had become a widely accepted management strategy' (Horton 1999 p149). This was continued with the change of government in 1997 (Cabinet Office 1998). In 1998, the former Citizen's Charter Unit became the Service First Unit. Two new units, The Performance and Innovation Unit (PIU) and the Centre for Management and Policy Studies (CPMS) were added in October 1998. The PIU in particular called upon civil servants and outsiders to work in project teams, which disbanded at the end of each scrutiny. The Major government's benchmarking exercise which aimed at identifying best practice not only between public and private sectors but also internationally, had also been continued and developed by the Blair government (Horton 1999).

But management practice in the last 20 years or so has not been totally pre-occupied with these external generically defined practices. The efficiency scrutinies in the early 1980s led by Sir Derek Rayner (a board member of Marks and Spencer, later chief executive) and his efficiency unit had a significant impact in raising the profile and importance of efficiency and resource management, and paved the way for much that followed. The literature on this suggests that Rayner's success was largely due to his working with the internal machinery and structures in place, gaining the support of permanent secretaries and realising in particular the ambiguous, diffuse and political nature of the senior civil servant's job (Bray 1988; Theakston 1999). Other changes in management in the 1980s actually re-focused attention at the internal/institutional level. The traditional national collective bargaining system in the public sector (a tradition dating back to post-first war introduction of Whitleyism) still had some force: in 1990, 78% of employees were covered by collective bargaining (WIRS 3 1990). Yet this was being challenged by the introduction of performance related pay, first introduced in 1986 for senior staff but covering all civil servants by 1992. At the same time there was an extension of flexible working, with increases in part-time working, fixed term and more variable contracts (Mueller Report 1987). The introduction of 'human resource management' (HRM) into the public sector with a shift from a 'rule bound culture' to a 'performance based culture' from the 1980s has been well documented (Shim 2001). These trends inevitably led to greater discretion and scope for internal managerial action at the local or institutional level rather than at an external-national level. However, implementation was patchy and variable and subject to dynamic shifts: in large agencies in the civil service such as the employment service, where union resistance was substantial, managers were unable to implement as many innovations and varied employment policies as smaller agencies where unions were weaker (Corby 1993; 1997).

The public sector reform thrust of governments after 1997 and the resulting research and literature provides an interesting range of material. There is a rather mixed picture of the extent and nature of the impact of externalisation approaches to the management of the civil service and central government. On the one hand there is the view that the entire ministerial, political environment is in severe danger of capture by a managerial ethos, ironically often 'originating from civil servants or consultants' (Walker 2003 p 3). Citing parliamentary and cabinet office documentation Walker claims there is a growing view 'suggesting ministers should acquire the same analytical and quantitative skills as civil servants, ignoring the political and presentational role of ministers' (Walker 2003 p. 3, citing Cabinet Office 2000; Public Administration Committee 2001). Other research on civil service reform in the wake of the civil service management board reform programme directed at achieving improved managerial processes within the civil service, casts doubt on the convergence of practice as a result of attempts to introduce generic management reforms, but rather stresses the slow and context specific nature of changes in practice (Bovaird and Russell 2003). There is other evidence indicating the power and persistence of 'traditional' internal institutional practices. The Fraser Inquiry into the Scottish Parliament Building highlighted the traditional generalist skills at middle and senior ranking levels in the Scottish end of the UK civil service, accompanied by a lack of the technical management-in this case specific skills required to deal with large external construction projects-a claim reminiscent of Fulton some 35 years previously (Fraser Inquiry 2004). There is also a range of literature indicating that where change has occurred through externalisation strategies, there has not always been evidence of comprehensive adoption of managerial change. For instance, research on executive agencies has shown many such bodies adopting a managerial performance based regime, but change is much less evident in the parent civil service departments (Bichard 1999;Talbot 2004). However there is research showing the successful introduction of a range of generic HRM practices in central government departments (Gould-

Williams 2004), but perhaps ironically, this giving greater discretion to management and other internal stakeholders. Finally, there is a body of literature addressing the hypothesis that there is a 'post-new public management' model emerging which is neither about the transfer of externally referenced practice (usually meaning transferred from the private sector) nor a polarisation between traditional bureaucratic or marketised models, but more about new forms of managerial practice and models clustering around new organisational forms, partnerships and patterns of leadership (Pettigrew and Fenton 2000; Poole, Boyne and Mendes 2002; Andreescu 2003). Much of the primary research to date is focused on the commercialising or quasi-autonomous parts of government rather than civil service or government departments.

Local Government

The scope for local authorities to exercise managerial autonomy in the provision of services within their area reached its zenith by the 1970s. This was reflected in the role described by Sir George Sharp as 'area monopolist' (Sharp 1970), the authority being the sole provider of a range of services in its area. Central government's relationship with local authorities was generally benign, and it underpinned local authority activity, with central exchequer funding contributing 50-60% of local government spending. By the 1980s, the relationship was characterised by financial strain, often political hostility, and by the late 1990s less than 20% of local government expenditure was determined by local government (Wilson and Game 1998; Painter and Isaac-Henry 1999).

The managerial environment by the late 1990s was categorised as one of governance, necessitating external relationships with a plethora of agencies. The 1980s and 1990s saw the rise of the 'local unelected state' and a range of local public spending bodies (LPSBs). Traditional local authority services were now in some cases shared with others (these services ranging from education to refuse collection) while newer services (e.g. local economic development) were often the responsibility of completely separate bodies. A leading authority on local government summarised the situation:

> The overall effect can be summarised as a shift from a system of local government to a system of local governance. Local authorities now share to a greater extent than before 1979 service provision and---decision making responsibilities with other agencies. (1)

On the one hand there was clearly a 'democratic deficit' implied in these arrangements (Painter et al 1996), though some of the new agencies developed a more open, consultative style of decision-making and evolved new forms of participation (Painter et al 1994). The privatisation agenda spearheaded by compulsory competitive tendering (CCT) had a deep impact on local councils' management creating difficulties for the leadership role of senior local authority managers. The managerial role changed significantly from managing council committees and the elected member inter-face (Clarke and Stewart 1991).

Research indicated that senior managers spent more than half their time in meetings with 'community partners' and in networking with local institutions (Travers, Jones and Burnham 1997).

The externalisation of management in councils continued, despite a change in government in the late 1990s. According to Prime Minister Blair:

> There can be no monopoly of service delivery by councils; the 1970s will not be revisited. Delivering quality services means that councils must forge partnerships with communities, agencies and the private sector. (2)

Indeed, it was argued the striking post-1997 development was that where previously much partnership and networking arrangements were often ad-hoc responses to the dysfunctional consequences of local institutional fragmentation, now collaboration had become intentional strategy (Painter and Clarence 1998).

Local authority education provision   Specific illustration of local authority education management is important given the radical and dramatic change which occurred from the late 1980s.   There was a reduction in education authority management responsibilities, with the Local Management of Schools (LMS) statutes devolving resources to schools. This was followed by 'opt-out' legislation and funding arrangements for schools, which had chosen to remove themselves from local council control. School governors managed schools, though the local education authority (LEA) remained the legal employer of those working in LEA maintained schools. Although there was (eventually) similar legislation in Scotland, experience was markedly different, with virtually no take-up of opt-out provision (any enthusiasm for this only surfaced with closure plans) and a continued strong role for local authorities in school management as the case study 4 shows. (3) The management of education was indeed complex especially when government's target for opt-out schools (1500 by 1994) was not achieved by 1997. Yet the management of schools, especially the larger ones, was increasingly the responsibility of a management hierarchy under the head teacher in the school. There has also been an increasing tendency for additional and supplementary resource to go directly to school management rather than via local education authorities. (4)

The local authority role in the management of further education colleges also changed. The Further and Higher Education Act 1992, and parallel legislation in Scotland, removed further education from direct local authority control. Colleges were to be run by independently appointed boards of management with a majority of members coming from the private sector, funded centrally as a LPSB on the basis of an agreed business plan prepared on unit costed student activity. This made colleges in many senses archetypal new managerial institutions. Further education is presented as a case study in chapter 11.

Lack of definition, indeed role loss, is the most accurate way to describe the local authority role in school education after the Education Reform Act of 1988 and its associated legislation devolved resource and managerial responsibility to school governors and managers. As case study 5 shows, the internal and external management arrangements in further education changed dramatically after the 1992 Further and Higher Education Act. Colleges were now funded directly by central government on the basis of a business plan, and had full responsibility for all aspects of managing that plan with no intervening structure or layer in local education authorities. Externally, college networks developed between institutions, central government and other bodies with little reference to local councils. Previously, councils had been the key part of these networks, often to the exclusion of colleges themselves.

The difficulties for LEAs, given the combined effect of schools and further education legislation were recognised by the Audit Commission:

> The dispersal of LEA powers encourages central government to take more powers for itself and to use these powers more actively; which in turn limits the scope and incentives for LEAs to act of their own volition; which in turn encourages central government to assume more powers of direction and co-ordination; which in turn reduces the LEA role still further. (5)

Government thinking in the final years of the 1990s and early 2000s appeared to provide some role clarity though envisaged only limited pupil specific services. The main managerial concerns for LEAs are to facilitate the work of others (e.g. schools and OFSTED) to improve standards. Externalisation of management practices will be important in the development of Department of Education approved local development plans, with which LEAs are charged (Holloway, Horton and Farnham 1999). The situation is in a state of flux in Scotland. The removal of a policy advisory role from Her Majesty's Inspectorate in 2001 raised the possibility of an enhanced role in policy for senior education professionals in schools and local education authorities. (6) However the Scottish Executive in 2003 and 2004 appeared to be giving greater autonomy to school heads rather than (perhaps at the expense of) local authorities.

However, in local authorities more generally, internal management practices were still important. Research indicated that financial pressures on local government led to the internal development of performance management measures by the late 1980s and early 1990s and consequently the government's requirement of the Audit Commission to publish performance indicators for councils was hardly necessary, though there was some council hostility to the number of measurement indicators proposed by the Commission. According to Kerley, by the early 1990s, 'assessing performance [became] so entrenched in commonsense practice as to be almost value free and not for political debate and comment'. (7) Changes in employment relations practices had in some instances given local authority managers the power to set arrangements internally: 34 local authorities in England and Wales opted out of national agreements for non-manual employees in the late 1980s and 1990s (Bryson et al 1993); this never occurred in Scotland. Somewhat ironically, although CCT led to the externalisation of management practices (e.g. in the management of external contractors), and thereby led to a reduction in the scope of internal management in manual services, it significantly increased local management control over pay and work, since these could be specified by management in the external contracts drawn up, unlike those nationally (externally) negotiated (Sheaff 1987; White and Hutchinson 1996). This management control though was severely limited by the application, since the mid-1990s, of the European Court of Justice interpretation of the Transfer of Undertakings (Protection of Employment) Regulations 1981, insisting that terms and conditions of employees who transfer employers were protected in public sector environments.

The replacement of CCT with Best Value in 1999 has maintained the local authority external focus since there is still the presumption of market/competitive comparison (Flynn 2002). But this must be balanced against the possibility of discretion internal to the local council: there has also been scope for individual local authority variation in management of service provision within the Best Value regime despite the fact that Best Value is considered to be more detailed and comprehensive in its objectives than other managerial reforms in the public sector (Geddes and Martin 2000; Boyne, Martin and Walker 2004); the 2001 Local Government White Paper has introduced the concept of 'earned autonomy' albeit within the context of new managerial freedoms rather than any enhancement of local democratic autonomy (Lowndes and Wilson 2003).

National Health Service

The attempt to introduce general management into the NHS after the late 1970s was based on and attempt to strengthen internal management practices by altering the prevailing system of consensus management: the attempted reforms of the mid to late 1970s were largely negated by the unanimity required before local health authorities could reach decisions-a triumph, as one writer has put it for medical syndicalism (Klein 1995). The Griffiths enquiry in 1983 found an organisation in which there was little that could be recognised as management, and his report concluded with a phrase much repeated since:

> If Florence Nightingale were carrying her lamp through the corridors of the NHS today she would almost certainly be searching for the people in charge. (8)

As a result, general managers were introduced into the NHS and were responsible for defined units of management within a unified management reporting structure. Other aspects of NHS governance were changed. The internal management structure was strengthened by external pressure. For example, the introduction of performance measures in 1983 allowed health authorities to be compared on the basis of value for money; in the same year the government set manpower targets for all staff; Rayner efficiency studies were introduced into the NHS, and competitive tendering was introduced for laundry, domestic and catering services, driven by a desire to support NHS management vis-à-vis powerful public sector trades unions, and help management reduce NHS costs (Mailly et al 1989). Unlike the marketisation programme in local authorities, these were not core NHS services. In this sense, the concept 'mixed economy of health care' (Klein 1995), was rather dramatic: although there was a substantial increase in private external earnings for a number of NHS consultants (though much skewed by geography and specialism-Monopolies and Mergers Commission 1994) as case 3 shows, key elements of the mixed economy, including the building of a private hospital, were opposed by Scotland's largest health authority. And there was one area of traditional governance as yet untouched, individual clinician autonomy. One leading writer on the NHS put it thus: 'In short Griffiths and related reforms set out to challenge the professional domination of the NHS but they did not dent clinical freedom' (Corby 1999). The area of clinical freedom, as shown below, was only systematically addressed from the latter years of the 1990s.

In 1990, the government intensified its attempt to influence management and alter the governance of the NHS by introducing an internal market. By so doing, it intended to strengthen the position of managerialism in the health service. It wished to assert managerial practices over clinical ones and create a mimic market of purchasers (health authorities) and providers (hospitals). This was later extended to the GP service with the introduction of fund-holding status where GPs purchased care on behalf of their customers (patients). These moves were all complemented by the attempt to denationalise pay bargaining, designed to support internal management by giving to managers greater discretion over wage and labour relations. By 1996, 31% of staff were on individual NHS Trust contracts (Income Data Services 1997); however, attempts to introduce local bargaining for nurses and paramedics led to a major industrial dispute with the moderate Royal Colleges of Nursing and Midwives repealing their rules prohibiting strike action. A face-saving device for government was put in place but the attempt at local pay bargaining for nurses was abandoned just before the general election of 1997 (Income Data Services 1998).

The final piece of the governance jigsaw was to address the embedded nature of professional interests, arguably the most powerful influence in NHS internal management. Government clearly wished to tackle this, and in particular the notion of individual clinician autonomy. It was clear to Griffiths that the process of individual clinician autonomy committed resources difficult for managers to control. This required to be addressed; otherwise the rest of the reforms, ranging from internal markets to regulating performance and industrial relations, were peripheral.   Attempts were made by the NHS in Scotland to embed the management of clinical decision and resource usage in existing internal structures through the Scottish Health Service Planning Council (SHSPC), a body not replicated elsewhere in Britain. This is elaborated in case study 3. Important though it was, the SHSPC was short lived, but its role and function were reenergized through other bodies (e.g. the Clinical Resource and Audit Group, and later the Scottish Health Technology Board and successor bodies).

In other parts of Britain, though somewhat later than in Scotland, engagement with professional clinician interests to address the clinical autonomy/resource usage interface was evident. In the face of a government determined for change, it was in the medical profession's interest to engage in the process. Otherwise, the profession as a whole could be excluded from the change process. An accommodation was indeed reached between professional autonomy and central government concern for resource usage. After 1990, many protocols on good practice were issued by the Royal Colleges, which retained medical audit within professional hands, counter-balancing individual clinician autonomy (Klein 1995). This was more apparent earlier in Scotland with the creation in the late 1980s of the Clinical Resource and Audit Group under the chairmanship of the Chief Medical Officer (Scottish Office 1997). In addition, NHS management engagement with the medical professional was formalised through the creation of part-time clinical director posts, which enabled managerial and clinical functions to co-exist for the post holders (Ashburner 1996).

In 1997, the in-coming government retained the purchaser/provider split, clearly believing that this provided the strongest way to manage health care though no longer titled an internal market-contracts now being called funding agreements. De-centralised management in NHS trusts remained too, though the number of trusts was reduced (Dept of Health 1997; Scottish Office 1997; Welsh Office 1998). In Scotland, trusts were abolished and their functions subsumed with the area health boards. Primary care groups run by GPs were to provide the commissioning of health care for localities. These groups required strong management and there was early indication that some GPs were less than comfortable with the 'gate-keeping for health care' role implied (GP 1998). The primary care groups also had a strong external management requirement: as well as commissioning health care, they were required to work closely with social services, the voluntary sector and others to contribute to the local health improvement programmes required for all local health authorities (Dept of Health 1997; Scottish Office 1997). The most recent trends in NHS management have three key features. First, an intensification of partnership working between various parts of the health care and local authority run social services systems. Second, the introduction of localism with the creation of Foundation Hospitals in England. Third, divergence within the UK. Post-devolution, Scotland's system appears to focus more on partnership management with the creation of community health partnerships, bringing together health boards and local authority services with the abolition of hospital trusts and no plans for foundation hospitals. Some writers have indicated this departure represents more than differential management arrangements, that it is about Scottish adherence to traditional NHS values from which the rest of the UK is departing (Greer 2003). In this context it is perhaps worth noting that the 1980s and 1990s concept of a mixed economy of health care has taken a step forward in 2003. Since then, there has been an increased use of private medical care but this involves NHS purchasing on behalf of NHS patients: this however is much less well developed in Scotland.

At the clinical/resource interface, an increasingly important component of health service practice was in the strategic management of clinical quality and standards. Inevitably, this involved relationships between managers, central government and professionals. The management of these relationships required the co-option of medical professional and other interests. The strategy to achieve this was threefold. First, the establishment of the National Institute for Clinical Excellence (NICE), in Scotland the Scottish Health Technology Board, with a membership drawn from medical and other health professionals as well as health economists and patient representatives. These agencies were charged with establishing a programme of new evidence-based national service frameworks setting out patterns and levels of service to be provided for patients with certain medical conditions. Second, the creation of a Commission for Health Improvement drawn from medical professional and patient representatives to spot-check local arrangements, monitor and ensure clinical quality and with power to remove chairs of NHS trusts (and non-executive directors too) where there was evidence of systemic failure. Third, 'clinical governance' was to be instituted to ensure clinical standards at local level as a result of which trust chief executives, in addition to financial responsibilities, were given a duty for the quality of care. At the clinical/resource inter-face professional accommodation with external stake-holders appeared to be the defining objective, rather than professional control underpinned by individual clinician autonomy.

The future will tell whether these initiatives become grounded in NHS management practice and the degree of tension with professional self regulation. As the British Medical Association (BMA) stated:

> the requirements of professional self regulation and outcomes driven performance assessment required by NHS management can be mutually incompatible'. (9)

Nevertheless, there is accumulating research indicating the key role played by clinical directors in accommodating the worlds of managerial and professional power. Far from de-professionalisation in the face of managerialism, a process of re-professionalisation seems to be occurring (e.g., Thorne 2002).

Summary and Conclusion. Internal Management and External Influence

Considerable pressure was exerted on public expenditure in the wake of the 1970s oil crises. New right thinking gave a particular ideological twist to this, eulogising the benefits of a managerial ethos in the public sector, aimed at making public sector management more efficient. New managerialism systematised this and introduced consumerism, devolved managerial responsibility at the delivery level while attempting to centralise strategy and policy making. This represented a clearly articulated attempt to alter and redirect prevailing management practices.

In the civil service, the formation of 'next steps' agencies and market testing represented a real external dimension to civil service management. This has been maintained up to the present through benchmarking exercises with a range of external organisations. The continuation of initiatives like the Private Finance Initiative (PFI, now Public Private Partnership, PPP) in some instances goes beyond the accessing of private money for public sector controlled projects, including shared management with external (often private sector) bodies. Such initiatives are currently planned for Air Traffic Control and London Underground. Yet much of the change has been focused on the executive agencies rather than in central government or civil service practice. Internal management still retained a presence: from the work of Rayner's efficiency unit in the 1980s to the deregulation and increased flexibility in local bargaining of labour conditions to the introduction of HRM and other practices, internal management has in some ways strengthened its position. It will also be interesting to see if this continues in the light of any newly emerging post new public management models and approaches.

In local government, the significant changes of the 1980s and 1990s from CCT to legislation affecting control of schools and colleges have altered the focus of management to the governance of a range of external relations including those with agencies in the private sector, LPSBs and neighbourhood organisations. In some instances, there has been role reduction for local authority management, for example in further education, where local authorities now have little input, and in schools where increasing autonomy and resource flows have by-passed local education authorities. In management of schools, Scottish and English experience diverged, with the former country retaining more local council control over schools management. Yet in local authority management in general, internal management and the local discretion this implies remains of considerable importance.

Management in health was subjected to external influences from the late 1970s. Managerialism was introduced and super-imposed upon professional interests, reaching its apotheosis with the creation of an internal market and the external marketisation of a range of non-clinical support services. Much of this has been retained, even though the terminology of internal market has altered: indeed from late 2003 there has been an increased use of the external market with NHS purchasing from the private medical sector for a range of treatments. More subtly, external influence on clinician autonomy as a guiding principle in the management of the health service has been evolved to the present with bodies like the National Institute for Clinical Excellence, the Commission for Health Improvement and the Scottish Health Technology Board apparently operating embodiments of an accommodation between internal professional interest and an external governmental agenda, which couples clinical decision and resource allocation. There is some evidence this may represent a successful attempt by internal professional interests to retain a key influence and control of key aspects of NHS management – but only time will tell.

Notes

1. Stoker, G. (1997), 'Quangos and local democracy' in M. Flinders, I. Harden and D. Marquand (eds) *How To Make Quangos Democratic,* London: Charter 88, p. 53.
2. Blair, A. (1997), 'Next on the list: clean up the councils' in *The Guardian*, 3 November, p. 5.
3. According to Andrew Neil then a key executive employed by News International this was only because Downing Street bludgeoned an unenthusiastic Scottish Office. Neil claims to have played a key role in this when Strathclyde Regional Council proposed closure of his old school Paisley Grammar. He worked on Brian Griffith, head of the Downing Street Policy Unit (who is reported to have said, 'Rifkind [Secretary of State for Scotland] is in the pocket of the Scottish Office, and there are not many Tories there') to get the following response from the Prime Minister: "furious with Rifkind she [the Prime Minister] instructed him to issue a new regulation giving the Scottish

Office powers to 'save' schools where 80% of parents disagreed with a local authority closure plans". Neil, A (1996), *Full Disclosure*, London: MacMillan, p. 239-243.

4. *Financial Times* 9 October 1999; *Times Education Supplement* 14 March 2001.

5. Audit Commission (1996), *Trading Places, The Supply and Allocation of School places*, London: HMSO. p. 39.

6. *Scotland Times Higher Education Supplement* 12 January 2001.

7. Kerley, R. (1994), *Managing in Local Government*, London: Macmillan, p. 140.

8. Klein, R. (1995), *The New Politics of the NHS*, third edition, London: Macmillan, p. 147.

9. British Medical Association (1998), Letter to Chairman of Professional Regulation Working Group, 8 May, unpublished. Cited in Corby, S. (1999), 'The NHS', in S. Horton and D. Farnham (eds) *Public Management in Britain,* London: Macmillan, p. 192.

Chapter 9

Case Study 3: The Hospital Service in Greater Glasgow 1947-1987

Synopsis

Management of hospitals in the newly created NHS was entrusted to the Regional Hospital Boards (RHBs). Boards had executive powers, were funded directly from the Scottish Office and had substantial representation from the medical profession. Western Regional Hospital Board's (WRHB) archive revealed the way in which strong internal professional control of the system was established in the formation years; this was also supported and re-inforced by government at political and administrative levels. The two decades after 1960 were years of central government search for rational and planned approaches to management of the public sector. Much of the initiative in this area was internally generated by the RHB itself but reliance on internal structures, which were bounded by professional control, had limitation. In the Health Service generally throughout the UK, external change initiatives were focused in two dimensions. First, there was a brief flirtation with the notion of an additional player (local government) in the provision of health care and second, the introduction of general management and aspects of managerialism into the running of the NHS. These initiatives were largely unsuccessful: institutional exclusiveness was not seriously challenged and there was general failure to introduce key elements of managerialism. All this was of course observed in the case. But here (and in Scotland as a whole) there was a stronger resistance to change: the administrative-political community was more strongly and cohesively aligned with medical interests to resist change, in contrast to England.

Evolving from the 1970s, a key dimension of change-the introduction of managerialism-was a major focus of externally generated change by central government in the 1980s. It will be shown that the application of managerialism in the Greater Glasgow Health Board (GGHB), WRHB's successor, was dominated by the cost control part of that agenda to the exclusion of other features of managerialism. Finally, a major component of managerialism was alteration of Health Service governance and this is examined: the development of medical managerialism witnessed the involvement of professional clinicians with government and NHS at the centre as a means of retaining professional control, though the relationship between medical audit, clinical governance and resource management could not, in the period of the case, be termed 'settled'. Another aspect of centrally influenced change, use of marketisation and the encouragement of a mixed economy of health care, is in evidence in the case. This however was adopted in a less than enthusiastic manner. A key dimension to earlier thinking on change – consideration of local authority input – was settled, the outcome being NHS institutional monopoly. Yet ironically, institutional exclusiveness was more difficult to sustain in light of legislation affecting social and personal care, yet the case evidence did not suggest an easy accommodation with more collaborative arrangements.

- NHS creation: internal management and professional control
- 1960-1980: search for rational approaches to management
- 1980-1987: externalization of management?

NHS Creation. Internal Management and Professional Control of the Hospital Service

> *[since 1949] effective beds are up 6%; inpatients admitted are up 29%; the ratio of treatment to beds is up by 22% and the waiting lists are down 11%.* (Derek Walker Smith, Conservative Minister of Health 1958). (1)

The settlement which saw the NHS established was the result of much negotiation, discussion and not a little acrimony between various senior figures in the Labour government and medical interests ranging from the BMA to the Royal Colleges and within the civil service, between alternative scenarios for the implementation of a socialized health care system. (2)

For the hospital service, there were two key elements. First, the management of hospitals would be devolved to Regional Hospital Boards (RHBs). The board used in this study, the Western RHB (WRHB) had responsibility for hospitals in the Greater Glasgow area as far east as Lanarkshire and as far south as Dumfries. Second, RHBs were funded entirely from the health component of the Secretary of State for Scotland's territorial budget. Significant was the fact that RHBs had executive and not merely advisory powers (the latter had been considered in discussions prior to legislative enactment). This meant that from the outset, RHBs had a concern for the efficient use of resources in hospitals: this concern for efficiency was mirrored in other parts of the public sector.

From the early 1950s there is ample evidence of the Board making cost comparisons between different hospitals on admissions, bed usage, out-patient attendance and staffing levels. (3) Also clear is that the Secretary of State for Scotland's investigation of staffing and associated costs in the hospital service, sparked by the attention of the Public Accounts Committee, was supported and executed by the RHB. (4)

But by far the most significant aspects of hospital management were the structure and modus operandi created in the newly formed RHBs. These were established in such a way that the primacy of professional control at executive level was embedded from the outset. Internal management was synonymous with professional control.

Professional Control of Hospital Management Structures.

> *The NHS after 1948 can thus be seen simply as the re-emergence of organizational routines anchored in particular on the incorporation of interest groups in the process of decision- making* (Klein 1995). (5)

The important and vital element of policy after 1947 was the executive (rather than solely advisory) powers given to RHBs, membership of which was dominated by local medical professional interests. There-by a key interest group was incorporated into the decision making process (see Middlemass 1979, for an account of this in the policy process in Britain). This in effect amounted to government compliance with professional control of the system and led directly to, as one author has put it, professionals being turned into the state's agents for rationing scarce resources" (Klein 1995). The case has indicated how professional control was achieved at the local level in the greater Glasgow area.

Medical professional representation on the WRHB was significant. Throughout the 1950s the typical Board contained 25-35% medical representation (6) though a per-centage figure was never written into statute. Important key committees of the Board (e.g., the Hospital Staffing Committee and the Hospital Medical Specialists' Committee) had medical representation in excess of 50%. The medical professional interest was fully locked into and influenced the management of the system in four key aspects: first in execution and management of resource distribution; second, in the organisation of the medico-administrative system; third in the creation, maintenance and development of medical professional hierarchies and fourth, in the mediation of relationships with other parts of the hospital medical profession. How this was done will be briefly explored.

First, in the management of resources, the RHB performed two functions. The Board had responsibility for maximising financial allocations from the centre for the hospitals within its area. The financial difficulties faced by the government in 1951 (Aldcroft 1986) led to pressures on public expenditure: referring to a meeting between hospital boards of management and the secretary of state for Scotland,

> Most of the discussion related to estimates for 1951 / 52 and substantial reductions expected in budget allocations-- . (7)

This group of hospitals was informed of a budget cut of some 7%. Inter-cession on the group's behalf by the RHB restored this cut. (8) A second function of the RHB was to drive for resource usage efficiencies in its hospitals, very often in concert with central government.

Second, the way in which medical and administrative systems were designed indicated medical professional primacy in the system. All the evidence appears to suggest that in Scotland, in some contrast to the rest of Britain, the RHBs placed priority on using resources for medical rather than administrative or managerial personnel. A paper for the Scottish home and health department (SHHD) in the early 1960s (in response to the Wright Report on Medical Staffing) indicated the position, which had evolved in the 1950s:

> The striking point which emerges is that overall the present scale of consultant staffing in relation to the population is very much higher in Scotland than in England and Wales, the difference being about 50%. (9)

At the same time, the number of administrative and managerial staff was considered less than the UK average:

> The ratio of Scottish to English administrative staff numbers should be 1:8 in comparison of the expenditure on hospital services, 1:7 on bed numbers. The actual ratios for general administrative grade is 1:14, senior administrative grade 1:12, hospital secretaries 1:30. (10)

The SHHD was very clear that this was a situation, which had been deliberately pursued by the RHB:

> There seems to be a major question here of priorities-- disparity [re. the situation in the rest of the UK] has been evident ever since the figures became available after 1948. Regional Boards in Scotland have chosen to devote a substantial part of their development money each year to the creation of new consultant posts. (11)

The frenetic jostling for position and the uneasy balance of power between the component parts of health care administration (that is to say medical, lay and financial administrators) which appeared elsewhere (Ham, 1981) was slanted noticeably in favour of medical administration in Scotland, largely due to the importance of the post of medical superintendent in Scottish hospitals. (12) The RHBs wished to make it clear from the outset that the medical superintendent was seen as the chief officer in hospitals, with responsibility for all staff: a circular and deputation from most of the medical superintendents in the Western RHB area led to the board's general purposes committee deciding

> to recommend to the Regional Board that a medical superintendent of a hospital should be regarded as the chief officer within his hospital. (13)

The challenge to the medical superintendent's power and autonomy appeared to have come from the hospital secretary (or treasurer) with friction

> only being avoided by secretaries in many cases not carrying out their duties---. (14)

Once primacy had been won by medical superintendents the growth of managerial, administrative and functional infrastructures and hierarchies developed as growth made necessary. For instance, work study evaluation was carried out in several areas, technician training with systematic day release provision was put in place, and supervisory structures and training were also implemented in a range of activities from catering to hospital cleaning. (15) However, despite the powerful role of the medical superintendent, such support structures grew up almost independently without medical superintendents assuming (or apparently wishing) parallel managerial responsibility for them. Understandably, the medical superintendent's role was seen by the post-holder as primarily a medical position: some positions were in fact filled on a part-time basis to enable the post-holder to continue with clinical duties and responsibilities. (16) It was only much later that the wish to draw senior members of the medical profession into 'management' of the NHS was seen as a major issue for NHS management (Griffiths 1983).

Third, the control which the medical profession held over the creation, maintenance and development of medical/professional hierarchies, was significant. Much of this represented modernisation and a clear improvement on previous practice. In a memorandum to the WRHB, Professor J. W. Howie of the Bacteriology Department, University of Glasgow stated:

> Compared with the state of affairs before the National Health Service was instituted, the policy of selection and appointment of Registrars by committee confers the great benefit of open competition for posts. There is no longer any question of patronage or of arbitrary selection or exclusion of candidates. In the past some chiefs may have had virtually sole powers in this matter, and I am glad that this state of affairs has ended. (17)

In fact doctors' representatives at hospital level were an important force in pressing for appointments to occur at RHB rather than hospital level:

> It would seem necessary that the Regional Board itself should retain in its own hands the responsibility for Registrars' appointments. To place this obligation upon Boards of Management would lead to inequities in practice. (18)

All senior appointments (registrars and above) were handled by the specialist staffing sub-committee of the Western RHB. The concern was not only with appointments per se but in managing professional and medical career routes. The hospital staffing sub-committee of the RHB took the position that

> in view of the few opportunities for promotion, the total number of senior registrars in the region must be limited,

with the caveat,
> --so far as is consistent with the efficiency of the service. (19)

The medical establishment sub-committee pushed for the

> creation of 'X' grade to indicate a senior registrar whose training is regarded as completed and who is to be continued until a suitable permanent grading is available. [recommend] The creation of junior consultant and senior hospital

medical officer posts (five) and reduction of five consultant posts to achieve this. (20)

The medical appointments and career management system was certainly within the locus of the medical professional representatives of the WRHB, so much so that this preoccupation caused some concern with the SHHD:

> The Regional Board members should spend less time on senior medical appointments-- the time of medical members of the Regional Board could better be spent on other matters of medical and hospital policy.

The RHB board members would have none of it:

> In view of the importance of senior clinical appointments, the attendance of medical members of the Regional Board at meetings of committees dealing with these appointments [was considered] to be one of their most important functions. (21)

The fourth dimension to the retention of the professional control of health care delivery was in the policing of rival local power sources and interests. The establishment of a National Health Service was very much on the basis of central government's policy for hospitals being executed through local health boards. These bodies were therefore expected as part of the incorporation 'deal' to bring under their control, or at least mediate with, the various elements of the system in the locale. (22) There was considerable evidence of WRHB cooperating in alliance with the SHHD as the main agent in driving efficiencies in hospitals. RHBs distributed resources to hospitals on behalf of government without any requirement to justify the settlement. It was not until the 1960s that the Association of Scottish Hospitals could receive from RHBs the following transparency in the allocation of funding for hospital running costs (and only then after a very hostile resolution at the Association's AGM)

> Since 1948 the procedure followed by the Secretary of State in distributing money for hospital running costs has been adapted and improved. The procedure now is that the annual provision for each regional hospital board is based on the previous year's grant; allowances are made for wage and price changes; and, in addition, provision is made for development of the hospital service. (23)

It was also established that devolution of financial responsibility to hospitals was very much at the discretion of RHBs, with even the powers of virement tightly defined. (24) The RHB also made it very clear that the key issue of employment contracts for senior medical staff was the Regional Board's responsibility:

It is the duty of the RHB to enter into formal contracts with senior medical and dental staff as may be appointed to serve at hospitals and clinics throughout the region. While the final responsibility for the distribution of appointments made to the specialist service must remain within the regional board, the latter hopes to carry all Boards of Management with it. (25)

In addition to the above factors, the power of the medical profession was reinforced by the institutional exclusiveness of the NHS, which eliminated power sources or interests to rival medical professional control. Prior to NHS creation, the idea that a national service should have a strong input from local authorities was seriously considered. However, such involvement was not to be, although local authorities could be represented on health boards. This role, though, was restricted in Scotland as well as in England, as a letter from the department of health for Scotland indicated:

Appointment of Members to Regional Hospital Boards

Each regional hospital board has appointed various professional and technical advisory committees and experience has confirmed that it is through membership of these committees rather than of the board itself that the advice of professional and technical officers of local authorities and similar bodies can best be given. (26)

The pattern of professional control at regional level was underwritten by a party political consensual environment (see Kendall, Moon et al, 1996). Two issues where political consensus could have fractured were the issues of pay beds in NHS hospitals (the existence of which was enshrined in the legislation) and the representation on health authorities of classes of health service employee other than medical professionals (a proposal very quickly squashed when the TUC tried to raise the issue with Bevan). (27) The pay bed issue rarely arose within the WRHB. One occasion where it did was in a memorandum to the medical superintendent of the Southern General Hospital in Glasgow, in which the Medical Staff Association wrote,

Consultants in this hospital are to an extent penalised by the lack of hospital facilities for private patients' care. We believe that the provision of pay beds would be of value to this hospital group. (28)

The RHB replied cautiously but without commitment:

The Committee instructed the Secretary to advise the Medical Staff Association that while they did not consider that suitable pay bed accommodation could be provided by adaptation to existing ward accommodation, careful consideration would be given in any future planning of ward accommodation. (29)

The scale of pay beds indicated the insignificance of pay beds as an issue some twenty years later - Greater Glasgow Health Board area (broadly equivalent to the WRHB area prior to 1974) in its entirety had 40 pay beds (and 550 consultants). (30)

The issue of doctors being the only class of employee with representation rights on executive boards could raise temperatures. For instance, the consultants' group in the WRHB area felt they had an 'excellent working relationship with the WRHB' but expressed

> Concern at adverse reports in the Press on the appointment of a surgeon at the Royal Alexandra Infirmary in Paisley, especially reports suggesting the Regional Consultants and Specialists' Committee were trying to dictate to the Board over which grade of staff be appointed. The Regional Board should review more closely the composition of the Board to ensure individuals who consistently made irresponsible statements about senior medical staff were not re-appointed.

This provoked certain members of the board:

> Mr. Jack pointed out that the medical profession rightly or wrongly had been given a very privileged position under the Act in that they were heavily represented on Regional Boards and Boards of Management in a way not granted to other staffs in the NHS. Responsibility lay on members of the Board to ensure this is not abused.

The board minute indicated an attempt to lower the temperature:

> [The Board] was pleased that the relationship between the Regional Board and the Regional Consultants was regarded by the latter as satisfactory but the Board had no wish to interfere with the rights of members of the Board to express their views at meetings or to the press. (31)

The archive material indicates that such conflicts were rare; or if they did arise were not significant enough to be recorded. The administrative machinery of government also re-inforced the internal structures and practices establishing and legitimizing professional control, as well as being underpinned by party political consensus. The SHHD did this by practicing a consensual approach to mediating powerful (and sometimes opposing) local interests within the RHB. This was well exemplified in the proposed creation by the department of health, Scotland, of a Scottish School of Radiotherapy. The initial proposal was for a school with an institute in Edinburgh concentrating on x-ray work and one in Glasgow concentrating on isotope development.

> Dr. Johnstone [Dept. of Health] made it clear that money would not be available for 2 units in the western region. (32)

There were currently two units operating in Glasgow, one at the Western Infirmary and one at the Royal Infirmary. Professor McKay of the Royal made his views known on the possible sacrifice of his unit:

> The creation of one such unit at the Western Infirmary and the removal of the more advanced techniques from the Royal Infirmary's Radiotherapy Department meant in his view the upgrading of the Western at the expense of the Royal----Dr Morrison [also of the Royal Infirmary] suggested if the Royal Infirmary surgeons had to send cases for radiotherapy to an institution at the Western Infirmary they would inevitably hesitate before doing so. (33)

The proposals were referred to the cancer committee of the Scottish health service advisory council, which was serviced by very senior Scottish Office civil servants. The scheme, which was approved the following year by the SHHD, was presented in medical/scientific terms but one cannot overlook the political-consensus making elements of the settlement:

> The Cancer Committee were of the opinion that while it was very desirable that the Institute should be closely associated with a teaching hospital or hospitals, this did not necessarily mean that it should be on the same site. (34)

Both the Royal and Western were teaching hospitals. The justification for the two sites was elaborated:

> The conception of the scheme as originally envisaged by the Dept. of Health had been changed by development in radiotherapy-- [then], cobalt therapy was still in an experimental stage-- [the Royal Infirmary specialised in this field]-- the urgent need at present, agreed by the Department, is to upgrade firstly the Western Infirmary's Radiotherapy Department and secondly the Royal Infirmary's Radiotherapy Department-- £400,000 has been earmarked for these two purposes. (35)

The Search for Rational Approaches to Health Care: Internal and External Management

The years from 1960 were typified, as discussed above, by growing concern in government for public sector efficiency and financial control (Lowe 1996, 1997).

This was also an era when policy makers were concerned with rational and efficient practices (Heclo and Wildavsky 1981). Part of this policy thinking was the application of 'management' and 'business' practices in the health service (Webster 1988; Klein 1995). Did this affect the internally established professional control model established in the creation years?

The development of techniques of administrative rationalism and efficiency in the public sector was accelerated in the late 1950s when the House of Commons select committee on estimates criticised the control of public expenditure. This resulted in the Plowden Report (1961) which recommended radical changes in the planning and control of spending and introduced the idea of management as a central activity (Horton 1996). This framework of thinking led to various initiatives like the public expenditure survey committee (PESC) system; planning, programming, budgeting (PPB), and programme analysis review (PAR). There was also a debate about the way government was managed, leading eventually to the Fulton committee report which (inter alia) attacked the failure of the civil service to address managerial as distinct from policy advice concerns (Fulton 1968), placing faith in the production of a professional corps of administrators/managers. These prevailing concerns for management and efficiency had an impact on the NHS: within 5 years of the NHS's existence, the Guillebaud committee had investigated resource efficiency; shortly thereafter another committee-the Bradbeer Committee-investigated resource management in the hospital service; in 1959, the Ministry of Health set up an advisory committee for management efficiency and in the four years after 1963 expenditure on hospital efficiency studies rose from £18,000 to over £250,000 per annum (Klein 1995). (36) Allied to this was the belief in the transferability of current business managerial practices to the health service: a 'new rationalism' (Heclo and Wildavsky 1974), which held to the belief that government and business were not so different, and they both required modern management. Indeed, the Farquarson-Lang Report of 1966 (Farquarson-Lang was a member of the North Eastern Regional Hospital Board in Scotland) addressed many of the managerial issues tackled by the Thatcherite inspired Griffiths enquiry in the 1980s, leading at least one commentator to say that Farquarson-Lang predated Griffiths in all the key elements by 20 years or so (Hunter 1986).

Internal Management of the Hospital Service

These concerns articulated by central government were transparently in evidence in the internal management of the hospital service explored in the case. This was in a sense inevitable given an often ambiguous role which RHBs had, an integral part of being incorporated into a central government funded health care system. RHBs argued for resources in their own hospitals, yet in some instances allied with government concerns over resource management. The latter role can be seen from a minute of a meeting of RHB Chairmen in 1969:

> Referring to the situation [i.e., of nurse shortage and high turnover of trained nurses] in the Western Region, Mr Stevenson [Chairman of WRHB] doubted if

> Boards of Management [of hospitals] were doing enough to ensure that existing staff resources were used efficiently-- some evidence that some Boards of Management were unreasonable if not irresponsible as in one case where a Board was pressing for approval for new development when the general nursing staffing situation was on a knife edge-- some Boards expressed concern about RHB involvement in what was ostensibly a Board of Management field. Mr. Millan [Minister of State at the Scottish Office] agreed that a period of staff shortage might be the best opportunity for securing changes to which there might ordinarily be initial resistance. (37)

The general introduction of resource efficiency tools into hospitals did proceed apace in the 1960s, initiated by RHBs and hospital management. There was a gradual shift from subjective to functional costing in hospitals. The former was defined as a cost analysis system based on costs being allocated 'subjectively' under three sub-headings of salary and wages, supplies and services to give an overall cost per in-patient week and per out-patient day attendance. This was changed to a departmental or functional basis, with over one third of hospitals in WRHB operating this in 1960. (38) There was also a substantial growth in the application of work study, supported generally by trade unions and administrators in the hospital service. (39)

There were other internally driven initiatives designed to improve and rationalize management. There is ample evidence that medical administration training was taken seriously: from the mid to the late 1950s, there was a regular flow of senior medical administrators attending an eight week course on medical administration at the London School of Hygiene and Tropical Medicine; (40) the Scottish College of Commerce ran day release and evening classes as well as distance learning routes for examinations of the Institute of Hospital Administrators. (41) From the early 1960s, managerial positions and supervisory hierarchies were established in the 'domestic' aspect of hospital management with, for example, the appointment of domestic superintendents. (42) Hierarchies and training systems were also in place in the finance function by the early 1960s, and the appointment of clerical grade trainees in the WRHB's treasurer's department was

> on the understanding that it be made a condition of appointment that a course of accountancy study with a view to obtaining a suitable qualification be undertaken. (43)

There was a substantial investment in management training for nurses: 'top' management courses were organised under the auspices of Strathclyde University and were well supported by WRHB. 'Middle' management courses were offered with the Royal College of Nursing in Edinburgh, and first line management courses were undertaken in house. The nursing services sub-committee of WRHB

> noted the position with satisfaction-- [that] during the last year 460 ward sisters and charge nurses had undertaken first line management courses and that a further

180 would have undertaken the courses between 1 January and the end of April this year. (44)

This followed on from a total of 696 ward sisters and charge nurses planned to attend similar courses between January 1968 and December 1969. (45) The WRHB was well advanced and perhaps a pioneer in the introduction and application of electronic computing in the hospital service. The board held the first 'symposium on the application of electronic and digital computers in the hospital service' on 23 November 1965. (46) By the end of 1969 WRHB had a department of 44 in its computer unit with a hierarchy running from manager through to systems designers, programmers, supervisors and operators. (47) The Board encouraged work study and organisation and methods studies in hospitals and created its own infrastructure to facilitate developments in these fields. In 1967, a senior post was created at assistant secretary grade, 'the first of its kind in Scotland and enthusiastically supported by the SHHD'. (48) With an establishment of 25, this department organised training for other RHBs and was visited by a range of bodies including North West Metropolitan RHB London, Leeds RHB's Windsor Hospital Group, United Cambridge Hospitals, Ministry of Social Services Paris and the Construction Industry Training Board.

Improved rationalistic technocratic approaches were used on capital projects. In 1962, a radical change was made to the WRHB's capital project appraisal system. Previously, each project had been viewed on its own merits; now a set of criteria was established and a priority rating system used against a decennial build programme with bi-annual review. (49) WRHB, like other RHBs in the 1960s was confronted with a rapid development of the hospital build programme and a serious craft skills shortage exacerbated by periods of overheating in the economy, and its response was business-like in approach:

> Steps have been taken to speed up the work of planning new hospitals include the creation of a separate planning department and the introduction of new techniques known as 'critical path analysis' which I believe has been more highly developed in this region than by any other in Britain and with considerable success. (50)

The Board was also quick to use systems building with the use of standardised components for the building of new wings and units in hospitals. This use of industrialised building methods, due to the higher initial overhead costs incurred by firms operating such methods, also called for negotiated and 'market tested' tendering procedures. WRHB and SHHD jointly operated a selective tendering process to enable the speedy use of such building methods as well as satisfying accountability controls for public funding. (51)

The internal management, which was established, always within the context of medical-professional control, did have limitations. There was a 'negative' grip and influence which professional interests could hold on rational planning, as the following extract from a meeting between the Greater Glasgow Health Board (GGHB, WRHB's successor) and the Secretary of State for Scotland reveals:

Dr McKay thought that the definition of bed usage was too rigid. Many acute beds were occupied for long periods by elderly patients. There were professional problems about whether they should be under the care of general physicians or geriatricians. There was a need for the profession to consider this because both specialties were doing a similar job-- the Secretary of State reiterated that there must be a rationalisation and that the Board could not afford to wait for this to happen in an undetermined way-- the Board should formulate its plans.

The chairman accepted the Board had a responsibility in this matter but thought it would be very difficult to get the various interests to accept an overall plan. (52)

There was, too, continuing concern at the use of medical manpower. The following was all the more significant since it was a response of the GGHB's area medical committee (overwhelmingly composed of senior medical figures) to the government's enquiry into the use of resource in the NHS:

> There is as yet little evidence of the functional integration and still plenty of evidence of '2 doctors doing 1 doctor's work'-- nurses could take on new functions formerly discharged by doctors; what has to be determined is the person who can most appropriately deal with a particular situation and it may not always be a doctor. (53)

Existing practices were in a sense re-inforced by the funding regime. An aide memoire drawn up in 1970 indicated that hospital revenue expenditure would be based on existing expenditure as a base-line, added to which would be guaranteed increases to cover pay awards, other price increases and any improvements or expansions during the year. This meant that a large element of hospital expenditure was in effect outwith the strategic control of the board, having been determined historically. (54)

The focus on internal management contextualised by professional control of the hospital service seems to have been an inhibitor for a wider perspective on the purpose and function of NHS resources. This was particularly poignant in Glasgow. GGHB's area medical committee in its response to the aforementioned enquiry referred to this very point:

> Para. 15 of the government's document refers to information services but these are to be limited to manpower statistics. The Committee would like to see this comment strengthened to refer to information services on the health needs of the community. The NHS as a whole is sadly deficient in knowledge of what is actually required to meet the needs of the people in a given area and so enable objectives to be defined. There has been too little examination of the genuine priorities in terms of needs and of whether limited resources should be spent on the promotion in the NHS of highly technical and very costly services if this can only be done at the expense of more ordinary and less glamorous but perhaps more needed services. A better information service might provide the data on which these difficult value judgments and decisions should be based. (55)

And in Glasgow's view, the newly proposed funding system some 2 years later would not address these specific needs. Information short-comings leading to serious policy and resource deficiencies had particular focus with the publication of the Scottish Health Authorities Resource Equalisation (SHARE) report. A paper approved by the policy and planning committee and later the full GGHB Board concluded:

> The Board does not dispute the principle of establishing a pattern of distributing available revenue funds on the basis of population but the major defect of the report is the failure to take account of the effects of urban deprivation. It is agreed there is a lack of data, the only alternative would seem to be a political judgment and initiative designed to give special attention to the joint health and social requirements of an area such as Glasgow-- [also] the outpatient flow into Glasgow is high e.g. because of workers in the city using A and E. Social services in deprived areas are overworked, there is a greater burden on the health services. (56)

External influences on management?

There were two significant attempts in the late 1960s and 1970s, consistent with then contemporary thinking on 'rational' business-like approaches to public sector management, which represented attempts to exert substantial external influence on traditional management of the NHS: the challenge to NHS institutional exclusiveness; and the introduction of managerialism into the NHS.

The 'institutional exclusiveness', in effect the key decision to isolate any potential local authority input, was (at least theoretically) challenged from the late 1960s. Much of the thinking behind local government reform (the subject of royal commissions in England and Wales, chaired by Redcliffe Maude and in Scotland, Wheatley) was that the local fragmentation of council activity required to be addressed by the creation of larger authorities able to play a strategic role in the development of their areas (Wilson and Game 1994; Midwinter 1982). For health planning purposes the logic of a link with the newly created local authorities was understood by policy makers (Klein1995). (57) Submissions to the Wheatley royal commission from some of the RHBs in Scotland indicated an appreciation of the value of some form of integration with post reform local council structures. The North Eastern RHB made the following submission:

> [currently there are] three tiers, the hospital and specialist service, general medical and dental, local health authority. It is in the best interests of the community if a new type of authority were created to exercise all functions at present allocated to RHBs, Executive Councils and Local Health Authorities-- the whole expenditure of such an authority being met from Exchequer funds. (58)

However, significantly the WRHB and other RHBs made no submissions. And the consensus view recognised in the legislation was that local authority and health care should be institutionally discrete areas of public policy. The RHBs Chairmen's view in 1970 was:

> The second English Green Paper left open for consideration the possibility of some contribution by local authorities-- [we express] profound dismay at this. It has been one of the main strengths of the hospital service since 1948 that it has been able to concentrate development in the areas of greatest need without concern about questions of local finance. Any provision that prejudices this principle will be to the detriment of the health service in the new structure and would be strongly opposed by the chairmen. (59)

This view held sway despite a strong rearguard action by John MacKintosh MP in favour of local government administration of health services in the final stages of the debate on the NHS (Scotland) Act, which received royal assent in August 1972 (Webster 1996).

Government aims for reform and the introduction of managerialism, from the views expressed in the Farquarson-Lang report to Labour's 1968 Green Paper, the Conservatives White Paper in 1972 and legislation the following year strongly emphasised effective management of the health service rather than professional representation and control, despite protestations from some politicians. Richard Crossman, previously a Labour health secretary referred to the proposed reforms in 1973 as excessively managerialist and 'terrifying' (Klein 1995). The British Medical Journal commented:

> A case for such a drastic curtailment of the participation of the profession in the management of the NHS might be made simply in the interests of efficiency. But there is a limit to the extent to which the principles of organisation and methods should be introduced into a medical service. (60)

However the legislation, which passed and led to the 1974 reorganisation undoubtedly deferred to the professional representation principle. The executive group was embedded in the structure. This group was dominated by medical professionals (though finance and administrative officers were also included) and unanimity was required, 'giving medical professionals virtual veto rights'. Although these arrangements applied in both Scotland and England, the picture, which emerged in England, was recognition by government of the day of the importance and power of professional interests. As a leading authority put it:

> The basic unit of management gave the medical representatives veto rights. These extensive concessions should be seen not so much as a victory for the corporate organisations of the medical profession as an acknowledgment of the reality of medical syndicalism-- it seemed only logical to build the participation of the medical profession into the process of the decision making machinery. Participation followed effective power. (61)

Klein in fact referred to at best a 'political fudge' and at worst a reluctant acceptance of the situation by government. (62) The picture which emerged in the case studied (and by extension, to Scotland as a whole) was rather different in tone, with an apparently closer link between professional interests and the central government policy machine on the one hand, and on the other little enthusiasm for the managerial ideas which drove the reform agenda. In a sense this was ironic given the significant input made by Farquarson-Lang - an important Scottish health administrator - to much of the prevailing managerial thinking. Indeed, the response of the SHHD in 1972 to Farquarson Lang's proposals for the creation of chief executives with direct managerial accountability and responsibility made the point:

> Para. 12 of Farquarson Lang believed the advantages of a single channel of management and administration outweighed the public disadvantages and recommend that a chief executive post should be established at each type of Board Para. 14-- there are more fundamental difficulties in the use of chief executives to administer affairs of health board—other officers must be able to advise the board; it remains to be determined whether the executive of the board's functions is most appropriately performed through a hierarchy in which relationships are essentially those of superiors to subordinates.
>
> The rationale of the executive group is that a service pursuing a wide range of objectives with the help of a number of professions can be administered better by a multi disciplinary group than by a single chief executive-- an executive group may provide a more suitable point of contact and communication with clinical divisions than a chief executive particularly since these divisions will include many doctors who are independent contractors. (63)

Management consultants whose concerns will generally tend towards managerial and business prescriptions were not used in the lead up to the 1970s reforms in Scotland (Hunter 1986; Maxwell 1975).

Throughout the 1970s, management of the NHS in Scotland appeared to be more cohesive than in England. There is circumstantial evidence that this was due in some measure to the links between senior representatives of the medical profession and government administration in the Scottish Office. Aspects of this were seen in the case material.

In the various pre-reform discussions the SHHD appeared much stronger in its attempt to exclude or marginalise local authority involvement than was the case in England. In addition, the chief medical officer in Scotland took a key role in deliberations and was largely responsible for the creation of the Scottish Health Service Planning Council. This contrasted to the strongly managerial tone of the pre White Paper and subsequent deliberations in England, where the consultancy firm McKinsey and leading management writers and researchers like Elliot Jacques were invited into the process by government (Webster 1996). Keith Joseph, the Health Secretary, attempted to alter some initial drafting of the Scottish White Paper-a key area being his wish to avoid professional advisory committees gaining a statutory right to consultation: the SHHD declined to make these changes and the right was eventually conceded in England. (64) It has been suggested that some of the 'difficulties' in relationships between doctors and government was due to some features of the administration in the Department of Health in London: not staffed by the 'best' people (Kogan 1969) or, perhaps more accurately, staffed by civil servants who had reached their final post 'having gone through much of the rigours of creation'. (65) The most senior positions in SHHD were usually staging posts for 'career movers' moving up the Scottish Office hierarchy in the key period of the late 1950s to the late 1970s. This has been quantitatively documented by Webster (1996) and McTavish (2000). (66)

The political environment which underpinned the management of the health service in the 1960s and 1970s still appeared to contain much of the post-creation consensus in contrast to England. The conflicts which hit the NHS there from the late 1970s, industrial relations disputes and the issue of pay beds, were much less significant in Scotland (Hunter 1986). In the period 1976 to1977 and again 1979 to 1980, the NHS suffered severe cash limits; Scotland too was affected by this but 'cushioned' to the extent that health was more generously funded in Scotland anyway. The issue of pay beds saw the medical profession and Labour government from 1974 locked in ideological conflict. Under 1976 legislation, phasing out of pay beds was to occur (the decision to be taken by an independent board with half of its members from the medical profession) and four years later the number of pay beds in England had fallen from 3,444 to 2,533. Yet in the entire GGHB area, covering over one third of Scotland's population there were only 50 pay beds in total. (67)

There is other evidence of Scottish and English divergence in the 1970s. The management structures after the 70s reforms differed, with an additional regional tier put in place in England to the almost immediate criticism of over bureaucracy. In England, the medical profession's control (and in this sense the maintenance of the post war settlement) has been portrayed rather negatively, as a reluctant political 'fudge' and the veto rights (the unanimity condition) at district management team level 'a recognition of medical syndicalism' (Klein 1995). In Scotland, the unanimity principle was also in place (in fact the idea appeared to originate in the SHHD-Webster 1996) but the first post reform health authority in Glasgow had a much stronger medical representation (40%), (68) than was the case in England (Klein 1995) and with little apparent evidence of reluctance from policy makers.

However, the continuation of at least one element of a kind of Scottish particularism which continued to underpin the post-war consensus (pay beds) was questioned by some, given trends in other parts of Britain:

> The existing level of private practice carried out in Glasgow hospitals is comparatively small-- only 40 beds can be used at any one time. The implications of [the government's] Consultative Statement will not result in any major problems in the Greater Glasgow Area. It would however be wrong to assume that the demand for private treatment will not increase as more professional and trade union groups are being covered by private insurance and it may well be that Scotland will follow the trend in the rest of Britain. (69)

Externalisation of Management?

If Florence Nightingale was carrying her lamp through the corridors of the NHS today she would almost certainly be searching for the people in charge (Griffiths Report 1983). (70)

> *The efficiency programme is ahead of schedule – overspending has been cured---financial and manpower controls are in place – strategy reviews are progressing* (GGHB General Manager 1987). (71)

Conservative Caution and a Change Agenda

As the new political administration led by Mrs. Thatcher approached the 1980s the key feature of NHS management was typified by the incorporation of local medical interests into decision making and delivery of health care services within a national policy framework. The cost of the service was borne by the exchequer, the main exception to this being prescription charges. Although not without significant managerial and administrative support systems and structures, managerialism and managerial accountability could hardly be said to be the key to understanding the management of health care. Sir Roy Griffiths' report in the early 1980s (Griffiths 1983) produced the now famous phrase, which, if rather extreme, at least made the point:

> If Florence Nightingale was carrying her lamp through the corridors of the NHS today she would almost certainly be searching for the people in charge. (72)

Rather, the balance of power was with the medical representatives at local level, even if only exercised as a veto, due to the unanimity principle accepted in the 1970s reforms. The governance of the system was completed by an institutional exclusiveness in the sense that other bodies (most notably local authorities) had little role other than minor representation on local health boards or health councils and that many non-medical support services were provided in house; there was the overwhelming preponderance of free provision at the point of care, and local boards operated on consensual grounds. These features were much in evidence in the WRHB case.

Thatcher's policy of state roll-back, which in theory could have been executed in a service overwhelmingly funded from the centre, was engaged very cautiously and as will be seen, in a very circumspect fashion. Some commentators have explained this in terms of the acute political antennae of some leading Conservative principals of whom the most significant was the leader herself (Micklethwaite and Wooldridge 1996; Moon 1994; Kavanagh 1990; Lawson 1993; Fowler 1991). Key evidence of this was seen with the publication of the central policy review staff's paper examining the options for cutting public expenditure. Included in these options was the replacement of the tax financed NHS by a system of private insurance. This idea was quickly 'lost' by Norman Fowler (Klein 1995). This is not to suggest that the government then left the NHS alone. No government has ever been able to do this even if the desire is there. The final part of the case will examine the way in which broad policy thrusts up to 1987 affected the management of health care in Greater Glasgow.

External Influence and the New Managerial Agenda

The symbiotic incorporation-based relationship between the local delivery mechanisms (the health boards) and central government showed a marked shift in the 1980s. There was now an accentuation of the board's role as central government's delivery arm, a strong emphasis on control of costs and the attainment of managerial objectives. This did not occur dramatically. Indeed, there were some clear examples of GGHB successfully resisting government pressures to re-focus the medical professional advisory function away from board to unit management level:

> Proposals are made to simplify the medical advisory system by concentrating it at unit management level-- to enable the medical profession to develop an incisive role in management, doctors must be prepared to give their representatives sufficient authority to state the medical view without necessarily having to resort to prior consultation on every issue. (73)

However, the Board's area medical committee continued to operate at board and area levels. The following year the board, led by its area medical committee, seemed to be playing a brinkmanship game by resisting the full adoption (including medical participation) of unit general management. A circular from the NHS made it quite clear that,

> there should be a unit medical committee corresponding to each unit of local management [and that] senior members of medical staff will be identified to take part in unit management. (74)

The board, however, decided to

> homologate its previous decision to accept advice of the Area Medical Committee and to agree that SHHD be advised that the Board while accepting that the proposed arrangements might be applicable in other parts of Scotland, adhere to the views already submitted to the Department. (75)

The board was finally instructed by the secretary of state to institute unit management, though

> The Board had through the chairman put up a strong case for districts to be maintained but a final decision had been for uniformity throughout Scotland. (76)

The important point to note is that despite unit management being introduced elsewhere in Scotland three years previously, GGHB could hold out for well over half of a parliamentary term. Central government though did appear to be in control of the agenda and were able to influence practices adopted by GGHB. This was not done by reducing medical representation on the board or by any obvious intensification of the process of placing more politically sympathetic voices on the board, but by re-focusing the board's agenda and activity on issues of cost and managerial control. This occurred in Glasgow's case after an attempt to gain extra funding, to reflect higher health care costs due to the city's deprivation, was unsuccessful. Instead, GGHB was informed that it had

> Expenditure greater than its proportion of Scotland's population-- it was also recognised that [due to this] the 1.6% growth in the Scottish Health Service allocation was not applicable to GGHB. GGHB's growth rate was somewhat less than this. (77)

This environment contributed to a very difficult financial situation for Glasgow and provided the context for the managerialist approach, which undoubtedly took hold in GGHB from 1985 just shortly after unit management was put in place. It also became apparent that the financial pressure would intensify. The board's allocation under the Scottish health authorities' resource equalisation (SHARE) formula was to decrease each year for the next five years (from 1986) -- 'an estimated reduction in real terms of £5 million over the next 4-5 years'. (78) The philosophy and ideology of the 'new managerialism' had two important dimensions. First, it addressed local managerial accountability, control of cost and performance and was in this sense presented as devolutionary. But second, strategy would be controlled from the centre. Central government in fact wished to have control over decision making while at the same time de-centralise activity (Hoggett and Hambleton 1988; Hood 1991; Pollitt 1993; Harrison and Wood 1999). This represented a re-configuration of the 1948 settlement which was based largely on a relationship with the centre that prioritised localism as the price required to commit medical professionals to the NHS. In addition to introducing managerial and cost control there was another important aspect of the agenda. The government attempted to alter the governance framework of the NHS by introducing a mixed economy of health care, in effect meaning an increase in private medicine and the privatisation of some non-clinical support services. Another key element too was to be found in the Griffiths Enquiry: the desire for full engagement of medical professionals in the management of health care rather than simply responsibility for distribution of centrally generated funding, a process clearly dis-engaged from medical decisions which were always in the sphere of individual clinician autonomy. The underlying aim behind Griffiths' thinking has been termed 'medical managerialism' (McTavish 2000). Did all this in actual fact change the management of health care in the case studied?

External influence and managerialism   Aspects of managerialism were implemented and to this extent the answer is in the affirmative. Tight cost control and savings were implemented. Given the financial environment which existed, the introduction of such measures were almost a self fulfilling prophecy: a forecast shortfall of c. £ 9 million from 1986-87 saw the board identify savings of up to £ 13 million. The over-riding managerial objective of the unit managers accountable to the board general manager was to 'ensure that the Board would not exceed its projected cash limited allocation in that year'. (79) In these narrowly defined ways the measures were indeed successful:

> The efficiency programme is ahead of schedule-- overspending had been cured-- financial and manpower controls are in place but need refinement-- strategy reviews are progressing but require extra resources to accelerate. (80)

However, the degree and extent to which control measures were accompanied by devolution of control and responsibility to unit managers is questionable. The following statement from the board's general manager is revealing:

> I have been asked several times on visits to unit management teams whether if they make savings in one area they can spend in another. The question reveals a totally niaive misunderstanding of both the present and future difficulties-- all savings will of necessity be taken to the centre and used to reduce the overall Board deficit. (81)

If the board's managerial activities were tightly structured rather than devolved to the level of unit management, what of the other main plank of the new managerialism, strategic control from the centre? The Scottish health authorities' priority for the eighties (SHAPE) framework seemed to provide the machinery for this. The intention was to frame policy and spending in key areas like geriatric care, care for the mentally ill and primary care in support of a preventative programme (McGirr 1988). However, the documentation on the monitoring of this initiative indicated little in terms of targeted programmes set against specifically measurable aims and objectives; concern was almost exclusively on cost and expenditure control. (82) The conclusion was inescapable. A central government focus on managerialism was (in part) implemented. The dominant theme was cost control levered by financial 'encouragement' from the centre, with other elements of the new managerial agenda absent.

Externalisation and Health Service governance   There were three main elements in the attempt to alter governance. The first was the degree to which medical professional interests were to be committed to the clinical/resource management inter-face, medical managerialism. In terms of the continued strong professional control of health service provision this was vital. It was clear that if the department of Health was trying to target clinical cost, then failure of professional clinicians to engage with this process would create difficulties for their continued clinician control of medical interventions and procedures: one extreme outcome could be the centralised categorization and imposition of acceptable procedures in specific circumstances. The second element was the shift from institutional exclusiveness to more collaborative approaches, by their nature representing a shift to external management, and the third, the creation of a mixed economy of health care, which by definition implied a dilution of the NHS's near monopoly of its internal management of health provision.

Medical managerialism   Representatives of the medical profession were very lightly represented on the GGHB group, which drew up and implemented the savings and costs in year 1986-87. (83) The difficulties of doctors assuming managerial roles was succinctly put by the GGHB's area medical committee:

> The importance of involving clinicians in management is recognized [by the SHHD]. While medical involvement in management is essential it is highly unlikely that many hospital consultants or GPs would be interested in a full time role as unit general managers in view of the difficulties of returning to medical practice. (84)

The notion though of medical-professional disengagement and distance from management is mis-leading. The board's area paramedical committee representing dieticians, occupational therapists, radiographers, speech therapists and physiotherapists was, 'in total agreement with the basic criteria for the establishment of general management arrangements and hope to play a full part'. (85) Research elsewhere in Britain has shown a medical professional accommodation to managerialism (Ashburner 1996), largely achieved through the creation of part-time clinical director posts enabling managerial and clinical functions to co-exist for the post holders. There was certainly evidence of a number of such posts in the GGHB area. Fitzgerald (1996) also found evidence of clinicians becoming more involved in management. There were indications too of professional acceptance of some aspects of managerialism: Dr Sam Galbraith MP made a speech in 1988 complimenting GGHB on the 'production of management information on waiting times for specialist appointments supplied to GPs on a regular basis'. (86) As a neuorosurgeon and opposition MP there would be no particular motivation for him to praise such an initiative were it controversial amongst doctors in the health service.

But key was the extent to which medical professionals seem to have exerted some control of medical managerialism in issues like medical audit, the key area of inter-face between clinical and resourcing decisions. The Scottish health services planning council was established in the late 1970s and started to fully function in the 1980s. This had the remit of advising the Secretary of State for Scotland and was composed largely of senior medical figures as represented on all 15 health boards in Scotland. There was no equivalent elsewhere in the UK (Hunter 1986). It was indeed an initiative from this body, which led to consultants' waiting lists becoming available to GPs, the initiative which was praised by Sam Galbraith and referred to above. The council also undertook in-depth studies of various sectors and services. A successful example was its study of the management of orthopaedic services in Scotland ranging from administrative procedures to case management and liaison between medical and para-medical professions. (87) This type of approach touched the critical resourcing issues of clinical practice, which the previous dominance of individual clinician autonomy never could and was crucial to the medical profession retaining key input to medical and clinical audit procedures. It mirrored in many ways the situation post-1990 when many of the protocols on good practice were issued by the royal colleges, thereby retaining medical audit within the boundaries of professional control (Klein 1995). The evidence suggested this was more apparent earlier in Scotland, accounting for the view taken in the 1997 White Paper on the NHS in Scotland that the country led the way with the creation since the late 1980s of the Clinical Resource and Audit Group under the chairmanship of the chief medical officer (Scottish Office Department of Health 1997). It would, however, be inaccurate to suggest by extension to the present that medical audit and resource management are comfortably coupled (see chapter 6).

From institutional exclusiveness to collaboration   After exclusion of local authorities from significant input to the NHS in the 1970s reforms, attempts were made to encourage liaison between health and local authorities in the planning of local provision. In 1980 a small financial allocation (£1m) was made available to GGHB ' to encourage the continuation of co-ordinated planning of services between the NHS and local authorities'. (88) Major collaboration of course was required with the implementation of the Griffiths Review's recommendation that responsibility for funding long stay care be given to local authorities. A collaborative spirit, though, was hardly in evidence in Glasgow:

> We cannot have a blanket policy on funding-- must be negotiated on a scheme by scheme basis. At the heart of the Regional Council's [i.e., the local authority's] paper is the desire to have a long term commitment to transfer resources with patients as they move from hospital into the community, an example being the dowry system when a price is put on the head of individual patients. To safeguard the Board's interests this should be contracted with a specification of the service to be provided rather than being added to the Regional Council's general coffers where value for money will be difficult to determine and where it would be difficult to know if the Council was subsidising other services by reducing the content of the care in the community service. (89)

There was little to suggest that greater Glasgow or Scotland was different from other parts of the UK.

Mixed economy of health care   There were two aspects of the creation of a mixed economy of health care: private care and the provision of support services. In the 1980s, doctors' private care earnings soared, though much skewed by specialism and most certainly by geography (Monopolies and Mergers Commission 1994; Klein 1995). The use of private care was relatively insignificant in Glasgow (in the rest of Scotland too), and there seemed little concerted enthusiasm amongst doctors in support of private care as the following episodes illustrated. In 1982 the chairman of the consultants committee of the Institute of Neurological Sciences in Glasgow attempted to gain GGHB approval for private treatment in the department of neuro radiology at the Southern General Hospital. Approval for this was given by the area medical committee of the GGHB on the understanding that government guidelines were adhered to. (90) The key guideline was 'Principle 2' of NHS guidelines: 'subject to clinical considerations earlier private consultation should not lead to earlier NHS admission or to earlier access to NHS diagnostic procedures'. The main issue was the interpretation of the time to be 'added on' after a private inpatient had been diagnosed. Three of the seven consultants supported the application. One of the remaining four, Sam Galbraith received clarification from the Scottish Office:

> The effect of Principle 2 is that a patient should not be admitted more quickly following a private consultation than if he or she had remained under the NHS throughout, taking account of the patient's relative urgency. I would agree with your interpretation that a private in patient in the case you quote would also have to wait 6 months for admission. (91)

Clearly the GGHB had to rescind its earlier approval, which it did. (92) The significant point was that that fewer than half of the consultants supported the initial application for private treatment, hardly a resounding endorsement, though views were clearly divided.

In the creation of a mixed economy of health care support services, the broad NHS dominance (if not monopoly) consensus, which epitomised health board governance through the 1950s and 1960s and most of the 1970s, mirrored at peak political level, was strained. Privatisation provided an adversarial arena as indicated by a letter from the Opposition spokesman on the NHS in Scotland to GGHB:

> It will not have escaped your notice that the circular on behalf of the Secretary of State for Scotland does not quote any section of the Health Service Act which gives him the power to privatise domestic catering and laundry services in the NHS-- the first three words of the circular says 'the circular asks'. (93)

The chairman of the board referred to this letter at another meeting, this time with the Scottish Trade Unions Congress (STUC),

> While the actual wording of the circular might not use the term 'instruction' it was clearly intended as a directive to health boards-- in his view it would be necessary to carry out the Secretary of State's instructions. (94)

Nevertheless, the privatisation of many support services did go ahead as it did elsewhere.

However, the board did show total consensus in its opposition to central government's plans for a private hospital in Clydebank run by a private for profit international health care organisation, Health Care International:

> It is generally accepted that nurse recruitment would be a problem in the 1990s – scepticism of the chairman that all HCI's nursing staff will be met from overseas recruitment – medical staff required by HCI likely to be recruited from among top consultants creating considerable medical staffing problems in NHS hospitals – also shortage of trained paramedical staff – the development was not seen as one which could be considered as prestigious for the Glasgow area as it did not introduce facilities or techniques not already available.

The Committee agreed to recommend to the board that this development would significantly interfere with the provision of NHS services or operate significantly to the disadvantage of NHS patients. (95)

The board agreed with this recommendation but the HCI development still went ahead with considerable support from central government including derelict land grants and a range of other supports. The political consensus at peak level, which underpinned so much of health delivery in earlier periods, was certainly not in evidence.

Summary and Conclusion

The legislative enactment of the NHS gave executive powers to RHBs to manage hospitals. Medical professional control of this key component of health service management was implemented and realised through the power of resource distribution, the representative structures adopted and the influence of the medical profession in the creation of administrative and professional structures surrounding all areas of RHB activity. This settlement was re-inforced by a party political consensual support for the NHS at peak political level and the internal management practices were underpinned by the institutional exclusivity of the NHS, thereby excluding powerful alternative institutional interests like local authorities.

While existing internal practices were strengthened in the 1960s - with a strong rationalistic and businesslike focus to many non-clinical areas of management as well as increased training and support in some clinical, administrative and medical areas - there were instances of rigidities in internal practice inhibiting the effective use of resources.

Attempts were made in the 1970s to alter internal management arrangements by external influence. The reform agenda and consultative process raised the possibility of local government influence on health care, not welcomed by existing structures and not implemented. There was also an attempt to introduce general management across the UK: while in the event this did not challenge existing professional control, since medical professional representatives on executive bodies were given veto rights, the research indicated substantial differences in Scotland's approach to reform. Here there was a greater cohesiveness and resistance to encroachments on existing internal management practices and processes.

The final period of the case was 1980-1987. In these years systematic efforts were made to disturb the prevailing internal arrangements and introduce change by central government initiation. There were various components some of which were initially witnessed in the 1970s. First, the introduction of cost and management disciplines at executive delivery level. Second, the introduction of a mixed economy of health care and a challenge to institutional exclusiveness. Third, the inclusion (or absorption) of medical professional interests into the managerial clinical decision process. This was a radical departure from the 1948 settlement which separated clinical decision making and execution of resource distribution:

while both were professionally controlled they were institutionally separated with ramifications for cost and resource control

The case illustrated very emphatic managerial controls, not surprising given financial pressures from central government. The evidence also indicated less enthusiasm than other parts of Britain for the introduction of privatized aspects of health care both medical and non-medical, though the health board was required to follow a UK government policy agenda. Institutional exclusiveness was challenged by legislation which gave funding for long stay care to local authorities, though collaborative frameworks between council and health board to implement did not proceed smoothly in this case.

Finally the external attempt to engage clinicians in management and in the clinical/resourcing inter-face was seen in the case. Although externally influenced, a key implementation instrument, the Scottish health service planning council, was as much a creation of the medical profession in Scotland as it was of central government. This was crucial to medical professionals retaining key in-put to medical and clinical audit procedures. This process was developed further in Scotland and other parts of the UK after 1987.

Notes

1. Cited in Klien, R. (1995), *The New Politics of the NHS*, London: Longman   p. 28.
2. The establishment of the NHS is a fascinating study indicating evolutionary developments towards some form of national system from the 1920s and 1930s boosted particularly in Scotland with emergency war time hospital provision (Davidson 1947, Johnston 1952, Klein 1995, Bartrip 1996), rifts between different parts of the medical profession at key times (Klein 1995, Webster 1988) political posturing and a degree of hostility (from the BMA in particular) towards the post war Labour government, not quite matched by hostility to its policies per se (Bartrip 1996). There was also serious debate within the Labour government between Herbert Morrison who wished a strong role for local authorities in the new service (backed by some thinking in the civil service) and Bevan who did not (Klein 1995; see also footnote 25).
3. HB 16/1/2 Minute of WRHB meeting 19 June 1951; HB16/1/3 Minute of WRHB meeting 30 May 1952.
4. RHB 16/1/3. Notes of a meeting of Chairmen of Boards of Management 4 December 1952.
5. Klein, R. (1995), *The New Politics of the NHS*, London: Longman p 29.
6. HB 28/2/1-2/12. Minutes of WRHB meetings, various 1950-1958.
7. HB 16/1/2. Minute of Board of Management Glasgow South Western Hospital (GSWH) 30 January 1951.
8. HB 16/1/2. Minute of Board of Management GSWH 24 April 1951.
9. HB 28/2/63 Paper on the Wright Report on Medical Staffing, SHHD 11 September 1963.
10. HB 16/1/5. Minute of Association of Scottish Hospitals Board of Management September 1964.
11. HB 28/2/63. Paper on the Wright Report on Medical Staffing, SHHD 11 September 1963.

12. Doctors filled the posts of medical superintendents in Scottish hospitals. See for example, HB 28/2/11.
13. HB 28/2/11 Minute of general Purposes Committee WRHB 9 July 1948.
14. HB 28/2/1. Letter from the Association of Secretaries and Treasurers of Boards of Management of Hospitals in the Western Region of Scotland 17 November 1948.
15. HB 16/1/14-15. Minutes of Staffing Committee WRHB, various 1952-1958.
16. HB 28/2/4. Paper presented to Medical Staffing Committee WRHB September 1953.
17. HB 16/1/5. Agenda item for WRHB meeting 27 April 1954. Letter from Professor J Howie re Selection Procedures for Registrars and Senior Registrars.
18. HB 28/2/9. Paper presented by AK Bowman Senior Administrative Medical Officer to WRHB Hospital Staffing Committee 7 February 1956.
19. HB 28/2/3. Minute of WRHB Hospital Staffing Sub Committee 7 August 1950.
20. HB 28/2/4. Minute of WRHB Medical Establishment Sub Committee 16 October 1951.
21. HB 28/2/12 Minute of Special Meeting of WRHB General Purposes Committee to Discuss Dept. of Health Memorandum 'Some Problems of Organisation and Policy for Regional Hospital Boards' 14 July 1959.
22. The General Practitioner service was organized and funded separately. GPs were self employed and contracted independently with the NHS. These arrangements are still in place, though the Scottish Executive is considering establishing and funding a number of employed GPs to target provision in certain postal code areas (2001).
23. HB 16/1/15. Agenda Item 5 for Association of Scottish Hospitals Boards of Management Meeting with Regional Board Chairmen 29 December 1964.
24. HB 16/1/1. Minute of WRHB 25 April 1950.
25. HB 16/1/1. Letter from WRHB Chairman to Hospital Boards of Management 10 May 1949.
26. HB 16/1/1. Letter from Norman W Graham, Department of Health Scotland to WRHB 9 December 1949.
27. Public Record Office MH 77/73, letter dated 18 July 1946, cited in Klein (1995).
28. HB 16/1/10. Memorandum on Pay Beds to Dr Charles McKay, Medical Superintendent Southern General Hospital from G Timbury, Secretary of the Medical Staff Association, 26 January 1961.
29. HB 16/1/11. Minute of WRHB 30 May 1961.
30. HB 55/M/43. Consultative Paper on Private Practice, presented to GGHB meeting 17 July 1979.
31. HB 28/2/10. Joint Meeting Between WRHB Hospital Staffing Committee and Western Regional Consultants and Specialists Committee 20 November 1956.
32. HB 28/2/9. Minute of a Meeting Between Representatives of WRHB and Department of Health, 16 May 1956.
33. HB 28/2/9. Minute of a Meeting Between Representatives of WRHB and Board of Management of Royal infirmary and Associated Hospitals to Discuss Regional Radiotherapy Unit, 16 April 1956.
34. HB 28/2/10. Minute of Meeting WRHB Hospital Services Committee 11 February 1957.
35. HB 28/2/10. Minute of Special Meeting WRHB, re Radiotherapy Service 11 April 1957.
36. There is ample evidence, in both primary and secondary sources to suggest that resource management and concern for efficiency was considered very important in health service thinking prior to the 1960s.

37. HB 28/2/8. Note of a Meeting Between RHB Chairmen and Mr. B Millan, Scottish Office Minister, 17 December 1969.
38. HB 28/2/62. WRHB. Paper on Departmental Costing, 23 April 1961.
39. HB 28/2/19. WRHB Establishment Committee. Report on Work Study and Relations With Trade Unions, 7 July 1966.
40. HB 16/1/10. Minute of WRHB Meeting 24 February 1959.
41. HB 16/1/10. Minute of Meeting, Association of Scottish Hospital Boards of Management, 25 April 1959.
42. HB 16/1/13. Minute of WRHB Meeting 14 March 1961.
43. HB 2/15. Minute of WRHB Establishment Committee Meeting 3 May 1962.
44. HB 28/2/3. WRHB Nursing Services Sub Committee Report on Management Courses, 23 April 1970.
45. HB 28/2/22. Minute of WRHB Nursing Services Sub Committee meeting 2 June 1969.
46. HB 28/2/18. WRHB Symposium on the Application of Electronic and Digital Computers in the Hospital Service, 23 November 1965.
47. HB 28/2/22. Minute WRHB Meeting 25 November 1969.
48. HB 28/2/20. Minute WRHB Establishment Committee Meeting 6 July 1967.
49. HB 28/2/15. WRHB. Procedure for Considering Proposals for Capital Projects Submitted by Boards of Management, 5 September 1962.
50. HB 28/2/20 WRHB. Chairman's Comments on the Period 1963-1967.
51. HB 28/2/17 WRHB. Notes of a Meeting Between the Major Buildings Progress Sub Committee and Representatives of SHHD, 21 December 1966. This approach to increased output needs in an era of labour shortage and constraints (and consequent cost pressures) was in contrasting to the shipbuilding, which continued in the 1960s to build conventionally, tied to the craft system (see chapter 3 case study 1). Industrial building in the construction industry was not new: this had been pioneered by weir in the 1920s in the west of Scotland though only had limited success (se chapter 1).
52. HB 55/M/42. GGHB. Notes of a Meeting With the Secretary of State for Scotland, Mr. B Millan, 4 December 1978.
53. HB 55/M/38 GGHB. Enquiry on the Use of Resources in the NHS. NHS Circular 1976(Gen) 16: Response of GGHB Area Medical Committee, ND.
54. HB 28/2/70. Working Party on Hospital Revenue Expenditure 2 June 1970.
55. Ibid.
56. HB 55/M/41 GGHB. Paper for Consideration by the Policy and Planning Committee on SHARE Report 6 March 1978.
57. It is however perhaps significant that the English Royal Commission was chaired by Redcliffe-Maud and not one of the country's leading academics in public administration, Sir Norman Chester. It is suggested by Fry (1999) that part of the reason for the appointment of Redciffe-Maud rather than Chester was that the latter was thought to wish hospitals brought into the sphere of local government.
58. HB 28/2/65. WRHB. North East Regional Health Board's Submission to the Royal Commission on Local Government in Scotland, 28 October 1966.
59. HB 28/2/68. WRHB. Regional Hospital Boards Scotland, Administrative Reorganisation of the Scottish Health Service, 19 August 1970.
60. *British Medical Journal*, Editorial Comment 3 June 1970.
61. Klein, R (1995) *The New Politics of the NHS*, p.87 London: Longman.
62. Other perceptions however assess that the government's approach, if not the final outcome, was well crafted, bringing together and including professional structures and rationalistic planning approaches. See Harrison and Wood (1999).

63. HB 28/2/25 WRHB. Reorganisation of the NHS. Draft Discussion Paper, SHHD 28 March 1972.

64. Confidential information given to me suggests that the background of un-enthusiasm for much of the managerial agenda in health in the Scottish Office was accounted for by the Chief Medical Officer in Scotland (Sir John Brotherston) 'vetoing behind the scenes movement towards the implementation of the Farquarson Lang Report'.

65. Klein, R (1995) *The New Politics of the NHS*, London: Longman   p. 39.

66. The importance of health in the Scottish political-administrative structure is interesting, perhaps linked traditionally to the significant contributions made to medicine by Scottish practice from the late nineteenth century - in both clinical and public health arenas. A leading Scottish historian has referred to the latter part of the nineteenth century as the golden age of Scottish medicine (Devine 2000). The role played by the 'formidable' group of Medical Officers of Health in the same period (in Glasgow, Aberdeen and Edinburgh) has been commented on: ' they led the battle for cleanliness, drainage, public parks, civic fever hospitals, better housing and collection of statistics to the continued embarrassment of the City Fathers' (Crowther, 1990 p. 285). After creation of the NHS, the position and status of health in Scotland and England differed. In England, after Bevan became Minister of Labour in 1951, the Department of Health's responsibility was reduced and the Ministry lost cabinet status. It was not until Enoch Powell was promoted to Cabinet in 1962 that cabinet status was restored, a situation however that was not permanent: Harold Wilson's first cabinet in 1964 excluded health and only in the late 1960s when the Ministries of Health and Social Security were merged under Richard Crossman that permanent cabinet membership was established. Absence from the cabinet denied health a heavy weight presence in standing up to Treasury pressure. The situation in Scotland was different. Here health always had a strong champion in cabinet through the territorial remit of the Secretary of State for Scotland, always a cabinet position. This political contrast is mirrored in the administration of health in Scotland. In England, health was seen, in the early years of the NHS as a relatively unattractive proposition for a civil service career and was therefore avoided by the high fliers needed to take the new machinery forward and negotiate strongly with the Treasury (Kogan 1969). The evidence for this is strong: all permanent secretaries at the Department of Health prior to Sir Bruce Fraser's appointment in the 1960s were occupying their last career posts; the firm civil service career pattern which existed by the mid 1960s whereby the majority of permanent secretaries had spent time at the Treasury, had not been replicated in health. The contrast with Scotland was marked. The head of the Department of Health for Scotland / SHHD was usually seen as a staging post in the Scottish Office: John Anderson was recruited from the SHHD, served as Secretary of the Department of Health 1956-59, became secretary of the Scottish Home Department and in 1963 chairman of the Board of Customs and Excise. When Anderson left the Scottish Health Department in 1959 Douglas Haddow who had risen through the ranks of the Health Department, transferred to SDD in 1962 and in 1965 succeeded Sir Wiliam Murie as permanent Under Secretary at theScottish Office succeeded him. If Health was the place for mobile career movers in England, this was not so in Scotland (Webster 1996).

67. HB 55/M/43. GGHB. Consultative Paper on Private Medicine, 17 July 1979.

68. HB 28/2/26. GGHB. Paper on NHS Reorganisation in Scotland: members of Glasgow board 1973. This percentage was almost as high as the peak medical representation identified in the WRHB archive from 1947 through the 1950s and 1960s.

69. HB 55/M/43 GGHB. Paper for Consideration by the Policy and Planning Committee, 3 September 1979.
70. Griffiths Report (1983), NHS Management Enquiry: Report to the Secretary of State for Social Services, p.12, London: DHSS.
71. HB 55/M/53 GGHB Policy and Planning Committee Report: Managerial and Financial Review-One Year On, 1 June 1987.
72. Griffiths Report (1983), NHS Management Enquiry: Report to the Secretary of State for Social Services, p12, London: DHSS.
73. HB 55/M/46. GGHB. Medical Advice and Management in the Scottish Health Service. A Consultative Paper, SHHD, June 1981.
74. HB 55/M/53 GGHB Policy and Planning Committee Report: Managerial and Financial Review-One Year On, 1 June 1987.
75. HB 55/M/47. GGHB. Minute of Policy and Planning Committee meeting, 6 December 1982.
76. HB 55/M/49. GGHB. Minute of meeting between GGHB and South Eastern Local Health Council, 9 April 1984.
77. HB 55/M/47. GGHB. Note of a meeting between GGHB and Parliamentary Under Secretary of State Mr. J Mac Kay, 2 September 1982.
78. HB 55/M/51. GGHB. Policy and Planning Committee, Paper No. 86/23, GGHB Strategy Review, 7 April 1986.
79. HB 55/M/50. GGHB. Policy and Planning Committee, Paper No. 85/113 Confidential, 11 November 1985.
80. HB 55/M/53. GGHB. Policy and Planning Committee, Report: Managerial and Financial Review- One Year On, 1 June 1987.
81. HB 55/M/51. GGHB. Policy and Planning Committee, Paper No. 86/23 Strategy Review, 7 April 1986.
82. HB 55/M/47. GGHB. Policy and Planning Committee, Paper on NHS Circular No. 1981 (Gen) 46-Monitoring of Programmes Towards Implementing the SHAPE Priorities, 5 April 1982.
83. HB 55/M/50. GGHB. Policy and Planning Committee Paper: Financial Situation 1986-87. Confidential, 11 November 1985.
84. HB 55/M/51. GGHB. Minute of Special Board Meeting to Discuss General Management at Unit Level and the Development of Senior Management Structures, 1 September 1986.
85. Ibid. Response from Paramedical Committee.
86. HB 55/M/54. GGHB. Minute of Policy and Planning Committee-ref to speech made by Mr. Sam Galbraith MP, 14 June 1988.
87. HB 55/M/54. GGHB. Report prepared for Policy and Planning Committee: Future of Health Service Planning Council, 11 January 1988.
88. HB 55/M/45. GGHB. Minute of Policy and Planning Committee re Joint Planning and Support, Financial Arrangements NHS Circular (Gen) 5, 6 May 1980.
89. HB 55. GGHB. Strategy Review. Memorandum from P Wilson Unit general Manager to L Peterkin General Manager. In Confidence, 2 September 1988.
90. HB 55/M/47. GGHB. Minute of Policy and Planning Committee, 4 May 1982.
91. HB 55/M/47. Letter from LC Cumming, SHHD, to Sam Galbraith, 10 July 1982.
92. HB 55/M/47. GGHB. Minute of Policy and Planning Committee, 7 February 1983.
93. HB 55/M/48. GGHB. Letter from H Ewing MP to Chairman, GGHB, 19 September 1983.
94. HB 55/M/49. GGHB. Note of a Meeting Between Representatives of STUC and GGHB, 31 July 1984.

95.   HB 55/M/53. GGHB. Minute of Special Meeting of Policy and Planning Committee, 17 August 1987.

Chapter 10

Case Study 4: Education in Glasgow and Strathclyde 1955-1992

Synopsis

The case studied the management of education departments in Glasgow and Strathclyde from 1955-1992. Themes were researched in three distinct time periods: 1955 to the post Wheatley Royal Commission restructuring of local government in 1976; from the introduction of corporate management until the end of the 1980s; the new managerial environment from 1989 to 1992. In the first of these periods, internal management of the education department in Glasgow was considerably strengthened and the methods used to achieve this were the development of 'exclusive' links between senior managers and the elected member education committee of the council, the growth of managerial support structures and an increasing centralisation of management. This was contextualised within the traditional administrative structures of the local authority, which as far as education were concerned included elements of external management of the relationship in with central government's Scottish Office education department. In the corporate era, located in this case within Strathclyde Regional Council, from the mid-1970s to the late-1980s, the management of the education department was significantly affected by rivalry and division between the council's corporate centre and education department. Education maintained its strong traditional external links and external management was an important part of the operation of the department in these years. In the new managerial period, external influence on management was part of a political drive from central government to introduce generic approaches to management. Departmental management at the end of the 1980s did not appear well equipped for such and environment. This however changed after 1989 when there was a further external focus to council management which saw a shift from 'local authority government' to 'governance', and ultimately role reduction with many activities previously internally managed by councils becoming externalised (or devolved) to other agencies: the response of the education department in its attempt to retain internal control and management of schools was of particular significance.

- Strengthening of internal management: 1955-local government reform

- Corporate structures and departmental management 1976-1989:internal and external management
- New managerialism 1989-1992: externalisation of management?

The Strengthening of Internal Management: From 1955 to the Restructuring of Local Government

> *Education administration exists to meet the needs of the children in our schools and therefore must be directed by officials who have first hand experience of these needs* (Director of Education, Glasgow Corporation 1955). (1)

Internal management of the education department in Glasgow was considerably strengthened in the two decades after 1955. This was achieved in three broad ways: by cultivating a strategy of exclusive links between senior management in the department and the education committee of the council; by the growth of managerial and bureaucratic support structures; centralisation of management.

Exclusivity of Links Between Senior Management and the Education Committee.

Significant evidence exists to indicate a close and direct link, developed and maintained between committee and senior staff. A major review of the department in 1955, advised a splitting of the roles of educational administration and policy-making with the latter being the preserve of the director of education and his senior professional staff and the former re-defined as managerial rather than educational. The director in a report written and presented to the education committee carefully rebutted this proposition on two grounds.
First,

> The recommendations are founded on the fallacy that it is possible to divide educational administration into two separate spheres, matters which have a teaching implication and those which do not-- educational administration exists to meet the needs of the children in our schools and therefore must be directed by officials who have first hand experience of these needs.

And second,

> I [the Director] consider that I have the right to advise the Committee on how the services of the deputes appointed to assist me in exercising these powers and duties may best be deployed; I am convinced that the *intervention of a third party in* this matter would have an unfortunate and crippling effect on the direction of policy.

Lest it was thought that the most senior official could be an administrative or managerial functionary, the director pointed out,

It is significant that the Advisory Council have stressed that senior officials in educational administration should have higher educational qualifications. Since the passing of the Education Act in 1945 it has been the invariable practice of authorities both in England and Scotland to require that Directors and their Deputes should possess both educational and administrative experience. (2)

Just over a decade later there was further evidence of the strategy of maintaining a clear and unified line between senior staff and committee, during the creation of boards of management for the city's further education colleges. The parameters for these boards were set out in a letter from the director to Baillie John Mains of the education committee on 25 November 1963:

With the increasing number of further education colleges to be opened in Glasgow the future pattern of administration in these colleges will inevitably be the establishment of Boards of Management as advisory bodies to assist the Education Committee-- the dominant partner in the management of further education colleges would however be the Education Committee whose members are publicly elected and responsible to rate payers for education policy and expenditure. (3)

The subsequent management of the boards was interesting. Some boards were indeed high powered, containing some of the most senior figures in industry, commerce and the trade union movement. In 1966 the board of Anniesland College included a director of Yarrow shipbuilders, a director of WS Gordon a Glasgow engineering company, the divisional works director of L Sterne and Co. Ltd. and the Scottish Secretary of the National Union of General and Municipal Workers. (4) Such a powerful Board would presumably wish to exercise some influence over matters such as appointments. However there was no doubt where the power lay: between senior education officials and the education committee.

The present position is that Boards interview candidates for posts as Assistant Teachers and make a recommendation to the FE Department. In the case of promoted posts, the sub committee on promoted posts conducts the interview to which the Principal of the college and chairman of the Board *are invited*-- it is suggested that the functions of the Board be extended to consider a list of applicants for promoted posts and to recommend and leet to the Committee. Director recommends this *provided that the Convenor of the sub committee retained the right to add other applicants to this list.* [italics in original document] (5)

Growth of Managerial and Bureaucratic Support Structures

The development of managerial and bureaucratic hierarchies occurred to a considerable extent against a background of growth in the school building programme and the significant expansion from the 1960s of the further education sector. The proliferation of further education provision was accompanied by a promotional hierarchy to support growth. The increase in full-time students was over 100% between 1960 and 1966 (2,025-4,061), part-time day students just under 100% (9,123-17,925) and full-time teachers by 136% (313-740). In 1966 plans were approved for 4 new colleges in Glasgow to service 31,250 day release places. Four new senior managerial/professional appointments were made at the Glasgow Corporation headquarters. (6) A promotional hierarchy was created within further education colleges on the basis of '1 promoted to 4 un-promoted'.

There was though an element of external involvement in this: while the education committee was presented with a case and argument for these structures and at the end of the day had the right of approval, the key 'permission' sought for the implementation of proposed structures was from central government through the Scottish Office Scottish Education Department. (7) The role played by other parts of the council (e.g., the town clerk's department) or advice given by organisation and methods staff (located in the town clerk's department) must be considered marginal, even as far as non-teaching posts and hierarchies were concerned: an organisation and methods review of non-teaching staff requirements was undertaken in 1962. The director of education's report on this to the sub-committee noted that,

> notes made by the O and M review did not reflect an understanding of the educational process of which non teaching work is an essential and integral part, although they gave a fair picture of mechanical aspects in terms of clerical work. (8)

At departmental level there was also significant investment in human resource through training which compared very favourably with many private sector practices at the time: it would indeed be ironic were it to be otherwise in one of Britain's largest education departments. Officials were involved in design, and as participants in, a part-time Diploma in Public Administration offered at Glasgow University from the mid 1960s; attempts were made to vocationalise this course and tailor to the specific needs of participants:

> the vocational aspect of the course is now being emphasised and among several planned changes third year students specialise in such subjects as 'administration of health services', 'administration of physical planning', 'administration of an education service' etc. (9)

Staff in the City's colleges participated in a programme of training and development activities at the Further Education Staff College serving England and Wales, (10) including: courses in the management of office and registration services in colleges; 'Improvement of Efficiency and Economy of Teaching in Technical Colleges. Methods, Organisation, Buildings and Equipment'; (11) refresher courses in industry for further education teachers were institutionalised -some of these programmes had important learning transfer spin offs between teachers, the colleges and the companies involved; (12) there was also a steady, if small, stream of individuals in both colleges and schools being seconded to pursue higher education qualifications. In 1967, several college registrars were supported to attend a college registrar's course at the F.E Staff College the objective of which was 'to enable registrars understand basic techniques of organisation and methods study and to define the areas of work where the technique can best be used'. The participants on return cascaded the programme throughout other colleges. (13)

Centralisation of Management

The centralisation of managerial control was another key feature of departmental supremacy. A proposal in 1955 that many services including school painting, transport and the up-keep of schools' grounds should be transferred to other parts of the council or de-centralised within the department was strongly resisted. This resistance was justified on the grounds that,

> they are part of the common services to the schools by the education department. They have been developed to what is admitted to be a high degree of efficiency in the closest association with the requirements of our schools-essentially because they have been an integral part of the education service over the years. We are convinced that to decentralise them would be a retrograde step, which would reflect ultimately on the efficiency of the schools.

Other seemingly innocuous measures of de-centralisation were resisted:

> We disagree with the view expressed that 'one of the few regular jobs of reasonable calibre performed by school clerks is janitor paybill work'. We do not agree that absence records of janitors, cleaners and dining attendants should be transferred to schools; it would lead to duplication of records.

Suggestions to devolve the ordering of school supplies to schools was opposed,

> since extra responsibility is being placed on the schools----and this deflects from the main task of the teaching profession

Overall control by the directorate and through it the education committee can also be identified in the arguments used by the director against the proposal that teacher appraisal and review should be done by exception. The director stated:

> It is not agreed that it is sufficient to have a report only on the teachers who are regarded as unsatisfactory. In our view it is essential that the Committee should receive annual reports on each member of its teaching staff. (14)

Interview procedures for senior appointments in both schools and colleges also symbolised centralised control. A letter from the depute director to a senior councillor indicated his views that appointment to promoted posts in further education should not be devolved to college boards of management:

> I am inclined to the view that the sub committee should continue to interview for promoted positions. It is a most important aspect of educational administration

and it is a basic tenet of democratic local government that such vital issues should be determined by elected representatives. Using this procedure, the sub committee we currently have naturally acquires valuable insight into the entire field, becomes familiar with staff who are seeking promotion and can use their knowledge to make the most appropriate appointments. A Board [of a college] concerned with one college will never achieve such an insight into the whole field. (15)

Archives also showed a close involvement of the directorate in selection and appointment of all posts above basic teacher/lecturer and in some cases there was hands on involvement. Symbolically all candidates for senior positions were in no doubt where power and control lay: all interviews were held in the education department headquarters not in the institution where the post was located.

The evolution of this strengthening management structure led to an interesting juxtaposition on the eve of local government reform and the creation of a corporate structure within the new Strathclyde Council. These strong departmental structures were not simply demolished along with Glasgow Corporation. Prior to the reorganisation, there was a series of Local Government Reorganisation Working Party Reports. The education report was particularly focused on education rather than corporate approaches to service delivery per se:

> There is a great need for co-ordination of the development plans of different services in the timing of new education projects, location of new premises in the deployment of architectural and other services. The chief concern is with the educational aims and philosophy, curricular content and teaching methods. This also means providing teachers and other staff with an advisory service with in service training, and gearing the administrative machine to draw upon and pool experience and to disseminate ideas, undertaking research and keeping in touch with educational developments. (16)

Importantly, a significant number of key personnel in Glasgow's education department transferred to Strathclyde. (17)

Corporate Structures and Departmental Management 1976-1989: Internal and External Management

> *The proposed arrangements [for the introduction of corporate structures] would appear to diminish the authority of the head of the education department. This is unsatisfactory* (Director of Education, Strathclyde Region 1976). (18)

The newly formed Regional Council with its fledgling corporatist structure and evolving chief executive's department at the centre also housed Scotland's largest education authority. The strengthening of the education department in these years must be viewed to a large extent in the context of a rivalry with the corporate centre of the council as represented through the chief executive's department; but also in the context of the education department's management of external relationships which the department often used to shape its position within the council.

The organisational structure and the consequent managerial practices in education occurred without much reference to the corporate centre, but with much reference to the department's own headquarters. This was in a sense inevitable since the education department had its own structure in place well before there was a chief executive's support infrastructure let alone a fully formed department. Correspondence with senior staff and with the external consultants appointed to advise on structures indicated strongly that arrangements were driven by the director himself. For example, in a communication with PA Consultants the director stated:

> I would be prepared to allow divisional education officers a certain amount of discretion in practice though they would require to convince me-- as you can see I favour an allocation of responsibilities by function rather than the branching system contemplated by Mr McFarlane [Director of Policy Planning and very close to the chief executive]-- my system is better because it allows one officer to specialise in a particular field such as staffing, curriculum development, buildings etc. (19)

This divisional matrix structure was adopted in education and persisted for the entire life of the council. Like most matrix structures it was messy and led to a mix of operational and policy (later to be called strategic) issues being taken at both headquarters and divisional levels. Such confusion in matrix structures has been well documented and criticised (Jacques 1989). By the mid-1980s the relationship between the headquarters and divisions seemed to be well defined in matters of devolved financial management: a disciplinary situation for mal-administration in Glasgow division in 1985 indicated considerable de-centralisation of financial accountability. In a memorandum to the divisional education officer for Glasgow an overspend of £750,000 had been identified; the memorandum highlighted the degree of responsibility permitted at divisional level. The name of the disciplined individual has been omitted.

> Although information from finance was constantly misleading, there is nonetheless mal-administration by x who concluded in 1984 that supplies would be under spent by £895,000 and refuted contrary views and proceeded to spend without taking steps to monitor or control this expenditure-- no choice but to hold a disciplinary hearing. (20)

The budgeting and policy options process at various times indicated a very clear divergence between the approach of the chief executive's and education departments: this was more than just a departmental haggling over resources, but more a fundamental disagreement about the policy options and budgeting processes organised through the chief executive. For instance, in a communication with the chief executive 17 October 1978, the director stated:

The crucial question of the initial resource allocation to the department of education is crude and simplistic, and I do not have any confidence in the budgetary control system. (21)

A potentially explosive clash between the two departments in 1986 clearly illustrated that the education department was a serious alternative point of power and influence within the council. In January 1986 a demand for additional £2.5 million of financial savings was requested from the education service. On 8 January the director wrote to the senior depute chief executive:

> I am now unable to proceed further since the chairman, Councillor Green, is unwilling to discuss and agree the complete package of savings with me. I attach a note from the chairman and one of his vice chairmen refusing to follow procedures-- hey make it clear I would have no political support from them for any cuts additional to those already approved. (22)

These additional cuts were not imposed and the budget for 1987-1988 gave

> an extra £ 1.5 million for education. A much greater injection was required but I [the director] am very pleased and much happier about the manner in which the exercise has been conducted this year. (23)

There were other instances of this department having a perspective different on occasion to that emanating from the corporate centre. Some gentle advice was given to a department secondee on placement in the chief executive's department:

> I would caution you strongly not to become involved in so called 'issues' which appear to interest certain members of the Chief Executives office such as 'economies which could arise from de-segregation of schools' and 'overlap / duplication in the service provided by the social work department and community education'. (24)

The education department used the external relationships it had with the wider educational community, including with central government, to its advantage. Early in the life of Strathclyde, an ambitious pitch was made to capture the very core of the department's activity for the attainment of council's corporate objectives. A review of departmental structures in 1976 recommended

> that the Regional Council should negotiate with the Scottish Education Department (SED) clarifying questions of accountability and authority.
> -- that the education service in Strathclyde be subjected to far greater scrutiny than at present-- on balance it is recommended that an inspectorial force be employed by the Regional Council. Negotiations with the SED would be required to clarify the respective roles of the Council and the SED. The review group believes that control of the inspectorial function should rest with the body which is accountable for education in the region viz the Regional Council; that the present dominant role

of the SED both in curriculum and inspection leads to confusion of accountability and weakness of management. (25)

The director evidently saw little problem in the current arrangements, saying in a communication with the chief executive,

> In recent years there has been an increasing relaxation of central government controls in respect of education services and I do not consider any of the present practices of the SED restrictive or interference in the independent action of an education authority. (26)

The following month the director stated a view divergent with the policy review group on possible council role in inspection:

> On the issue of advisory / inspection functions in relation to the education service, it is my view that HM Inspectorate perform a valuable advisory / inspectorial role in the education service and that we learn much from a wider knowledge which they can bring on educational matters. (27)

So clearly the director of education was not of the same view as the corporatists (as expressed in the policy review group) for an activist council role vis a vis the SED. At this time an enhanced council role in inspection did not occur; and as will be seen later, when it did become council practice a decade later under differing circumstances it was very much led, not resisted, by the department, with the chief executive's very much a minor player.

The external relationships which the department had, appeared to be efficient and sometimes more so than the chief executive's. Of considerable significance when assessing differing perspectives was the observation of differing policy networks (developed over a long period of time) within which the education department officials operated. Records show the director having regular (formal and less formal) meetings with the chief HMI, Mr Clark, at the Scottish Office. This was hardly surprising but the informal networks which the education department had with the Scottish Office were often more efficient than the formal mechanisms used by the council 'officially' through the chief executive, a point made by the director. In a memorandum to the chief executive marked 'private and confidential' re the capital budget 1981-1982, he wrote:

> Mr Halliday has regular informal meetings with appropriate colleagues in the SED and the Department of Architectural and Related Services re the building programme. I initiated these meetings in 1975 as a constructive alternative to the annual set piece confrontation. These meetings have been consistently fruitful and have given us a clear understanding of the problems of central government officials and vice versa.
>
> Recognising the unprecedented difficulties in 1980-81, officials at the SED indicated informally at one such meeting that our overspending of £2million could be met by Lothian's under spend of £3 million. Before this could be effected, you and Mr Paterson had discussed the matter at a higher level within the Scottish Office, and in the light of that discussion our informal arrangement had to fall. (28)

There were other instances of education policy networks being used to shape the council's education agenda. The director attended a very significant conference of the Society of Education Officers in 1986. The importance of this conference was revealed in a communication between the director and his depute:

> The final speaker at the conference was Mr Chris Patten a relatively new Minister of State for Education with responsibility for England and Wales. I found him refreshingly open and willing to consider contrary points of view-- he indicated that *legislation* will be introduced and that by the end of 1986 the DES will ask LEAs what they have done about HMI Reports over the last three years. I feel sure the Scottish Office will follow suit and we should make sure we have been pursuing our policy of monitoring and following through on HMI Reports. (29)

The standards/quality agenda was the one which (as will be argued later) shifted the focus from the corporate policy centre to departmental level. The recipient of the above memorandum was the next and last education director of Strathclyde.

Yet despite all this, the department appeared to have been ill-placed for the concerns of a more managerialist-consumerist environment. A major consultancy study on Strathclyde education department was carried out in 1988 and prepared jointly by the Institute of Local Government Studies and the School of Education, University of Birmingham (Strathclyde Regional Council 1989). (30) The department was criticised for being 'over bureaucratic', (31) 'too driven by administrative regulation'. (32) There was little evidence 'apparently of the new environment of quality assurance, performance indicators being addressed'. (33)

New Managerialism and Strathclyde Education Department 1989-1992. Externalisation of Management?

> *The moment to change had taken place, believing it to be irrevocable, believing there was less mischief in frankly submitting to it than seek to disturb it---I have laboured to extract the good and to mitigate the danger* (Sir Robert Peel, 1837, reflecting on the Great Reform Act of 1832). (34)

> *This [Strathclyde's introduction of Direct Management of Resources policy for schools] reflects our own policy proposals which were met with shock and dismay when we introduced them, but which are becoming an accepted part of the education thinking in Scotland* (M Forsyth, Scottish Education Minister 1990). (35)

The Political Context

The political context within which local authority management was conducted was especially important from the early to the mid-1980s. At first glance it would appear to be externally driven, employing an 'area governance' rather than 'government' view of council activity. A Conservative government re-elected for a second term was much influenced by ideas and ideologies of de-intervention of rolling back the state. Local government was very much part of this thinking (Newton and Karan 1985). At one extreme, the withdrawal from the governmental scene of a number of local authorities (The GLC and Metropolitan English Counties) was rather crudely party political (Elcock 1991). Although at this time no local authorities in Scotland were abolished, councils had to be managed within an enforced choice framework, adopting policies which were forced from central government and with which they fundamentally disagreed (Johnson and Scholes 1998): there was much policy congruity between Scotland and the rest of the UK (Midwinter 1995) with central government control instruments similar (in aim if not in detail)-e.g., restrictions on council revenue raising powers, unified business rates, marketisation, legislation introducing compulsory competitive tendering.

This was the political context of management, not simply state roll back, but concurrently (and somewhat ironically) a stronger grip from the centre (Hoggett 1996). Despite this, until the mid-1980s at least, the only area where the new right agenda had been achieved was in the privatisation of nationalised industries, public utilities and in the local authority arena housing, largely because the government did not understand how to implement its policies through the correct policy networks (Marsh and Rhodes 1992). Nonetheless, what can now be stated without challenge was that external management was clearly evident: combination of political hostility (defined as antagonism towards much state activity including much of what local government did), fragmentation of public expenditure and policy instruments (through the increasing use of quangos), alternative sources of public sector funding (e.g. through European funded programmes and initiatives) meant that the area monopoly model of local authority (Sharp 1970) was no longer appropriate. Much more important was the concept and practice of area governance, and the management and governance of networks (King and Stoker 1996; Painter, Isaac-Henry, Rouse 1997).

The sheer size of Strathclyde made 'governance' as distinct from government difficult: it was by far the largest local authority in Scotland with almost 50% of the country's population within its boundaries. Even so, Strathclyde up to a point was able to operate effectively within governance networks. For example, one such included parts of the council, the European section of the department of employment and several directorates of the European Commission, and the council was able to use its participation in this network to lever considerable European funding for major infrastructural and other projects in Strathclyde. (36)

Archive material from the education department showed the council's membership (sometimes management of) such networks. A memorandum from the depute director made this clear:

Subject: Meeting with Stuart Gullivar, Chief Executive, Glasgow Local Enterprise
Company

I outlined our general willingness to work with third tier bodies in Lanarkshire, the
East End of Glasgow and elsewhere-- re the joint economic initiatives, I indicated
to Mike Greig of the Chief Executive's that the Department of Education would
wish to be represented at this, and that you might wish to attend personally the
session on future arrangements for the schemes as we had been giving a lot of
thought to the issues. (37)

Two other initiatives provide further evidence. The Scottish Wider Access
Programme, a multi institution approach to widening access in higher education
was led by Strathclyde and involved other local authorities and higher education
institutions; the responsive college programme, a UK-wide project involving
other local authorities, central government agencies aimed at developing quality
measures in further education colleges:

> The formation of the West of Scotland Wider Access consortium in partnership
> with all the institutions of higher education in the west of Scotland and Dumfries
> and Galloway Regional Council to develop access programmes which will provide
> a non traditional route to higher education. This builds on the work started by the
> Regional Council in collaboration with the Universities of Glasgow and
> Strathclyde and with Paisley and Glasgow Colleges. This work was used for the
> Scottish Wider Access Programme (SWAP).
> The Responsive College Programme, a UK project funded by the Training Agency
> and organised by the FE Staff College. The focus in the Strathclyde project
> colleges has been on developing measures of quality control and after sales service.
> (38)

The second key aspect of the political context was the 'new managerialism',
with its focus on managerial accountability the features of which included: an
emphasis on the de-centralisation of managerial responsibility and functions
including financial management and devolved budgetary controls; efficient
resource usage; use of performance indicators; the development of consumerism
and market discipline cultures and processes; the assertion of managerial
responsibility and control (Pollitt 1990,1993; Farnham and Horton 1996).

Focus on Departmental Management

The two key contextual factors were, at the macro-level, the altered relationship
vis a vis central government with central control over aspects of local
government power (especially revenue raising) and a re-definition of local
councils' government and governance; and at the micro-level, a managerial
focus on local devolved financial resource management as well as the increased
use of output, performance and quality measures, in other words managerial
accountability. For management, this represented a radical shift from the
situation prevailing at the time of reform in the mid 1970s: here the focus was
on corporatism, processes whereby local authorities through strong centres of
management and administration could direct, co-ordinate and plan their

functions and departments; now by the mid-1980s, the focus was on the actual outputs and resource usage of service departments. This subtly shifted managerial attention away from chief executives' and central co-ordinating departments to service departments where the actual delivery took place. This was a point not lost on Strathclyde's director of education:

Budget Preparation 1990-91 and 1991-92

It is superficially tempting to propose savings by diluting and diverting the restructuring of the education department in train as the regional council's response to the Inlogov Report-- that this would be a false economy is borne out by the Audit Commission's occasional Paper, 'Losing an Empire, Finding a Role: the Local Education Authority of the Future'.

There is a need for authorities increasingly to support education departments in delivering the curriculum to secure and provide public assurance of quality and to provide accessible information to parents, staff-- [there will be] new costs incurred in 'inspection and advisory services, training and development and information exchanges' [quotation from the above mentioned Audit Commission Report]. (39)

How did this re-focus on departmental service provision shape the configuration of internal and external management of education in Strathclyde? This can be analysed through three initiatives between 1985 and 1992: the development of quality measures and performance indicators; the evolution of a management system within schools; devolution of resource management to schools, in Strathclyde known as direct management of resources (DMR). There appeared to be a dominant and recurring objective of management in the department when managing the three initiatives-the desire to maintain internal management control of the education delivery process by 'outdoing' and in some cases pre-empting a central government directed agenda. (40) These council initiatives all spear-headed by the education department provide a strong counter-weight to the view that the 1980s and early 1990s local government environment was comprehensively externally driven.

Management in Schools

Following an HM Inspectors' report 'Learning and Teaching in Scottish Secondary Schools-Schools Management' in 1984, the council established a working party which produced a report just over one year later (Strathclyde Regional Council 1986).

The deliberations of this working party indicated, as expected, specific regional council concerns. For example the collective duty of senior staff in schools serving 'areas for priority treatment' 'to address the educational consequences of deprivation', concern about reporting lines through the department's divisional structure to headquarters. However two other features of the working party were of some significance. First, its membership included a representative from the Scottish Office (H.M. Inspector, George Gordon), surely the best way of assessing and testing the most important aspect of the external environment, central government's thinking. This was no doubt linked to the second significant feature of the working party's discussions and final report that is, the extent to which the findings were in tune with government favoured new managerial thinking. For example, the very clear view of managerial accountability was much more emphasised than ideas of participation and consultation, as illustrated:

> The principle of management can be summarised: the formulation of clear aims and objectives, devising the means of their implementation, regular and thorough monitoring and evaluation of practice-- in some schools an attempt has been made to broaden the base of senior management by involving other members of staff. These extra members are sometimes chosen by the head teacher but in other cases they are elected by their peers: this extension requires clarity. Senior members of staff have specific responsibilities which are ultimately derived from the authority and which render them accountable to the authority. The inclusion of representatives of the staff changes the nature of the meeting in a manner which could make it unreasonable to adopt management perspectives and responsibilities. (41)

With further education colleges, managerial accountability was taken one stage further when they were removed from local authority control. College managers were directly accountable to the college board of management and the main funder, central government. Colleges were given responsibility for developing business plans and controlling resources within the constraints of funding received.

The report continued not with hostility to participation but with a clear distinction between this and the managerial accountability of the schools' most senior management:

> Perhaps the best and most regularly employed channel for participation in management decisions and on discussion of professional issues is the departmental meeting. (42)

Case 5 examines managerial accountability in further education and the role of professional teachers in this managerial environment.

Development and Introduction of Quality Measures and Performance Indicators

There was a commitment to the introduction of performance measures from the middle of the 1980s. This was evident from the level of seniority of staff involved: a performance indicators working party was operating in the wake of the Inlogov Report and consisted exclusively in the first instance of the depute director and one tier below. (43) This built on work initiated two years earlier in the further education sector (the Responsive College Project) working with the Further Education Staff College in England and Wales and the central government agency, the Manpower Services Commission. Central government funding was given to the regional council to appoint staff through this initiative with the aim 'to develop with colleges measures of quality control and customer satisfaction'. (44)

Although the commitment to such initiatives seemed from the records to be unequivocal, much of pressure for the development of published indicators (e.g., exam results tables for general release to the public) may well have been at elected member level as well as council official or central government level. A note from the director to one of his deputes gave such an indication:

Meeting with Councillor Ian Davidson, 15 March 1989

According to Ian Davidson there is a need to produce information on examination results in FE. I understand he was thinking in terms of HNC and other courses-- he seemed particularly adamant that he was going to pursue this matter-- some statistics have been produced. He has assured me he is not interested in raw statistics. (45)

But the over-riding objective behind the entire initiative seems clear in an exchange between the depute and senior depute director:

In order to discharge the quality control function I would suggest that our Advisory Service must take on the role of local inspectorate-a role which they should always have had in my view-to enable them to perform the authority's current duties to provide an adequate and efficient education service. *If we do not move quickly to make this change we may well have a national curriculum and assessment foisted upon us* (emphasis in memorandum). (46)

Devolved Management of Resources

The School Boards (Scotland) Act of 1988 was the first tentative step towards the legislative enactment of substantial devolution of resource management to schools. This Act established the principle of delegated powers for expenditure of resources allocated for books and classroom material. Actual cost estimates had to be made available to each school board, which was also given the right to have financial questions answered. This was followed by the Self Governing Schools Etc. (Scotland) Act (1989), which made possible 'opt-out' from local authority control. Three years later the Scottish Office education department issued a consultative paper (SOED 1992) and the following year circular 6/93 with guidelines for devolved management arrangements (SOED 1993).

Strathclyde's management of this was interesting. After the initial 1988 legislation, the education department actually went much further than the legislation required. An education budget unit was set up which identified cost centres; 24 pilot schools were selected; a computerised budget system (SEEMIS) was implemented 'which could handle allocation methods based on formulae and actual costs to individual establishments'. (47) It can be assumed that in all of this the education department had a particularly 'close eye' on the external political environment: as early as 1988, Cooper and Lybrand consulting firm (with the Department of Education and Science as the client) was working with the education department and reporting back to the DES on progress (Cooper and Lybrand 1988).

The entire approach of the department (supported by the council as a whole) was a response to external influence from central government and in this sense external management. But the objectives were strongly influenced by internal management concerns. Indeed it is not exaggerated to state that the department's very raison d'etre was at stake and the department and authority was engaged on an exercise to maintain control of the educational resourcing at local authority level. (48) The Education Committee approved the DMR system at a meeting 31 January 1990 in the following terms:

> The aim of any scheme to be introduced by Strathclyde must be to maximise the potential benefits of decentralised control while minimising the dangers inherent in the mechanistic approach south of the border. Schools, colleges and other educational establishments should be able to enjoy a very high level of control over their own resources while still benefiting from the services of a very large local authority. (49)

Some saw the issue in slightly different terms as expressed more bluntly in private at an education department staff seminar: 'to reduce the incentive [for schools] to opt out'. (50)

Just how far DMR had developed by late 1991 was made clear in a memorandum from the director to an assistant chief executive:

> Target date of DMR is to all schools by August 1994. By August 1992, 25% of all primary and secondary schools will be covered.
>
> The scheme gives heads the power to vire up to £5000; £5000-£10,000 approved by divisional director; amounts beyond £10000 are referred to headquarters. But regional council staff levels and conditions must be maintained. Subject to these constraints 87% of a secondary school's and 85% of a primary school's budget is devolved locally.
>
> This contrasts with the non DMR position where only the detailed expenditure of per capita allocation for teaching and learning materials lies within the head teacher's power and that is itself subject to power of the School Board (1991-92 £20.19 per pupil in the primary sector; £52.88 in secondary. (51)

Schools were maintained within council control in Scotland and managed internally by the local education authority. This diverged from experience in England.

Summary and Conclusion

From the mid-1950s to its demise in the wake of local government restructuring, the education department of Glasgow Corporation actively sought to strengthen its internal management position within the council. It ensured minimal intervention between senior departmental figures and the education committee of the council, developed bureaucratic support structures especially evident in the growing further education sector, and generally centralised control within the department. However despite this evident strengthening, Glasgow was not considered a particularly strong or influential player in the Scottish educational policy community (see footnote 7).

The management of education in the newly created Strathclyde Regional Council indicated interesting trends. In Strathclyde's first ten or so years internal management of the education department was largely explained by rivalry with the central co-ordinating role of the chief executive's department. Education maintained strong external links, and could on occasion use management of these links and relationships to strengthen its own position against the chief executive's department in the council. However by the end of the 1980s, education seemed ill-prepared for the externally influenced new managerial and new right agenda. At that time, the department was criticised by external consultants for being too inward, over administered and over bureaucratic with little grip on the emerging requirements of a consumerist or accountability environment.

The emerging environment represented an externally government driven agenda redefining the role of local authorities, who required now to work in governance arrangements with others; introducing the establishment of a performance and accountability regime in education; overseeing a considerable role reduction for councils in the management of schools. While this environment and agenda were to an extent externally driven, it led to the focus of educational management being firmly located in the education department rather than elsewhere in the council. The education department in Strathclyde was proactive in implementing large parts of this change agenda and in so doing had a very clear aim of retaining control of schools and other parts of the managerial accountability agenda within the internal management of the local authority education structure.

Notes

1. D-ED.8/1/1. Review of Education Department by O and M Section of Town Clerk's Department, 1955.
2. Ibid.
3. D-ED 12/1/38. Letter from Director to Baillie John Mains, 25 November 1963.
4. D-ED 12/1/42. Minute of Meeting, Further Education Sub Committee, 6 April 1966. In fact, such seniority was never to be systematically seen again on boards of management or college councils until the era of incorporation and removal of colleges from local authority control in the early 1990s.
5. D-ED 12/1/47,48. Minute of Meeting, Education Sub Committee, October 1966.
6. D-ED 12/1/47,48. Review of Establishment of Teaching and Professional Staff, Further Education. Report by the Director, 8 August 1967.
7. D-ED 12/1/39. Minute of Meeting, Education Committee, November 1966. However, it should be noted that a key feature of Glasgow's Education

professional network was that it was never considered at the very core of Scottish education's professional governing elite at this time (McPherson and Raab 1988). According to these authors much of the prevailing value system in Scottish education was based on notions of a national identity focused on almost pre urban community values having little interaction or relationship with priorities facing a Clydeside conurbation. This was compounded by the fact that school building needs in the post war period in Glasgow often took a lower priority than Glasgow's pressing housing problems: for example, land released for building often saw housing gain access to the easier developable land for schools often more expensive and difficult. This did not endear Glasgow to the Scottish Education Department. According to an under secretary at the SED: *'Stewart McKintosh* [Glasgow's Director of Education] *didn't carry great weight because he was Stewart McKintosh but because he was director of Glasgow. But he did have his point'* (cited in McPherson, A and Raab, C.D 1988, Governing Education, Edinburgh: Edinburgh University Press p. 450).

8.   D-ED 12/1/32. Report to the Education Sub Committee 23 March 1962.
9.   D-ED 11/1/23. Directorate Correspondence 1963-74.
10.   There was no equivalent body in Scotland at this time.
11.   D-ED 12/1/37. Report to the Further Education Sub Committee 29 November 1963.
12.   Seconded staff from Stow College in Glasgow helped established a joint venture with Alexander Stephens shipbuilders. This venture provided craft and technician training and developed welding and profile cutting equipment.
13.   D-ED 12/1/45,46. Minute of Meeting, Education Sub Committee, 7 April 1967.
14.   D-ED 8/1/1. Review of Education Department, O and M Section Town Clerk's department, 1955.
15.   D-ED 12/1/42. Letter from Mr Scollin, depute Director of Education to Councillor G Moore, 12 August 1966.
16.   SR 10.9.416. Local Government Reorganisation, Strathclyde Region. The Administration of the Education Service Working Party Report to the Joint Advisory Committee 1972.
17.   Many of the senior departmental personnel including director (E Miller) and depute (G Bain) were from Glasgow Corporation. The first chief executive of Strathclyde (L Boyle) was from Glasgow Corporation too. Later, on the creation of a chief executive's department, former Glasgow education department figures gained senior positions there, including a depute chief executive (I Stuart) with responsibility for personal services (encompassing education). Miller's early appointment to Strathclyde gave him the opportunity to advise the external consultant appointed to advise the council on departmental and management structures. The archive indicates an active part being played here by the new director. For instance, see footnote 18.
18.   SR3 Policy Review Group, Departmental Structures, Education. Director's Response to Recommendations.
19.   C1125 Box 4, 6336. Letter from E Miller to J Angus Clark, PA Consultants, 10 September 1974.
20.   C1125 Box 6, Memo. From E Miller to P Drake, Divisional Education Officer Glasgow, 18 September 1985.
21.   C1125 Box 4, 6336. E Miller to L Boyle, Chief Executive 17 October 1978.
22.   C1125, Box 6. E Miller to I McFarlane, Depute Chief Executive 8 January 1986.
23.   C1125 Box 6. E Miller to Councillor Green, 17 December 1987.

24. C1125 Box 5, 6337. E Miller to Mr Cranston, 21 January 1982. The two issues referred to were of interest. Community Education employed community education workers throughout the region; community development staff were also employed by the council, but through the Social Work Department. There was obvious duplication here. The other issue was the position of separate Roman Catholic schools provided for under the 1918 Education Act. While the council's official position was to maintain the status quo with no plans to review this, there was a strong body of opinion within the chief executive's department which wished to open the matter for debate in the context of falling school rolls, heavy maintenance costs and the possible opportunities presented for rationalisation. The education director 'informally' resisted this body of opinion. Information provided in a private interview with an employee of the chief executive's department at this time (in confidence).

25. SR 3. Policy Review Group, Departmental Structures, Education. Recommendations 1976.

26. C1125, Box 4. 6336. E Miller to L Boyle, Chief Executive, 30 December 1976.

27. C1125, Box 4. 6336. E Miller to I McFarlane, Director of Policy Planning, 21 January 1977.

28. C1125, Box 5 6337. E Miller to R Calderwood, Chief Executive, 'Private and Confidential', 11 June 1981.

29. C1125, Box 6. E Miller to F Pignatelli, Assistant Director of Education, 31 January 1986.

30. Strathclyde Regional Council (1989), Report on Education in Strathclyde Undertaken by Inlogov and the School of Education University of Birmingham, Glasgow: SRC. The study team was star studded and contained some of Britain's leading writers and researchers on local government. The team included Stewart Ranson, Peter Ribbins, Kieron Walsh, Howard Davis, Mary Davis, Tony Travers and Professor Ken Young. It was also indicated to me in a private interview with Frank Pignatelli, then an assistant director (later director) of education of Strathclyde, that this study was initially commissioned directly by senior councillors without the knowledge of the most senior figures in the education department.

31. Ibid para. 5.18.

32. Ibid para. 5.77.

33. Ibid paras. 4.59, 4.60, 4.62.

34. Peel, Sir Robert (1937), A Correct Report of the Speeches Delivered by the Right Honourable Sir Robert Peel, Bart, M.P, on His Inauguration into the Office of Lord Rector of the University of Glasgow, January 11 1837 and at the Public Dinner at Glasgow, January 13 1837. Glasgow University Special Collections.

35. ET. The Scottish Education Minister is quoted in the Evening Times 5 May 1990, p 7. This was drawn to my attention by Frank Pignatelli.

36. Strathclyde was considered one of the UK's most successful local authorities in accessing European funds for the restructuring of depressed manufacturing areas in the 1980s. It was one of the first to develop an integrated development operation ranging over several European funding regimes and was the first local council in the UK to have a permanent representative office in Brussels staffed by a senior official (Norman McGrail). The current head of Scottish Enterprise's representative office in Brussels indicated that the Strathclyde experience provided a working model for the Scottish Office's initial ventures in this field (The Herald 21 September 1999), now much expanded with the activities of the Scottish Executive and a permanent Scottish representative presence in Brussels.

37. C1676, Box4/7, John McPherson, Depute Director to F Pignatelli Director of education, 10 October 1990.
38. SR 10.9.129. Memo from F Pignatelli Director of Education to R Calderwood, Chief Executive, 20 April 1989.
39. C2261, Box1/9. Memo. From F Pignatelli Director of Education to R Calderwood Chief Executive 20 July 1990.
40. In a private interview with Frank Pignatelli, this was made very clear. In Scotland, although opt out was legislatively possible, the pattern was for state schools to remain overwhelmingly within local authority control. In England, many areas used the legislation and this led to some substantial geographical blocks of grant maintained school provision. Information given to me suggests that the education policy community in Scotland (with Strathclyde playing a leading part in the influential Association of Directors of Education in Scotland-an influence never accorded to Glasgow's education department prior to local government restructuring) was able to maintain local authority control in large measure due to the strategies pursued by Strathclyde and others. This may qualify Midwinter's (1995) thesis on policy congruity throughout the UK. It has also been suggested that strands of the Scottish policy community (including some elected members of the government) were recognised, at the highest levels of the UK government, as being less enthusiastic about the Thatcherite agenda than the Prime Minister desired (Neil 1996).
41. Strathclyde Regional Council (1986), Report of Working Group on Learning and Teaching in Secondary Schools in Strathclyde: SRC para 1.10.
42. Ibid para 3.05.
43. The Performance Indicators Working Party in October 1989 consisted of J McPherson, J Traviss, D Montgomery, D Thomas, K Bloomer, and P Drake. (C 1975, Box 1/2. Education in the Community: Implementation Plan. Performance Indicators Working Party).
44. C 1517, Press Advert, 5 September 1986.
45. C 1676, Box 5/7. F Pignatelli, Director of Education to J McPherson, Depute director, 20 March 1989.
46. C1517. J McPherson, Depute Director of Education to D Burns, Assistant Director, 19 August 1987.
47. SR 10/9/141. Working Papers on DMR 1988-1989.
48. See also footnote 40.
49. Strathclyde Regional Council (1990), Minute of a Meeting of the Education Committee 31 January: SRC.
50. SR 10/9/41. Education Directorate Seminar Notes, 12 December 1988.
51. C 2261, Box 1/9, F Pignatelli, Director of Education to D Peutherer, Chief Executives Department 30 August 1991.

Chapter 11

Case Study 5: Y College

Synopsis

The new managerial environment which altered the traditional configuration of internal and external management was typified in the further education sector. Under the terms of the Further and Higher Education and the Further and Higher Education (Scotland) Acts of 1992. colleges were removed from the internal management of local authorities. Henceforth, college internal management was to be focused at institutional level and considerably strengthened, with the key external relationship now with central government. To this end, colleges were given authority over considerable areas of managerial activity, including wage and salary negotiations, though central government retained financial and aspects of strategic control, as well as reserving considerable powers of intervention.

This study of Y College reveals that significant aspects of the new managerial agenda were implemented in the internal management of the college, though substantial areas of the pre-existing collegiate and professional approaches were still in place. The management of external relationships, traditionally organised through council education departments was very significant in Y as in other colleges. Relationships between further education and central government, private companies, public sector and quasi-public sector agencies like enterprise companies, European Union funding agencies were now the responsibility of individual colleges. Study of external relationships in Y indicated first, institution specific explanations behind the externalisation and outsourcing of key activities like estates and property maintenance, cleaning and catering; second, the development of collaborative partnerships with external bodies (often other colleges) evolving from limited to systemic and symbiotic networks; third, the exterior relationships with governmental institutions indicated a complex picture, with the fragmentation of public policy and service provision (a key feature of the new managerialism according to some commentators) apparent in some levels of college governance but not others; and fourth, while the externalisation of colleges from local council control led to the virtual demise of a local council locus on further education colleges, there were considerable external linkages between colleges, locality based organisations and policy making networks and partnerships at the centre of government. There was in fact considerable evidence of an active further education policy community, which linked colleges and central government, and also many examples of engagement with local participatory and consultative bodies. There was, however, fluidity in arrangements between colleges and the major external stakeholder, central government, regarding the balance of centralisation, the importance of partnership and local institutional integrity. It is in the nature of public policy that these arrangements are likely to remain central and dynamic.

- The Context: Colleges and the New Managerial Environment
- Y College: Internal and External Management in the New Managerial Environment

Colleges and the New Managerial Environment

External Management

The management of relationships between colleges and external agencies was altered dramatically with the 1992 legislation. Colleges were removed from the control of local authorities. This was in part motivated by the belief in the superiority of quasi-market mechanisms, the appropriateness of generic management and the view that locally appointed college boards of management would be best placed to respond to a locality's post-16 training and educational needs (Elliot and Crossley 1997; Randle and Brady 1997). It has also been argued that there was a (Conservative) party-ideological hostility to local government (Ainley and Bailey 1997).

The government saw the 1992 legislation as a key enactment of the series of White Papers set out in 1991 (Department for Education 1991a; 1991b). According to the government, the Act was to introduce

> Far reaching reforms designed to provide a better deal for young people and adults and to increase still further participation in further and higher education. (1)

That a substantial degree of local autonomy was required to achieve this was also evident:

> our aim is to give colleges much greater freedom to manage their own affairs and, through a funding regime, a powerful financial incentive to recruit additional students and thereby expand participation. (2)

The method by which colleges were to achieve growth (successfully in many cases) was by market competition with others in the sector. Government's funding methodology for 1992 was based on student numbers assessed by a student unit of measurement (the equivalent of 40 hours of teaching) and critically, targeted efficiency savings. Due to the level of unit funding set, growth was the only way to achieve savings by reducing unit costs and this inevitably led to competition within the sector. This was subsequently recognised:

> The Department [since 1992] wanted to achieve convergence in levels of college grant in aid funding per unit of student activity. For many colleges convergence has meant a reduction in funding. The funding methodology encourages growth. Assuming that overall funding for the sector remains stable, then individual

colleges need to achieve at least the sector average for growth if they are to maintain their level of funding in the previous year. This emphasis on growth has also encouraged many colleges to adopt a competitive approach to student recruitment and to delivery of their provision. (3)

Implicit in the legislation was a belief that it was college boards of management, locally based, who were best placed to oversee this process: significantly, these were to be focused on individuals from a business, commercial or professional background, with the number of local authority members (who were de-barred from holding the chair) limited to two and mandatory membership for the local enterprise company (in England, training and enterprise council).

The second dimension of external management was the role of central government and its relationship to colleges. There have been differing emphases placed on government's role in the new managerial environment. There was the 'rowing/steering' analogy of Osborne and Gebler (1993) where central government gave a strategic steer to policy; the rowing, that is operations, was carried out at a more localised, often de-centralised level. Others have emphasised a much sharper delineation between centre and locality/operations with a strong centralisation of strategy and policy formation, with operations and service delivery devolved to managers (Pollitt 1993). There is some evidence for the validity of the rowing/steering analogy. On the one hand, government put in place a funding mechanism creating a range of incentives to achieve the policy aim of increased student participation rates, yet left the colleges free to decide how best to achieve this. Further, college development plans (in effect business plans) outlining projected student activity rates. were 'merely' submitted to, and not approved by, central government. On the other hand, the 1992 legislation enabled considerable strategic for the centre. The Act removed the responsibility for further education from local authorities to the Secretary of State for Scotland (in England the Education Secretary); gave the Secretary of State power to establish new colleges, merge two or more colleges, close colleges, and establish a Further Education Funding Council. It also gave the power to require a college board of management to publish information regarding the educational provision for students, the achievements of students and subsequent destination. The English and Welsh legislation altered the inspection regime from Her Majesty's Inspectorate to a Further Education Funding Council appointed by the Secretary of State. In fact, government intention was for greater central power than was actually enacted: according to the Paymaster General, Section 56 of the Act (England and Wales) regarding 'direction' by the Secretary of State,

> is founded on the proposition that the Secretary of State needs a long-stop power of intervention in order to protect taxpayers' interests in the considerable sums of public money that do flow and will flow into further education in the form of grant to the funding councils. (4)

As a result of the concern about the effects of such a power on the academic freedom of individual institutions, amendments were introduced in the House of

Lords to divide the intervention power of the Secretary of State into more circumscribed powers to issue general directions to the funding council (Section 56); and to intervene in individual institutions in the event of mis-management or breach of duty (Section 57). (5)

Internal Management

Equally important to the removal from local council control was the strengthening of college institutional management. Section 12 of the 1992 Act made it clear that each college was responsible for determining its own strategy. This necessitated strong internal management, indicated by the fact that the college principal was designated accounting officer (for what in effect were substantial public funds) and the board of management given ultimate responsibility for all that took place under the college's auspices. In almost 50% of Britain's colleges, principals were designated as chief executives or 'principal and chief executive' (Harper 2000). This was formalised and incorporated into the language used in key further education documentation:

> As chief executive of a college, its designated accounting officer, the principal is charged with delivering the college's strategy. (6)

Pre-incorporation management structures typically had a pyramid shape with lecturers supervised by heads of department who in turn usually reported to one vice or depute principal. This changed significantly, with an increase in second tier managers usually designated as directors or assistant principals; beneath them were programme area directors, managers or programme area leaders, and then team or section leaders. Not only did these titles replace the old (for example, heads of department, deputy heads) but their functions were defined in terms of resource control and/or product development or quality: in short, in managerial terms (Harper 2000). Other research has indicated that considerable management resource was deployed in resource efficiency post-1992 (Warner and Crosswaite 1995). Further, a pilot study in Scotland in 1998 found that all colleges included in the study had senior finance personnel and that resource management responsibilities were being cascaded down managerial layers (McTavish 1998). An institutional governance framework (an independent board of management) oversaw this process though there were significant differences between Scotland and England. In the former, boards were more inclusive of the college community: the Scottish legislation indicated that staff and student representatives had a statutory right of board membership, whereas, in the latter, discretion was given to individual colleges. Survey work has shown that only 50% of English colleges opted for staff representation on boards, and considerably less than this for student representation (Gee 1997). Arguably, this inclusiveness gave greater strength to boards in Scotland.

A final aspect of the internal strengthening of institutional management was in the specific autonomy given to negotiate salary and other employee matters. While the 1992 Act fell within the Transfer of Undertakings (Protection of Employment) Regulations 1981 (TUPE)-existing college staff were transferred from council to college employment on existing collective agreements-the national regulatory framework was weakened in that college negotiated contracts were given to new staff, and negotiations for salary, wage increases and changes to existing agreements were college responsibilities. What followed created a very fragmented picture: almost as soon as colleges were given internal responsibility and autonomy there evolved a College Employers Forum in England and in Scotland the Association of Scottish Colleges. In both cases these were created by the sector itself to provide nation-wide frameworks. Most colleges adopted a policy of offering new flexible contracts to new appointments and promotions while others negotiated new contracts for all staff, though the position in Scotland was less turbulent. Change was facilitated by government, which in both Scotland and England had held back some funding to colleges in 1994-96 (7) dependent on new contracts (Hewitt and Crawford 1997). This led to a protracted two year contract dispute, the result of which was a patch-work of practices: in some colleges a majority of staff were on new contracts, in others only new appointments. In others still, entire departments were on contracts, others not (Hewitt and Crawford 1997). Nevertheless, college managers were now given powers to negotiate and arrange wage and salary levels, a function previously carried out at national level.

Fundamental or Incremental Change?

It was clear - and governments can rarely be clearer than when they pass legislation like the Further and Higher Education Act 1992 - that government action in removing colleges from local council control was policy driven by new managerial thinking. The case of further education contributes to the debate about whether the 'Conservative revolution' was achieved pragmatically and incrementally (Barberis 1995) or with more strategic deliberation (Fry 1984) (see also chapter 8). There is evidence for the incrementalist view. Many of the new managerial features in terms of internal and external management of further education, were observed in evolution through the new managerial era prior to the 1992 legislation. While there was no attempt to remove further education from local authority management, there were attempts to exteriorise aspects of management away from local authority domination. Throughout the 1980s, legislative change was significant: at the beginning of that decade the Education (Scotland) Act made clear that further education was the responsibility of LEAs; the Education Reform Act (1988) led to a measure of autonomy for colleges in the requirement of LEAs to delegate budgets to colleges (Basset-Jones and Brewer 1997). This went further with the Self Governing Schools Etc. (Scotland) Act 1989 with the establishment of college councils to which were delegated certain local council functions. Throughout the 1980s, increased amounts of college funding came through central government and its agencies, particularly the Manpower Services Commission and its successors (Drodge and Cooper 1997).

Prior to 1992 there was also significant development of internal institutional management in colleges. The college councils established under the 1989 legislation contained a majority of representatives from business, commercial and professional sectors; in many cases these councils became the core of the new post 1992 college boards of management. (8) However, the influence of the LEA was still apparent: college councils could be, and usually were, chaired by representatives of the LEA. (9) But the evidence of institutional management strengthening was limited. While the growing use of performance indicators and consumerist measures were evident (e.g., student achievement and other measures were drawn up and published for all of Strathclyde's further education colleges), the following extract indicated that the pressure to do this appeared to come from within the local authority, at elected member level (as indicated in Chapter 10 when discussing schools):

Meeting With Councillor Davidson 15 March 1989

According to Ian Davidson there is a need to produce information on examination results in further education-- he seemed particularly adamant that he was going to pursue this matter. (10)

In one key respect, the 1992 legislation was far from incremental and represented a complete break with the past: the removal of local authority control and management. Although the part played by local authorities in management of colleges prior to 1992 should not be overstated (for example, wage negotiations were carried out at national not local government level) it was significant. In addition to the statutory position where all college staff were council employees, the limited research which has been done on the policy formation process in further education (Leech 1994; Humes 1994) has shown that though there was college participation in policy networks, these networks were largely driven through local authorities and organisations like the Association of Directors of Education Scotland. (11) But after 1992, there was very little local authority involvement in the further education policy community. Furthermore, this should be viewed in the context of some hostility between central and local government, leading to the abolition of the English Metropolitan Counties, the Greater London Council (Newton and Karan 1985; Wilson and ˙Game 1994) and a review of local government in Scotland not welcomed by the local authorities (Midwinter 1995). The role of local councils in the management of further education was terminated, and in this sense the incorporation of colleges was part of a radical rather than incremental agenda.

Y College. The New Managerial Environment: Internal Management

A research and literature base on the impact of the 1992 legislation on internal management of colleges has been rather slow to develop, though much has been written in the educational press (e.g., Austin 1997; Crequer 1998; McGavin 1998; Mackney 1998; Mansell 1996; Ward 1996). Some empirical research has been carried out under the auspices of the Further Education Development Agency (e.g. Levacic and Glatter 1997) and the Scottish Further Education Unit (e.g., McTavish

1998), and a wider range of research now appears to be developing (e.g., Elliot 1996; Harper 2000).

The strengthening of institutional management can be observed and analysed in three key aspects of college operations. First, there is the extent to which the governing body or board of management and senior managers formulated strategy at college level. Second, management arrangements as articulated through managerial/hierarchical structures and the execution of business and professional functions can be observed. Of particular interest here was the extent to which professional and collegiate approaches were replaced by managerial ones. Third, we can assess how institutional control was exerted over key aspects of human resource management.

First, there is little doubt that since 1992, colleges advanced considerably to take substantial control over college strategy (Drodge and Cooper 1997). This was inevitable given the operating guidelines which the legislation put in place: colleges were required to provide central government with a development plan, outlining proposed student activity based on student units of measurement. Research undertaken in 1998 in a range of Scottish colleges indicated clear college control of this process, though there was considerable variation of practice and sophistication in methodology used (McTavish 1998). In Y College, it is clear that the board monitored and approved the college's strategic plans and that the preparation of the plan was co-ordinated by the senior management team acting with divisional heads who drew up targets. (12) A considerable degree of strategic control was exercised at college level, though as seen later, this was not without qualification. The National Audit Office spelt out the expectation of institutional control:

> Section 12 of the Act [the Further and Higher Education (Scotland) Act 1992] makes it clear that it is each college's responsibility to determine its own strategy. The Department requires colleges to submit their development plans but does not approve them. (13)

Second, there was major change in internal management structures and arrangements after 1992. Direct responsibility for revenue and budgeting necessitated the creation of a finance function (if not hierarchy) quite different from the 'bursar' or 'registrar' of the pre-incorporation era. In Y College, the finance director was graded as an assistant principal, reporting directly to the principal and with a staff of seven. In addition, there was considerable devolution of financial responsibility to the level of divisional head. On the other hand, costing systems were less well developed (most reliance being placed on historic costing and on staff in-put costs). This was not surprising, since 50% of all colleges had (in 1999) no costing processes at all, and

> even where college costing systems were relatively well developed, they tended to focus on staffing inputs and costs. None of the colleges reported recharging for the use of capital assets such as accommodation or teaching equipment, even though expenses relating to these items are part of the cost of teaching and other college activities in any one academic or financial period. (14)

Management structures and responsibilities recognised concerns for quality, marketing and information systems. This was reflected in the shape of the managerial hierarchy. Prior to incorporation in this college (like most others-see Harper 2000) there was a pyramidal structure for academic staff where lecturers were supervised by a head of department who reported to a vice principal immediately below the principal. Now there were four managers at second tier level, with managers of discrete curricular areas no longer part of a senior management team (see Figure. 11.1). Yet those with responsibilities for curricular areas were clearly given a remit distinct from an exclusively 'educational' one.

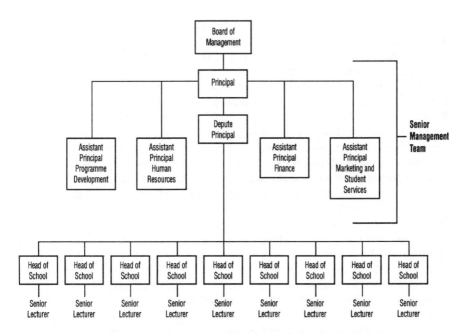

Figure 11.1 Y College Management Structure 2001

Harper's research found this to be the case in over 90% of the colleges studied in her English sample (Harper 2000). When the Principal of Y College resigned in 1997, his 'valedictory address' made the point:

> The Principal noted that the Curriculum Management Team had been progressing and working with the model and structure and this was tested each day-- he noted that Heads of School had been put in place to deliver growth and that this had been an adventure for all-- he asked if Heads of School were ready to address the issues which underpin the productivity gains which will be required. An alert institution will be able to identify low productivity and will be prepared to address the underlying issues. (15)

There were practices in a number of colleges that could dilute 'traditional' professional/collegiate arrangements in favour of more managerial approaches. Lower cost teaching staffs have been used in a number of Scottish and English colleges to deliver part of the curriculum, and there has been an increased use of less expensive support staff (National Audit Office [NAO] 1999), although this has not occurred in Y college. A particular area where colleges have not been strengthened as anticipated has been in marketing. Research found that while most colleges undertook marketing activity,

> Few had actually moved this to the strategic level in the organisation-- use of local market information in strategic planning process is poor. (16)

In Y College, while there was an assistant principal responsible for marketing, this was one of the post holder's several responsibilities. There was only a thin staff complement in this area of activity; publicity and media relations services are bought-in from an external agency.

Third, the extent to which the institution's management controls key aspects of human resource is an important indicator of internal management strength. Research and survey work found that in many colleges significant gaps existed in the human resource function. Survey work also found that only in a minority of colleges has human resource management been integrated with the strategic level of college management (SFEFC 2000). In Y, the introduction of the human resource management into the strategic focus of the senior management team is a relatively recent practice with the appointment early in 2001 of an assistant principal with specific human resource management responsibilities. This college did have particularly strong human resource policies and procedures in a number of areas from staff training to health and safety and equal opportunities, the strength of which had been recognised with Charter Mark, National Training Award and other external recognition. Other aspects of the college's approach to human resource management gave an indication of the extent of internal management strengthening in line with HRM approaches and philosophy. The 'democratisation' of the human resource management discourse (see McKinlay 1998) with individual manager 'empowerment' and self-managing teams has been cascaded, with divisional heads given responsibility for part-time staffing budgets and large areas of curricular development and implementation. On the other hand, a key aspect of HRM, the alignment of professional resources (i.e. teaching staff) to managerial/business goals may be limited given the absence (at the time of writing) below senior management level of performance appraisal or any other formal mechanism to assess individual and organisational goals.

A final aspect of human resource management in the college was salary and employment contract negotiations with teaching and non-teaching staff. The extent to which this gave discretion to institutional management was variable. In some colleges, the negotiating environment was regulated and heavily collectivised (though not nationalised) with considerable density of union membership (in Y college over 90%, the Scottish average approaching 60%), and the existence of a standard teaching contract with pro rated benefits for part-time staff. Only a small number of employees, the most senior, had individually negotiated contracts. Senior managers in this college were exploring the re-creation of external negotiating machinery through the Association of Scottish Colleges (ASC), feeling that any benefits gained in local negotiations were far outweighed by the necessity to devote considerable managerial resource to the process. (17) However, local negotiation is likely to remain the norm.

Y College. The New Managerial Environment: External Management

The definition and configuration of external management changed dramatically in 1992. Prior to this, colleges were part of the local authority management infrastructure, with professional hierarchies at institutional level reporting to and implementing policies of the local authority. The key external relationships were between local authority education departments and the policy and professional community focused largely on the Scottish Office Education Department and its successors (McPherson and Raab 1988; Humes and MacKenzie 1994). The externalisation of further education from local authority control in 1992 was not 'simply' like another marketisation/competitive tendering exercise, where contract oversight was maintained within the council and operational management migrated to operational or institutional level. Operational management did certainly migrate and became internalised within colleges as the preceding section outlined. But unlike CCT and similar initiatives, the external relationships were no longer within the scope of local authorities, but the colleges themselves. (18) Colleges developed external relationships with central government agencies like enterprise companies, and European funding bodies. In Scotland, this process commenced very quickly after incorporation (Pignatelli 1994).

There were two types of external relationship. First, those with external bodies either in a market setting (e.g., private companies providing services to the college under contract) or in a professional partnership context (usually with other colleges). Second, there was the key external relationship between the college and the main funder/stake-holder (i.e. central government).

The first of these saw college Y contracting with the previous local authority provider for a range of support services like cleaning and catering; other support services were tendered widely (e.g., property maintenance and refurbishment) and the college employed its own specialist staff to manage and monitor these activities and external contractual relationships. The decision over which activities should be externalised and which should be kept in-house gives some support to the concept and notion of 'asset specificity' (see Williamson 1975): for example, this college and most others retained control of janitorial services because of the necessity of extended hours surveillance, familiarity with aspects of the college estate and in some instances the desirability of 'live in' facilities in college owned residential property. Yet not all colleges have outsourced the same activities and this is difficult to explain without reference to particular institutional, historical or cultural factors: for example, Y externalised catering due to the belief that this was not an area of activity where it wished to develop competence, though it was acknowledged that experience of other colleges indicated in-house cost savings. Detailed research on outsourcing in other sectors has revealed a similar pattern (Ritson 2000).

The college was involved in a broad range of collaborative arrangements with other colleges. For example, it held membership of city-wide, national and European partnerships. The nature of these partnerships and the management role played by the college reflected a very broad typology of relationship. Similar to many organisations in the private sector, there were examples of collaborative arrangements to reduce financial risk and to gain entry to blocked markets (Hax and Majluf 1991; Kotler 1992): these, along with resource dependency theory (Alter and Hage 1993) help explain the key involvement in a city-wide educational technology project and another nationally focused partnership aimed at the development of open learning resources and materials (Colleges Open Learning Exchange Group - COLEG). The partnership network (from which the educational technology project was born) has developed substantially since it was researched four years ago. Then it was categorised as 'limited' due to the unequal distribution of power within the network (Finlay, Holmes and Kydd 1997 – research carried out in 1995); subsequently, the network has evolved to have a resource winning role with a greater equality of power within the partnership, moving in the process from a limited network towards one which appears to display aspects of the systemic and symbiotic (Alter and Hage 1993). (19)

The second type of external management relationship was between the college and its key funder and stake-holder, central government. There were three dimensions to this exteriorisation, typical of the new managerialism. First, it is argued that an evacuation of service provision from public policy values has occurred, with service provision, (particularly in LPSBs like further education colleges), overwhelmingly dominated by managerial and business-strategic issues, leaving little attention to policy and 'public values' at service delivery level (Greer and Hoggett 1999). This view has been partially challenged by other studies of LPSBs (mainly in the field of local economic development), which describe the emergence of a new 'consensual' discourse highlighting a synthesis of public-private sector values, which comprise a new public management ethos (Brereton and Temple 1999). According to this perspective, there was a shift from a traditional public sector ethos of integrity of process and procedures, of professionally self-referencing definitions of efficiency, towards concerns about service outputs and outcomes rather than those solely business or cost focused, and to consumer consultation and procedural transparency (Brereton and Temple 1999). In college Y an analysis of proceedings at board of management meetings certainly indicated an overwhelming concentration on business-management and strategic issues which focused on business planning, property and estates matters, costs, audit and financial affairs, and on occasion organisational structures; discussion on educational matters was framed very much within this business-managerial framework. However, this picture was partial, since in terms of strategy development and implementation a very important instrument of college governance was the curriculum management team (previously the board of studies). Here there was a different pattern of proceedings: a greater mix of 'traditional' public sector issues framed by bureaucratic process and procedure; professionally referenced issues, and a range of discussions best described (to use Brereton and Temple's language) as a new consensus bringing together business related cost and resource issues and educational client-based ones. Added to this, the senior management team meeting, held fortnightly sometimes weekly, addressed an amalgam of the issues discussed by the board and the curriculum management team but in much greater detail and with more immediacy. In addition, these senior management team meetings included a range of issues untouched by others e.g. specific areas of staffing.

The second dimension (relationships between college and its main funder/ stake-holder, central government) surrounded the stated objective of the 1992 Act, domain clarification in the management of college and central government relationships:

> Our aim is to give colleges much greater freedom to manage their own affairs and, through the funding regime, a powerful financial incentive to recruit additional students and thereby expand participation. (20)

In other words, governments could use the funding methodology to achieve policy objectives (recruiting additional students) but gave considerable authority to colleges to develop and implement strategy themselves. The optimal effectiveness of the funding methodology in achieving policy objectives (even when these were as narrowly defined as increased student numbers) was questionable: effectiveness could only be maximised if the operation of the funding regime was transparent to the key agents, and this was not necessarily the case. According to a board of management minute, Y College,

> The Principal stated that from the analysis of SOEID funding, it had emerged that 11 Scottish colleges had required to be safety netted [that is, not subjected to the complete application of the funding formula since this would take college funding below an acceptable level, a figure determined by the SOEID] with only 2 colleges receiving more than 5% increase. Y College would receive an increase of 3.12%. The new methodology had not proved to be very transparent. [Italics added by author for clarification] (21)

Subsequent documentation also highlighted the idealised domain clarification stated in the 1992 Act (e.g. SFEFC 2000; NAO 1999). However, implementation and practice showed a more fluid and dynamic situation. The legislation gave ministers more than a 'steering' role: further education was now the responsibility of the Secretary of State who was given power to establish new colleges, (22) merge or close colleges; (s) he could also require boards of management to publish information on student attainment and subsequent career destination. There were instances of these powers being used, illustrating at times a rather direct central government role in college strategy: in 1994, colleges were instructed by the Scottish Office education and industry department, under Conservative administration, not to offer any more Higher National Certificate courses

(McTavish 1998). More recently, despite government's objective of increased access to higher education, a cap was placed on the number of higher education students to be funded in further education colleges, (23) and the Secretary of State for Scotland vetoed a proposed merger of two city-centre colleges in Glasgow in 1999. Although central government did not play an active role in the appointment of senior college staff (there was no mention of this in the Act), all principals before appointment must be deemed as suitable 'accounting officers' to the appropriate government department, giving central government in effect a long stop veto, a power as yet unused. (24) In Scotland it could also be assumed that the National Audit Office's 1999 report on Scottish further education with its strong message that many of the cost variations between different colleges were within the control of managers along with its recommendation that colleges should benchmark with others in the sector, could lead to a pull towards centralisation and standardisation (NAO 1999). However in practice this has not happened to the extent some would have hoped. In 2004, the Scottish Parliament Audit Committee made trenchant criticisms (to the Scottish Further Education Funding Council) about the lack of centralised information on colleges' performance indicators, the level of benchmark information and the lack of centrally held information on unit costs (Scottish Parliament Audit Committee 2004).

A third dimension, which some commentators highlighted as a consequence wrought by new managerialism, was a bifurcation of public policy. This went even further than the view that service provision and public values were decoupled (Greer and Hoggett 1999). What occurred, according to some, was a restriction and closure of discussion on alternative policy approaches, given (for example) the role limitation of democratically accountable local authorities (Clarke and Newman 1997). A full evaluation of this view is beyond the scope of this book, but the work of Painter et al (1994) provides evidence that new forms of local community participation developed alongside the role diminution of local councils. This was reflected in Y's engagement with local community organisations: a major estate and capital expenditure initiative in 2000 was heavily influenced by the training and education services to be provided for an active 'Social Inclusion Partnership'. (25) The college participated in a range of local economic and community development bodies whose governance remit included local neighbourhood consultation, representation and participation. (26) It is also clear that a complete fracturing of service provision and policy formation at the centre had not taken place. Although local authorities were in the main no longer part of the further education policy community, there is much evidence since the mid-1990s of individual college staff throughout Scotland being involved in participative and consultative networks over matters such as curriculum change, management of student bursaries, design of the funding regime and other policy matters (McTavish 1998). Although there is not yet the volume of research to match the schools sector (e.g. McPherson and Raab 1988; Humes 1986; 1994; 1997; Levacic 1993), enough exists to identify a distinct further education policy community with strong representation from colleges (in England, Riley 1997; Scotland, Leech 1994). (27) Colleges were represented on bodies like the Scottish Qualifications Authority and the Scottish Further Education Funding Council, Community

Learning Scotland, Scottish Further Education Unit. The principal had a strong role (as chair) in Community Learning Scotland, a non-departmental body (NDB) with advisory and other responsibilities for community education, and other aspects of adult and post-compulsory education in Scotland. She is also a member of the new deal taskforce (along with one other from further education) (28), a body comprising senior public and private sector figures, charged with advising government on the strategy of training and work placement programmes for unemployed young people. The depute principal was a member of the FEFC funding methodology working party. The chairman of the board of management was a member of FEFC Review of Management Steering Group, and another board member was active on the Funding Council's Strategy Development Committee. The evidence suggests that this college was not atypical or exceptional. (29)

Summary and Conclusion

The internal management arrangements and practices forged in the new managerial environment continued after the passage of the 1992 Further and Higher Education Act. The management and control structures were required for the running of independent cost and revenue centres. In Y college, with a turnover of almost £8 million, it is inconceivable that it could survive, let alone thrive, without an accounting/control capacity well managed and resourced; or that development planning could take place without academic divisions and schools having some control over the inputs and outputs of their work areas. However, although academic and management structures look rather different from the pre 1992 situation, it is over simplistic to refer to this as a dilution of traditional professional academic approaches. In all of Scotland's colleges, principals had a professional teaching background, and only in the area of finance was there a significant movement of people into senior management from non-teaching backgrounds. (30) In Y College, all senior management team members, with the exception of one, were professional teachers; in the entire management cohort of 30, only 4 were non- teachers. (31) This is a position not dissimilar to the NHS, where a range of non-clinical and managerial responsibilities were structured in such a way that professional clinicians could apply for managerial-clinical posts, thus retaining professional control of key aspects of the managerial hierarchy (Ashburner 1986). In this college, basic grade professional teachers have been retained with similar contractual terms for full time and part time staff: this tends to be commonplace in Scotland, but less uniform in other parts of the UK where a number of professional teaching posts were redesigned as instructor or support posts.

Relationship with the key external stake-holder, central government, was re-defined after the 1992 legislation. It is clear that post-1992, central government used the funding regime to achieve policy ends, while apparently leaving strategic management to colleges at institutional level, though in practice the situation was rather more fluid and dynamic. Conceptually, this model has continued though government's policy objectives have changed: where administrations from 1992-

1997 used a competitive funding model to increase student numbers, the post-1997 model has been re-structured to encourage collaboration between colleges (SOEID 1999) with 'strategic funding' made available for colleges to explore areas of collaboration and joint action. Where the post-1992 government focus was on increasing student numbers, the policy from the late 1990s has been is to increase numbers from under-represented groups with a funding premium attached to students from specific postal code areas.

Lying behind these central government policy concerns was the hypothesis that the removal of bodies like further education colleges from local authority control had led to the migration of policy discussion and debate and indeed public policy values from service delivery. This hypothesis was tested in Y College, and was not entirely borne out.

The key feature of central government-college management was inter-action between the institutional and central government policy arenas. This was observed in Y college. For the sector as whole, a Scottish Executive/Scottish Parliament perspective on further education was evident. This raised the possibility of greater (Scottish) central government control, given sharper focus by the fact that education is a key area of spending by the devolved government. There are some indicators of this with the parliament's lifelong learning committee scrutinising the SFEFC Chief Executive and others after the publication of the 1999 National Audit Office report on further education management (National Audit Office 1999) and on-going reviews of the college sector by the parliament's audit committee. However, there was little evidence to suggest strong policy and strategic control from the centre (Scottish Further Education Unit 2004). The participation of senior college personnel in the policy process is unlikely to change. Recent work highlights the key part played by institutions, including Y college, in the further education policy networks (McTavish 2003).

The presence of collaborative and partnership practices rather than central government dominated landscape in the external management of colleges was widespread. All the evidence to the end of the study period indicated this was likely to continue if not intensify. The creation of the Learning and Skills Council (LSC), operational from April 2001 in England has brought further education, training and enterprise funding under the one organisation: the LSC, with a £8 billion budget, a series of 'local arms' and the model adopted was one of collaborative working at local level aimed at enabling and institutionalising further education into local economic development/training governance structures and networks. In Scotland this model was not adopted, though the map is still one that emphasises partnership working. Here the further education funding body was merged with the higher education funding council creating a merged Scottish Further and Higher Education Funding Council, reflecting the significant degree of higher education provided in the college sector and the Scottish Executive's aim of producing strong collaborative links between further and higher education institutions.

Notes

1. *Hansard HL* Vol. 532 Col. 1022, Lord Belstead, Paymaster General.
2. *Ibid* Col. 1023.
3. National Audit Office (1999), Scottish Further Education Colleges: Managing Costs, London: HMSO. The Minister of State at the Scottish Office in 1997 (Rt. Hon Brian Wilson MP) referred to the 'folly' of an over competitive environment in further education. Speech delivered at the June 1997 meeting of the Association of Scottish Colleges (see McTavish 1998).
4. *Hansard HL* 1991 Vol. 533 Col 7.
5. This was brought to my attention by Professor J Bell, University of Leeds.
6. Scottish Further Education Funding Council (2000), *The Way Ahead. Management Review of Scottish Further Education Colleges,* Edinburgh: The Stationary Office.
7. The power of government to do this was questioned by the National Audit Office (NAO 1995). See also Hewitt and Crawford, 1997.
8. The College Council of Y College provided 60% of the first College Board of Management.
9. Information received from the Scottish Further Education Unit.
10. C1676 Box 5 / 7, F Pignatelli to J McPherson 20 March 1989.
11. This has also been indicated in a private interview with Mr Frank Pignatelli the last Director of Education Strathclyde Region, and Mr Tom Kelly Chief Executive of the Association of Scottish Colleges who in 1980 was a Scottish Office civil servant with responsibility for further education. Attempts were made to strengthen college involvement in policy through a comprehensive programme operated by Strathclyde Region, which saw the secondment of middle and senior managers from colleges to the LEA.
12. This is a fairly conventional view of strategy formulation-a rational approach (see Johnson and Scholes 1998) necessitated to a large extent by the guidance framework outlined by the SOEID and most recently the SFEFC (2000). In Y College however, there were also indications of other approaches to strategy formulation e.g., strategy formed by a process of 'strategic stretch' (Hamel and Prahalad 1994) and by the management of networks and partnerships (Miles, Snow and Coleman 1992; Kay 1993).
13. National Audit Office (1999), Scottish Further Education Colleges: *Managing Costs,* London: HMSO para. 1.10.
14. Ibid para. 3.6.
15. Y College, Minute of Curriculum Management Team Meeting, Note of Principal's Valedictory Address, 28 January 1997.
16. Scottish Further Education Funding council (2000), *The Way Ahead. Management Review of Scottish Further Education Colleges,* Edinburgh: The Stationary Office paras 7.32; 7.33.
17. These views are repeated in the 10 colleges in the Glasgow Colleges group. However, outwith this grouping, there is not a consensus for the recreation of national negotiating machinery according to Tom Kelly, chief Executive of the Association of Scottish Colleges. The position in England is rather different where there is national negotiating machinery (through the Association of Colleges) though local variation in implementation. About 50% of colleges in England engage with this national negotiating body.
18. Colleges were not completely hollowed out from local authority activity. Colleges can be considered part of an authority's governance network: Local authority education

departments for a time retained control over student bursaries; currently, funding for child care arrangements in colleges is channelled through local authorities; in some colleges, training and education is provided for local authority funded community and economic development projects requiring a functioning external relationship between college and council.

19. Finlay et al's original research looked at the relationship of the 5 partnership colleges (since increased to cover all Glasgow's colleges –10). The dominant agenda was the relationship between colleges and the city's universities and the movement of students from further into higher education. Unsurprisingly, the research found that this was not a partnership of equals but that the universities dominated the network as a whole as well as the relationship between individual colleges and university. The same partnership organisation (The Glasgow Colleges Group) has increased to include al the city's colleges; the agenda is no longer dominated by the movement of students from further to higher education, but is focused on a range of issues, the most significant of which (at the moment) is the accessing of funding from the European Commission. Although each college has individual aims and objectives in bidding, there are clear areas of collaborative rather than competitive bidding. The Group now has a small full time executive staff funded by the member colleges.

20. *Hansard HL* (1991) Vol. 532 Col. 1023, Paymaster General.

21. Y College, Board of Management meeting 3 March 1998.

22. The Secretary of State for Scotland in 1996 did just that. A new further education facility was approved and funded through the Private Finance Initiative in the Secretary of State's constituency, Stirling.

23. Y College, Board of Management meeting 8 June 2000.

24. Conceptually, domain definition and the respective roles of central government and service delivery institutions is also an issue for non departmental public bodies (NDPBs). A 'maximalist' decentralisation-autonomy position seems to have been adopted at least until the summer of 2000 in the Scottish Qualifications Authority (SQA). Written evidence by the Scottish Executive Enterprise and Lifelong Learning Department to the Enterprise and Lifelong Learning Committee states that:
    In general policy terms, the power of direction is viewed as a measure of last resort, to be used only in exceptional circumstances where there is lack of cooperation by or conflict within the organisation concerned - Scottish Executive (2000), *A Review into Examination Results Issues Concerning the Scottish Qualifications Authority, First Report*, 30 October, para.4.2, Edinburgh.
    This is rather different in emphasis to the way central government's powers have been used in further education in Scotland as outlined in the text. There could of course be an element of political pragmatism and opportunism in the above report. An experienced journalist and observer of the Scottish political scene has indicated that this is an example of devolution of responsibility to the point of least resistance (Kemp, 2000).

25. Y College Board of Management meeting 9 October 2000.

26. The college is represented on several such bodies ranging from those (like Scottish Enterprise, Glasgow) with a central government-nomination based membership to others (like Drumchapel Opportunities) with elements of local community representation in its governance structure.

27. The speed with which college principals and others stepped into the policy network vacuum after local authority removal was significant. This was partly explained by the transitional arrangements put in place to implement the 1992 legislation. Scottish Office Education and Industry Department (SOEID) set up a number of 'core groups' to address various aspects of post incorporation college management. These core

groups had strong representation from college principals and other senior college staff. The groups were in fact an indication of the formation of a new restructured policy network (Howgego 1993).

28. Y College Board of Management Meeting October 1988.
29. Information from Tom Kelly, Chief Executive, Association of Scottish Colleges.
30. All principals in Scotland's further education colleges except for 4 have a further education teaching background. These four have backgrounds in other education sectors. Information from Tom Kelly.
31. This is not uncommon. Information from Tom Kelly.

Chapter 12

Conclusion

Management is about the co-ordination of resources to achieve purposes----among the key areas of management are physical, financial and human resources---defining the needs, planning and acquiring. (Drucker 1954). (1)

Management is an activity that performs certain functions to obtain and utilise physical and human resources to accomplish some goal (Wren 1994). (2)

Business and Public Sector Management: A Generic Approach?

The above views on management, expressed by one of the twentieth century's leading management writers and by a leading academic specialist on management thought would appear to apply to both areas of this study, the business and public sectors. There are indeed long historical antecedents for a view of the transferability of management practice suggesting the appropriateness of generic approaches:

> The management of private concerns differs from that of public concerns only in magnitude---those who understand how to employ men are successful directors of public and private concerns and those who do not err in the management of both. (Socrates 469-399 BC, translated by Marchant (1968)). (3)

The book indicated ample evidence of management practices common to both public and private sectors. Considerable effort in the public policy arena from the late 1970s was aimed at ensuring (what were considered) generic practices were applied in the public sector.

However, such a universal view fails to grasp the contextual complexities of management in both sectors. Rather than view management as a generic activity, the book adopted a twin foci out-lined in Part A and Part B. In Part A, business management was analysed in the context of performance in the competitive-market environment. Many of the key debates were about the extent to which internal management developed appropriately or whether market co-ordination and performance were achieved through external mechanisms. The categories used were internal and external management respectively. There was however another category, a sub-set of external management, which assessed the extent to which external management encompassed a wider societal dimension.

Part B recognised a contrast with the business sector. The contextual under-pinning of the public sector was the political policy arena rather than the competitive-market environment. However, the study of internal and external management was significant and appropriate. The internal practices used to manage resources made available by government were key to understanding public management. The way in which traditional administrative and professional structures managed the strong resource growth post-1945 was a key area of the work and the particularistic approaches of different parts of the public sector were fundamental. The book explored the dynamic of internal management, especially the extent to which changes in political and public policy direction disrupted internal management practices and arrangements and led to the import and introduction of external management.

So while the 'internal' and 'external' were valuable as categories for researching management in business and public sectors, this analysis recognised the different contextual environments of each .

Business Management

The elements of focus were the internal and external management of business. The analysis of external management was sub-divided into business and wider societal aspects.

The Growth and Development of Internal Management

Business management practice was analysed in the context of the market imperative: companies first and foremost perform in the market place, a key feature of which around the start of the twentieth century was the increasing scale of business organisation. Vertical and horizontal integration was significant, requiring from companies an increased attention on throughput to achieve efficiency in the management of the firm. From around 1900, the most significant changes in management were found most obviously in the USA since it led the way in size and scale of business operation. In relative terms, Britain was distanced from this: though similar trends were clearly seen here, the country's interface with the international competitive environment, especially in the 40 or so years after 1930, was such that in large sections of business, competitive exposure was not a particularly strong instrument of change.

There was a strengthening of structures to accommodate market led integration of value chain activities with subsequent exertion of control on the market place. This was typified by the evolution of the hierarchically structured multi divisional (M) form from the early decades of the twentieth century. Similar developments occurred in Britain, too, but in a less uniform and systematic manner and often later. The Chandlerian paradigm of development (investment in internal management practices and structures and the shift from external co-ordination strategies to the managerial 'visible hand') was not experienced in the shipbuilding case. Here, external often personalised managerial practices typical of 'personal capitalism' persisted with robust internal management supports and structures either non-existent or under-developed by any objective comparative standard. Yet this industry was internationally competitive in the first two decades of the twentieth century. And there is a strong continuing body of research and literature in UK business history questioning the apparent limitations of personal capitalism per se as an engine of business development.

Contemporary management of throughput has a very different focus. Attention turned from the internally integrated organisation to co-ordination through managing relationships with suppliers, contractors and other external bodies; in terms of organisational structure, the writing and research now refers to the 'post-M Form'. Clearly this reflects a shift from internal to external management, and has been underpinned by changes in the market environment which gained momentum after 1970.

The book focused on a range of internal management practices, specifically those relating to the management of people. First, the craft-technical system so important in Britain was often considered in many ways an externally modulated system: with the 'craft' (which was external to any individual company) rather than internal company management assuming key responsibilities for training. In addition, the craft system often contested managerial control of certain work processes. Nonetheless the value and benefit of this system for internal management of business was obvious: self regulating, the craft community itself providing recruitment and training, obviating or minimising the need for employers to invest in these areas of activity; in sectors particularly subject to the vicissitudes of the business cycle (for example, shipbuilding and some heavy engineering sectors) a plentiful supply of skilled labour was a disincentive to increasing the intensity of capital investment; important too was the key part played by the 'craft leader' (the foreman) in management control, studied in some detail in the shipbuilding case. Given the factor mix in shipbuilding (low capital and high labour intensity) with production dominated by the craft system, the foreman as a front line manager was a key element in managerial control. Various practices and incentives were used to engage the managerial and company identity of the foreman from housing to relative job security, longevity and advancement of employment opportunities. The system however, especially after 1960, had severe limitations for the strength and efficiency of internal company management with much evidence of shortcomings in the shipbuilding case studied. There was a rather different experience in the contemporary case: in X plc the craft technical resource in the engineering division was in fact a considerable strength for company management.

Second, the conventional view that managerial training was considered largely informal (indeed often non existent) relative to other countries until the last quarter of the twentieth century was not entirely borne out by archive material from the Weir group in the early 1950s. The cases showed that in shipbuilding, managers were well trained technically (e.g. with special emphasis on world class naval architecture training). But while managerial training was not ignored, there did appear to be institutional barriers to the training, development and mobility of craft-technical personnel into management beyond supervision, compounding a well recognised shortage of managerial skill in the industry by the late 1960s. In the contemporary case, X plc, a lack of attention to managerial training and education was identified by a government funded agency (Investors in People) a situation that the company later addressed.

Third, many of the approaches used in managing the firm's human resource were intended to strengthen managerial control, and in this sense strengthen internal management. Welfare schemes were often introduced in antagonism to trade union growth, though in shipbuilding these were targeted at white collar staff, particularly foremen. 'Human relations', while having a concern for the personal and psychological development of employees was influenced by a managerial control agenda. No evidence of such practices was apparent in the shipbuilding case, not surprising since the anti-pluralistic underpinnings of human relations ran counter to the trade union regulated workplace environment, a traditional feature of shipbuilding.

The growth and development of HRM practices had the potential to internally strengthen management. HRM attempted to integrate personnel management, training and development with the strategic and other goals of the organisation, at the same time giving individual managers devolved and de-centralised responsibilities. Greater internal management control occurred from the 1980s within an altered industrial relations environment, but chapter 4 showed that the impact of HRM was mixed. Case research in X certainly identified a less than comprehensive approach to the implementation of HRM. Indeed large-scale surveys in the 1990s have indicated that one of the key aims of HRM, gaining commitment of employees to organisational goals, has not been achieved comprehensively throughout UK industry.

From Internal Management Control to Externalisation?

From the 1970s changes in the business-competitive environment and the related fall from grace of the vertically integrated internally managed corporate structure, invite the question, business management: from internal management control to externalisation? There is broad agreement that the transaction costs of internalisation increased relative to external market co-ordination for a wide range of businesses. This was particularly apparent in firms with high volume throughput and extended value chains that were subject to international competition and susceptible to upward pressure on wages. Companies in manufacturing and oil refining exemplified this. In addition there was a significant growth in inter-firm trade in the major multi-nationals whose strategies moved significantly from regional integration to globalisation and a sharing of business risk between companies in research and development. In contrast with pre-1970 years, British business was not isolated from the competitive environment's ability to act as a driver of change: this was demonstrated in X plc as well as more generally through the experience and effects of foreign direct investment into the UK since the1970s. Yet X plc showed that while there was considerable evidence of the management of external linkages in the supply and value chain, there were very strong elements of internal management - for example of the craft and technical resource.

Such market pressure towards externalisation and away from the M form was indeed ironic for large areas of British business activity, occurring just when it seemed that US styled internally integrated M form structures had been well deployed in Britain after a slow start. However there had always been much managerial success in British companies which used external strategies (or at least strategies and practices quite different from the integrated M form), lending support to Penrose's (1959) view of the importance of managerial action rather than Chandler's (1979; 1990) somewhat over deterministic and perhaps ethnocentric structure-based perspective. (4)

Despite increased external management and co-ordination of business up to the present, management control within companies was still important, though less likely to occur solely within the boundaries of the firm: writing and research on management in the post-M form environment has appreciated the requirement to design practices which integrated rather than internalised management. Practices were focused on the integration of structures that gave more authority and devolved responsibility to business units and entities removed from the centre. Case research of X plc indicated that while the decentred 'federal' or devolved status of the post-M form model as portrayed by Bartlett and Ghoshal did not apply to X's joint venture operating companies, integration was nonetheless strong: in fact stronger than it appeared to some of X's managers (who viewed relationships with headquarters in Brussels almost like the typical H form with financial control but little integration of management practices). The part played by managerial roles in integration of activities was not fully in accord with Bartlett and Goshal's model, though it was shown that market imperative and management control were still the key drivers of practice in the post-M form environment, albeit that control was more focused on integration rather than internalisation.

External Management of Business: The Societal Dimension.

The wider societal engagement of business, which spanned the entire period from 1900 to present, was an important aspect of external management. This too was viewed in terms of market context and management control. There were a range of motivations for business figures extending activities beyond the narrowly defined confines of business management; these motivations included philanthropy and civic mindedness. However, the activities of Weir, Lithgow and others in the period up to and beyond 1945 was viewed largely in terms of securing markets for companies (or indeed even narrower self-interest in some instances). There was little evidence that wider societal engagement compromised companies' control of management or business practices at company level even in the high water mark years of corporatism. The 'post-corporate era' after 1980 saw the rise to prominence of the 'stake-holding company'. Conceptually, this could have implications for corporate governance, diluting notions of managerial control in the sense that wider groups (that is, stakeholders both internal and external to the organisation), had an active interest and focus on the company's activities. Stake-holding theory also legitimised on the one hand business managers extending their sphere of influence to areas which have hitherto been the preserve of the public sector, by playing an important role in the governance of public funded bodies; on the other hand, companies being introduced with some compulsion into the wider social arena and encouraged to audit a range of activities (e.g., in the social, community and environmental arenas) which impact on stakeholders. In the contemporary case, a key internal stake-holder (employees) were in fact not included in the institutional governance of the company, in contrast to the parent group's institutional practice in Belgium. The divergence was explained by Britain's legislative exclusion from certain EU directives. Senior managers of X on the other hand were involved in non-executive governance of a number of public funded bodies. Other company activities also indicate a wider stake-holder perspective, for example X's preparation of an 'Environmental Account and Audit Statement' in addition to its financial report. X appeared to illustrate and exemplify the position of many leading companies in Britain. That is, a broad recognition of the stake-holder perspective in terms of broader social and community engagement but no settled consensus with regard to the balance of stake-holder rights in terms of the privileging of share-holders' over others' interests. Nor is there agreement on the measurement and implementation regime to assess business management activity in this area (see below).

Public Sector Management

Public Sector Management 1945-1970s.

Although in the public sector, many management practices were driven by concerns similar to those in firms (e.g., all areas of the public sector after 1945 had practices to address resource efficiency), the key contextual differences between the sectors were fundamental. In business, the two drivers of management practice were market imperative and management control. In the public sector it was the political environment shaped by government policy and legislative enactment, and secondly (certainly from 1945 to the 1970s) the co-option of existing administrative and professional structures to operate and manage public services.

Public Sector Management: The Importance of Internal Structures and Systems

The dominant role played by the political process was in the provision of resource to achieve political objectives. This is not to deny that attempts were made to influence the internal running of public services. The NHS in particular was riddled with examples of ministers and civil servants seeking to influence the internal management of the service. But to little effect (Klein 1995). In the three main parts of the public sector, the NHS, local government and civil service, administrative and professional structures provided a better explanation of management practice. These structures were particularistic. In the civil service the attention of senior civil servants was focused on policy advice to ministers and an understanding of the legislative process (allied to observance of expenditure limits voted by parliament), rather than the achievement of outputs. This led to the triumph of the generalist. By contrast in local government, particularly in the education management case studied, the post-1945 years saw the growth of specialist control within the council in the sense that the most senior education officials developed practices and strategies to retain control of service delivery. NHS practices were typified by professional medical control at executive level as embedded in the founding legislation. Analysis of the recognised particularisms and diversity in management was deepened by original archival research on NHS hospital service management and on education management in two local authorities, as well as research of the contemporary case, Y College.

NHS founding legislation was based on the executive control of resources at local level. This gave power and control to, in large measure, the medical profession. The study of the greater Glasgow hospital service indicated how professional control over hospital resources was established. The attempt by central government to introduce change into these internal professional systems in the 1970s by the introduction of 'rational' approaches to management was, despite rigorous attempts, largely unsuccessful in disturbing prevailing management and professional arrangements. The archival research of the Western Regional Hospital Board and associated bodies indicated a less enthusiastic approach to change by central government administration in Scotland. Reasons for this different approach in Scotland were explored.

The traditional ethos of civil service management which (at senior civil servant level) was encapsulated by the giving of policy advice to ministers rather than management of departmental resources and outputs, the custodianship of public finances and the supremacy of the generalist, was comprehensively scrutinised by the Fulton Royal Commission in the late 1960s. Fulton recommended some changes to traditional internal management. In particular, greater use was to be made of specialists. Also recommended was a shift from the senior civil servants' preoccupation with policy advice to prioritising the achievement of policy objectives and outputs. However, although some changes to existing internal practices were made, traditional departmental structures remained intact and some commentators argued that serious change was circumvented.

The third pillar of the public management study, local government, was a key element of state sector growth after 1945, since it was the key provider of the new and expanded services in housing, education, personal and social services. Growth occurred through existing internal structures, though with considerable diversity between local authorities. Research showed considerable divergence of practice within one local authority, Glasgow Corporation. The case research also showed that the proposed changes from traditional departmental and other organisational arrangements to more corporate approaches as outlined in the Royal Commission on Local Government in Scotland were strongly supported by the council's internal management. In addition, the local authorities themselves influenced the implementation machinery. However, the extent to which corporatism was actually implemented is questionable based on the evidence of one local authority (Strathclyde Regional Council). The archive based research of education management in Glasgow and Strathclyde councils 1955-1992 (supported by a small number of interviews) showed the continuing strength of departmental control until 1989, despite attempts from the mid to late 1970s to introduce a centralising and co-ordinating corporate overlay to this.

Public Sector Management. The 1980s to the Present: Politically Driven Change and the Import of External Management in the Public Sector?

From the 1980s, the politically driven aspects of management change were significant. Considerable political energy was expended in attempting to alter and disturb pre-existing internal management. There were attempts to import generic approaches, the new managerialism, into the public sector, there-by undermining pre-existing internal management and control.

New managerialism in the public sector had twin foci: the control of policy and strategy at the centre, and the devolution of operational decision making and resource/cost management to local managers at delivery level. The former would diminish the power of professional groups and service providers, since policy would be centralised (and therefore substantially controlled) at governmental level. Government would be helped in this by giving more power to managers rather than professionals, inevitable given the focus on cost and resource control. Pressure for change was intensified with compulsory competitive tendering, marketisation and subsequent governance changes, which led to fragmentation of service provision. An important consequence of the centralisation of public policy was the dis-association of policy discussion and development from service provision. This was particularly important in local government with the removal of democratic control and accountability from a range of local initiatives and services previously provided by councils. According to some writers, these were precisely the aims of governments in the 1980s and 1990s (Greer and Hoggett 1999).

The long-lasting impact of these 'imported' changes was assessed. As expected, there was differential impact. In the civil service, a considerable number of functions were transferred out and subjected to market and cost disciplines, though the extent to which internal practice changed was variable. In local government, while much had been taken from local council control with local authorities now functioning in an environment of 'governance' rather than 'area government', some aspects of the new managerial agenda gave councils greater control over service provision (for example, the ability to specify pay and work conditions in tendered services, this previously being subject to national union negotiation). The case study on the management of education provision in Strathclyde indicated that the council used aspects of the new managerial agenda actively from 1987 to retain traditional local education authority and professional control of schools. This contrasted with experience in English schools management. Strathclyde education directorate papers clearly indicated that senior managerial activity was motivated by a desire to retain control of key aspects of education management within the local authority. The council's initiative in devolving resources to individual schools (Direct Management of Resources, DMR) was given approval by the council precisely to pre-empt central government action, thereby minimising loss of local authority locus on the management of school resources.

In the health sector, the case study illustrated that elements of the new managerial agenda were applied but (at least until 1987) skewed significantly towards local resource management/cost control. Attempts to alter NHS governance appeared to have led to an accommodation between powerful professional interests and the strategic clinical/resourcing concerns of government, with the professionals' power base maintained.

Y College was a particularly interesting and compelling case, given the position of colleges as typical new managerial bodies, deliberately removed from local education authority control and given considerable operational autonomy in the planning and use of their own finances. College (non executive) boards of management were heavily dominated by those from a business or commercial background. Although the power of the traditional council providers was clearly diminished, chapter 11 indicated that an important part of the management and provision of further education was professionally controlled by educators, despite the creation of a managerial infrastructure. While the direct funding of colleges from central government could imply control from the centre, what was found was college participation in policy and resourcing networks, and a fairly fluid and dynamic relationship between institution and central government. This is likely to continue. Control of many externally managed relationships migrated not from local authorities to central government but collectively to colleges. Finally, the fracturing of public policy from service provision and democratic accountability was accurate only in the sense of loss of democratically elected local authority control of colleges. The research showed college involvement in a range of neighbourhood and other organisations; it also showed that while board meetings were dominated by business rather than education service issues, this was not the case in other very important college governance bodies.

British Management in Public and Business Sectors 1900-2003. Towards an Engagement of Internal and External Management

This book was based on a representative study of British management practice, studying both business and public sectors, using a range of primary researched case studies and utilising current literature.

There were clear differences in the context of management in both these sectors. The key objectives of each sector differed, the public sector conditioned by governmental and public policy aims, the business sector by the over-arching requirement to perform in the market environment. Nonetheless, internal and external management were the key practices in both sectors, key to understanding and analysing managerial practice.

In British business, the growth and development of Chandlerian type internal management structures and controls was limited, though nonetheless evident in some firms and sectors. But many parts of British business undertook successful management practices typified by alternative strategies ranging from external market co-ordination to personalised and network based approaches. The shipbuilding case indicated management appropriate to the factor endowment mix of the industry and its wider environment, though this led to rigidities and a management infrastructure eventually incapable of modernisation.

After the 1970s a range of business and economic factors shifted the focus from internally integrated management to external management. This occurred alongside other changes affecting internal management of business including a de-regulation of workplace relations and the development of HRM and other management led initiatives like TQM, all strengthening internal management. In fact, the key literature as well as the case research of X plc indicated a dynamic consensus between external business relationships and internal management control, suggesting a synthesis of internal and external management, depicted as the integration of dispersed activities. While there is ample evidence of this synthesis taking place, it is important to note fissures in the process. Research in X plc and elsewhere has indicated only a partial success of HRM practices achieving the objective of integration, with pluralistic perspectives and employee quiescence stronger than commitment to strong internal management practices. In X, an inappropriate choice of organisational structure to manage increased global sourcing and other internationalised external activities could make integration and synthesis difficult to achieve.

Throughout the entire period studied, the wider societal engagement of business was an important aspect of management. The societal dimension has been separated from the sphere of internal management in the sense that there has been little relationship between societal engagement activities and internal management of the business, even in the high tide years of corporatism. However, currently there are strong themes of synthesis between internal business management and societal engagement. The extension of business managerial activity into many areas of public policy interest, supported by stake-holding theories of the firm, has integrated more closely the internal management of the business and indeed legitimised companies' wider societal engagement. However, X plc showed that some management practices considered illustrative of a stake-holding perspective (e.g., employee representation and participation) were shaped most significantly by a key external factor, the national legislative framework: this explained the different approaches to employee representation in X plc and other parts of the multinational group. This it could be argued suggests that governmental and legislative action will be as important a driver and shaper of managerial activity than business management generated activities by themselves. The wider stake-holder perspective of business is, it could be argued, at a crossroads particularly with regard to the effectiveness of current approaches to measurement and implementation of the wider societal impacts of business activity. There is a recognition that company management should be publishing an 'Operating and Financial Review' providing non-financial information and analysis of the company's operations. There is however caution expressed by some (e.g., Sikka 2004) that this will be ineffective in stimulating real business management-societal engagement due to the fact that the Companies Acts will not specify indicators, leaving this to business led negotiation processes through the Accounting Standards Board.

In the public sector, the substantial resource increases after 1945 were managed by particularistic practices based on internal administrative and professional structures. There were attempts to introduce change and modification to these practices in the 1960s and early 1970s by a process of external scrutiny. However, the extent to which this led to changes in practice was limited. In the civil service some external change was introduced but was limited in scope. In the NHS little change occurred in terms of the medical-professional executive management of the hospital service. In local government, while structural change took place, it was shown that the driver of this change had significant internal support. Yet, as the Strathclyde case showed, the structural change which took place (in the form of the introduction of corporate management structures) did not comprehensively replace existing internal practices.

Major public policy initiatives from the late 1970s gave force to the introduction of external management in three parts of the public sector studied. There were two main aspects of external management change. First, the importation of a generic managerialism with a strong emphasis on cost and resource control. Second, an attempt to reconfigure public sector management by giving the centre strategic control of policy while devolving operations and cost control responsibility to the service deliverers. There is a strong body of research literature on the implementation experience of these changes. There is evidence of the successful transfer of HRM and other practices into parts of the core executive (Gould-Williams 2004). On the other hand, the experience of partnerships between public and private sectors indicates that the highly context specific nature of partnership activity highlights not simply the import of generic private sector practices into the public sector (as much 'new right' thinking anticipated and encouraged), but more particularistic approaches (Pollitt and Talbot 2004). Even one of the more detailed and prescriptive initiatives, 'Best Value' in local government has experienced considerable local authority discretion and diversity (Geddes and Martin 2000). In addition, large swathes of public sector management activity (most clearly displayed in the NHS) has not seen de-professionalisation in favour of managerial interests, but an accommodation of professional interests to the management of service delivery, more accurately described as re-professionalisation.

The reality of central government's relationship with the devolved management of service delivery also paints a complex picture. Executive agencies have gained operational autonomy (and have delivered service improvements) but the strategic control of these from the centre has been questionable (Bichard 1999; Talbot 2004). Indeed, government policy after 1997 (and arguably before then) by shifting emphasis from markets to strategic target based approaches often attempted to increase centralised strategic control of service delivery (with, for example, the use of treasury driven public service agreements) has had limited impact with the relevant government departments and service deliverers (James 2004). There may currently be a trend to more local initiative and discretion with the concept of 'earned autonomy' (in for instance English local authorities and foundation hospitals) indicative of a 'new localism' (Lowndes and Wilson 2003): this suggests an engagement between centre and service deliverer, rather different to a simple division of activity attributing strategy and policy to the centre, delivery and operations to the locale or institution.

All the primary researched cases revealed there was no simple importation of external practices into internal management arrangements. The research findings showed a synthesis of internal and external management. In all three public sector cases the outcome of external change was not a simple usurpation of internal management structures, practices and controls. The hospital service case indicated some loss of individual clinician freedom, but a process of co-option where professional interests retained much of the execution of policy. The concept of medical managerialism was noted. The case study on education management in Strathclyde displayed that while the new managerial agenda was introduced, it was executed and implemented in such a way that professional and local government control was maintained. Y College too showed evidence of considerable professional retention of key aspects of institutional management.

The second aspect of external change, the fracturing of policy and service delivery, was analysed in some detail in Y College. In one sense there was clear indication of externally driven dominance submerging pre-existing internal arrangements: the removal of the further education sector from local authority control eliminated local government from the policy discourse on post-16 education, leading to claims of democratic deficit. Yet the case lent support to the theme of internal and external management synthesis. College management participated actively in external (often central government initiated) policy networks. There was also active management engagement in policy discourse at local level through a range of local participatory and community based bodies.

Notes

1.   Drucker, P. (1954), *The Practice of Management*, New York: Harper and Row, p. 125.
2.   Wren, D.A. (1994), *The Evolution of Management Thought*, fourth edition, New York and London: Wiley p. 10.
3.   Socrates, *Memorabilia and Oeconomicus*, trans E.C. Marchant (1968), Cambridge MA: Harvard University Press p. 189.
4.   According to Penrose (1959), size and structure are not key determinants of business effectiveness. Her view is of the firm as a pool of resources organised within an administrative framework with managerial action fundamental to success. This in fact is conceptually close to current resource based views of strategy (e.g., Prahalad and Hamel 1989; 1993; Stalk, Evans and Schulman 1992; Tece, Pisano and Shien 1990; Kay 1993).

Bibliography

Primary Archive Sources

DC 96 Series. Papers of Viscount Weir based in the Scottish Business History Archive.

UCS Series. Business Records of John Brown Shipbuilders and Fairfield Shipbuilding and Engineering Company, located in the Scottish Business History archive and Glasgow City Archive.

TD Series. Shipbuilding Employers Federation and Clyde Shipbuilders and Engineers Association Records in Glasgow City Archive.

D-CF
D-ED   Glasgow Corporation Departmental Records in Glasgow City Archive.
D-OM
D-WS

HB and RHB Series. Greater Glasgow Health Board Records in Greater Glasgow Health Board Archive.

C1125; C1676; C2261; C1571 Boxed Papers. Strathclyde Regional Council Directorate Papers, based in Glasgow City Archive.

SR Series. Other Strathclyde Regional Council records based in Glasgow City Archive.

THES. Times Higher Education Supplement.
ET. Evening Times.
FT. Financial Times.

Books and Journals

Aaronovitch, S. and Sawyer, M. (1975), *Big Business*, London: Macmillan.
Abraham, N. (1974), *Big Business and Government. The New Disorder*, London: Macmillan.
Ackrill, M. (1988), 'Britain's Managers and the British economy, 1870s to the 1980s', *Oxford Review of Economic Policy*, Vol. 4, No. 1 pp. 59-73.
Ackroyd, S. and Proctor, S. (1998), Models of Manufacturing: Understanding Change in Contemporary British Industry, *Proceedings Managing Innovative Manufacturing Conference*, Nottingham.
Adams, I.H. (1978), *The Making of Urban Scotland*, London.
Adler, P.A., Adler, P. and Fontana, A (1987), 'Everyday life sociology' in K Plummer (ed), *Symbolic Interactionism: Vol. 1. Foundations and History*, Brookfield, VT.
Adler, P.S. and Cole, R.E. (1993), 'Designed for learning: a tale of two plants' *Sloan Management Review*, Vol.34, No. 3. pp. 32-44.

Ainley, P. and Bailey, B. (1997), *The Business of Learning*, London: Cassell.

Albertson, N. (1998), 'Postmodernism, post Fordism and critical social theory', Environment and Planning D: *Society and Space*, No. 6. pp. 17-36.

Aldfcroft, D.H. (1986), *The British Economy, Vol. 1, The Years of Turmoil 1920-1951*, Brighton: Wheatsheaf.

Aldcroft, D.H.(1992), *Education, Training and Economic Performance 1994-1990*, Manchester: Manchester University Press.

Alexander, K. (1970), *Fairfields: A Study of Industrial Change*, London: Allen Lane.

Alford, B.W.E (1998), *British Economic Performance 1945-1975*, London: Macmillan.

Allen, W.T. (1992), 'Our schizophrenic conception of the business corporation' *Cardoza Law Review*, Vol. 14, No. 2.

Alter, C. and Hage, J. (1993), *Organisations Working Together*, London: Sage.

Amdam, R.P. (ed) (1995), *Management Education and Business Performance*, London: Routledge.

Andreescu, F. (2003), Post- New Public Management Models? New templates and possible lessons from a British commercialising public organisation, *Conference paper, British Academy of Management annual conference*.

Ansoff, I. (1988), *Corporate Strategy*, London: Penguin.

Argenti, J. (1997), 'Stakeholders. The case against', *Long Range Planning*, Vol. 30 No. 3. pp. 442-445.

Arnold, D., Birkinshaw, J. and Toulan, O. (2000), Implementing Global Account Management in Multinational Corporations, *MSI Working Paper 00-103 and London Business School Working Paper* 57/99, London.

Ashburner, L. (1996), ' The role of clinicians in the management of the NHS' in J. Leopold., I. Glover. and M Hughes, *Beyond Reason? The National Health Service and the Limits of Management*, Aldershot: Avebury.

Ashworth, W. (1991), *The State in Business, 1945 to the mid 1980s*, London: Macmillan.

Atkinson, J. (1984), 'Manpower strategies for flexible organisations' *Personnel Management*, August.

Atkinson, J. and Meager, N. (1986), 'Is the flexible firm just a flash in the pan?' *Personnel Management*, September.

Audit Commission (1996), *Trading Places, The Supply and Allocation of School Places*, London: HMSO.

Austin, M. (1997), 'Old lags must find ways to break the funding shackles' in *Times Educational Supplement*, 20 June.

Babson, S. (1993), 'Lean or mean: the MIT model and lean production at Mazda' Labour *Studies Journal, 18. (Summer)* pp. 3-21.

Bacon, R. and Eltis, W. (1978), *Britain's Economic Problem: Too Few Producers*, second edition, London: Macmillan.

Balasubramanyan, V.N. (1993), 'Entrepreneurship and the growth of the firm: the case of the British food and drink industries in the 1980s' in J. Brown and M.B. Rose (eds), *Entrepreneurship, Networks and Modern Business*, Manchester: Manchester University Press.

Bains Report (1972), *The New Local Authorities: Management Structures*, London: HMSO.

Barberis, P. (1995), 'The civil service from Fulton to Next Steps and beyond; two interpretations: two epistemologies' *Public Policy and Administration* Vol.10, No.2, pp. 34-51.

Barberis, P. (1996), *The Elite of the Elite: Permanent Secretaries in the British Higher Civil Service*, Aldershot: Dartmouth.

Barker, J.R. (1993), 'Tightening the iron cage: coercive control in self managing teams', *Administrative Science Quarterly* Vol.38, Sept. pp. 408-437.

Barnett, C. (1986), *The Audit of War: The Illusion and Reality of Britain as a Great Nation,* London: Macmillan.

Barrell, R. and Pain, N. (1997), 'Foreign direct investment, technological change and economic growth within Europe', *Economic Journal* 107 pp. 1770-1786.

Bartlett, C. and Ghoshal, S. (1989), *Managing Across Borders: The Transnational Corporation,* Harvard MA: Harvard Business School Press.

Bartlett, C. and Ghoshal, S. (1990), 'Matrix management: not a structure, a frame of mind', *Harvard Business Review,* Vol. 68 No. 4 pp. 138-145.

Bartlett, C. and Ghoshal, S. (1998), 'Beyond the M form: towards a managerial theory of the firm' in S. Segal-Horn, *The Strategy Reader,* Oxford: Blackwell.

Bartrip, P. (1996), *Themselves Writ Large. The British Medical Association 1832-1966,* London: BMJ Publishing Group.

Basset, P. (1986), *Strike Free – The New Industrial Relations in Britain,* London: Macmillan.

Basset-Jones, N. and Brewer, R. (1997), 'Strategic management and competitive advantage' in R. Levacic and R Glatter (eds), *Managing Change in Further Education,* London: Further Education Development Agency.

Baxter, J.L and McCormack, J.B. (1984), 'Seventy per cent of our future: the education, training and employment of young people' *National Westminster Bank Quarterly Review,* November, pp. 8-21.

Bean, C. and Crafts, N. (1996), 'British economic growth since 1945: relative economic decline and renaissance?, in N. Crafts and G. Toniolo (eds) *Economic Growth in Europe Since 1945,* London.

Beatson, M. (1995), Labour Market Flexibility, *Employment Department Research Series* 48, April.

Beaumont, P.B. (1985), 'The diffusion of human resource management innovations', *Relations Industrialles (Canada),* Vol. 40.

Beesley, M.E. and Littlechild, S. (1986), 'Privatisation: principles, problems and priorities' in J.A. Kay, C. Mayer and D. Thompson (eds), *Privatisation and Regulation: the UK Experience,* Oxford: Clarendon.

Bendix, R. (1956), *Work, Authority and Industry: Ideologies of Management in the Course of Industrialisation,* London: Wiley, Chapman Hall.

Berg, N.A. (1969), 'What's different about conglomerate management?' *Harvard Business Review,* Vol. 47, No. 4, pp. 112-120.

Bettis, R.A. and Hall, W.K. (1983), 'The business portfolio approach: where it breaks down in practice' *Long Range Planning,* Vol. 16, No. 2, pp. 95-104.

Bichard, M. (1999), Performance Management-Civil Service Reform: A Report to the Meeting of the Permanent Heads of Department, London: Cabinet Office.

Birkinshaw, J. (2000), *Entrepreneurship in the Global Firm,* London: Sage.

Birkinshaw, J., Hood, N. and Jonson, S. (1998), 'Building firm and specific advantages in multinational corporations: the role of subsidiary initiatives' *Strategic Management Journal,* 19, pp. 221-241.

Birkinshaw, J. and Hugstrom, P. (2000), The Flexible Firm: *Capability Management in Network Organisations,* Oxford University Press: Oxford.

Black, J. and Dunning, J.H. (eds) (1982), *International Capital Movements,* London: Macmillan.

Blackburn, J.A. (1982), 'The vanishing UK cotton industry' *National Westminster Bank Quarterly Review,* Nov. pp. 42-52.

Blackford, Mansel G. (2003), 'British business history: a review of the periodical literature for 2001', *Business History,* Vol. 45, No.2, April.

Booth, A. (1996), 'Corporate policies and the search for productivity: the British TUC and the politics of industrial productivity 1947-1960' in J. Melling and A McKinlay, *Management, Labour and Industrial Politics in Modern Europe*, Cheltenham: Edward Elgar.

Booth, A. (2000), 'Inflation, expectations and the political economy of Conservative Britain' *The Historical Journal* Vol. 43. No.3 pp. 827-847.

Booth Committee (1918), *Report on Shipping and Shipbuilding After the War*, Cmnd 9092.

Booz-Allen and Hamilton Report (1973), *British Shipbuilding*, Department of Trade and Industry, London.

Bostock, F. and Jones, G. (1994), 'Foreign Multinationals in British Manufacturing 1950-1962' *Business History* Vol. XXXVI, No.1, pp. 89-126.

Boticelli, P. (1997), 'The British engineering press during the second industrial revolution: responses to corporate capitalism', *Business History Review*, Vol. 71, No. 2, pp. 260-286.

Bovaird, T. and Russell, K. (2003), Civil service reform: evolution or revolution?, *Conference paper, British Academy of Management annual conference.*

Bowden, S., Foreman-Peck, J. and Richardson, T. (2001), 'The post war productivity failure: insights from Oxford (Cowley)', *Business History* Vol. 43, No. 3, pp. 54-78.

Bower, J.L (1970), *Managing the Resource Allocation Process*, Boston MA: Harvard Graduate School of Business Administration.

Boyce, G. (1992), 'Corporate strategy and accounting systems: a comparison of developments at two British steel firms 1898-1914' in C Harvey and G Jones (eds) 'Organisational capability and competitive advantage', Special Issue, *Business History* Vol. XXXIV, No. 1, pp. 42-65.

Boyce, G. and Lepper, L. (2002), 'Assessing information quality theories: the USS Co. joint venture with Wm. Holyman and Sons and Huddart Parker Ltd. 1904-1935', *Business History*, Vol. 44, No. 2 pp. 19-39.

Boyne, G., Martin, S. and Walker, R. (2004), 'Explicit reforms, implicit theories and public service improvement', *Public Management Review* Vol. 6, No. 2, pp. 189-210.

Braverman, H. (1974), *Labour and Monopoly Capital*, New York: Monthly Review Press.

Bray, A. (1988), The Clandestine Reformer: A Study of the Rayner Scrutinies, Glasgow: *Strathclyde Papers in Government and Politics*, No. 55.

Brereton, M. and Temple, M. (1999), 'The new public service ethos: an ethical environment for governance' *Public Administration* Vol. 77, No. 3, pp. 455-474.

Brewster, C. (1995), 'Towards a European model of human resource management', *Journal of International Business Studies*, Vol. 26, No. 1, pp. 1-26.

Briggs, A. (1979), *The Age of Improvement*, London: Longmans.

British Medical Association (1998), Letter to Chairman of Professional Regulation Working Group, 8 May, unpublished. Cited in Corby, S (1999) 'The National Health Service' in S. Horton and D. Farnham (eds) *Public Management in Britain*, London: Macmillan.

British Medical Journal (1970), Editorial Comment, 3 June, cited in R. Klein (1974), 'Policy making in the National Health Service' *Political Studies*, Vol. XXII, No. 1 pp. 114.

Broadberry, S.N. and Crafts, N.F.R (1992), 'Britain's productivity gap in the 1930s: some neglected factors' *Journal of Economic History* Vol. 52, No. 3, pp. 531-558.

Broadberry, S.N. and Crafts, N. (2001), 'Competition and innovation in 1950s Britain', *Business History*, Vol. 431, Winter, pp. 97-118.

Broadberry, S.N. and Marrison, A. (2002), 'External economies of scale in the Lancashire cotton industry 1931-1939', *Enterprise and Society*, Vol. 3 No. 1, pp. 51-77.

Brown, J. and Rose, M.B (eds) (1993), *Entrepreneurship, Networks and Modern Business*, Manchester.

Bryson, C., Gallagher, J., Jackson, M., Leopold, J. and Tuck, K (1993), 'Decentralisation of collective bargaining: local authority opt outs' *Local Government Studies*, Vol.19 No.4, pp. 114-132.

Buckley, P. and Casson, M. (1988), 'The theory of co-operation in international business' in F. Contractor and P. Lorange (eds) *Co-operative Strategies in International Business*, Lexington, MA: Lexington Books.

Budhwar, P.S. (2000a), 'A reappraisal of HRM models in Britain', *Journal of General Management*, Vol. 26 No. 2, pp. 72-133.

Budhwar, P.S. (2000b), 'Strategic integration and devolvement of human resource management in the British manufacturing sector', *British Journal of Management* Vol. 11, No. 4, pp. 285-302.

Butler, R. (1994), 'Reinventing British government: a symposium', *Public Administration* Vol. 72 No. 2, p. 263.

Burn, D. (1961), *The Steel Industry 1939–59*, Cambridge: Cambridge University Press.

Buxton, N.K. (1968), 'The Scottish shipbuilding industry between the wars. A comparative study' *Business History* 10, Nos. 1 and 2, pp. 101-120.

Byrne, T. (1994), *Local Government in Britain: Everyone's Guide to How it all Works*, London: Penguin.

Cabinet Office (1991), *The Government's Guide to Market Testing*, London: HMSO.

Cabinet Office (1997), *The Government's Response to Comments on the Green Paper, Government Direct*, London: The Stationery Office.

Cabinet Office (1998), *Modern Public Services for Britain: Investing in Reform*, Cmnd. 4011, London: The Stationery Office.

Cabinet Office Performance and Innovation Unit. (2000), *Adding it Up: Improving Analysis and Modelling in Central Government*, London: Cabinet Office.

Cameron, R. (1997), *A Concise Economic History of the World. From Paleolithic Times to the Present*, third edition, Oxford: Oxford University Press.

Campbell, A. (1997), 'Stakeholders: the case in favour', *Long Range Planning*, Vol. 30 No. 3, pp. 446-449.

Campbell, A., Fishman, N. and McIlroy, J. (eds) (1999), *British Trade Unions and Industrial Politics Vol. 1*, Aldershot: Ashgate.

Campbell, R.H. (1980), *The Rise and Fall of Scottish Industry 1707-1939*, Edinburgh.

Cannon, T. (1994), *Corporate Responsibility*, London: Pitman.

Carew, A. (1991), 'The Anglo-American Council on Productivity (1948-1952): the ideological roots of the post war debates on productivity in Britain' *Journal of Contemporary History* Vol. 26, No.1, p. 49.

Casson, M.C. (1987), *The Firm and the Market: Studies of Multinational Enterprise and the Scope of the Firm*, Oxford: Blackwell.

Casson, M.C. (1995), 'Information costs and the organisational structure of the multinational enterprise', *University of Reading Discussion Papers in International Investment and Business*, Series B V11. No. 193.

CBI (1999), *Employers Survey*, Confederation of British Industry, London.

Chandler, A.D. (1962), *Strategy and Structure: Chapters in the History of American Industrial Enterprise*, Cambridge MA: MIT Press.

Chandler, A.D. (1976), 'The development of modern management structures in the US and UK', in L Hannah (ed), *Management Strategy and Business Development. An Historical Perspective*, Macmillan: London.

Chandler, A.D. (1977), *The Visible Hand: The Managerial Revolution in American Business*, Cambridge MA: Belkins Press.

Chandler, A.D. (1980), 'The United States: seedbed of managerial capitalism' in A.D. Chandler and H. Daems, (eds), *Managerial Hierarchies: Comparative Perspectives on the Rise of the Modern Industrial Enterprise*, Cambridge, M.A.

Chandler, A.D. (1990), *Scale and Scope: The Dynamics of Industrial Capitalism*, Cambridge MA: Harvard University Press.

Chandler, A.D. and Daems, H. (eds) (1980), *Managerial Hierarchies: Comparative Perspectives on the Rise of the Modern Enterprise*, Cambridge, M.A.

Channon, D.F. (1973), *The Strategy and Structure of British Enterprise*, London: Macmillan.

Chapman, R and Greenaway, J. (1980), *The Dynamics of Administrative Reform*, London: Croom Helm.

Chapman, R. and O'Toole, B. (1995), 'The role of the civil service: a traditional view in a period of change', *Public Policy and Administration*, Vol. 10. No. 2, pp. 3-20.

Checkland, S.G. (1975), *Scottish Banking: A History, 1695-1973*, Glasgow: Collins.

Chester, D.N. (1975), *The Nationalisation of British Industry 1945-1951*, London: HMSO.

Chick, M. (1990a), 'Marginal cost pricing and the peak hour demand for electricity 1945-51' in M. Chick (ed) *Governments, Industries and Markets*, Aldershot: Edward Elgar.

Chick, M. (ed) (1990b), *Governments, Industries and Markets*, Aldershot: Edward Elgar.

Chick, M. (1994), 'Nationalisation, privatisation and regulation' in M.W. Kirby and M.B. Rose (eds) *Business Enterprise in Modern Britain From the Eighteenth to the Twentieth Century*, London: Routledge.

Chick, M. (1995), 'The political economy of nationalisation: the case of electricity distribution' in R. Milward and J. Singleton (eds), *The Political Economy of Nationalisation in Britain 1920-1950*, Cambridge: Cambridge University Press.

Child, J. (1969), *British Management Thought: A Critical Analysis*, London: George Allen and Unwin.

Christopher, M. (1998), *Logistics and Supply Chain Management: Strategies for Reducing Cost and Improving Service*, London: Pitman.

Church, R. (1993), 'The family firm in industrial capitalism: international perspectives on hypotheses and history' *Business History* Vol. XXXV, No.4, pp. 17-39.

Church, R. (1994), *The Rise and Decline of the British Motor Industry*, London: Macmillan.

Citizen's Charter (1991), *Raising the standard*, Cmnd. 1599, London: HMSO.

Citizen's Charter (1994), *Second Report of the Citizen's Charter Unit*, Cmnd. 2540, London: HMSO.

Clark, P. and Tann, J. (1986), 'Cultures and corporations: the M form in the USA and Britain', *Paper presented to the International Academy of Business Conference 1986.*

Clarke, J. and Newman, J. (1997), *The Managerial State: Power, Politics and Ideology in the Remaking of Social Welfare*, London: Sage.

Clarke, M. and Stewart, J. (1991), *The Role of the Chief Executive*, Luton: Local Government Management Board.

Clarke, R. (1971), *New Trends in Government*, London: HMSO.

Clarke, T. and Clegg, S. (1998), *Changing Paradigms. The Transformation of Management Knowledge for the Twenty First Century*, London: Harper Collins.

Clarkson, M. (1995), 'A stakeholder framework for analysing and evaluating corporate social performance' *Academy of Management Review*, Vol. 20, No.1, pp. 80-110.

Clay, H. (1957), *Lord Norman*, London: Macmillan.

Clegg, S.R. and Palmer, G. (1996), *The Politics of Management Knowledge*, London: Sage.

Clutterbuck, D. and Crainer, S. (1988), *The Decline and Rise of British Industry*, Mercury Books.

Coase, R.H. (1937), 'The nature of the firm', *Economica*, New Series 4; reprinted in Supple, B.E. (ed) *The Rise of Big Business*, Aldershot: Edward Elgar.

Coleman, D.C. (1973), 'Gentlemen and players', *Economic History Review*, Vol. XXVI. No. 1, pp. 92-116.

Coleman, D.C. (1987), 'The uses and abuses of business history', *Business History* Vol. XXIX. No. 2, pp. 141-156.

Collins, M. (1995), 'The growth of the firm in the domestic banking sector' in MW Kirby and MB Rose (eds), *Business Enterprise in Modern Britain From the Eighteenth to the Twentieth Century*, London: Routledge.

Collins, B. and Robbins, K. (ed), *British Culture and Economic Decline*, London: Weidenfield and Nicholson.

Constable, J. and McCormick, R. (1987), *The Making of British Managers*, London: British Institute of Management.

Cooke, P. and Morgan, K. (1993), 'The network paradigm: new departures in corporate and regional development' Environment and Planning D: *Society and Space* Vol. 11, No. 5, pp. 543-564.

Cooper and Lybrand (1988), *Report on Delegated Management in Schools*, London: Department of Education and Science, Cooper and Lybrand Consultants.

Corby, S. (1993), 'How big a step is 'Next Steps'? Industrial relations developments in executive agencies', *Human Resources Management Journal*, Vol. 4 No. 2.

Corby, S. (1998), 'Industrial relations in civil service agencies: transition or transformation', *Industrial Relations Journal*. Vol. 29. No.3 pp. 194-206.

Corby, S. (1999), 'The National Health Service' in S. Horton. and D. Farnham, *Public Management in Britain*, London: Macmillan.

Cox, H. (1997), 'Learning to do business in China: evolution of BAT's cigarette distribution network 1902-1941' *Business History*, Vol. 39 No. 3, pp. 30-64.

Crafts, N.F.R. and Woodward, N.W.C. (1992), *The British Economy Since 1945*, Oxford: Blackwell.

Crequer, N. (1998), 'Fearful principals sought mergers', *Times Educational Supplement* 16 October.

Crewe, I. (1982), 'The Labour Party and the electorate' in D. Kavanagh (ed), *The Politics of the Labour Party,* London: Allen and Unwin.

Cross, J. (1995), 'IT outsourcing: British Petroleum's competitive approach' *Harvard Business Review*, Vol. 73 No. 3, pp. 94-104.

Cross, M. (1990), 'Contracting out in UK manufacturing industry: recent developments and issues' in H Ormuson and D Ross (eds), *New Patterns of Work*, St Andrews: St Andrews Press.

Crowther, M.A. (1990), 'Poverty, health and welfare' in W.H. Fraser and R.J. Morris (eds), *People and Society in Scotland, Vol. 11, 1830-1914*, Edinburgh.

Daly, A., Hitchens, D.M.W.N. and Wagner, K. (1985), 'Productivity, machinery and skills in a sample of British and German manufacturing plants', *National Institute Economic Review* 111, p. 48.

Damer, S. (1980), 'State, class and housing: Glasgow 1885-1919' in J. Melling (ed), *Housing, Social Policy and the State*, London: Croom Helm.

Dassbach, C.H.A.C (1989), *Global Enterprise and the World Economy*, New York: Garland.

Davidson, A. (1947), *Scottish Experiments in Social Medicine*, Johns Hopkins.

Day, P. and Klein, R. (1985), *Accountabilities*, London: Tavistock.

Department for Education (1991a), *Access and Opportunity: A Strategy for Education and Training,* Cmnd. 1530, London: HMSO.

Department for Education (1991b), *Education and Training for the Twenty First Century*, Cmnd. 1536, London: HMSO.

Department of Health (1997), *The New NHS, Modern and Dependable*, Cmnd. 3807, London: HMSO.

Department of Health in Scotland (1943), *Health and Industrial Efficiency. Scottish Experiments in Social Medicine*, Edinburgh: HMSO.

Devine, P.J. (1976), 'The Firm', 'Corporate Growth' and 'State Intervention' in the private sector' in P.J. Devine., R.M. Jones., N. Lee. and W.J Tyson (eds), *An Introduction to Industrial Economics*, London: George Allen and Unwin.

Devine, P.J., Jones, R.M., Lee, N. and Tyson, W.J. (eds) (1976), *An Introduction to Industrial Economics*, London: George Allen and Unwin.

Devine, T.M. (1999), *The Scottish Nation 1700-2000*, London: Penguin.

Digby, A. (1999), *The Evolution of British General Practice 1850-1948*, Oxford: Oxford University Press.

Drewry, G. and Butcher, T. (1994), *The Civil Service Today*, second edition, Oxford: Blackwell.

Drodge, S. and Cooper, N. (1997), 'The management of strategic planning in further education colleges' in R. Levacic and R. Glatter (eds), *Managing Change in Further Education*, London: Further Education Development Agency.

Drucker, P. (1954), *The Practice of Management*, New York: Harper and Row.

Drummond, D.K. (1995), *Crewe: Railway Town, Company and People 1840-1914*, Aldershot: Scolar Press.

DTI (1998), *Our Competitive Future: Building the Knowledge Driven Economy. The Competitiveness White Paper: Analysis and Background*, Department, London: The Stationery Office.

Dunkerley, J. and Hare, P.G. (1992), 'The nationalised industries' in N.F.R. Crafts and N.W.C Woodward (eds) *The British Economy Since 1945*, Oxford: Clarendon.

Dunleavy, P. (1991), *Democracy, Bureaucracy and Public Choice*, Hemel Hempstead: Harvester Wheatsheaf.

Dunleavy, P. and Hood, C. (1994), 'From old public administration to new public management', *Public Money and Management*, Vol.14, No.3, pp. 9-16.

Dunning, J.H. (1970), *Studies in International Investment*, London: George Allen and Unwin.

Dunning, J.H. (1985), 'The United Kingdom' in J.H Dunning (ed) *Multinational Enterprise, Economic Structure and International Competitiveness*, Chichester: Wiley.

Dunning, J.H. (1986), *Japanese Participation in British Industry*, London: Croom Helm.

Durnin, J. and Peck, F. (1999), 'Inter firm networks and the relevance of proximity: the case of Cumbria'. *Paper presented to the 39th European Congress of the European Regional Science Association*, 22-27 August 1999, University College, Dublin.

Dyas, G.P and Thanheiser, H.T. (1976), *The Emerging European Enterprise*, London: Macmillan.

Dyos, H.J. and Aldcroft D.H. (1974), *British Transport: An Economic Survey from the Seventeenth Century to the Twentieth*, Harmondsworth: Pelican.

Eckstein, H. (1958), *The English Health Service*, Cambridge MA: Harvard University Press.

Edwards, P.K., Hall, M., Hyman, R., Marginson, P., Sisson, K., Waddington, J. and Winchester, D. (1998), 'Great Britain: from partial collectivism to neo liberalism to where?' in A. Ferner and R. Hyman (eds), *Changing Industrial Relations in Europe*, Oxford.

Edwards, P.K. and Whitson K. (1989), 'Industrial discipline, the control of attendance and the subordination of labour: towards an integrated analysis' *Work, Employment and Society*, Vol.3, No.1, pp. 1-28.

Egelhoff, W.G. (1984), 'Patterns of control in US, UK and European multinational corporations' *Journal of International Business Studies*, Vol.15, Fall, pp.73-84.

Elbaum, B. and Lazonick (eds) (1986), *The Decline of the British Economy*, Cambridge: Cambridge University Press.

Elcock, H. (1994), 'The parlous state of British democracy', *Public Money and Management,* Vol.1, No.4, pp. 4-5.

Elcock, H., Fenwick, J. and Harrop, K. (1998), Partnerships for Public Service, *Local Authority Unit Discussion Paper:* Newcastle Upon Tyne Polytechnic.

Elliot, D.C. and Gribbin, J.D. (1977), 'The abolition of cartels and structural change in the United Kingdom' in A.P. Jacquemin and H.W. de Jong (eds), *Welfare Aspects of Industrial Markets,* Leiden: Leiden University Press.

Elliot, G. (1996), 'Educational management and the crisis of reform in further education', Journal of Vocational Education and Training, No. 48, pp. 26-35.

Elliot, G. and Crossley, M. (1997), 'Contested values in further education', *Educational Management and Administration,* Vol. 25, No.1 pp. 79-92.

European Journal of Industrial Relations (1998), Vol. 4, No. 1.

Fairburn, J. (1989), 'The evolution of merger policy in Britain' in J. Fairbairn and J. Kay (eds), *Mergers and Merger Policy,* Oxford: Oxford University Press.

Farnham, D. and Giles, L. (1996), 'Education' in D. Farnham and S. Horton (eds), *Managing People in the Public Services,* Basingstoke: Macmillan.

Farnham, D. and Horton, S. (eds) (1996), *Managing the New Public Services,* second edition, London: Macmillan.

Farnham, D. and Horton, S. (eds) (1996), *Managing People in the Public Services,* London: Macmillan.

Farnham, D. and Horton, S. (1999), 'Managing public and private organisation' in S. Horton and D. Farnham (eds), *Public Management in Britain,* London: MacMillan.

Farquarson Lang Report (1996), *Administrative Practice of Hospital Boards in Scotland,* Edinburgh: HMSO.

Ferner, A. and Hyman, R. (eds), (1998), *Changing Industrial Relations in Europe,* Oxford.

Findlay, P., Hine, J.A., McKinlay, A., Marks, A. and Thompson, P. (2000), 'Flexible when it suits them' in S. Proctor and F Mueller (eds), *Teamworking,* London: Macmillan.

Findlay, P., McKinlay, A., Marks, A. and Thompson, P. (2000), 'In search of perfect people: teamwork and team players in the Scottish spirits industry', *Human Relations* Vol. 53, No. 12, pp. 1549-1574.

Finer, S.E. (1956), The Federation of British Industry, Political Studies Vol. 4. pp. 61-68.

Finlay, I., Holmes, S. and Kydd, L. (1997) 'Institutional boundary management: experiences in Scottish colleges since incorporation' in R. Levacic and R. Glatter, *Managing Change in Further Education,* London: Further Education Development Agency.

Fitzgerald, L. (1996), 'Clinical management: the impact of a changing context on a changing profession' in Leopold, J., Glover, I. and Hughes, M. (eds), *Beyond Reason? The National Health Service and the Limits of Management.* Stirling Management Series, Aldershot: Avebury.

Fitzgerald, R. (1988), *British Labour Management and Industrial Welfare 1846-1939,* Croom Helm.

Fitzgerald, R. (1993), 'Industrial training and management education in Britain; a missing dimension' in N. Kawake and E Daito (eds), *Education and Training in the Development of Modern Corporations,* Tokyo: Tokyo University Press.

Fitzgerald, R. (2000), 'Markets, management and merger: John MacKintosh and Sons 1890-1969', Business History Review, Vol. 74, Winter, pp. 555-610.

Flinders, M., Harden, I. and Marquand, D. (eds) (1997), *How to Make Quangos Democratic,* London: Charter 88.

Flynn, N. (1997), *Public Sector Management,* third edition, London: Prentice Hall.

Foreman-Peck, J. (ed) (1991), *New Perspectives on the Late Victorian Economy,* Cambridge: Cambridge University Press.

Foreman-Peck, J., Bowden, S. and McKinlay, A. (1995), *The British Motor Industry*, Manchester: Manchester University Press.

Foreman-Peck, J. and Federico, G. (eds) (1999), *European Industrial Policy: The Twentieth Century Experience*, Oxford: Oxford University Press.

Foreman-Peck, J. and Hannah, L. (1999), 'Britain: from economic liberalism to socialism-and back?', in J. Foreman Peck and G Federico (eds), *European Industrial Policy: The Twentieth Century Experience*, Oxford: Oxford University Press.

Foreman-Peck, J. and Milward, R. (1994), *Public and Private Ownership of British Industry 1920-1990*, Oxford: Clarendon.

Foster, J. and Woolfson, C. (1986), *The Politics of the UCS Work-In*, London: Lawrence and Wishart.

Fowler, N. (1991), *Ministers Decide: A Memoir of the Thatcher Years*, London: Chapman.

Fraser Inquiry. (2004), *A Report by the Rt Hon Lord Fraser of Carmyllie QC on his Inquiry into the Holyrood Building Project*, SP paper 205, Edinburgh: Scottish Parliament Corporate Body.

Fraser, W.H. and Maver, I. (eds) (1996), *Glasgow Vol. 11: 1930-1912*, Manchester: Manchester University Press.

Fraser, W.H. and Morris, R.J. (eds) (1990), *People and Society in Scotland, Vol. 11, 1830-1914*, Edinburgh.

Franco, L (1976), *The European Multinationals*, London: Harper and Row.

Franco, L. (1978), 'Organisational structures and multinational strategies of continental European enterprises' in M. Ghertman and J. Liontiades (eds), *European Research in International Business*, Amsterdam: North Holland.

Freeman, R.E. and Reed, D.L. (1983), 'Stockholders and stakeholders: a new perspective on corporate governance', *California Management Review*, Vol.25, No. 3.

Friedman, M. (1962), *Capitalism and Freedom*, Chicago: University of Chicago Press.

Fry, G. (1969), *Statesmen in Disguise*, Macmillan: London.

Fry, G. (1984), 'The development of the Thatcher government's 'grand strategy' for the civil service: a public policy perspective', *Public Administration*, Vol. 62, No.3 pp. 322-335.

Fry, G. (1999), 'More than 'counting manhole covers': the evolution of the British tradition of public administration', *Public Administration*. Vol. 77, No. 3. pp. 527-540.

Fulton Report (1968), *The Civil Service, Vol. 1*, Cmnd. 3638, London: HMSO.

Gallie, D. and Felstead, A. (2001), 'Employer policies and organisational commitment in Britain 1992-1997', Journal of Management Studies, Vol. 38, December. pp. 1053-1080.

Garside, W.R. and Greaves, J.J. (1997), ' Rationalisation and Britain's industrial malaise: the interwar years revisited', *Journal of European Economic History*, Vol. 26 No. 1, pp.37-68.

Geddes, M.N. and Martin, S.J. (2000), 'The policy and politics of Best Value: currents, cross-currents and under-currents in the new regime', *Policy and Politics*, Vol. 28 No.3, pp. 377-394.

Geddes Report (1966), *Shipbuilding Enquiry Committee 1965-1966*, London: Cmnd. 2937 HMSO.

Gee, R. (1997), 'Introduction' in R. Levacic. And R. Glatter (eds), *Managing Change in Further Education,* London: Further Education Development Agency.

Geertz, C. (1973), 'Thick description: toward an interpretative theory of culture' in C Geertz, *The Interpretation of Cultures*, New York: Basic Books.

Geertz, C. (ed) (1973), *The Interpretation of Cultures*, New York: Basic Books.

Ghoshal, S. and Bartlett, C.A. (1994), 'Linking organisational context and managerial action: the dimensions of quality of management' *Strategic Management Journal*, Summer Special Issue.

Glaister, K.W. and Buckley, P.J. (1997), 'Task related and partner related selection criteria in UK international joint ventures', *British Journal of Management*, 8, pp. 199-222.

Glynn, S. and Booth, A. (1996), *Modern Britain, An Economic and Social History*, London: Routledge.

Gospel, H.F. (1992), *Markets, Firms and the Management of Labour in Modern Britain*, Cambridge: Cambridge University Press.

Gospel, H.F and Littler, C.R. (eds) (1983), *Managerial Strategies and Industrial Relations*, London: Heinemann.

Gould-Williams, J. (2004), *'The effects of 'high commitment' HRM practices on employee attitudes: the views of public sector workers'*, Public Administration, Vol. 28, No.1, pp. 63-81.

Gourvish, T.R. (1972), *Mark Huish and the London and North Western Railway*, Leicester: Leicester University Press.

Gourvish, T.R. (1980), *Railways and the British Economy, 1830-1914*, London: Macmillan.

Gourvish, T.R. (1987), 'British business and the transition to a corporate economy', *Business History* Vol.29, No.4, pp.18-45.

Gourvish, T.R. (1991), 'The rise (and fall?) of state owned enterprise' in T. Gourvish and A. O'Day (eds), *Britain Since 1945*, London: Macmillan.

Gourvish, T. and O'Day, A. (1991), *Britain Since 1945*, London: Macmillan.

G.P (1998) Editorial 'We are facing crisis', 15 May, 36.

Grant, W. (1993), *Business and Politics in Britain*, Basingstoke.

Greasley, D. (1995), 'The coal industry: images and realities on the road to nationalisation' in R. Milward and J. Singleton (eds), *The Political Economy of Nationalisation in Britain 1920-1950*, Cambridge: Cambridge University Press.

Greaves, J.I. (2002), 'Competition, confusion and collusion: the state and the re-organisation of the British Cotton industry 1931-1939', *Enterprise and Society*, Vol. 3 No. 1 pp. 48-79.

Green, F. (2001), 'Its been a hard day's night: the concentration and intensification of work in late twentieth century Britain' *British Journal of Industrial Relations*, Vol.39, No.1, pp. 53-80.

Greer, A. and Hoggett, P. (1999), 'Public policies, private strategies and local public spending bodies' *Public Administration*, Vol. 77, No. 2, pp. 235-256.

Greer, S. (2003), Policy divergence. Will it change something in Greenock?, in R Hazell (ed), *The State of the Nations 2003: The Third Year of Devolution in the United Kingdom*, London: UCL Constitution Unit.

Greenwood, R. and Stewart, J.D. (eds) (1974), *Corporate Planning in English Local Government*, Birmingham and London: Inlogov and Charles Knight.

Greenwood, R., Walsh, K, Hinings, C.R. and Ranson, S. (1978), *Patterns of Management in Local Government*, London: Martin Robertson.

Grey Book (1972), *Management Arrangements for the Reorganised NHS*, London: HMSO.

Gribbin, J.D. (1978), *'The post war revival of competition as industrial policy'* Government Economic Service Working Paper 19.

Griffiths, R. (1983), *Report of the NHS Management Enquiry*, London: Department of Health and Social Security.

Hague, D. and Wilkinson, G. (1983), *The IRC-An Experiment in Industrial Intervention*, London: Allen and Unwin.

Hall, P.A. (1986), 'The state and economic decline' in B Elbaum and W. Lazonick (eds), *The Decline of the British Economy*, Oxford: Clarendon Press.

Ham, C. (1981), *Policy Making in the National Health Service*, London: Macmillan.

Hamel, G. and Prahalad, C.K. (1994), *Competing for the Future*, Cambridge MA: Harvard Business School Press.

Hamill, J. (1991), 'Strategic restructuring through international acquisition and divestments', *Journal of General Management* Vol.17, No. 1, pp. 27-44.

Hammersley, M. and Atkinson, P. (1995), *Ethnography: Principles in Practice*, second edition, London.

Hampel Report (1998), *Corporate Governance*, London: Committee on Corporate Governance and Gee Publishing.

Handy, C. (1988), *Making Managers*, London: Pitman.

Hannah, L. (1974), 'Managerial innovation and the rise of the large scale company in interwar Britain' *Economic History Review* 27, pp. 252-270.

Hannah, L. (1976a), *Management Strategy and Business Development. An Historical and Comparative Study*, London: Macmillan.

Hannah, L (1976b), 'Strategy and structure in the manufacturing sector' in L. Hannah (ed) *Management Strategy and Business Development. An Historical and Comparative Study*, London: Macmillan.

Hannah, L. (1977), 'A pioneer of public enterprise: the Central Electricity Board and the National Grid 1927-1940' in B. Supple (ed) *Essays in British Business History*, Oxford: Clarendon Press.

Hannah, L. (1980), 'Visible and invisible hands in Great Britain' in A.D. Chandler and H. Daems (eds), *Managerial Hierarchies: Comparative Perspectives on the Rise of the Modern Industrial Enterprise*, Cambridge, M.A.

Hannah, L. (1983a), *The Rise of the Corporate Economy*, London: Methuen.

Hannah, L. (1983b), ' New issues in British business history', *Business History Review*, Vol. 57, No. 2, pp. 165-174.

Hansard (1991), House of Lords (HL), Vols. 532 and 533.

Harper, H. (2000), 'New college hierarchies? Towards an examination of organisational structures in further education in England and Wales', *Educational Management and Administration*, Vol. 28 No.4, pp. 13-29.

Harrison, S. and Wood, B. (1999), 'Designing Health Service organisation in the UK 1968-1998: from blueprint to bright idea and manipulated emergence', *Public Administration*, Vol. 77. No. 4, pp. 751-768.

Hawkins, K. (1976), *British Industrial Relations 1945-1975*, London: Barrie and Jenkins.

Hayek, F.A. (1974), *Law, Legislation, Liberty Vol 3: The Political Order of a Free People*, Chicago: University of Chicago Press.

Haz, A.C. and Majluf, N.S (1991), *The Strategy Concept and Process*, London: Prentice Hall.

Heclo, H. and Wildavsky, A. (1974), *The Private Government of Public Money*, first edition, London: Macmillan.

Heclo. H. and Wildavsky, A. (1981), *The Private government of Public Money*, second edition, London: Macmillan.

Heilbroner, R.L. (1972), *In the Name of Profit*, New York: Doubleday.

Hennessy, P. (1989), *Whitehall*, London: Secker and Warburg.

Hertner, P. and Jones, G. (1986), *Multinationals: Theory and Practice*, Aldershot: Gower.

Heseltine, M. (1980), 'Ministers and management in Whitehall', *Management Services in Government*, No. 35.

Hewitt, P. and Crawford, M. (1997), 'Introducing new contracts: managing change in the context of an enterprise culture' in R. Levacic and R. Glatter (eds), *Managing Change in Further Education*, London: Further Education Development Agency.

Higgs Report (2003), Review of the Role and Effectiveness of Non Executive Directors, London: Department of Trade and Industry.

Hofstede, G. (1984), *Cultures Consequences*, London: Sage.

Hoggett, P. (1991), 'A new management in the public sector?, *Policy and Politics*, Vol. 19, No. 4, pp. 243-250.

Hoggett, P. (1996), 'New modes of control in public service' *Public Administration*, Vol. 74, No. 1, pp. 9-32.

Hoggett, P. and Hambleton, R. (1988), *Decentralisation and Democracy*, Bristol: School of Advanced Urban Studies, University of Bristol.

Hollis, P. (1987), *Women in English Local Government 1865-1914*, Oxford: Clarendon Press.

Holloway, D., Horton, S. and Farnham, D. (1999), 'Education' in S. Horton and D. Farnham (eds), *Public Management in Britain*, London: Macmillan.

Honeyman, K. (2000), *Well Suited, a History of the Leeds Clothing Industry*, Oxford: Oxford University Press.

Hood, C. (1991), 'A public management for all seasons', *Public administration*, Vol. 69 No.1, pp. 3-19.

Horton, S. (1996), 'The civil service' in D. Farnham and S. Horton (eds), *Managing People in the Public Services*, London: Macmillan.

Horton, S. and Farnham, D. (1999), 'New Labour: legacies, impacts and prospects' in S Horton and D. Farnham (eds), *Public Management in Britain*, London.

Horton, S and Farnham, D. (eds) (1999), *Public Management in Britain*, London: Macmillan.

Howe, G. (1981), *Privatisation: The Way Ahead*, Conservative Political Centre.

Howgego, J. (1993), *The Incorporation of Colleges of Further Education in Scotland. A Personal Account of the Former HM Chief Inspector*, Edinburgh: SOEID.

Howlett, P. (2000), 'Evidence of the existence of an internal labour market in the Great Eastern Railway Company 1875-1905' *Business History*, Vol. 42 No. 1, pp. 21-40.

Hubert, F. and Pain, N. (2001), 'Inward investment and technical progress in the UK manufacturing sector', *Scottish Journal of Political Economy*, Vol. 48 No. 2, pp.134-147.

Huczynski, A.A. (1994), *Management Gurus. What Makes Them and how to Become One*, London: Routledge.

Hughes, A. (1976), 'Company concentration, size of plant and merger activity' in M Panic (ed), *The UK and West German Manufacturing Industry 1954-1972: A Comparison of Structure and Performance*, London: HMSO / NEDO.

Human Relations (1947-1948), 'Editorial Policy', Vol.1.

Human Relations (1965), 'Restatement of Editorial Policy' Vol. 18.

Humes, S. (1993), *Managing the Multinational*, Hemel Hempstead: Prentice Hall.

Humes, W.M. (1986), *Leadership and Class in Scottish Education*, Edinburgh: John Donald.

Humes, W.M. (1994), 'Policy and management: mending the fracture' in W.M. Humes and M.L MacKenzie (eds), *The Management of Educational Policy: Scottish Perspectives*, London: Longman.

Humes, W.M. (1997), 'Analysing the policy process', *Scottish Educational Review*, Vol.29, No. 1, pp. 20-29.

Hunter, G. (1957), The Role of the Personnel Officer: A Group Review, London, *IPM Occasional Paper No. 12*.

Hunter, J.J. (1986), *Managing the National Health Service in Scotland: Review and Assessment of Research Needs*, Edinburgh: SHHD.

Income Data Services (1998), *Pay in the Public Services: Review of 1997, Prospects for 1998*, London.

Ingham, G. (1984), *Capitalism Divided? The City and Industry in British Social Development*, London: Macmillan.

Isaac-Henry, K. and Painter, C. (1991), 'The management challenge in local government: emerging trends', *Local Government Studies*, Vol.17 No.3, pp. 69-90.

Isaac-Henry, K., Painter, C. and Barnes, C. (eds) (1997), *Management in the Public Sector,* London: Chapman and Hall.

Jackson, N. and Carter, P. (1998), 'Labour as dressage' in A. McKinlay and K. Starkey (eds), *Foucault, Management and Organisation Theory*, London.

Jacobs, M. (1997), 'The environment as stakeholder' *Business Strategy Review* Vol. 8, No. 2, pp. 25-28.

Jacquemin, A.P. and de Jong, H.W. (eds) (1977), *Welfare Aspects of Industrial Markets*, Leiden: Leiden University Press.

Jacques, E. (1951), *The Changing Culture of a Factory*, London: Tavistock Publications.

Jacques, E. (1981), *Requisite Organisation*, Arlington, VA.

James, O. (2004), 'The UK core executive's use of Public Service Agreements as a tool of governance', Public Administration, Vol. 82, No. 2, pp. 397-419.

Jeremy, D.J. (1998), *A Business History of Britain 1900-1990s*, Oxford: Oxford University Press.

Johnman, L (1991), 'The Labour Party and industrial policy 1940-1945' in N. Tiratsoo (ed), *The Attlee Years*, London: Pinter.

Johnson, G. and Scholes, K. (1998), *Exploring Corporate Strategy*, fourth edition, Hemel Hempstead: Prentice Hall.

Johnston, I. (2000), *Ships for a Nation. John Brown and Company Clydebank*, Glasgow: West Dunbartonshire Libraries and Museums.

Johnston, R. (2000), *Clydeside Capital, 1870-1920: A Social History of Employers*, East Linton: Tuckwell Press.

Johnston, T. (1952), *Memories*, Glasgow: Collins.

Jones, B. and Keating, M. (1985), *Labour and the British State*, Oxford: Clarendon Press.

Jones, C.S. (1992), 'The attitude of owner managers towards accounting control systems following management buyout', *Accounting, Organisation and Society*, Vol. 17 No.2, pp. 151-168.

Jones, E. (1978), *A History of GKN, Vol. 1, Innovation and Enterprise 1759-1918*, London: Macmillan.

Jones, G. (1986a), *British Multinationals: Origins, Management and Performance*, Aldershot: Gower.

Jones, G. (1986b), 'The performance of British Multinational enterprise 1890-1945' in P. Hertner and G. Jones (eds), *Multinationals: Theory and Practice*, Aldershot: Gower.

Jones, G. (1993), *British Multinational Banking 1830-1990*, Oxford: Clarendon Press.

Jones, G. (1994), 'British multinationals and British business since 1850' in M.W. Kirby and M.B. Rose, *Business Enterprise in Modern Britain From the Eighteenth to the Twentieth Century*, London: Routledge.

Jones, G. (1996), *The Evolution of International Business*, London: Routledge.

Jones, G. (1997), 'Some British paradoxes' *Business History Review*, Vol. 71 No. 2, pp. 291-298.

Jones, G. and Kirby, M.W. (eds) (1991), *Competitiveness and the State: Government and Business in Twentieth Century Britain*, Manchester: Manchester University Press.

Jones, G. and Rose, M. (1993), 'Family capitalism', *Business History* Vol. XXXV, No. 4, pp. 1-16.

Jordan, G. (1993), 'Next Steps: from managing by command to managing by contract', *Aberdeen Papers on Accountancy, Finance and Management*: University of Aberdeen.

Kanter, R.M. (1983), *The Change Masters*, London: Routledge.

Kay, J. (1993), *Foundations of Corporate Success: How Business Strategies Add Value,* Oxford: Oxford University Press.

Kay, J. (1997), 'The stakeholder corporation' in G. Kelly, D. Kelly and A. Gamble, *Stakeholder Capitalism,* Basingstoke: Macmillan.

Kay, J. and Thompson, D. (1986) 'Privatisation: a policy in search of a rationale' *Economic Journal,* 96, pp. 18-31.

Kay, J.A., Mayer, C. and Thompson, D. (eds) (1986), *Privatisation and Regulation: The UK Experience,* Oxford.

Kavanagh, D. (ed) (1982), *The Politics of the Labour Party,* London: Allen and Unwin.

Kavanagh, D. (1987), *Thatcherism and British Politics,* Oxford: Clarendon Press.

Kavanagh, D. (1990), *Thatcherism and British Politics: The End of Consensus,* Oxford: Oxford University Press.

Keeble, S.P. (1992), *The Ability to Manage: A Study of British Management 1890-1990,* Manchester: Manchester University Press.

Kellner, P. and Crowther-Hunt (1980), *The Civil Servants,* London: MacDonald.

Kelly, G., Kelly, D. and Gamble, A. (1997), *Stakeholder Capitalism,* Basingstoke: Macmillan.

Kemp, A. (2000), 'Devolution and responsibility?', *The Observer,* 5 November.

Kendal, I., Moon, G., North, N. and Horton, S. (1996), 'The National Health Service' in D. Farnham and S. Horton (eds), *Managing the New Public Services,* London: Macmillan.

Kennedy, M.M. (1979), 'Generalising from single case studies', Evaluation Quarterly, No. 1, pp. 24-36.

Kerley, R. (1994), *Managing in Local Government,* London: Macmillan.

King, D. and Stoker, G. (1996) (eds), *Rethinking Local Democracy,* Basingstoke: Macmillan in association with ESRC Local Programme.

Kirby, M.W. (1987), 'Industrial policy' in S. Glynn and A. Booth (eds). *The Road to Full Employment,* London: Macmillan.

Kirby, M.W. (1994), 'The corporate economy in Britain. Its rise and achievements since 1900' in M.W.Kirby and M.B. Rose (eds), *Business Enterprise in Modern Britain,* London: Routledge.

Kirby, M.W. and M.B. Rose (1994), *Business Enterprise in Modern Britain From the Eighteenth to the Twentieth Century,* London: Routledge.

Klein, R. (1974), 'Policy making in the National Health Service', *Political Studies* Vol. XX11, No. 1, pp. 10-25.

Klein, R. (1995), *The New Politics of the NHS,* third edition, London: Longman.

Knights. D. and Morgan, D. (1990), 'Management control in sales forces: a case study from the labour process of life insurance', *Work, Employment and Society,* Vol. 4, No.3, pp. 369-389.

Knox, W.W. (1999), *Industrial Nation. Work, Culture and Society in Scotland 1800-Present,* Edinburgh: Edinburgh University Press.

Knox, W.W. and McKinlay, A. (1999), 'Working for the Yankee Dollar: American inward investment and Scottish labour 1945-1970', *Historical Studies in Industrial Relations,* Vol. 7, Spring, pp. 1-26.

Kochan, T., Katz, H. and McKersie, R. (1986), *The Transformation of American Industrial Relations,* New York: Basic Books.

Kogan, M. (1969), 'Social services: their Whitehall status', *New Society* 21 August, pp. 282-285.

Kotler, P. (1992), 'Megamarketing' in D. Mercer, *Managing the External Environment,* London: Sage.

Kramer, D.C.(1988), *State Capital and Private Enterprise,* London: Routledge.

Kreiger, J. (1986), *Reagan, Thatcher and the Politics of Decline,* Cambridge: Polity Press.

Krubasik, E. and Lautenschlager, H. (1993), 'Forming successful strategic alliances in high-tech businesses' in J. Bleeke and D. Ernst, *Collaborating to Compete: Using Strategic Alliances and Acquisitions in the Global Market Place*, New York: Wiley.

Lane, H.W. and Beamish, P.W. (1990), 'Cross cultural co-operative behaviour in joint ventures in LDCs', *Management International Review*, 30, pp. 87-102.

Lawson, N. (1993), *The View From No. 11*, London: Corgi Books.

Lazonick, W. (1991), *Business Organisation and the Myth of the Market Economy*, Cambridge: Cambridge University Press.

Lazonick, W. and O'Sullivan, M. (1997), 'Finance and industrial development part 1: the USA and UK', *Financial History Review*, Vol. 4, No. 1, pp. 7-29.

Leavy, B. (1999), 'Organisation and competitiveness-towards a new perspective', *Journal of General Management*, Vol.24 No. 3, pp. 33-51.

Lee, C. (1990), 'Corporate behaviour in theory and history: 1. The evolution of theory', *Business History*, Vol. XXXII, pp. 17-31.

Leech, M. (1994), 'Corporate Caledonia: the management of policy in further education' in W.M. Humes and M.L. McKenzie (eds), *The Management of Educational Policy, Scottish Perspectives*, London: Longman.

Legge, K. (1995), *Human Resource Management: Rhetoric and Realities*, Chippenham: Macmillan.

Leopold, J., Glover, I. and Hughes, M. (1996), *Beyond Reason? The National Health Service and the Limits of Management*, Aldershot: Avebury.

Levacic, R. (1993), 'The coordination of the school system' in R. Maidment and G. Thompson (eds), *Managing the United Kingdom. An Introduction to its Political Economy and Public Policy*, London: Sage.

Levacic, R. and Glatter, G. (1997), *Managing Change in Further Education*, London: Further Education Development Agency.

Lewchuk, W. (1987), *American Technology and the British Vehicle Industry*, Cambridge: Cambridge University Press.

Lewchuck, W. and Robertson, D. (1996), 'Working conditions under lean production: a worker based benchmarking study?', *Asia Pacific Business Review*, Vol. 2 No.4, pp. 60-81.

Littler, C. (1982), *The Development of the Labour Process in Capitalist Societies: A Comparative Study*, London: Heinemann.

Littler, C. (1985), 'Taylorism, Fordism and job design' in D. Knights, H. Wilmot and D. Colinson (eds), *Job Redesign: Critical Perspectives on the Labour Process*, Aldershot: Gower.

Littler, C.R. and Salaman, G. (1984), *Class at Work*, London: Batsford.

Littlewood, J. (1998), The Stock Market: 50 Years of Capitalism at Work. London.

Locke, R. (1984), *Management and Higher Education Since 1940*, Cambridge: Cambridge University Press.

Locke, R. (1993), 'Education and entrepreneurship: an historian's view' in J. Brown and M.B. Rose (eds), *Entrepreneurship Networks and Modern Business*, Manchester: Manchester University Press.

Lorange, P. and Roos, J. (1992), *Strategic Alliances*, Oxford: Basil Blackwell.

Lorenz, E. (1991), *Economic Decline in Britain: The Shipbuilding Industry 1890-1970*, Oxford: Clarendon Press.

Lorenz, E. and Wilkinson, F. (1986), 'The shipbuilding industry 1880-1965' in B. Elbaum and W. Lazonick (eds), *The Decline of the British Economy*, Oxford: Oxford University Press.

Lovell, J. (1992), 'Employers and craft unionism: a programme of action for British shipbuilding, 1902-1905, *Business History*, Vol. XXXIV No. 4, pp. 38-58.

Lowe, R. (1996), 'The core executive and the historical development of the welfare state: modernisation and the creation of PESC 1960-64', Paper given to *ESRC Whitehall Programme Conference, Birmingham.*

Lowe, R. (1997), 'Milestone or millstone: the 1959-61 Plowden Committee and its impact on British welfare policy', *Historical Journal* Vol. 40, No. 2, pp. 463-491.

Lowndes, V. and Wilson, D. (2003), 'Balancing revisability and robustness? A new institutionalist perspective on local government modernisation', Public Administration, Vol. 81, No. 2 pp. 275-300.

Lynch, M. (1991), *Scotland. A New History*, London: Pimlico.

MacDonald, C.M.M. (2000), *The Radical Thread. Political Change in Scotland. Paisley Politics 1885-1924*, Scottish Historical Review Monographs series No. 7, East Linton: Tuckwell Press.

MacInnes, J. (1987), *Thatcherism at Work: Industrial Relations and Economic Change*, Milton Keynes: Open University Press.

Mackie, R. (2001), 'Family ownership and business survival: Kircaldy 1870-1970', Business History, Vol. 43, July, pp. 1-32.

MacKney, P. (1998), 'Move on after the misery', *Times Educational Supplement*, 3 April.

Mailley, R., Dimmock, S.J. and Setha, A.S. (1989), 'Industrial relations in the National Health Service since 1979' in R. Mailley, S.J. Dimmock and A.S. Setha (eds) *Industrial Relations in the Public Services*, London: Routledge.

Maidment, R. and Thompson, G. (eds) (1983), *Managing the United Kingdom. An Introduction to its Political Economy and Public Policy*, London: Sage.

Malloch, H. (1997) 'Strategic and HRM aspects of Kaizen: a case study' *New Technology Work and Employment*, Vol. 12 No. 2, pp. 108-122.

Mansell, P. (1996), 'Changing your perspective' *F.E Now!* 30.

Marinetto, M. (1999), 'The historical development of business philanthropy: social responsibility in the new corporate economy', *Business History*, Vol. 41, No. 4, pp. 1-20.

Marchant, E.C. (1968), *Socrates Memorabilia and Oeconomicus*, Cambridge MA: Harvard University Press.

Marquand, D. (1988), *The Unprincipled Society*, London: Fontana.

Marsh, D. and Rhodes, R.A.W. (1992), *Implementing Thatcherite Policies*, Buckingham: Open University Press.

Martinez, J.I. and Jarillo, J.C. (1989), 'The evolution of research on coordination mechanisms in multinational corporations', *Journal of International Business Studies*, 20, pp. 489-514.

Martinez, M. and Weston, S. (1994), 'New management practices in a multinational corporation: the restructuring of worker representation and rights?', *Industrial Relations Journal*, Vol.25 No.2, p. 110-121.

Marwick, A. (1990), *British Society Since 1945*, London: Penguin.

Mason, G., Prais, S.J. and Van Ark, B. (1992), 'Vocational education and productivity in the Netherlands and Britain', *National Institute Economic Review*, No. 140, pp. 415-462.

Matthew, D., Anderson, M. and Edwards, J.R. (1997), 'The rise of the professional accountant in British management' *Economic History Review*, Vol. L, No. 3, pp. 407-429.

Maude Report (1967), *Royal Commission on the Management of Local Government*, London: HMSO.

Maver, I .(2000), *Glasgow*, Edinburgh: Edinburgh University Press.

Maxwell, R. (1975), 'Anomie in the NHS – a McKinsey view', *British Medical Journal*, 4 July.

McDowell, R.D. (1994), 'Devolved management of schools: myth or reality?' in W.M.Humes and M.L. McKenzie, *The Management of Educational Policy, Scottish Perspectives,* London: Longman.

McGavin, H. (1998), 'Cut salaries or lose jobs, lecturers told', *Times Educational Supplement,* 24 April.

McGirr, E.M. (1988), 'Reflections on the NHS in Scotland', *Scottish Medical Journal,* Vol. 33, No. 1. pp. 472- 476.

McGoldrick, J. (1983), 'Industrial relations and the division of labour in the shipbuilding industry since the war', *British Journal of Industrial Relations,* Vol.XX1, No. 2 pp. 197-220.

McKinlay, A. (1989), 'The inter war depression and the effort bargain: shipyard riveters and the workman's foreman', *Scottish Economic and Social History,* Vol. 9. pp. 55-70.

McKinlay, A. (1996), 'Management and workplace trade unionism: Clydeside engineering 1945-1957', in J. Melling and A. McKinlay (eds), *Management, Labour and Industrial Politics in Modern Europe,* Cheltenham: Edward Elgar.

McKinlay, A. and Melling, J. (1999), 'The shop floor politics of productivity: work, power and authority relations in British engineering, c. 1945-1957' in A. Campbell, N. Fishman and J. McIlroy (eds), *British Trade Unions and Industrial Politics, Vol. 1, The Post War Compromise 1945-1964,* Aldershot: Ashgate.

McKinlay, A., Mercer, H. and Rollings, N. (2000), 'Reluctant Europeans? The Federation of British Industries and European integration 1945-1963', *Business History,* Vol. 42, No. 4, pp. 91-116.

McKinlay, A. and Starkey, K. (1994), 'After Henry: continuity and change in Ford Motor Company', *Business History,* Vol.36, No.1, pp. 184-205.

McKinlay, A. and Starkey, K. (eds) (1998), *Foucault, Management and Organisation Theory,* London: Sage.

McKinlay, A . and Taylor, P. (1996), 'Power, surveillance and resistance: inside the factory of the future' in P. Ackers, C. Smith and P. Smith (eds), *The New Work Force and Trade Unionism,* London: Routledge.

McKinlay, A and Taylor, P. (1998), 'Through the looking glass: Foucault and the politics of production' in A. McKinlay and K. Starkey (eds), *Foucault, Management and Organisation Theory,* London: Sage.

McKinlay, A. and Zeitlin, J. (1989), 'The meaning of managerial prerogative: industrial relations and the organisation of work in British engineering 1880-1939', *Business History* XXX1 No. 2, pp. 32-47.

McLean, I. (1983), *The Legend of Red Clydeside,* Edinburgh.

McPherson, A. and Raab, C.D. (1988), *Governing Education,* Edinburgh: Edinburgh University Press.

McShane, H. and Smith, J. (1978), No Mean Fighter, cited in W.W. Knox (1999), *Industrial Nation. Work Culture and Society in Scotland, 1800-Present,* Edinburgh: Edinburgh University Press.

McTavish, D. (1998), 'Strategic management in further education colleges: a pilot study', *Scottish Educational Review,* Vol.30 No. 2, pp. 125-137.

McTavish, D. (2000), 'The NHS-is Scotland different?: a case study of the management of the hospital service in the west of Scotland 1947-1987', Scottish *Medical Journal,* Vol. 45, No. 5, pp. 155-162.

McTavish, D. (2003), 'Aspects of public sector management. A case study of further education, ten years after the passage of the Further and Higher Education Act', *Educational Management Administration and Leadership,* Vol. 31, No. 2, pp.173-185.

Melling, J. (1980a), 'Non commissioned officers: British employers and their supervisory workers 1880-1920', *Social History,* Vol. 5, No. 2, pp. 183-221.

Melling, J. (1980b), *Housing, Social Policy and the State*, London.

Melling, J. (1981), 'Employers, industrial housing and the evolution of company welfare policies in Britain's heavy industry: west Scotland 1870-1920', *International Review of Social History*, Vol. XXVI, pp. 255-301.

Melling, J. (1983), 'Employers, industrial welfare and the struggle for workplace control in British industry 1880-1920', in H.F. Gospel and C.R. Littler (eds), *Managerial Strategies and Industrial Relations*, London: Heinemann.

Melling, J. (1989), ' The servile state revisited: law and industrial capitalism in the early twentieth century', *Scottish Labour History Journal* Vol.24, pp. 68-86.

Melling, J. (1996a), 'Safety, supervision and the politics of productivity in the British coal mining industry 1900-1960' in J. Melling and A. McKinlay (eds), *Management, Labour and Industrial Politics in Modern Europe: The Quest for Productivity During the Twentieth Century*, Cheltenham: Edward Elgar.

Melling, J. (1996b), 'Management, labour and the politics of productivity: strategies and struggles in Britain, Germany and Sweden', in J. Melling and A. McKinlay (eds), *Management, Labour and Industrial Politics in Modern Europe*, Cheltenham: Edward Elgar.

Melling, J. and McKinlay, A. (eds) (1996), *Management Labour and Industrial Politics in Modern Europe: The Quest for Productivity During the Twentieth Century*, Cheltenham: Edward Elgar.

Mercer, D. (1991), *Managing the External Environment*, London: Sage.

Mercer, H. (1989), 'The evolution of British government policy towards competition in private industry 1940-1956' *Unpublished PhD thesis, University of London* (cited in Mercer 1994, in Kirby, M.W. and Rose, M.B. (eds) *Enterprise in Modern Britain from the Eighteenth to the Twentieth Century*, London: Routledge.

Mercer, H. (1991), 'The Monopolies and Restrictive Practices Commission 1949-1956: a study in regulating failure' in G. Jones and M.W. Kirby (eds), *Competitiveness and the State: Government and Business in Twentieth Century Britain*, Manchester: Manchester University Press.

Mercer, H. (1994), 'The state and British business since 1945' in M.W. Kirby and M.B. Rose (eds), *Business Enterprise in Modern Britain From the Eighteenth to the Twentieth Century*, London: Routledge.

Micklethwaite, J. and Wooldridge, A. (1996), *The Witch Doctors. Making Sense of the Management Gurus*, London: Heinemann.

Middlemas, K. (1979), *Politics in Industrial Society: The Experience of the British System Since 1911*, London: Deutsch.

Middlemas, K. (1983), *Industry Unions and Government. Twenty Years of the NEDC*, London: Macmillan.

Middlemas, K. (1986), *Power, Competition and the State, Vol. 1, Britain in Search of Balance 1940-1961*, London: Macmillan.

Midwinter, A. (1982), *Corporate Management in Scottish Local Government Policy Making*, Birmingham: Institute of Local Government Studies.

Midwinter, A. (1995), *Local Government in Scotland. Reform or Decline?*, London: Macmillan.

Midwinter, A., Keating, M. and Mitchell, J. (1991), *Politics and Public Policy in Scotland*, Basingstoke: Macmillan.

Miles, R.E., Snow, C. and Coleman, H. (1992), 'Managing the twenty first century network organisation', *Organisational Dynamics* Vol. 20 No. 3, pp. 5-20.

Milkman, R. (1997), *Farewell to the Factory: Auto Workers in the Late Twentieth Century*, Los Angeles: University of California Press.

Miller, D. and Stirling, J. (1998), 'European Works Council training: an opportunity missed', *European Journal of Industrial Relations*, Vol. 4 No. 1, pp. 35-56.

Milward, N., Woodland, S., Bryson, A. and Forth, J. (1999), *A Bibliography of Research Based on WIRS*, London.

Milward, R. (1989), 'Privatisation in historical perspective: the UK water industry' in D. Cobham, R. Harrington and G. Zis (eds), *Money, Trade and Payments*, Manchester: Manchester University Press.

Milward, R. (1991), 'The causes of the 1940s nationalisation: a survey', *Working Papers in Economic and Social History, University of Manchester* No. 10.

Milward, R. (1997), 'The 1940s nationalisation in Britain: means to an end or the means of production?', *Economic History Review*, Vol. L, No. 2, pp. 209-234.

Milward, R. and Singleton (eds) (1995), *The Political Economy of Nationalisation in Britain 1920-1950*, Cambridge.

Mohr, J. and Spekman, R. (1994), 'Characteristics of partnership success: partnership attributes, communication behaviour and conflict resolution techniques' *Strategic Management Journal*, Vol. 15 No.2, pp. 555-567.

Monopolies and Mergers Commission (1994), *Private Medical Services*, Cmnd. 2452, London: HMSO.

Moon, J. (1994), 'Evaluating Thatcher: sceptical versus synthetic approaches', *Politics*, Vol 14, No. 2. pp. 72-94.

Moore, C. (1996), 'Reskilling and labour markets in Britain c. 1890-1940: questions and hypotheses', *Historical Studies in Industrial Relations*, No. 2, pp. 93-110.

Morris, D. and Hergert, M. (1987), 'Trends in international collaborative arrangements' *Columbia Journal of World Business*, Vol. 22 No.2, pp. 15-21.

Mueller Report, (1987), *Working Pattern*, London: HMSO.

National Audit Office (NAO) (1999), *Scottish Further Education Colleges: Managing Costs*, London: The Stationery Office.

National Economic Development Council (NEDC) (1972), *Education for Management: A Study of Resources*, London: HMSO.

National Economic Development Office (1976), *A Study of UK Nationalised Industries: A Report to the Government*, London: HMSO

Neil, A. (1996), *Full Disclosure*, London: Macmillan.

Newton, K. and Karan, T. (1985), *The Politics of Local Expenditure*, London: Macmillan.

Newton, T. and Findlay, P. (1996), 'Playing God? The performance of appraisal', *Human Resource Management Journal*, Vol. 6, No.3.

Nicholas, S. (1991), 'The expansion of British multinational companies: testing for managerial failure' in J. Foreman Peck (ed), *New Perspectives on the Late Victorian Economy*, Cambridge: Cambridge University Press.

Norris, G.M. (1989), 'The organisation of the central policy capability in multi functional public authorities', *Local Authority Management Unit Discussion Paper 98/1, Newcastle Upon Tyne Polytechnic*.

O'Connor, E.S. (1996), 'Lines of authority: readings of fundamental texts on the profession of management', *Journal of Management History*, Vol. 2 No. 3, pp. 13-27.

O'Connor, E.S. (1999), 'The politics of management thought: a case study of the Harvard Business School and the Human Relations School', *Academy of Management Review*, Vol. 24. No. 1, pp. 117-131.

Oliver, N. and Wilkinson, B. (1988), *The Japanisation of British Industry*, Oxford: Blackwell.

Olson, M. (1982), *The Rise and Decline of Nations: Economic Growth, Stagflation and Social Rigidities*, New Haven CT: Yale University Press.

Ormuson, H. and Ross, D. (eds) (1990), *New patterns of Work*, St. Andrews.

Osborne, D. and Gaebler, T. (1992), *Reinventing Government*, Reading MA: Addison Wesley.

Pagnamenta, P. and Overy, R. (1984), *All Our Working Lives*, London: British Broadcasting Corporation.

Painter, C. and Clarence, E. (1998), 'Public services under New Labour: collaborative discourses and local networking', *Public Policy and Administration*, Vol.13 No.3, pp. 24 -45.

Painter, C. and Isaac-Henry, K. (1999), 'Managing local public services' in S. Horton and D. Farnham, *Public Management in Britain*, London: Macmillan.

Painter, C., Isaac-Henry, K. and Chalcroft, T. (1994), *Appointed Agencies and Public Accountability*, Birmingham: University of Central England.

Painter, C., Isaac-Henry, K. and Rouse, J. (1997), 'Local authorities and non elected agencies: strategic responses and organisational networks', *Public Administration*, Vol. 75 No.2, pp. 225-245.

Painter, C., Rouse, J., Isaac-Henry, K. and Mark, l. (1996), *Changing Local Governance: Local Authorities and Non Elected Agencies*, Luton: Local Government Management Board.

Panic, M. (ed) (1976), *The UK and West German Manufacturing Industry 1954-1972: A Comparison of Structure and Performance*, HMSO: NEDO.

Panic, M. (1982), 'International direct investment in conditions of structural disequilibrium: UK experience since the 1960s' in J. Black and J.H. Dunning (eds), *International Capital Movements*, London: Macmillan.

Parker, M. (2000), *Organisational Culture and Identity*, London: Sage.

Parkinson, J.R. (1960), *The Economics of Shipbuilding in the United Kingdom*, Glasgow: University of Glasgow Department of Economic and Social Research.

Parkinson, M. (1987), *Reshaping Local Government*, Bristol: Policy Journals.

Paterson Report, (1973), *The New Scottish Local Authorities: Organisation and Management Structures,* Edinburgh: HMSO.

Patton Report (1962), *Productivity and Research in Shipbuilding*. Report prepared under chairmanship of the joint committee of the Shipbuilding Conference, the Shipbuilding Employers Association and the British Shipbuilding Research Association.

Paulden, S.and Hawkins, B. (1969), *Whatever Happened at Fairfields?*, London: Gower Press.

Payne, P.L. (1967), 'The emergence of the large scale company in Great Britain' *Economic History Review*, Vol. XX, pp. 519-542.

Payne, P.L. (1979), *Colvilles and the Scottish Steel Industry*, Oxford: Clarendon Press.

Payne, P.L. (1985), 'The decline of Scottish heavy industries' in R. Saville (ed), *The Economic Development of Modern Scotland, 1950- 1980*, Edinburgh.

Payne, P.L (1988), *British Entrepreneurship in the Nineteenth Century*, London: Macmillan.

Payne, P.L. (1990), 'Entrepneurship and British economic decline' in B. Collins and K. Robbins (eds), *British Culture and Economic Decline*, London: Weidenfield and Nicholson.

Payne, P.L. (1992), Growth and Contraction. Scottish Industry c.1960-1990. *Studies in Scottish Economic and Social History*, Glasgow: Economic and Social History Society of Scotland.

Peck, F., Durnin, J. and Connolly, S. (1999), 'Changing structures for economic development in the English regions: the role of the new Regional Development Agencies', in J. Targalskiego (ed), *Przedsiebiorczosc a Localny Regionalny Rozwoj Gospodarczy, Wydawnicto Akademii Ekonomiczney*, Krakowie, Poland.

Peck, F., Holme, M. and Durnin, J. (1999), *'Corporate change and reinvestment in a peripheral economy: recent experience in Cumbria'. Paper presented to the ESRC*

Urban and Regional Economics Seminar Group, 6-8 January at University of Northumbria.

Peebles, H.B. (1987), *Warship Building on the Clyde: Naval Orders and the Prosperity of the Clyde Shipbuilding Industry*, Edinburgh: John Donald.

Peel, Sir Robert (1937), *A correct report of the speeches delivered by the Right Hon. Sir Robert Peel, Bart. M.P. on his inauguration into office of Lord Rector of Glasgow University, Jan. 11 1837*, London: J Murray (in Glasgow University Special Collections).

Penrose, E.T. (1959), *The Theory of the Growth of the Firm*, Oxford: Basil Blackwell.

Peters, T.J. (1992a), 'Rethinking scale, *California Management Review*, Fall, pp. 24 - 35.

Peters, T.J. (1992b), *Liberation Management*, New York: Macmillan.

Peters, T.J. (1994), *The Pursuit of Wow!*, London: Macmillan.

Peters, T.J. and Waterman, R.H. (1982), *In Search of Excellence*, London: Harper Collins.

Pettigrew, A. and Fenton, E. (2000), *The Innovating Organisation*, London: Sage.

Pignatelli, F. (1994), 'Market models and managerialism in education' in W.M.Humes and M.L McKenzie (eds), *The Management of Educational Policy, Scottish Perspectives*, London: Longman.

Plowden Report (1961), *Control of Public Expenditure*, Cmnd. 1432, London: HMSO.

Plummer, K. (ed) (1987), *Symbolic Interactionism: Vol. 1. Foundations and History*, Brookfield, VT.

Pollard, H.R. (1974), *Developments in Management Thought*, London: Heinemann.

Pollard, S. (1965), *The Genesis of Modern Management*, Harmondsworth: Pelican.

Pollard, S. (1989), *Britain's Prime and Britain's Decline: The British Economy 1870-1914*, London: Edward Arnold.

Pollard, S. and Robertson, P. (1979), *The British Shipbuilding Industry 1870-1914*, Cambridge MA.

Pollert, A. (1988), 'The flexible firm-fixation or fact?, *Work, Economics and Society*, 2(3).

Pollitt, C. (1990), *Managerialism and the Public Services*, first edition, Oxford: Blackwell.

Pollitt, C. (1993), *Managerialism and the Public Services*, second edition, Oxford: Blackwell.

Pollitt, C. and Talbot, C. (2004) (eds), *Unbundled Government: A Critical Analysis of the Global Trend to Agencies Quangos and Contractualisation*, London and New York: Routledge.

Poole, M. (1990), 'Human resource management in an international perspective', Editorial, *International Journal of Human Resource Management* Vol. 1. No. 1, pp. 1-15.

Poole, M.R., Boyne, G. and Mendes, P. (2002), Public and private sector managers: a test of the convergence thesis based on cross sectoral and longitudinal data, *conference paper, British Academy of Management annual conference.*

Porter, M.E. (1980), *Competitive Strategy: Techniques for Analysing Industries and Competitors*, New York: Free Press.

Popp, A. (2002), 'Barriers to innovation in marketing in the mid nineteenth century: merchant-manufacturer relationships', *Business History*, Vol. 44, No. 2 pp. 19-39.

Porter, M.E. (1985), *Competitive Advantage*, New York: Free Press.

Porter, M.E. (1990), *The Competitive Advantage of Nations*, London: Macmillan.

Poster, M. (1990), 'Foucault and databases: participatory surveillance' in M. Poster (ed), *Mode of Information: Post Structuralism and Social Context*, Cambridge: Polity.

Prais, S.J. (1976), *The Evolution of Giant Firms in Britain*, Cambridge: Cambridge University Press.

Prais, S.J. (1981), *Productivity and Industrial Structure*, Cambridge: Cambridge University Press.

Pratten, C.F. and Atkinson, A.G. (1984), 'The use of manpower in British manufacturing industry', *Department of Employment Gazette*.

Pryke, R. (1981), *The Nationalised Industries: Policies and Performance since 1968*, Oxford: Martin Robertson.

Public Administration Committee. (2001), *Third Report: The Ministerial Code: Improving the Rule Book, Session 2000-2001*, HC 235, London: The Stationery Office.

Pyke, F. and Sengenberger, W. (1992), 'Industrial districts and local economic regeneration', *International Institute for Labour Studies*, Geneva.

Quail, J.M. (1997), 'More peculiarities of the British: budgetary control in US-UK business to 1939', *Business and Economic History* Vol. 26, No. 2, pp. 617-631.

Randle, K. and Brady, N. (1997), 'Managerialism and professionalism in the Cinderella service' *Journal of Vocational Education and Training*, Vol. 50, No. 4, pp. 22-35.

Reader, W.J. (1971), *The Weir Group*, London: Weidenfield and Nicholson.

Reid, J.M. (1964), *James Lithgow. Master of Work*, London: Hutchinson.

Report (1960), *Royal Commission on Doctors' and Dentists' Remuneration*, Cmnd. 939, London: HMSO.

Rhodes, R.A.W. and Midwinter, A.F. (1980), *Corporate Management: The New Conventional Wisdom in British Local Government*, Glasgow: Centre for the Study of Public Policy, University of Strathclyde.

Rickets, M. (1987), *The Economics of Business Enterprise*: Wheatsheaf.

Richardson, R. (1992), 'Trade unions and industrial relations' in N.F.R.Crafts and N.W.C. Woodward (eds), *The British Economy since 1945*, Oxford.

Riley, K. (1997), 'Changes in local governance-collaboration through networks. A post 16 study', *Educational Management and Administration*, Vol. 25, No. 2, pp. 155-167.

Ritschel, D. (1991), 'A corporate economy in Britain? Capitalist planning for industrial self government in the 1930s' *English Historical Review*, 106, pp. 41-65.

Ritson, N. (1999), *Transaction Costs and Industrial Relations Strategy: Evidence From Mobil's Coryton Agreement*, ESRC Research Project No. R-000-22-1670.

Roberts, B.C. (1989), 'Trade unions' in D. Kavanagh and A. Seldon (eds), *The Thatcher Effect*, Oxford.

Roberts, R. (1984), 'The administrative origins of industrial diplomacy: an aspect of government-industry relations 1929-1935', in J. Turner (ed), *Businessmen and Politics. Studies of Business Activity in British Politics 1900-1945*, London: Heinemann.

Robson, W.A. (1977), 'The control of nationalised industries', *NatWest Bank Quarterly Review*, November, pp. 6-16.

Rodger, R. (1996), 'The labour force' in W.H. Fraser and I. Maver (eds), *Glasgow, Vol. 11: 1830-1912*, Manchester: Manchester University Press.

Rodger, R. (1996), 'Urbanisation in twentieth century Scotland' in T.M. Devine and R.J. Findlay (eds), *Scotland in the Twentieth Century*, Edinburgh: Edinburgh University Press.

Roethlisberger, F.J. and Dickson, W.J. (1939), *Management and the Worker*, Cambridge, MA: Harvard University Press.

Rogow, A.A. and Shore, P. (1955), *The Labour Government and British Industry 1945-1951*, Oxford: Blackwell.

Rollings, N. (2001), 'Whitehall and the control of prices and profits in a major war 1919-1939' *Historical Journal* Vol. 44 No. 2, pp. 517-540.

Rose, M.B. (1994), 'Investment in human capital and British manufacturing industry to 1990' in M.W. Kirby and M.B Rose (eds), *Business Enterprise in Modern Britain From the Eighteenth to the Twentieth Century*, London: Routledge.

R.S.A. Report (1995), *Tomorrow's Company*, London: Royal Society of Arts.

Rouse, J. (1997), 'Resources and performance management in public service organisations', in K. Isaac-Henry, C. Painter and C. Barnes (eds), *Management in the Public Sector*, London: Chapman and Hall.

Sabel, C. and Zeitlen, J. (1985), 'Historical alternatives to mass production: politics, markets and technology in nineteenth century industrialisation', *Past and Present*, 108, pp. 133-176.

Salmon Report (1966), *Senior Nursing Staff Structure*, London: HMSO.

Sanderson, M. (1972), *The Universities and British Industry 1850-1970*: Routledge.

Sanderson, M. (1988a), 'The English civic universities and the 'industrial spirit' 1870-1914', *Historical Research* Vol. LXI, pp. 90-104.

Sanderson, M. (1988b), 'Education and economic decline', the 1890s –1980s', *Oxford Review of Economic Policy* Vol. 4, No. 2, pp. 38-50.

Sandkull, K. (1996), 'Lean production: the myth which changes the world?' in S.R. Clegg and G. Palmer (eds), *The Politics of Management Knowledge*, London: Sage.

Savage, M. (1998), 'Discipline, surveillance and the 'career': employment on the Great Western Railway 1833-1914', in A. McKinlay and K. Starkey, *Foucault, Management and Organisation Theory*, London: Sage.

Saville, R. (ed) (1985), *The Economic Development of Modern Scotland, 1950-1980*, Edinburgh.

Saul, S.B. (1973), *The Myth of the Great Depression*, London: Macmillan.

Sawyer, M. (1991), 'Industrial policy', in M. Artis and D. Cobham (eds), *Labour's Economic Policies 1974-1979*, Manchester: Manchester University Press.

Sawyer, M. (1992), 'Labour's industrial policies in the 1970s: debates and deeds'. *Paper prepared for conference on 'Labour: The Party of Industrial Modernisation?' London School of Economics.*

Schmitz, C. (1993), *The Growth of Big Business in the United States and Western Europe*, London: Macmillan.

Scholes, E. and Clutterbuck, D. (1998), 'Planning stakeholder communication', *Long Range Planning*, Vol.31 No.2, pp. 227-238.

Schuler, R.S. (1992), 'Linking the people with the strategic needs of the business', *Organisational Dynamics*, Vol. 20 No. 2, p. 18-32.

Scott, A.(1994), *Willing Slaves? British Workers Under HRM*, Cambridge: Cambridge University Press.

Scottish Council (Development and Industry) (1970), *Oceanspan 1: A Maritime Based Development Strategy for a European Scotland, 1970-2000*, Edinburgh: Scottish Council (Development and Industry).

Scottish Executive (2000), *A Review into Examination Results Issues Concerning the Scottish Qualification Authority*, Final Report, 31 October.

Scottish Further Education Funding Council (2000), *The Way Ahead. Management Review of Scottish Further Education Colleges*, Edinburgh: Scottish Further Education Funding Council.

Scottish Further Education Unit (2004), *Report on the Strategic Management of the Scottish College Sector*, Stirling: SFEU.

Scottish Office (1997), *Designed to Care. Reviewing the NHS in Scotland*, Cmnd. 3811, Edinburgh: The Stationery Office.

Scottish Office Education Department (1992), *School Management. The Way Ahead*, Edinburgh: HMSO.

Scottish Office Education Department (1993), *Devolved Schools. Management Guidelines for Schemes*, Edinburgh: HMSO.

Scottish Parliament Audit Committee (2004), *Fourth Report, Scottish Further Education Funding Council-Performance of the Further Education Sector in Scotland*, Edinburgh.

Segal-Horn, S. (1998), *The Strategy Reader*, Oxford: Blackwell.

Shaiken, H., Lopez, S. and Mankita, I. (1997), 'Two routes to team production: Saturn and Chrysler compared', *Industrial Relations* Vol.36, No. 1, pp. 17-45.

Sharpe, L.J. (1970), 'Theories and values of local government' *Political Studies*, Vol. XV111 No. 2, pp. 153-174.

Shaw, V. and Kauser, S. (2000), 'The changing patterns of international strategic alliance activity by British firms', *Journal of General Management*, Vol 25, No. 4, p. 51-69.

Sheaff, M. (1988) 'NHS ancillary services and competitive tendering', *Industrial Relations Journal*, Vol.19 No.2, pp. 93-105.

Sheldon, O. (1930), *The Philosophy of Management*, London: Pitman.

Shim, D. (2001), 'Recent human resources developments in OECD member countries', *Public Personnel Management*, Vol. 30, No. 3, pp. 323-347.

Sikka, P. (2004), 'Revolution Chapter1', *The Giving List*, The Guardian in Association with Business in The Community, November 8: London.

Sisson, K. (1994), *Personnel Management*, second edition, Oxford: Blackwell.

Sjogren, H. (1997), 'Financial reconstruction and industrial reorganisation in different financial systems: a comparative view of British and Swedish institutions during the inter war period', *Business History*, Vol. 39, No. 4, pp. 84-105.

Slaven, A. (1975), *The Development of the West of Scotland 1750-1960*, London: Routledge and Kegan Paul.

Slaven, A. (1977), 'A shipyard in depression: John Browns of Clydebank 1931-1938, *Business History*, Vol. XIX No. 2, pp. 192-217.

Slaven, A. (1980), 'Growth and stagnation in British / Scottish shipbuilding 1913-1977', in Kuuse and Slaven, *Scottish and Scandinavian Shipbuilding Seminar: Development Problems in Historical Perspective, Glasgow.*

Slaven, A. (1986), 'Sir William Pearce' in A. Slaven and S. Checkland (eds), *Dictionary of Scottish Business Biography, 1860-1960: Vol. 11, The Staple Industries*, Aberdeen: Aberdeen University Press.

Stake, R.E. (1978), 'The case study method of social enquiry', *Educational Researcher*, Vol. 7, No. 2, pp. 44-68.

Stalk, G., Evans, P. and Schulman, L.E. (1992), 'Competing on capabilities: the new rules of corporate strategy', *Harvard Business Review*, Vol. 70, No. 2, pp. 57-69.

Stoker, G. (1997), 'Quangos and local democracy', in M. Flinders, I. Harden and D. Marquand (eds), *How to Make Quangos Democratic*, London: Charter 88.

Storey, J. (1989) (ed), *New Perspectives on Human Resource Management*, London: Routledge.

Storper, M. (1995), 'The resurgence of regional economies ten years later: the region as a nexus of untraded interdependencies', *European Urban and Regional Studies*, Vol.2, No.3, pp. 33-46.

Sako, M. (1992), *Prices, Quality and Trust*, Cambridge: Cambridge University Press.

Strathclyde Regional Council. (1977), *Executive Office Arrangements*, Glasgow: Strathclyde Regional Council.

Strathclyde Regional Council. (1986), *Report of Working Group on Learning and Teaching in Secondary Schools in Strathclyde*, Glasgow: Strathclyde Regional Council.

Strathclyde Regional Council. (1989), *Report on Education in Strathclyde*, undertaken by Institute of Local Government Studies (Inlogov.) and the School of Education, University of Birmingham: Strathclyde Regional Council.

Strathclyde Regional Council. (1990), *Minutes of Education Committee*, 31 January: Strathclyde Regional Council.

Strauss, G. (1992), 'HRM in the USA', in B. Towers (ed), *The Handbook of Human Resource Management,* London: Blackwell.

Supple, B.E. (1987), *The History of the British Coal Industry, Vol. 4,* Oxford: Clarendon Press.

Supple, B.E. (1992), 'Introduction' in B.E.Supple (ed), *The Rise of Big Business,* Aldershot: Edward Elgar.

Suzuki, Y. (1991), *Japanese Management Structures 1920-1980,* London: Macmillan.

Tailby, S. (2000), 'Taylorism in the mines? Technology, work organisation and management in British coalmining before nationalisation', *Historical Studies in Industrial Relations,* No. 10, pp. 71-98.

Talbot, C. (2004), 'Executive agencies: have they improved management in government?', *Public Money and Management,* Vol. 24, No. 2, pp. 104-112.

Taylor, F.W. (1903), *Shop Management,* New York: Harper and Row.

Targalskiego, G. (1999) (ed), *Przedsiebiorczosc a Lokalny i Regionalny Rozwoj Gospodarczy,* Wydawnicto Akademii Ekonmiczney, Krakowie, Poland.

Teece, D.J., Pisano, G and Shien, A. (1990), *'Firm capabilities, resources and the concept of strategy'. Mimeo. University of California at Berkely, Haas School of Business,* September.

Terry, M. (1986), 'How do we know if shop stewards are getting weaker?', *British Journal of Industrial Relations,* Vol.24, No.2 pp. 169-179.

Theakston, K. (1999), *Leadership in Whitehall,* London: Macmillan in Association with the ESRC Whitehall Programme.

Thomas, R.M. (1978), *The British Philosophy of Administration: A Comparison of British and American Ideas 1900-1939,* London: Longman.

Thomson, A.W. (2001), *Changing Patterns in Management Development,* Oxford: Blackwell.

Thorne, M.L. (2002), 'Colonising the new world of NHS management: the shifting power of professionals', *Health Services Management Research,* Vol. 15, No. 1, pp.14-26.

Tolliday, S. (1984), 'Tariffs and steel 1916-1934' in J. Turner (ed), *Businessmen and Politics: Studies of Business Activity in British Politics,* London: Heinemann.

Tolliday, S. (1986a), 'Steel and rationalisation policies 1918-1950' in B. Elbaum and W. Lazonick (eds), *The Decline of the British Economy,* Oxford: Clarendon Press.

Tolliday, S. (1986b), ' Management and labour in Britain 1896-1939',in S. Tolliday and J. Zeitlin (eds), *Between Fordism and Flexibility: The Automobile Industry and its Workers,* Oxford: Polity.

Tolliday, S. (1987), *Business, Banking and Politics: The Case of Steel 1918-1936,* Cambridge, MA: Harvard University Press.

Tolliday, S. (1991), *Government and Business,* Aldershot: Edward Elgar.

Tolliday, S. and Zeitlin, J. (1986), *Between Fordism and Flexibility: The Automobile Industry and its Workers,* Oxford: Polity.

Tolliday, S. and Zeitlin, J. (eds) (1991), *The Power to Manage? Employers and Industrial Relations in Comparative Historical Perspective,* London: Routledge.

Tomlinson, J. (1991), 'The failure of the Anglo American Council on Productivity', *Business History,* Vol. 33, No. 1, pp. 82-92.

Tomlinson, J. (1996), 'Productivity, joint consultation and human relations in post war Britain: the Atlee government and the workplace', in J. Melling and A. McKinlay (eds), *Management, Labour and Industrial Politics in Modern Europe,* Cheltenham: Edward Elgar.

Toms, S. and Wright, M. (2002), 'Corporate governance, strategy and structure in British business history', *Business History,* Vol. 44, No, 3. pp 98-106.

Toyne, B., Arpan, T.S., Ricks, D.A., Shimp, T.A. and Barnett, A. (1984) (eds), *The Global Textile Industry,* London: Allen and Unwin.

Travers, T., Jones, G. and Burnham, J. (1997), *The Role of the Local Authority Chief Executive in Local Governance*, York: Joseph Rowntree Foundation.

Turner, G. (1969), *Business in Britain*: Eyre and Spottiswoode.

Turner, J. (1984), 'The politics of business' in J. Turner (ed), *Businessmen and Politics. Studies of Business Activity in British Politics 1900-1945*: Heinemann.

Turner, J. (ed) (1984), *Businessmen and Politics. Studies of Business Activity in British Politics 1900-1945:* Heinemann.

Turner, J. (1985), 'Man and Braverman: British industrial relations', *History,* Vol. 70, pp. 236-242.

UCB (1999), *Annual Report 1999*, UCB, S.A., Brussels.

Urwick, L. (1922), 'Experimental psychology and the creative impulse', *Psyche*, Vol. 111 No. 1 (New Series) July.

Walker, D. (2003), 'Ministers and management', *Public Money and Management*, Vol. 23, No. 1, pp. 3-4.

Wallman, S.M.H. (1991), 'The proper interpretation of corporate constituency statutes and formulation of director duties' *Stetson Law Review*, No. 21, No. 1, pp. 163.

Wang, J.L. and Collinson (2003), Subsidiary Autonomy and Innovation Capability: A Pilot Case Study of Phillips Semi Conductor Plant in Taiwan, *British Academy of Management Conference Working Paper.*

Ward, L. (1996), 'Job losses outstrip last year's', *Times Educational Supplement*, 5 April.

Warner, D. and Crosthwaite, E. (1995), *Human Resource Management in Higher and Further Education*, Buckingham: Open University Press.

Watkins, B. (1975), *Documents in Health and Social Services: 1834 to Present Day*, London: Methuen.

Webster, C. (1988), *The Health Service Since the War, Vol. 1. The Problems of Health Care*, London: HMSO.

Webster, C. (1996), *The Health Service Since the War, Vol. 2. Government and Health Care*, London: The Stationery Office.

Weir Committee (1926), *Report of the Committee Appointed to Review the National Problem of the Supply of Electrical Energy*, London: HMSO.

Welch, H.J. and Myers, C.S. (1932), *Ten years of Industrial Psychology*, London: Pitman.

Welsh Office (1998), *NHS Wales: Putting Patient First*, Cmnd. 3841, Cardiff: The Stationery Office.

Westall, O. (1997), 'Invisible, visible and direct hands: an institutional interpretation of organisational structures and change in British general insurance', *Business History*, Vol. 39, No. 4, pp. 44-66.

Wheatley Report (1969), *Royal Commission on Local Government in Scotland*, Edinburgh: HMSO.

Wheeler, D. and Sillanpaa, M. (1997), *The Stakeholder Corporation*, London: Pitman.

White, G. and Hutchinson, B. (1996), 'Local government' in D. Farnham and S. Horton, *Managing People in the Public Service*, London: Macmillan.

White, L.D. (1933), *Whitley Councils in the British Civil Service*, Chicago, Illinois: University of Chicago Press.

Whitston, K. (1996), 'Scientific management and production management practice in Britain between the wars', *Historical Studies in Industrial Relations*, No. 1, pp. 47-75.

Wigham, E.E.L. (1973), *The Power to Manage: A History of the Engineering Employers Federation*, London: Macmillan.

Wilkins, M. (1986), 'Defining the firm: history and theory' in P. Hertner and G. Jones (eds), *Multinationals: Theory and History*, Aldershot: Gower.

Wilkins, M. (1989), *The History of Foreign Investment in the United States Before 1914*, Cambridge MA: Harvard University Press.

Wilks, S. (1981), 'Planning Agreements: the making of a paper tiger', *Public Administration,* Vol. 59, No. 3, pp. 399-419.

Williams, K., Haslam, C., Johal, S and Williams, J. (1994), *Cars: Analysis, History, Cases,* Oxford: Bergham Books.

Williamson, O.E. (1975), *Markets and Hierarchies,* New York: The Free Press.

Williamson, O.E. (1981), 'The modern corporation: origins, evolution, attributes', *Journal of Economic Literature,* 19, pp. 1537-1568.

Wilson, C. (1954), *The History of Unilever: A Study in Economic growth and Social Change, Vol. 1:* Cassel.

Wilson, C. (1965), 'Economy and society in late Victorian Britain', *Economic History Review* Vol. XXX11, pp. 183-198.

Wilson, D. and Game, C. (1998), *Local Government in the United Kingdom,* London: Macmillan.

Wilson, J.F. (1992), *The 'Manchester Experiment': A History of the Manchester Business School 1965-1990:* Paul Chapman.

Wilson, J.F. (1995a), *British Business History 1720-1994,* Manchester: Manchester University Press.

Wilson, J.F. (1995b), 'Modern management education in Britain: how to deal with business culture' in R.P. Amdam (ed), *Management Education and Business Performance,* London: Routledge.

Winstanley, M. (1994), 'Concentration and competition in the retail sector c. 1980-1990' in M.W. Kirby and M.B. Rose (eds), *Business Enterprise in Modern Britain From the Eighteenth to the Twentieth Century,* London: Routledge.

WIRS 3 (1990), Workplace Industrial Relations Survey, in N. Milward, S. Woodland, A. Bryson. and J. Forth (1999), *A Bibliography of Research Based on WIRS,* Policy Studies Institute, London.

Womack, J.P., Jones, D.T. and Roos, D. (1990), *The Machine That Changed the World,* New York: Rawson.

Working Party on Organisation of Medical Work in Hospitals (1967), Chairman Sir George Godber, London: HMSO.

Wren, D.A. (1994), *The Evolution of Management Thought,* fourth edition, New York and London: Wiley.

Yip, G. (1995), *Total Global Strategy,* London and New York: Prentice Hall.

Yoshino, M.Y. and Rangan, V.S. (1995), *Strategic Alliances: An Entrepreneurial Approach to Globalisation,* Boston: Harvard Business School Press.

Young, R.G. (1981), 'The management of political innovation-the Strathclyde experience of new devices for policy making' *Local Government Studies,* November / December, pp. 15-31.

Young, S. and Lowe, A.V. (1974), *Intervention in the Mixed Economy. The Evolution of British Industrial Policy 1964-1972,* London: Croom Helm.

Yui, T. (1998), 'Development, organisation and business strategy of industrial enterprises in Japan 1915-1935' *Japanese Yearbook on Business History,* 15.

Zeitlin, J. (1983), 'The labour strategies of British engineering employers 1890-1922' in H.F. Gospel. and C.R. Littler (eds), *Managerial Strategies and Industrial Relations,* London: Heinemann.

Index